LOS ANGELES PACIFIC
THE CLARENDON

Interurbans Special
63

THE STORY OF THE
LOS ANGELES PACIFIC RAILWAY

WILLIAM A. MYERS and **IRA L. SWETT**

TROLLEYS TO THE SURF

Interurbans

PO Box 6444
Glendale, California 91205

Publisher . . . . Mac Sebree
Editor . . . . Jim Walker

TROLLEYS TO THE SURF

Library of Congress Catalog Number 76-9685
ISBN: 0-916374-22-X

First Printing: Spring 1976

Contents

FRONTISPIECE PHOTO

The Los Angeles Pacific era in Southern California was a time of growth, buoyant good feelings and confidence in the future. The city was vibrant, the countryside green, and all was right with the world. And nowhere was this spirit better reflected than in the faces of the conductor of LAP's big, swift 726, and in the knickerbocker-clad youth waiting expectantly for the camera's click. The conductor knew his trade, and the young boy was already dreaming dreams of growing up in a world as yet uncomplicated by man's misadventures. It was a mighty good time to be alive. (Interurbans)

FRONT ENDSHEET PHOTO

LAP's haughtiest and finest equipment—the MU-equipped 700 series of passenger cars—was rolled out for this impressive lineup, location uncertain but probably on Hill Street in downtown Los Angeles. The white-capped train crew seems fully capable of handling these crowd-swallowers in fine style. (Interurbans)

BACK ENDSHEET PHOTO

Just a few days after the Great Merger of 1911 a train of LAP 700-series cars ventured off-line to handle a special movement. The train is seen parked at the Pacific Electric/ Southern Pacific depot in Pasadena. Repainting into PE red would be several months into the future. (Interurbans)

Introduction

Moses H. Sherman

Sherman Foundation

Eli P. Clark

Like railroads of much greater renown, the Los Angeles Pacific was to a large extent the extension of a commanding personality. The Union Pacific had its Harriman; the Great Northern its Hill; the Canadian Pacific its Van Horne—and the Los Angeles Pacific had Moses H. Sherman.

Sherman and his brother-in-law, Eli P. Clark, dominated the Los Angeles street railway scene for some two decades—the last of the nineteenth century and the first of the twentieth. They preceded Henry Huntington as a traction giant in the City of the Angels, but were to be later much eclipsed by Huntington. Their downfall as transit tycoons was occasioned by the entry of Southern Pacific into the Southern California transit picture. The SP, headed then by E.H. Harriman, bought control of LAP in 1906 and Sherman and Clark were eased out in 1911 when SP consolidated all of its Los Angeles area traction properties into the great Pacific Electric.

Clark was the front man. He had the title of President of LAP, and was often seen around the property—inspecting, riding the cars, talking to the passengers and shippers. But it was not the soft-spoken Clark that the financiers and industrial leaders came to see to get business done with the railway.

Sherman was the money man. Rather, he was the tall, lantern-jawed commanding presence who, exuding unbounded optimism, could always find a way to coax money from others to keep the LAP rolling and expanding. Sherman was a marked individualist who usually draped his 6'9" figure in a long frock coat. He always stood out in any crowd, and his mere entry into a room could bring conversation to a stop.

Moses Hazeltine Sherman was born December 3, 1853, in Vermont. In early life he was a teacher and when in 1874 he developed health problems he moved to Arizona to take up a teaching post in the territorial capital of Prescott. Within a few years the ambitious Sherman had become territorial superintendent of public instruction. He gradually shifted his base of operations to Phoenix, then the center of the territory's only prime agricultural area. Sherman invested in land, helped found what is today the state's largest bank (Valley National) and in 1887 took over the city's tiny horsecar system.

In 1876 Sherman's older sister, Lucy, joined him in Arizona and soon married Eli Clark who thereupon became Sherman's lifelong business associate. Sherman's political connections landed Clark the post of territorial auditor. Sherman also married while in Phoenix; he and his wife Harriet had two daughters and the General (Sherman used the title after serving a term as territorial adjutant general) adopted his wife's previous son, Robert. Sherman and Clark electrified the Phoenix street railways in 1893 and built an interurban to suburban Glendale. In 1890 the two turned their attention to Southern California.

As is noted in Chapter One, Sherman and Clark were Southern California's first true interurban builders, and were the very first to see the importance of providing swift, reliable, economical transportation to insure the area's economic vitality. Of course, as was typical of the era, the interurban builders had a heavy personal stake in that vitality; Sherman was one of Southern California's most aggressive land developers. He was instrumental in building up the Hollywood area and promoted one of the early high-class residential developments in the area: Hollywoodland. He also developed a large part of the southern San Fernando Valley and gave his name to Sherman Oaks and what is today one of the Valley's main business arteries: Sherman Way.

As was also typical of the era, Sherman found ways to expand his traction empire largely on borrowed money. He and Clark were frequently strapped for funds, but with creditors hard on their heels they pressed on, organized companies, printed stock certificates, shifted assets, bought supplies on credit, built rail lines, bought cars, and conducted grand openings. Then the whole process would be repeated on another line.

Many capitalists operated that way, but Sherman could be especially persuasive, and, as William O. Hendricks notes in his monograph on Sherman published by the Sherman Foundation, Corona del Mar, California, 1973: "Potential but reluctant investors, familiar with his powers, were sometimes known to flee when they saw him coming." A story told about the General at the time was that a perturbed creditor for $30,000 worth of railroad ties once called on Sherman to demand payment. On leaving, wrapped in a smile, he was asked by another man waiting in the anteroom whether he had been successful in collecting. "Oh, better than that," he happily replied. "I sold him $30,000 more ties!"

While the General had the ability, in the words of one contemporary, to charm the birds out of the trees, he also enjoyed a fight. The LAP's brief but furious struggle with rival traction magnates Abbot Kinney and William S. Hook in the summer of 1903 (see Chapter One) illustrates Sherman's will to win. Kinney and Hook proposed to build a competing electric line to the beaches, but Sherman and Clark fought them off both in the courts and in repeated face-offs by rival construction gangs. Kinney and Hook lost.

Sherman and Clark were finally coaxed into retirement from big-time traction railroading by Harriman money, but Sherman quickly got involved in a number of other big schemes, including the development of agricultural land on the Mexican side of the Imperial Valley; he helped form the Los Angeles Steamship Co. whose ships plied to San Francisco and Honolulu—and he served for a while on the board of directors of the Pacific Electric. Significantly, it was the management team that Sherman and Clark had developed on the LAP which largely took over the operation of the giant PE system.

Despite his hard-driving ways and constant financial scheming, it was unanimously held by Sherman's friends that he was personally honest and could, despite a hot temper, be extremely generous with friends and worthy causes alike. When he died on September 9, 1932, at age 78, he left an estate of several million dollars. Much of it went to universities, and a non-profit philanthropic Sherman Foundation was eventually founded by his heirs and his longtime personal assistant, Arnold D. Haskell. The foundation maintains, at Corona del Mar, California, a research library focusing on the Pacific Southwest.

* * *

One of *Interurbans'* most popular publications was Special 18, the original Los Angeles Pacific book published in 1955. This modest, softcover volume sold out in record time, as did a pictorial sequel, *Los Angeles Pacific Album,* published as Special 40 in 1966. It had long been the plan of Publisher Ira L.

Huntington Library

Henry E. Huntington

Union Pacific

Edward H. Harriman

Abbot Kinney

William S. Hook

Swett to bring out a bigger, better **LAP** book and, in fact, layout of the new volume was about to commence when the railfan world heard the shocking news of Swett's death in March of 1975.

Once set in motion, though, a project of this magnitude could hardly be stopped. Into the tremendous void of authorship created by the events of early 1975 stepped William A. Myers, "unofficial historian" of the Southern California Edison Co. Myers had long been collecting data on early-day Los Angeles traction companies and the Los Angeles Pacific was of especial interest. With the generous cooperation of the Edison Company, Myers set to work on the LAP project. Soon, a format for a new, larger, hardcover edition began to emerge. This would incorporate the rich pictorial lode appearing in both earlier books, the thousands of hours of patient research which had been done by Swett, and add improved typography and reproduction methods—and a hard cover to insure proper preservation of this, one of Interurbans' most serious historical studies. Myers was able to unearth much additional historical, operating and construction data, and enlisted additional contributors.

One of the new contributors to whom we owe a special debt of gratitude is the celebrated Southern California railroad artist, Harlan Hiney who, despite an extremely busy schedule, volunteered to draw four excellent historical maps of the **LAP** system. In addition to the fine draftsmanship which characterize these maps, they each contain a near-complete historical record of the salient geographical features up to the year they represent in the LAP chronology: 1910. This was the result of many hours of additional research by Hiney and others. Nor do we overlook the original cartographic contributions of Ray Younghans who did most of the original mapwork, some of which was retained in Special 63.

Another resident (like Hiney) of Santa Monica who put in much time as a labor of love of the area's rich transportation history was David G. Cameron, president of the Electric Railway Historical Assn. of Southern California, whose research turned up a considerable amount of new and corrected data on the building of the LAP. Still more research, especially into the LAP's rolling stock, was done by Rex B. Atwell of the mechanical department of the Orange Empire Trolley Museum. All car data in the earlier book was reviewed by Atwell, and corrected as necessary.

A twenty-one gun salute also must go to the many sources tapped for the original Specials 18 and 40 which have so enriched this volume. These include the Pacific Electric Railway Co., C.M. Pierce, manager of the Balloon Route Excursion, quite a number of Los Angeles area newspapers and libraries, the *Street Railway Journal, Electric Railway Journal, Poor's* and *Moody's* for historical and financial data on various Southern California street railways.

The Pacific Electric Official History compiled in 1914 by the company's chief engineer contained the data drawn on for the many corporate histories presented herein. Also of great value was an outstanding historical work on the west bay cities, "A Century History of Santa Monica Bay Cities," by Luther A. Ingersoll.

Photographs are credited individually, but an added note is appropriate concerning the many photos credited to the late T.L. Wagenbach, a former LAP and Pacific Electric official (he became PE General Manager in 1948) which originally appeared in Special 40. These photos were loaned to *Interurbans* by Carl Blaubach of the California Public Utilities Commission.

The Huntington Library and the Sherman Foundation Library were most helpful in the more recent researches on the LAP.

Spring, 1976   MAC SEBREE

Green Cars to

Chapter One

the Blue Pacific

Sherman and Clark

Started the Southland's

Great Traction Pageant

THE HISTORY OF THE LOS ANGELES PACIFIC SEEMS routine enough from a chronological point of view, but simplicity vanishes when one considers its frequently changing corporate structure.

No less than 26 different corporations were at one time or another in control of all or portions of the LAP system. To make matters more complex, certain merger and reorganization attempts were of doubtful legality, or were contested in the courts. A favorite device of the usually financially strapped owners, Moses Sherman and Eli P. Clark, was to set up a corporation for each new line extension. After the line was underway, the new company would be merged with the old, resulting in yet a third entity. These constant corporate machinations complicate the researcher's task tremendously.

Nevertheless, we have produced a "family tree" in this volume which reflects this corporate complexity. The technical legal descriptions of LAP and its corporate cousins and ancestors, as determined by the Pacific Electric Engineering Department in 1914 and researched by the late Ira L. Swett in 1955, appear as an Appendix later in this book where the reader may struggle through them at his leisure. This chapter will concern itself with a general history of the LAP and portray the men whose careers were interwoven with this pioneer Los Angeles electric railway and its big green trolleys to the beaches.

WHEN GENERAL Moses H. Sherman stepped off the train in Los Angeles in the summer of 1890, the city's newspapers were soon speculating as to the real reason behind the prominent Phoenix, Arizona, capitalist's visit to Southern California. Sherman was, the newspapermen knew, heavily involved with the budding streetcar system in his hometown. Was he seeking new transit vistas in Southern California?

The answer was not long in coming. Within weeks Sherman had purchased control of the primitive, rickety Pico St. electric railway line. From this beginning, he built, over the next five years, a network of electric street railway lines in the city under the name of the *Los Angeles Consolidated Electric Rail-*

OLD POSTCARD rendering, opposite page, depicts LAP car on Spring Street circa 1907. In those days, downtown streets were filled with people.   *(Magna Collection)*

STEAM DUMMY "Ivanhoe" and combine No. 5 pose in front of Sisters' Hospital, Sunset & Beaudry, about 1888. Passengers continued their journey into Los Angeles by walking over to the Temple Street Cable Railway.   (Security Pacific Bank)

THE BRIDGE at Ocean and Railroad Aves., Santa Monica, when horsecars rolled across it. A Southern Pacific steam train in the background is ready to leave for Los Angeles.   (Interurbans)

way Co. (LACE). The general brought his brother-in-law, Eli P. Clark, into the management as an associate, and gradually an effective working partnership evolved with Clark as the front man and Sherman as the money man.

This early-day dynamic duo of the Southern California railway scene, although often seriously hampered financially, operated in a lively—and usually successful—competition with the vastly more powerful Huntington-Hellman Syndicate (Los Angeles Railway and Old Pacific Electric) and the gigantic Southern Pacific, for some 16 years. Even after selling LAP to the SP, the two continued active in real estate and civic affairs for many years.

On April 11, 1894, Sherman and Clark incorporated the *Pasadena and Los Angeles Electric Railway Co.* (P&LA). At first planned as a subsidiary of their LACE to operate horsecar lines in Pasadena, P&LA in fact became the parent of the first interurban electric trolley line in the Southland. Within the space of a year, P&LA not only reconstructed Pasadena's horsecar lines into an excellent local trolley system, it also built a narrow-gauge line down the Arroyo Seco to connect with LACE's Sycamore Grove line, thereby forming an interurban line from Pasadena to Los Angeles.

In November, 1894, the partners incorporated the Pasadena and Pacific Railroad Company (P&P) to build another interurban line from Los Angeles to Santa Monica. Immediately the newspapers were full of stories about "Sherman's March to the Sea" as construction extended westward through the mustard fields toward the beach resort community.

It all proved to be too much, too fast. The extensions and reconstructions were having a disastrous effect on Sherman and Clark's fortunes. It must be remembered that although operating under their own names, the P&LA and the P&P were in effect subsidiaries of LACE, the partners' principal property which also was expanding at a vigorous rate. The two subsidiary companies were not yet profitable enterprises, as all revenues were being plowed back into construction. LACE, faced with staggering costs to replace cable-operated lines with electric lines and to extend new trolley routes to counter the competition of William S. Hook's *Los Angeles Traction Co.*, was also putting money into its subsidiaries' expansion efforts.

ECHO PARK AVE. horsecar, 1894; this photograph was taken where the modern-day Elysian Heights School was located. Louis Duni, the operator of the line, stands at left; the other man's girl took the picture.   *(Magna Collection)*

THE CAHUENGA VALLEY RAILROAD in steam days, two views: Above, a deluxe train on the CVR. The locomotive is the "Cahuenga," and the cars are spliced ex-cable trailers from the Second Street Cable Railway, Los Angeles. Bottom view from an old halftone places the CVR train in front of a gabled period residence.   *(Both, Security Pacific Bank)*

GRADING HOLLYWOOD BLVD. in 1899; this view looks west from approximately Bronson Ave. From Western Ave. to Highland Ave. the new electric line was a rebuild of the old Cahuenga Valley Railroad's steam line. (Security Pacific Bank)

As financial disaster loomed, an aroused bondholders group attempted to wrest control of the growing, but shaky, rail system away from Sherman and Clark. On March 19, 1895, LACE's bondholders organized the *Los Angeles Railway Co.* (LARy) for the purpose of taking over and operating the streetcar lines of LACE. Possibly because Sherman and Clark felt that an interurban electric railway network outside Los Angeles city ultimately would be far more profitable than the city lines (after all, the interurban lines would speed the sub-division and sale of the many tracts of land held by the two partners in the surrounding territory), they were willing to negotiate with the bondholders. LACE's city lines were turned over to LARy on March 23, 1895.

In return for this peaceful acquiescence, the bondholders allowed Sherman and Clark to retain full control of the two interurban subsidiaries, P&LA and P&P, including the Elysian Park and Daly Avenue lines that enabled the interurbans to enter L.A. (Quite possibly the new management believed the two interurban lines would never pay, pulling down the two promoters, but this is speculation.)

One clause in the agreement allowed Sherman and Clark to buy back the city operations at the end of three years (1898) if the bondholders proved unable to make a profit. As it turned out, the bondholders did go broke, but rather than re-turning the city lines to Sherman and Clark, they sold LARy to Henry E. Huntington.

Pasadena & Pacific

Having escaped the full wrath of the bondholders, Sherman and Clark were at last ready to devote their full energies to building their two interurbans. On May 4, 1895, the Pasadena line was opened, and construction of the extension to Santa Monica began. On May 3, the partners negotiated a trackage agreement with the new LARy management, enabling P&LA and P&P cars to reach the center of the downtown district. P&LA cars (curiously enough lettered "Pasadena & Pacific"!) were permitted to use LARy tracks on Sycamore Grove Avenue (Figueroa), Daly Street, Pasadena Avenue, Buena Vista (N. Broadway), Bellevue Avenue (Sunset), Main Street, and Spring Street to Fourth.

P&P cars, when they began regular service the following year, used LARy track from Fourth and Spring via Spring, Main, Bellevue to Bellevue and Buena Vista. At this time, P&P and P&LA shared a station at 222 W. 4th Street. Although the agreement included use of a loop via 4th, Broadway, 5th and Spring, no records survive to show if that route was ever used by either interurban to turn its cars. More likely, the cars changed ends in front of the station.

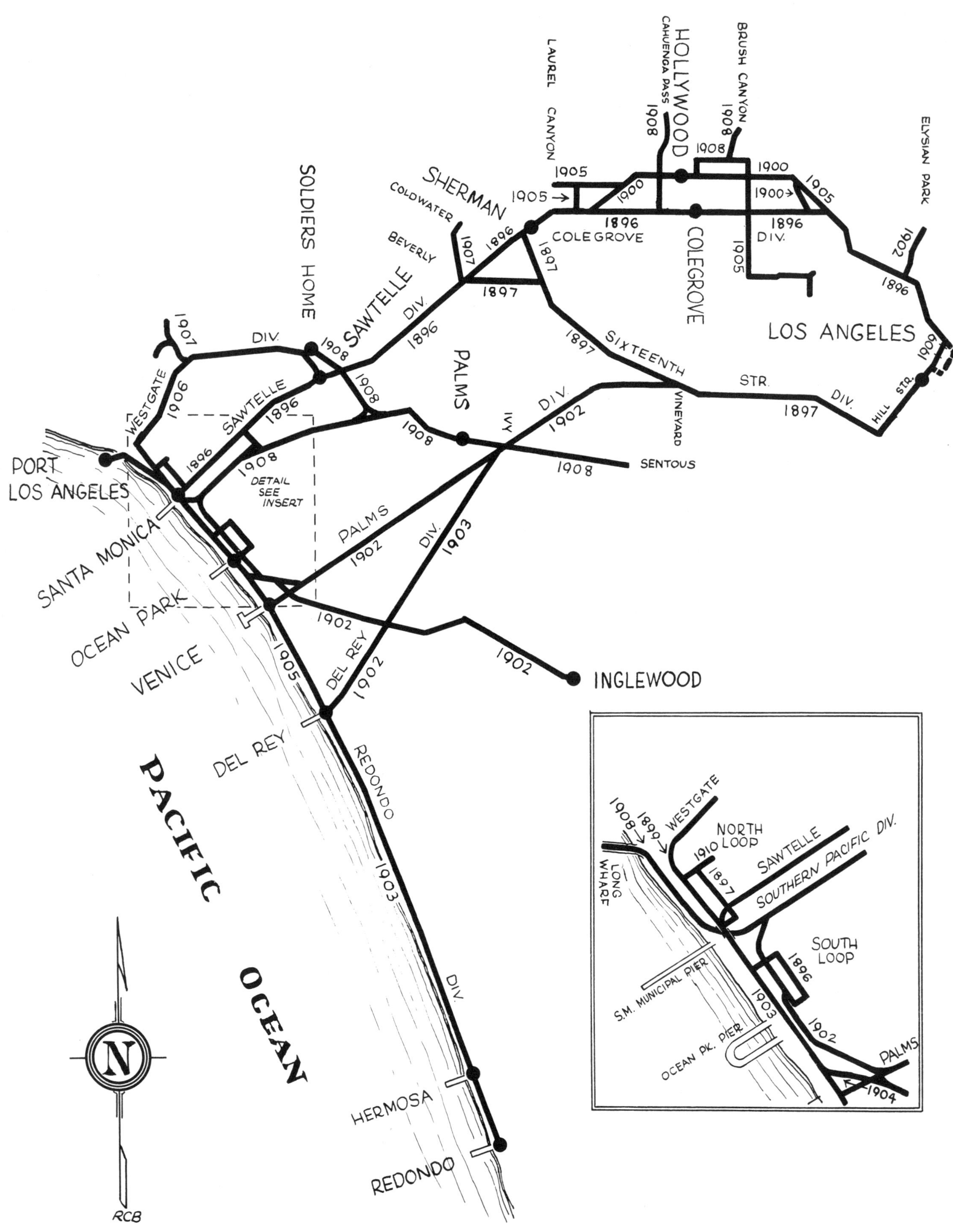
LAUREL CANYON
CAHUENGA PASS
HOLLYWOOD
1908
BRUSH CANYON
1908
1908
1908
ELYSIAN PARK
SHERMAN
COLDWATER
1905
1905
1900
1900
1900
1905
1896
COLEGROVE
1896
DIV.
1905
BEVERLY
1907
1896
1897
COLEGROVE
1902
SOLDIERS HOME
SAWTELLE
DIV.
1896
1897
1897
SIXTEENTH
1896
LOS ANGELES
1907
DIV.
1908
PALMS
1908
1897
STR.
1909
WESTGATE
1906
1908
1908
IVY
DIV.
1902
VINEYARD
1897
DIV.
HILL STR.
PORT
LOS ANGELES
1896
SAWTELLE
1896
1908
1908
SENTOUS
DETAIL
SEE
INSERT
SANTA MONICA
PALMS
1902
DIV.
1903
OCEAN PARK
1902
VENICE
1905
DEL REY
1902
1902
INGLEWOOD
DEL REY
REDONDO
1903
PACIFIC
DIV.
OCEAN
1903
N
HERMOSA
REDONDO
RCB
WESTGATE
1908
1899
NORTH
LOOP
SAWTELLE
SOUTHERN PACIFIC DIV.
1910
1897
LONG
WHARF
SOUTH
LOOP
1896
S.M. MUNICIPAL PIER
1903
OCEAN PK. PIER
1902
PALMS
1904

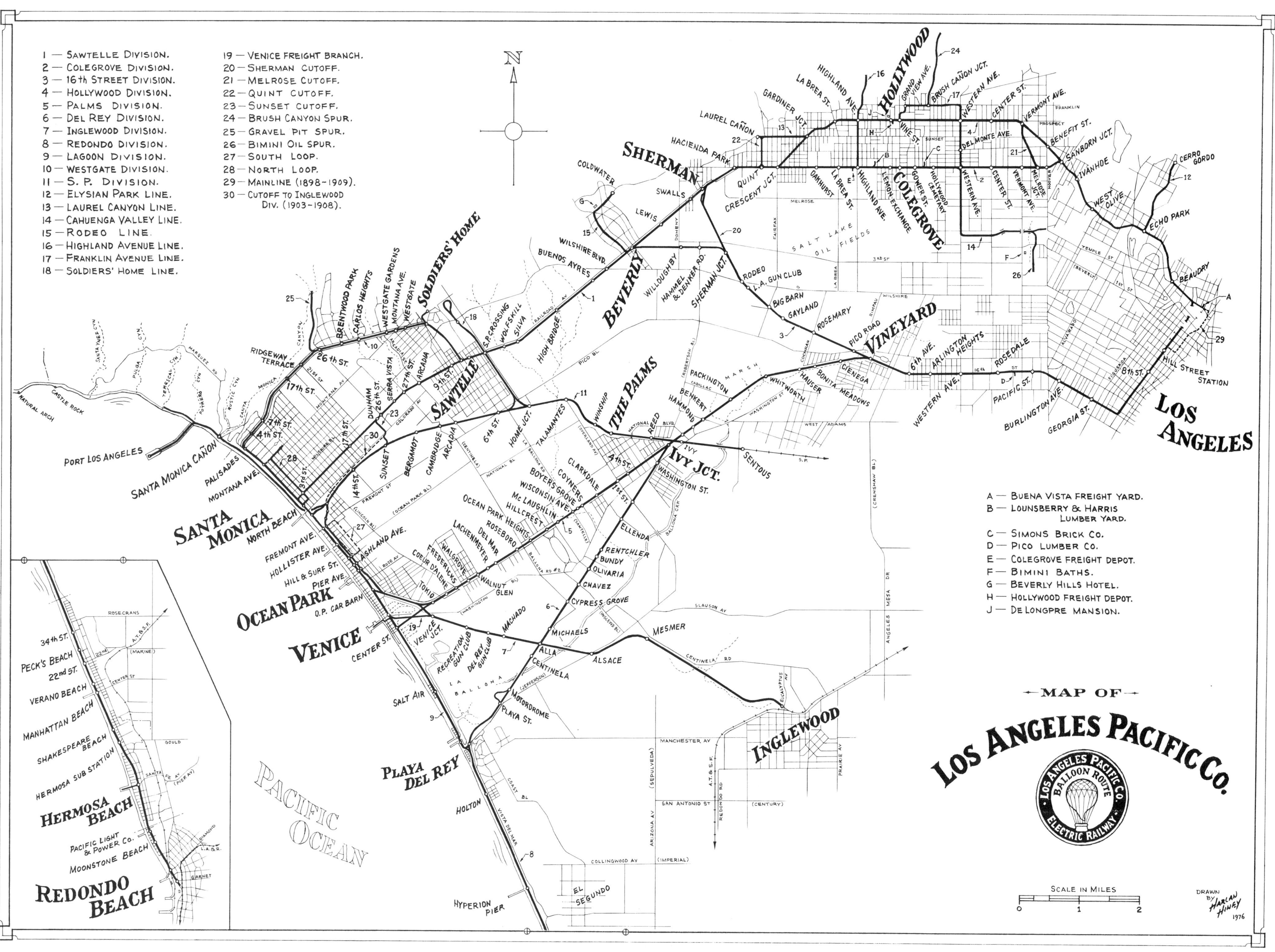

1 — Sawtelle Division.
2 — Colegrove Division.
3 — 16th Street Division.
4 — Hollywood Division.
5 — Palms Division.
6 — Del Rey Division.
7 — Inglewood Division.
8 — Redondo Division.
9 — Lagoon Division.
10 — Westgate Division.
11 — S. P. Division.
12 — Elysian Park Line.
13 — Laurel Canyon Line.
14 — Cahuenga Valley Line.
15 — Rodeo Line.
16 — Highland Avenue Line.
17 — Franklin Avenue Line.
18 — Soldiers' Home Line.
19 — Venice Freight Branch.
20 — Sherman Cutoff.
21 — Melrose Cutoff.
22 — Quint Cutoff.
23 — Sunset Cutoff.
24 — Brush Canyon Spur.
25 — Gravel Pit Spur.
26 — Bimini Oil Spur.
27 — South Loop.
28 — North Loop.
29 — Mainline (1898–1909).
30 — Cutoff to Inglewood Div. (1903–1908).
A — Buena Vista Freight Yard.
B — Lounsberry & Harris Lumber Yard.
C — Simons Brick Co.
D — Pico Lumber Co.
E — Colegrove Freight Depot.
F — Bimini Baths.
G — Beverly Hills Hotel.
H — Hollywood Freight Depot.
J — De Longpre Mansion.
N
HOLLYWOOD
SHERMAN
COLEGROVE
BEVERLY
VINEYARD
LOS ANGELES
SANTA MONICA
SOLDIERS' HOME
SAWTELLE
THE PALMS
OCEAN PARK
VENICE
PLAYA DEL REY
INGLEWOOD
PACIFIC OCEAN
REDONDO BEACH
HERMOSA BEACH
Port Los Angeles
Ivy Jct.
MAP OF
LOS ANGELES PACIFIC CO.
LOS ANGELES PACIFIC CO. BALLOON ROUTE ELECTRIC RAILWAY
SCALE IN MILES
0   1   2
DRAWN BY HARLAN HINEY 1976

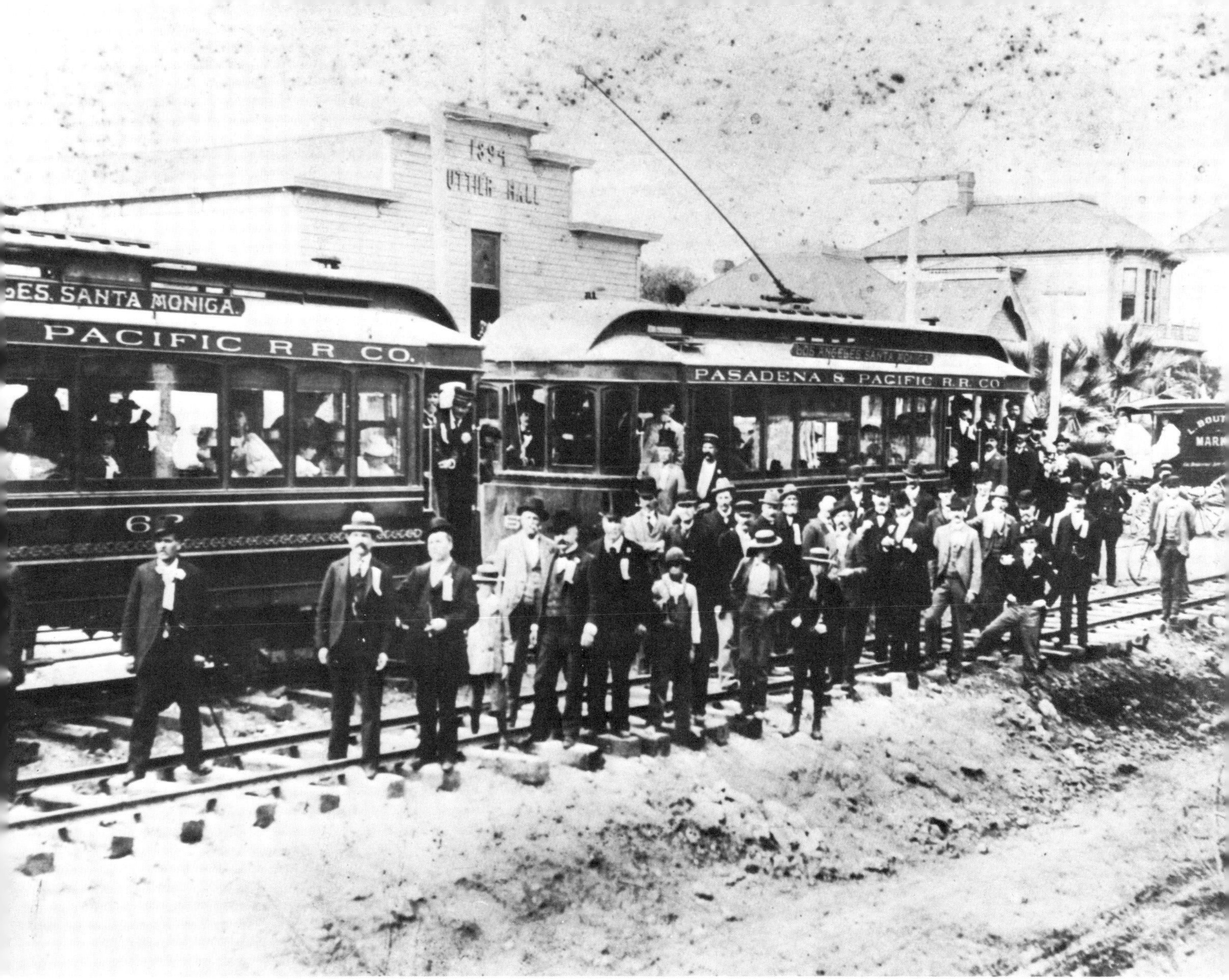

IT'S OPENING DAY on the new line to Santa Monica with two 60-class cars somewhere along the line. Note top-hatted dignitaries, and the absolute absence of ballast under the track. Wonder what top speed could have been?   (Interurbans)

Construction of the P&P was begun by the contractor, E.P. Clark, on June 11, 1895. From Bellevue (Sunset) and Buena Vista (N. Broadway), the new line was built on the roadbed of the old *Elysian Park Street Railway* as far as Echo Park Ave. From the latter point west, the abandoned roadbed of the *Los Angeles and Pacific Railway* was generally followed. This old steam-powered line had briefly offered through service to Santa Monica from the end of the Temple Street Cable Railway in late 1888 and 1889, before going bankrupt on December 1, 1889.

Utilizing in some instances the rusting 40-lb. rails of the old steam line, the P&P inched westward. From Echo Park Ave. to Hoover (on Sunset) the new line was double track; west of Hoover it was single track with several passing sidings. From Vermont Avenue west to the site of the new Sherman Shops (about today's Santa Monica Blvd. and San Vicente) the trolley line followed what became Santa Monica Blvd., rather than the Fountain Ave. alignment of the old steam road. From Soldiers' Home (Sawtelle) to Santa Monica, P&P electrified the tracks of the *Santa Monica and Soldiers' Home Railroad Co.'s* horsecar line, via Oregon Ave. (Santa Monica Blvd.).

In Santa Monica, the P&P built on the Soldiers' Home line to the bluff overlooking the ocean, where it turned south on Ocean Avenue. It continued south to Front (Pico), then east to 4th, south on Hill St. in Ocean Park, west on Hill to 2nd, where a small yard was built, and north on 2nd (Main) to a junction with its own line at 2nd and Front.

The new single-track interurban was built to the Los Angeles city 3'6" trolley gauge using 40-lb. rail, but overhead for a second track was erected; experience with the P&LA had shown Sherman and Clark that the upsurge in traffic following the line's opening would soon require extensive double tracking.

The completion of the P&P was heralded with a general public jubilation akin to the commotion a later generation would lavish upon the first successful space flight. The first trip was made on April 1, 1896, the first car into Santa Monica being No. 65, with "motoneer" Peter Reed at the controls. It arrived at 3:40 p.m., bringing city and county officials and prominent citizens, and was followed by a car loaded with tourists from Minnesota. A tremendous celebration followed, fueled with all the civic exuberancy typical of the era. Guns were fired, bands played, and the schools were let out. The trolley car had come to town: Santa Monica and environs were about to enter the Modern Age.

In May 1896, the P&P purchased the *Cahuenga Valley Railroad* for the valuable right of way franchises held by that steam road in the Hollywood area. From time to time over the next four years, portions of the Cahuenga Valley were converted to electric operation, but the last steam trains operated over the remaining trackage as late as 1915.

In May 1897, the first local line on the P&P was opened on Third Street in Santa Monica. Running from Oregon Ave. to Montana Ave., it was built on part of the horsecar line's roadbed. Thereafter the horsecar to the Soldiers' Home turned back at 3rd & Nevada.

An event destined to play a key part in the building up of the vast area between central Los Angeles and the Pacific Ocean occurred on November 9, 1896: the incorporating by Sherman and Clark of the *Pasadena & Pacific Railway Co. of California.*

This corporation at once began building an entirely new entry into Los Angeles from the original line at Beverly (Beverly Hills) Station. The new line ran on private right of way east from Beverly (now Burton Way-San Vicente Blvd.-Venice Blvd.) to Vineyard, entering the city limits at W. 16th St. (Venice Blvd.) & Arlington Ave. It then proceeded east on or adjacent to 16th St. to Hill St., then north on Hill to 4th and east on 4th to the P&P Station. The new line was somewhat better built, having 56 or 60-lb. rail, new redwood ties and decomposed granite ballast. More importantly it was about two miles shorter than the original line and took most of the beach traffic away from the old line along what was to become Santa Monica Blvd. through Colegrove. This new line was placed in service on July 1, 1897, and was called the "Santa Monica Short Line."

To permit cars from the new line to get to Sherman Shops expeditiously, a single track was built from Sherman Jct. to the shops; this became known as the "Sherman Cutoff."

Prior to the construction of the W. 16th line, the *Los Angeles Traction Co.* (LAT) had built a line over a part of that street from Burlington (then Bush St.) to Georgia St. P&P obtained trackage rights over this LAT trackage as well as LAT trackage on Hill St. between 4th and 8th Sts. In return, P&P gave LAT trackage rights over W. 16th from Georgia to Hill and on Hill from 16th to 8th Streets.

Los Angeles-Pacific

For a while, Sherman and Clark managed to finance the rapid expansion of their interurban system, but a national business depression in 1897 and 1898 plunged the two builders into a very turbulent period. The P&LA defaulted on its bond payments on July 7, 1897, and the line's other bond-

HUSTLE AND BUSTLE in Santa Monica's steam railroad days. This was the Southern Pacific's depot, circa 1890. Note hotel at right, old trestle heading toward oceanfront at left.

(Magna Collection)

holders forced the company into the hands of a receiver in January 1898. Sherman and Clark were then faced with the problem of divorcing the two interurban systems, while retaining what they could.

It is not clear the exact progression of steps they took, but in short order a bewildering succession of new corporations were formed, merged, and dissolved. When one merger appeared to be hazardous on legal grounds, it was followed by a subsequent reincorporation, a new merger, and so on, *ad infinitum*. P&LA was sold by the Court on April 27, 1898 and was reorganized as the *Los Angeles & Pasadena Electric Railway Co.* The elaborate corporate juggling act resulted in an eminently successful conclusion for the dynamic traction duo, for Henry E. Huntington eventually bought the *Los Angeles &*

THE COMPLETION of the P&P's line to Santa Monica brought a new pastime: trolley excursions. Here a motor of the 70 class arrives with three (!) trailers jammed to the roofs.
(Security Pacific Bank)

Pasadena from Sherman and Clark and, to quote Huntington: "General Sherman has made himself a nice profit."

The succession of legal corporations which bore either the P&P or LAP name during those troubled times need not be explained at this point; their histories are set forth in an Appendix later in this book. The next company to have an important part in expanding the LAP system was the *Los Angeles-Pacific Railroad Co.*, incorporated in California on June 4, 1898. Sherman and Clark headed it, with Clark the president. This company did several major things:

1. **It laid the second track** from Santa Monica to Beverly in 1898.
2. **It built the Ocean Ave.** extension in Santa Monica from Oregon Ave. to Montana St., and a line on Montana to 3rd where it connected with the 3rd St. Line; this formed what became known as the North Loop, and was opened on December 28, 1899.
3. **It built additional stretches** of second track on the original lines in Colegrove, and a complete second track between Beverly and Sherman.
4. **It built the Hollywood line**, using a part of the *Cahuenga Valley* roadbed, opening this line in April, 1900.
5. **The Oil Spur** and the Quint Cutoff were added to the Cahuenga Valley operation
6. **It built the first part** of the Trolleyway trackage—from Front St. to the Club House near Venice.
7. **The Palms Division** (Venice Short Line) was started. It

opened Aug. 16, 1902. This was eventually to become LAP's most important line to the beaches, outlasting all other routes.
8. **The Inglewood Line** of the Santa Fe was purchased.
9. **It built a second power house** at Ocean Park—plus a small car barn there.

By June 9, 1902, when this company was merged, the system had grown to a total of 102.635 miles of equivalent single track.

Sherman and Clark's growing trolley system took on a major new dimension when during September, 1902, work was started on a double track narrow gauge electric line from a junction with the Palms Division at Ivy (Culver City). The line ran down the coast through Playa del Rey, where the duo had important real estate holdings, to Manhattan, Hermosa and Redondo Beach. Opened to Playa del Rey on December 7, 1903 and through to Redondo late next summer, the line was built under the name of the *Los Angeles, Hermosa Beach and Redondo Railway Co.*, a non-operating subsidiary that was merged into yet another new company on June 16, 1903—the *Los Angeles Pacific Railroad Co. of California.*

Los Angeles Pacific Railroad Co. of California

This company was incorporated in California on June 16, 1903, and acquired about 132 miles of road from its constitu-

'TWAS A GALA DAY in Santa Monica when the first electric cars from Los Angeles rolled into town. Car 65 is shown leading two others of the 60 class on their inaugural entry into the beach city.   *(Security Pacific Bank)*

HILL STREET IN THE FLEDGLING DAYS: In the top photo, taken in 1906, the street ends abruptly at First St.; construction of the Hill Street tunnels was a year or so in the future. View was taken from near Fourth St. Bottom photo looks south on Hill from Fourth, also in 1906.   (Top: Interurbans; Bottom: Title Insurance)

Los Angeles & Pacific Railway Co.

MAIN LINE.

Santa Monica Time Schedule.

On and after February 23, 1889, trains will leave depot, corner of Bellevue and Beaudry Avenues, near Sisters' Hospital, for Santa Monica and way stations, as follows:

Leave LOS ANGELES	Leave SANTA MONICA
WEEK DAYS.	**WEEK DAYS.**
10:00 A. M.	8:00 A. M.
2:00 P. M.	12:40 P. M.
5:40 P. M.	4:20 P. M.
SUNDAYS.	**SUNDAYS.**
9:00 A. M.	8:00 A. M.
10:00 A. M.	10:10 A. M.
11:20 A. M.	11:25 A. M.
1:30 P. M.	3:30 P. M.
6:00 P. M.	4:30 P. M.

PACKAGES AND FREIGHT

Carried to Santa Monica and all points on the road at reasonable rates.

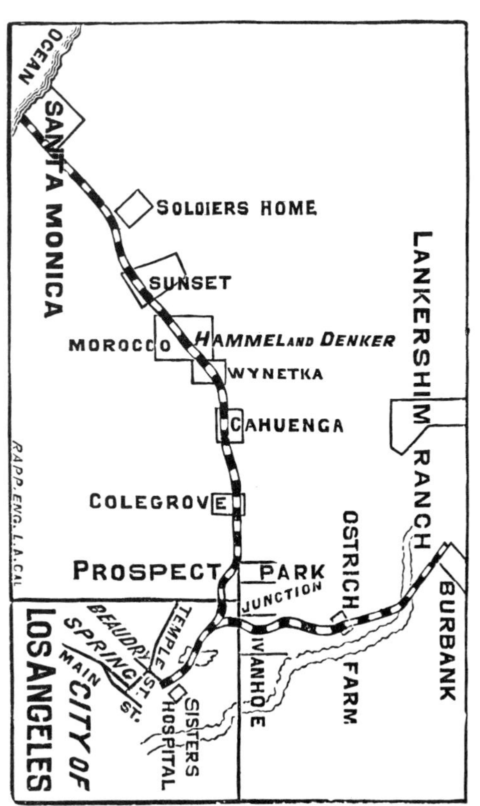

Los Angeles & Pacific Railway Co.

BURBANK DIVISION.

TIME SCHEDULE. On and after Feb. 23, 1889, trains will leave depot, corner Bellevue and Beaudry Avenues, near Sisters' Hospital, for Ostrich Farm and Burbank, as follows:

Leave LOS ANGELES	Leave BURBANK
WEEK DAYS.	**WEEK DAYS.**
7:00 A. M.	6:00 A. M.
10:30 A. M.	8:00 A. M.
1:45 P. M.	11:15 A. M.
4:00 P. M.	2:25 P. M.
6:00 P. M.	4:40 P. M.
SUNDAYS.	**SUNDAYS.**
10:00 A. M.	10:40 A. M.
*11:30 A. M.	4:40 P. M.
* 1:30 P. M.	**LEAVE OSTRICH FARM**
* 2:30 P. M.	ON SUNDAYS.
3:30 P. M.	12:00 M.
6:00 P. M.	2:00 P. M.
	3:00 P. M.
	4:52 P. M.

*Goes to Ostrich Farm only.

All trains stop at Ostrich Farm, going and returning.

Packages and freight carried to Burbank and all points on the road at reasonable rates.

RARE 1889 TIMETABLE of the old narrow-gauge Los Angeles & Pacific Railway Co., a narrow-gauge steam railway which went through Hollywood on what is now Fountain Ave. "Burbank Division" was the old Los Angeles & Ostrich Farm Ry. In 1887 the two divisions became the Los Angeles County RR; a year later the LA&P. Photo at bottom shows Sunset Blvd. in 1903. The horseless carriage has the road to itself. (Top: Huntington Library; bottom, Magna Collection).

ent companies: LA-P, the LA, HB&R, and the *Los Angeles-Santa Monica Railroad Co.* which was formed by Sherman and Clark on December 2, 1902, to build a line up the coast some 50 miles.

This corporation accomplished the following:

1. **Settled the intense rivalry** with the LAT by buying all stock of the LAT's interurban subsidiary, the *Los Angeles, Ocean Park & Santa Monica Railway Co.* This bitter interurban war raged from December 8, 1902 until July 13, 1903, dividing Santa Monica into two partisan camps; one backing Sherman and Clark, the other siding with rival traction tycoons William S. Hook and Abbot Kinney.
2. **Completed the Vineyard Power House**, started by LA-P.
3. **Constructed the Hollywood Cutoff** in the spring of 1905 whereby the Melrose Cutoff was replaced by a double track straight line from Vermont Ave. to Sanborn Jct.
4. **Built the balance** of the double track on the Colegrove (Santa Monica Blvd.) line between Sherman and Los Angeles.
5. **Extended the Lagoon Line** from just south of Venice to Playa del Rey.
6. **Electrified the Laurel Canyon Line** and the Western Ave. Line to Beverly & Alexandria (Cahuenga Valley Line).

On October 12, 1905, this company was merged into the LAP Company.

Sherman and Clark did not gain the lucrative Pacific beach traffic without a fight. And a colossal fight it was—for a while. Their old 1894 city line competitor William S. Hook and his

partner, Abbot Kinney, had incorporated the *Los Angeles, Ocean Park & Santa Monica Railway Co.* on December 8, 1902, to build to Santa Monica via a different route, using West Jefferson Street and going through Ocean Park.

THE FAMED HOLLYWOOD HOTEL, Hollywood Blvd. and Highland, prior to construction of the Highland Ave. car line in 1908.

(Southern California Edison)

That epic struggle, settled finally in the summer of 1903, was documented fully in the contemporary press—especially the *Santa Monica Outlook,* a newspaper ever on the alert to the prospect of the impending traction competition and its effect on the fortunes of rival seaside communities. Excerpts from the *Outlook* and other newspapers follow.

January 28, 1903: Grading has begun on LAT's new line. Houses are being moved from along the line of the LAP in Ocean Park and soon track laying will begin. The two roads will run parallel.

February 27: "At Ocean Park we want and will have the Traction road. Competition is the spice of life. LAT may be pepper to North Santa Monica but it is salt for us, and salt is a healthful life preserver." This from a realtor's advertisement.

March 4: LAT sues to condemn LAP lot on the east line of Surf St. LAP failed to use this property until the past week when work began on a depot. This long after the LAT line had been carried over the land.

March 18: Both LAP and LAT are bringing all available men into their track laying camps so as to be eligible to vote on April 13th. Three registrars have been working for the last 30 days and on March 4th the city registrations showed an increase of 343 votes over last November. The grading camp vote is estimated at 135, equally divided.

March 24: LAT rails are in place from Hollister St. to Pier Ave. Grading from Hollister to Bridge No. 2 (Pico) is about completed and ready for ties and rails.

April 16: LAP brings suit against LAT to restrain it from laying rails through Ocean Park.

April 19: The *Los Angeles Times* says LAT has been sold to Harriman of the SP. (Actual sale was April 14.)

May 14: *Los Angeles Times*—The $110,000 W. 6th St. franchise was bought last week by (E.H.) Harriman "to spank (Henry) Huntington and make him promise to be good." The alliance of Clark and Sherman with Huntington is such that it is well nigh inconceivable that LAP should oppose him in his plans. Huntington owns a large block of bonds in LAP and is closely identified in other ways with Sherman and Clark. General Sherman says, "Why, I don't own the franchise; there's not a word of truth in the story. I don't own the W. 6th franchise, I don't want it. It begins nowhere and ends nowhere." There will be a merger of the LAT with the Huntington system. This merger will be forced. There will be but one great streetcar system in Los Angeles. The details will be announced and arranged in San Francisco and New York City.

May 14: *Los Angeles Herald*—Sherman and Clark have bought the W. 6th St. franchise to be in better shape to talk business with LAT. LAT owns the tracks on W. 16th St. between Georgia and Bush (Burlington) and LAP was recently unsuccessful in getting its own franchise over this stretch.

May 21: In order to compete with LAP, LAT would be compelled to run over five blocks on Ocean Ave. Under its present franchise it cannot do this. If LAT proposes to lay a double track of its own along Ocean Ave. across the new bridge and on up through Utah Ave., the people might just as well abandon those streets entirely to the railway companies—there would be no roadbed left for the driving public.

GIANTS' MARBLES, or—as was popularly believed—dinosaur eggs? In excavating to straighten Sunset Blvd. just west of Silver Lake Blvd. in 1907, a treasure trove of these huge rock spheres was uncovered. Photo below shows electric shovel excavating north side of Sunset Blvd.
(Both, Russell Westcott)

June 10: LAT has won out in its suit against LAP involving LAP's right to erect a depot on the land adjoining its tracks near Hill St. LAP will appeal to the Supreme Court.

June 22: Clark, (Frederick) Rindge, Sherman and others sue LAT to prevent it from building across a lot owned by them. LAT's case for condemnation is now pending but LAT is preparing to build its roadbed now.

July 2: Henry E. Huntington, president of the Huntington-Hellman Syndicate (PE) will come into possession of LAT within the next 30 days. The transfer is set for the 15th and $1,750,000 will pass to the Hooks.

July 13: A sudden let-up four weeks ago by construction crews of PE toward San Pedro and LAT crews toward Pasadena corroborate the theory that the details of the LAT transfer to Huntington are completed.

July 14: The sale of LAT took place yesterday. It was Southern Pacific money which passed to the Hooks—$1,515,000 plus $200,000 already paid. (Kinney, however, refused to give up—as the following developments indicate.)

July 21: Mysterious railroad surveyors are at work in Santa Monica. Meanwhile, Kinney asks permission to unload ties on Ocean Ave. between Bridges One and Two and to establish a grading camp on the south side.

July 27: Kinney's grading crews at 4:00 a.m. Sunday, July 26, start laying track on Colorado Ave. and on 4th St. They refuse to stop at order of City Trustees. By nightfall a double track on Colorado from Ocean to 4th was laid on top of the street grade and some double track on 4th northward from Colorado. Today the crews began tamping and thus raised the grade of Colorado by nearly a foot, violating their franchise.

August 7: A gang of LAP track layers began work yesterday to close the gap in the track running through the south end of Ocean Park and connecting with Short Line Beach. This piece of track, 1,400 feet long, runs through land owned by the Ocean Park Improvement Co. (Kinney) and LAP had to sue to gain a right of way. The LAP completed its track

NATION'S FIRST TRACKLESS TROLLEY operated from the end of LAP's Laurel Canyon line up to Bungalowtown in the hills, 1910. Independent line bought power from LAP.
(Title Insurance)

below this point some time ago but until the condemnation suit was settled the work could not be finished.

August 8: General Sherman denies that LAP will be included in any merger. He says LAP is becoming more valuable every day. "We are spending thousands of dollars in new grades, heavier rails, additional power, more cars and a hundred and one other things. We employ nearly a thousand men."

August 20: Huntington now owns LAT and Kinney is said to be holding him to a contract made with Hook to get a competing line into operation to Santa Monica. But Huntington, at the time he purchased the Pasadena line, agreed with Sherman and Clark not to invade the Santa Monica field although repeatedly urged to do so. Huntington, it is said, after repeated conferences with Sherman, has got his consent whereby the SP Santa Monica Line will be electrified and connected to Kinney's line at the Arcadia Hotel. Sherman would get a slice of the revenue.

[Ed.: Kinney stubbornly held out for his competing line until March 9, 1904; he then sold his shares—except for one—to Sherman and Clark.]

With the Kinney-Hook feud settled, Sherman and Clark shifted the expansion of their LAP into high gear. Hollywood, West Los Angeles and the Beach cities were all growing now—thanks to their humming rail lines—and the LAP itself was swiftly becoming a heavy-duty suburban railway, a far cry from its humble beginnings as a wandering country trolley line. And big financial developments were looming.

In February, 1906, Clark emphatically denied the latest current rumor that President E.H. Harriman of the Southern Pacific had secured control of LAP. In discussing the affairs of the LAP, Clark said the company had just about completed the floating of a $10 million bond issue for the purpose of standard gauging and re-equipping of its system.

Despite Clark's denial, a week later the rumors had gained considerable ground. The price paid Sherman and Clark was said to be $6 million and the purchaser was said to be Harriman, together with Kuhn, Loeb & Co. and the Standard Oil Co. Henry E. Huntington was said not to figure in the deal, despite the theory that he had long held an option on the LAP.

Rumors became reality when in mid-March Sherman belatedly confirmed the fact that the control of the LAP had been purchased by Harriman. The public got its first proof of the transaction in a document filed with the Los Angeles County Clerk on March 14th revealing that Col. Epes Randolph, representing Harriman, held 76,500 out of LAP's total of 150,000 shares. This came to light as the result of LAP's stockholders' voting on a proposition to create $12 million of bonded indebtedness. However, Sherman and Clark were to remain in direct control of the company.

Harriman money began to show up on the LAP almost immediately. At once large expenditures began to be made improving the system. Besides the expansion of the Vineyard Power House, other major projects were:

1. **The Hill Street Tunnels.**
2. **The 4th St. Subway** and attendant cutoffs to Vineyard, Sherman Jct., Hollywood, Western Ave. and Occidental Blvd.
3. **Standard gauging** the LAP system.
4. **New standard-gauge MU cars.**
5. **Four-tracking** the Venice Short Line from Vineyard to Venice.
6. **Construction** of the Westgate Line.
7. **Enlarging** Sherman Yards.
8. **New lines** and extensions of old lines to total more than 500 miles; these projected lines were: Laurel Canyon Extension to Westgate line, up Santa Monica Canyon three miles, up the coast 26 miles to the Ventura County line, from Santa Monica Canyon to Santa Ynez Canyon via Rustic Canyon (6 miles), to Russell Canyon from Sunset & Occidental (37 miles), and the electrification of the Nevada Ave. horsecar line in Santa Monica.

Los Angeles Pacific Co.

Incorporated in California on April 4, 1907, by Southern Pacific, this company was capitalized at $21 million (210,000 shares at $100 each). A total of 107,100 shares were held by Epes Randolph for Harriman.

This company completed standard gauging the system, and built the following new lines: The Western Ave.-Franklin Ave.-Brush Canyon line, the Highland Ave. line, the Rodeo line, and did the preliminary work on the San Fernando Valley line and the 8th St. line in Santa Monica.

The LAP also built the Hill Street Station on 429 S. Hill St., Los Angeles. This was a standard gauge station and for a time LAP operated two stations: the old depot at 316 W. 4th St. for the narrow gauge lines (Hollywood & Colegrove), and the new Hill St. Station for the lines going out W. 16th St. The station on 4th St. was destroyed by fire on November 16, 1908, and thereafter all activities were centered at the Hill St. Station, with the LAP offices located next door in the former Masonic Temple which LAP hurriedly leased after the conflagration.

It was the announced intention of this company to construct a limit height depot and office building on its Hill Street property in conjunction with the building of the 4th St. Subway. However, a succession of uncontrollable events postponed both projects until they were overtaken by changing times: first came the 1907 Panic, then the Great Merger, then World War I, and finally the jitney bus and the private automobile.

A notable event occurred on March 30, 1908: the first LAP three-car multiple-unit standard gauge train left the Hill St. Station on a test run. The test was a success and the new cars

*BEVERLY HILLS,
as it looked in 1910.
(Security Pacific
Bank)*

TOKIO STATION, on the outskirts of Venice, is shown in bottom photo.   (T.L. Wagenbach)

(the 700 Class) entered regular service the following day to the beaches.

On July 1, 1908, LAP began operating its cars over the Southern Pacific's Santa Monica line and the Soldiers' Home branch. An April 4, 1908 lease made this line available to LAP from Sentous to Port Los Angeles and to Soldiers' Home. LAP electrified the line and thus added 13.49 miles of route.

Another big job was the building of the Ocean Park Station; it faced on the Trolleyway between Pier Ave. and Marine St. and was a one-story structure with an ornamental colonnade.

Undoubtedly the biggest event in the development of Hollywood (until the arrival of the movie industry) occurred on September 15, 1909. On that day LAP opened its two Hill

Street tunnels for service. At the same time, the Hollywood and Colegrove lines began standard gauge operation and changed their downtown terminus to the Hill St. Station.

By using the tunnels, the circuitous route over LARy tracks to Sunset Blvd. was eliminated and 10 minutes saved per trip. Hollywood celebrated with an extravaganza—its first—featuring a monstrous parade and a civic celebration at the home of celebrated artist Paul DeLongpre.

The Great Merger

The events leading up to the Great Merger which consolidated all the electric·interurban railways in the Los Angeles Basin into the great *Pacific Electric* system were triggered by an event which occurred in May, 1910. After Harriman secured control of LAP in 1906, Sherman and Clark remained as minority stockholders and continued as executive officers and directors. On May 28, 1910, the two Arizonans retired from active participation in LAP after selling all their remaining stock to the Southern Pacific Co. Once in complete control of LAP, SP pressed Henry E. Huntington to sell his 50 percent of stock in the other suburban electric railways of the Los Angeles area.

Huntington was willing to talk. A restructuring of the electric lines into narrow-gauge city and standard-gauge interurban systems was worked out and negotiations were successfully terminated by the following year. Huntington retired from the interurban field to continue as owner of the city street railway system of Los Angeles, in the process pocketing a cash bonus running into eight figures. Harriman did not live to see this happen, as he died in 1909 in Russia where he had gone seeking to acquire control of the Trans-Siberian Railway for his dream project: a round-the-world railroad.

LAP brought into the new PE the following: 204.67 miles of owned lines (equivalent single track), 26.20 miles of leased lines, 172 passenger cars, 194 freight cars and 25 service cars. It also brought into the new company $21 million in outstand-

HAPPY BALLOON ROUTE excursionists pose with cars 900, 901 at Playa del Rey in 1909.   (Interurbans)

ing capital stock, $14,201,000 in outstanding bonds—a total in excess of $35 million which was the largest of any of the constituent companies, exceeding that of Old PE itself by almost six millions.

Effective September 1, 1911, LAP was consolidated with seven other electric railways to form the *Pacific Electric Railway Co.* The familiar LAP green disappeared from its cars and the PE red replaced it. LAP's mighty 700-class cars were removed to the Pasadena line and gradually the LAP name disappeared. A PE Western Division was created to administer the former LAP lines and a track connection was installed at 6th & Hill Sts., Los Angeles, so cars of the Western Division could reach other parts of the PE system. A second track connection was built at Amoco Jct. on the Air Line late in 1911 after the remainder of that line had been leased and electrified.

The Los Angeles Pacific had played out its role in the Southland's traction pageant—and retired from the stage. The spotlight was now upon the Pacific Electric, whose Big Red Cars were destined to write a traction legend of heroic—if not everlasting—proportions.

LAP Chronology 1895 1911

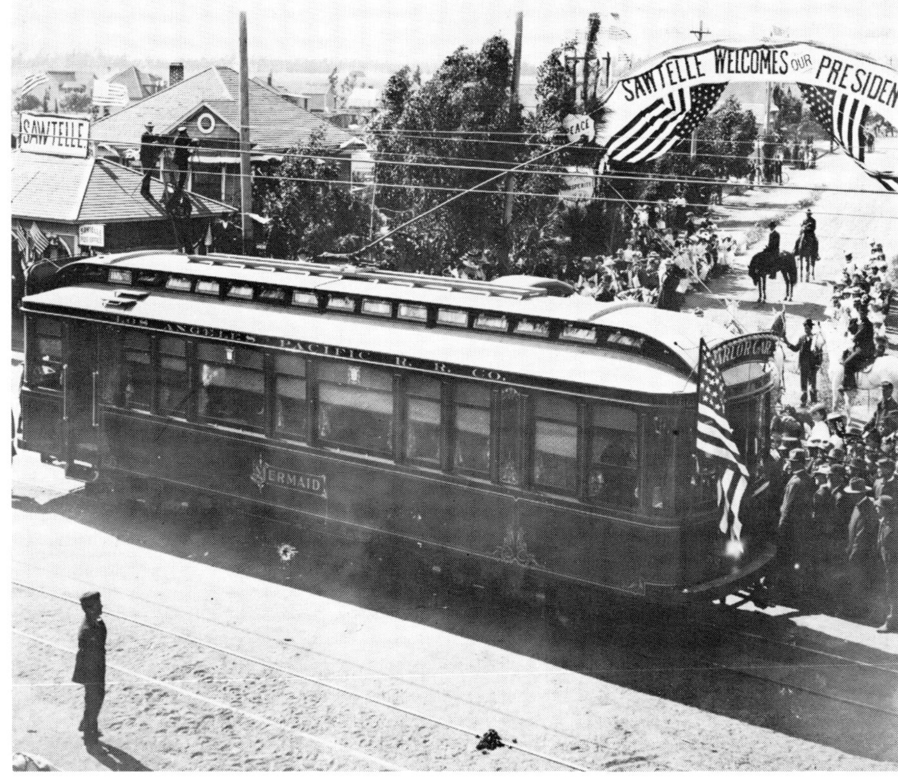

PROUDEST MOMENT FOR car "Mermaid" was the afternoon of Thursday, May 9, 1901, when it carried President McKinley and his cabinet to the Soldiers' Home. (Rudolph Brandt)

THE following brief news notes and comment have been culled from various sources including the daily newspapers, *Electric Railway Journal, Electric Railway Review,* and the official PE History. Entries have been kept as brief as possible; complete coverage of the items appears elsewhere in this work.

1895

May 2: The elegant new cars of the Pasadena & Los Angeles Electric Ry. are running today and they are labeled "Pasadena & Pacific." At present, however, if they get through as far as Los Angeles the Pasadena people will feel satisfied.

May 8: The handsome new P&LA cars reach Los Angeles bearing "Los Angeles & Santa Monica" labels. These have been replaced by titles reading "Pasadena & Pacific." That in itself is not bad for Santa Monica, for whenever those cars touch the Pacific shore it will be at SM.

1896

April 1: P&P opens its interurban line to Santa Monica via Hollywood.

July 1: South Loop operation starts.

First six months: Sherman Shops built.

1897

W. 16th St. line built, downtown L.A. to Beverly; first six months.

Third St. line, Santa Monica, opened in May.

Sherman Cutoff built, June and July.

Santa Monica Short Line opened July 1.

Sherman Cutoff opened late in July.

1898

Grading for second track between Santa Monica and Beverly.

1899

North Loop built late in year, opened Dec. 28.

Soldiers' Home horsecar partly abandoned.

1900

Second track completed between Beverly and Sherman.

Four miles of second track built on Colegrove line.

Hollywood line built and placed in operation in February.

Melrose Cutoff built; also Quint Cutoff and Oil Spur.

1901

Lagoon Line built, Santa Monica to Venice.

New Ocean Park power house built on Sunset Ave. adjacent to car barn; cost $25,000.

President McKinley visited Soldiers' Home; car "Mermaid" transported him.

1902

Venice Short Line built; opened on August 16.

Inglewood line purchased from Santa Fe on March 21; electrified.

Ivy Park-Del Rey line built; opened to del Rey on January 24, 1903.

Construction of Vineyard Power House begun in May.

Echo Park Ave. line electrified; opened on November 20.

No more will LAP allow its conductors to stop cars in the middle of the block when flagged by passengers, says the *Outlook* on July 5. Henceforth, cars will stop only at intersections.

1903

Line from Playa del Rey to Redondo completed; line placed in service late in summer.

Hook and Kinney build competing line on Trolleyway from Bicknell St. to Windward Ave., thence diagonally to connection with Inglewood Line in Venice.

Hook sells out his half interest in above line to SP representatives on April 14.

Work finished on new Vineyard power house.

Three bandits hold up LAP car on W. 16th near Normandie; one passenger shot dead, three others severely wounded.

As of June, LAP operates 129 miles of lines and 138 cars.

Bush St. substation built in July.

LAP condemning land in Redondo in September for a car house, shops and depot.

1904

LAP receives two shiploads of heavy steel rails, costing $100,000. Entire system to be put in shape to make fast time.

Vineyard power house being enlarged, and Ocean Park powerhouse converted into substation; this in March.

Hook-Kinney track on Trolleyway electrified and placed in operation.

President Clark returns from eastern trip and expresses himself as being heartily in favor of broad-gauging the system.

Lagoon line extended (double track) to a connection with Redondo line at Playa del Rey, opened August 26.

1905

Hollywood Cutoff built in spring.

Remainder of double-tracking on Colegrove line completed in summer.

Cahuenga Valley electrified from Western & Santa Monica to Beverly & Alexandria.

Venice Short Line Cutoff built (Venice) in latter part of year.

Vineyard powerhouse again enlarged.

Buena Vista freight house opened April; also del Rey depot.

Six express motors added in May.

7½ minute headway on Hollywood line and 15 minute headway on beach lines.

Two standard gauge freight locomotives completed at Sherman Shops in August; will haul SP and Santa Fe passenger trains to Venice from Sunset and Inglewood respectively.

Car 1552, just out of shops, jumps the track at Ivanhoe in November, tying up traffic.

1906

Harriman and the SP purchase a majority interest in LAP from Sherman and Clark for $6,000,000; this was revealed on March 14.

One hundred standard gauge interurban cars ordered, 25 of which will be trailers. (700 class.)

Sherman Yards enlarged and additional shop buildings constructed.

Surveys made for line up coast 15 miles from Long Wharf.

4th St. Subway revealed in July, along with projected cutoff lines from same to Vineyard, Sherman Jct. and Hollywood.

Hill St. tunnels also announced.

Plan to four-track Venice Short Line to Venice from Vineyard revealed in October.

Westgate Line constructed, "giving the public the most picturesque trolley ride in Los Angeles County," opened Feb. 14.

Linda Vista Station at North Beach opened in this year.

1907

Rodeo line built between April and August.

New shop buildings at Sherman built, May and June.

New yard and storage tracks built at the Buena Vista freight house during summer.

L.A. City Council by unanimous vote gives LAP permits for 4th St. Subway.

Ivy substation completed in July, as is new Sherman car house built to hold 100 cars.

LAP and LAIU secure injunction restraining City of L.A. from enforcing fender ordinance; city was arresting car crews and leaving cars standing in streets until new crews could reach them.

Gangs worked day and night standard gauging the system. Fifty new 700s to go in service as soon as Hill and W. 16th Sts. are standardized.

In December, LAP suspended all construction work and laid off 600 men temporarily. Most work in hand had been completed and no new work would start until financial conditions improve. Plans for subway and new downtown passenger station "not abandoned but temporarily postponed."

1908

Epes Randolph, representing Harriman, arrived in January to reorganize LAP.

Highland Ave. line opened from Santa Monica Blvd. to Cahuenga Pass.

Hill St. Station built between February and June.

Western-Franklin-Brush Canyon line constructed single track narrow gauge from January to April; standard gauged in May and June.

LAP's LAST BIG JOB was building through Cahuenga Pass to the San Fernando Valley. This 1911 photo shows the heavy construction that was necessary. Today one of the world's busiest freeways conducts thousands of automobiles through here hourly. (Security Pacific Bank)

Hill St. Tunnel No. 2 built between July and December.

4th St. Station and LAP offices burn on November 16.

Offices moved to Masonic Temple on Hill St. near Fifth in December.

Colegrove line standard gauged in May.

Santa Monica Air Line from Sentous to Long Wharf leased from SP on April 4; also Soldiers' Home Branch. Both were electrified and placed in operation in summer.

First three-car train operated from the Sherman Shops to Hill St. Station via W. 16th St. on March 30; test run.

700s enter regular service to Venice, Santa Monica and Redondo on March 31.

Electric service to Long Wharf begins on July 1.

Tunnel 2 completed on November 7.

New carhouse at Sherman built; also a new depot at Ocean Park.

1909

All interurban cars fitted with pilots in January.

Tunnel 1 completed, September.

Tunnel Day celebrated September 15; all major lines now standard gauge.

Hollywood line standard gauged, June.

1910

LAP places order for 125 large steel cars for use on Oakland-Alameda-Berkeley lines of SP, January.

SP purchases minority interest of Sherman and Clark in May; thereafter SP 100% in control.

Construction of line over Cahuenga Pass to San Fernando Valley started.

Borings for 4th St. Subway begin, June.

First American trackless trolley line began operation in Laurel Canyon in summer; got power from LAP.

South Loop abandoned in latter part of year and tracks taken up.

Portion of North Loop also abandoned.

Los Angeles Board of Public Utilities limits LAP cars to 20 mph on Sunset Blvd.

Sale of PE to SP, largest deal of its kind in the history of the west, was closed on November 8.

LAP discontinues use of Long Wharf for lumber handling on December 17.

Montana Ave. extension from 3rd to 7th St. built late in year.

1911

LAP electrified Air Line from Sentous to Clement Jct. in first half of year but did not place same in operation.

LAP head, Paul Shoup, assumed active management of New PE in January.

Management of PE and LAP merged on February 1. LAP men get most of key positions.

LAP begins exchanging tickets with Los Angeles & Redondo Railway at Redondo, effective April 1.

Venice Short Line and Hollywood line reconstructed in first half of year.

Consolidation of LAP, Old PE, Riverside & Arlington, Redlands Central, L.A. Interurban, LA&R, San Bernardino Interurban into the new Pacific Electric Railway Company became effective on September 1.

Western Division created September 1.

Hollywood Before

Chapter Two

First car through the Hill Street Tunnels, Sept. 23, 1909.　　　　*(Title Insurance)*

the Movies

LAP's Green Cars

Brought Boom Times

To the Future Film

Capital, to the

Beaches, and

Points in Beween

TO PROPERLY appreciate LAP, one must understand what it did for the country it served. This chapter directs the attention of the reader to the communities on the LAP's lines. Their history is, in most instances, as colorful as that of LAP itself.

The settlement of the land between Los Angeles and its west beaches took place in waves. The Great Boom of 1887 caused the first development of the rich territory; at that time such cities as Hollywood, Santa Monica, Palms and Redondo first appeared. When that boom ended in the summer of 1888, other cities founded less securely disappeared; among these were Sunset (where Westwood Village now flourishes) and Port Ballona (later to be resurrected as Playa del Rey).

In 1896 began the LAP Era. Frequent, dependable transportation at low cost via the clean, speedy electric cars resulted in new settlements springing up all along its system. Among these communities are Sawtelle, Venice, Playa del Rey, Manhattan Beach and Hermosa Beach. These cities all attracted permanent residents and today they flourish, although LAP's rails have disappeared.

LAP disappeared in the Great Merger of 1911, but its cities continued to grow. Under Pacific Electric operation, the LAP Country experienced steady progress; more new cities appeared: Culver City, Beverly Hills (founded in LAP's day, but its real development took place after 1912).

The San Fernando Valley is not included herein due to the fact that it was not an LAP area; although LAP's rails were being pushed deep into the valley over Cahuenga Pass in 1911, the Great Merger gave to PE the distinction of being the prime mover in the development of the Valley.

The LAP Country may be said to have consisted of three separate areas: (1) The Cahuenga Valley, from Hollywood to Santa Monica; (2) The string of beach cities, Santa Monica to Redondo; (3) The interior country between Venice and Vineyard. All three areas owe an enormous debt to LAP's green interurban cars.

Luther A. Ingersoll, in his *Century History of Santa Monica Bay Cities,* pays homage to LAP thusly: "It is safe to say that LAP caused the beach population to double inside of five years. So satisfactory has been their service that steam lines cannot compete. . . . We cannot question that our tremendous population growth and the growth of our electric railway mileage has a relation."

The Great Boom of 1886-87 merits a full description, for it was the foundation on which the LAP country was built. On

SHERMAN CAR HOUSE was out in the country when car 246 posed.   *(Interurbans)*

November 29, 1885, Santa Fe trains began entering Los Angeles from the east. The breaking of the Southern Pacific monopoly led to a rate war which was the first and greatest cause of the Boom. At first the rate from Chicago was dropped from $115 to $70 with freight rates mercilessly slashed. On February 21, 1886, tickets from Missouri River points to Los Angeles sold for $25. On March 6 the price fell to $20 from Chicago and $35 from New York City. For a few hours on March 8 tickets from Los Angeles to the Missouri River sold for $1! This was the climax. Naturally, such a travel bargain was seized upon by thousands of people who had never dreamed of seeing California and a great rush ensued. As this influx continued, prices of lots rose and real estate changed hands at prices which astonished oldtimers. Then the speculative fever seized old residents and newcomers alike and professional boomers and land sharks helped feed it.

Townsites were laid out anywhere and everywhere; if in the desert, they were health resorts; if in the mountains, mineral rights were emphasized; if at the shore, promises of gaudy resorts were the lure. Ads, auctions, bands and excursions helped the excitement along. Everyone expected to make up to 500% on their investment, and some actually did. One man decided to spend the day at the seashore but was sold a lot out in the Westlake district for $50 while walking to the station; upon returning that evening the same agent awaited him, eager to buy back the lot for $200! Many present cities were thus born and some survived, having real merit: Glendale, Garvanza, Glendora, Azusa, Alhambra. At the height of the boom in May, June and July of 1887, usually the dullest months, real estate sales amounted to more than $35,000,000. To help sell the tracts, promoters built steam dummy lines to serve them; thus LAP's predecessors came into being.

Hollywood

IT HAS BEEN SAID that "Hollywood" is the world's best-known proper noun, that the geographical location known by this name is the world's most famous city, although such a city doesn't exist (being but a part of a greater city). Be that as it may, the history of the Hollywood area is probably more interesting than is the majority of its celluloid masterpieces.

Earliest settlers found the land covered thickly with cactus. from whose thorny depths yowled the wildcat and howled the coyote. The Spaniards had a name for Hollywood: "La Nopalera," the area covered with cactus. Once cleared, the land was good only for grazing, as the water supply was almost nonexistent. In 1875 the Cahuenga Valley had managed to find some water, and here and there a windmill laboriously pulled the precious liquid up from the depths to be spread sparingly on the thirsty acres whereon grew barley. In 1879 a terrible drought hastened the end of the cattle era; sheep by the thousands died and starving cattle were stampeded in great herds over the cliffs into the sea. Then it was that experiments with oranges and lemons began. Slowly the area grew, but it was in a haphazard way with no incorporated city to lead the way. Forty acres were purchased near Hollywood Blvd. and Gower for $10 each.

In 1883 Horace H. Wilcox, ultimately the founder of Hollywood, came to Los Angeles from Topeka, Kansas, where he had made his fortune in the real estate business despite having lost completely the use of his legs as a result of typhoid fever. Wilcox purchased three tracts of land in Los Angeles and subdivided them. Much of the University district was built up through his efforts. Mrs. Wilcox was his constant advisor. Their

HOLLYWOOD, 1903, looking southwest from Beachwood Canyon.   (Security Pacific Bank)

only child passed away at the age of 19 months, and to solace themselves the Wilcoxes took long drives on Sunday afternoons. One of their favorite trips was out through the beautiful Cahuenga Valley. A certain fig and apricot orchard, centering at Hollywood Blvd. and Cahuenga Ave. (using today's names) was greatly admired by them and they purchased it. Shortly thereafter Mrs. Wilcox had to return East, and while on the train she became acquainted with a wealthy lady who often spoke of her country home named "Hollywood." The name pleased Mrs. Wilcox and when she returned to Los Angeles she so named her country place.

The Santa Fe Railway had been completed in 1885 and the wildest boom Southern California has ever known was upon the land. Wilcox made considerable money opening subdivisions but he sold little land in Hollywood. He moved one of his farmhouses to Cahuenga Ave., gave up his ornate Los Angeles home (on Hill Street, later the site of the LAP Hill Street Station), and moved to Hollywood permanently. To make Hollywood live up to its name, he imported two English holly bushes which were very carefully nurtured, to no avail. They did not thrive.

Wilcox was not frightened by the bursting of the boom in 1889. He cut up his 160-acre ranch with avenues running from Gower to Hudson and from Franklin to Sunset and lined his streets with pepper trees. A terrible drought came and his wells went dry. Watermelons were broken around the young pepper sprouts to keep them alive. Next year the whole country was flooded.

AT ABOUT THIS TIME Senator Cornelius Cole laid out Colegrove, now South Hollywood. He came to South Hollywood in 1880 after having received almost 500 acres there as a legal fee. The town he founded got a post office and became the address for most of the Cahuenga Valley.

Wilcox persuaded the Cahuenga Valley RR to extend its steam dummy line (see Unit 41) up Western Ave. and out Prospect Ave. (now Hollywood Blvd.) to Wilcox Ave. Tourists began to come, and some bought ranches, but not enough to keep the dummy line running. Then came E.C. Hurd, a wealthy Colorado miner. He bought acreage at the corner of Wilcox and Prospect and put in an immense lemon orchard, spending $50,000 for water. Hurd bought out the Cahuenga Valley Railroad and extended it to Laurel Canyon. This was somewhat of a help, but Hollywood was only a fair success. In

1892 Wilcox had died, land poor. Hurd followed him in a few years.

The Lean Nineties saw Hollywood engaged in a long and fruitless battle for water. Money was scarce, vegetable farmers were ruined, most people were land poor. Up to 1900 there were not more than 500 people in Hollywood and most of them came only after the electric cars began running through to Santa Monica from Los Angeles. The cars brought tourists, and at Cahuenga Ave. delivered them to C.M. Pierce (later to be the operator and chief guide of the Balloon Route Trolley Trip), who drove them around the valley in a tallyho and gave them a chicken dinner at the Glen-Holly Hotel, all for 75 cents. This hotel, a rambling frame structure, stood at Ivar and Yucca. After dinner, the tourists retook the car for the beach.

In the late Nineties Paul DeLongpre, the famous French painter of flowers, came to Los Angeles. In 1901 Mrs. Wilcox offered him three acres at the corner of Hollywood Blvd. and Cahuenga in exchange for three of his paintings; he readily accepted, and the DeLongpre Era began. He built a lovely home of Moorish architecture with a great gallery and planted a garden of flowers that was soon widely admired. The LAP Balloon Route excursionists always stopped at Cahuenga long enough to permit the tourists to go through the DeLongpre gallery and garden and there have their pictures taken. Many hundreds of permanent Hollywood residents were first attracted to this area through these excursions and DeLongpre's fame.

In 1903 Hollywood was incorporated as a city, whose boundaries were Normandie Ave. on the east, Fairfax Ave. on the west, Sunset Blvd. on the south, and the hills on the north. One of the first ordinances of the new city was one prohibiting

In Hollywood It Was Illegal To Drive Large Flocks of Sheep

bands of more than 2,000 sheep being driven through the streets at any one time. Another ordinance denied a liquor license to the Hollywood Hotel, the first wing of which was completed in 1902.

Rain was more plentiful in the 1900s and Hollywood experienced a steady growth. The high school was built in 1903; the

Bank of Hollywood (now Security Pacific) and the Board of Trade followed that same year. In 1905 the Wilcox Building was erected by Mrs. Wilcox. By 1909 there were about 4,000 people in Hollywood. It was a high-class community in every sense of the word. It was said that the high school baseball team was made up of boys of such refined rearing that never so much as a word of profanity had been overheard by bystanders! About this time Hollywood established the first motorized fire department in Southern California with two firemen on call at all times. In 1909 the LAP Hill Street Tunnels were placed in service, cutting ten minutes off the running time to Hollywood; "Tunnel Day" was celebrated at the DeLongpre garden by 10,000 visitors. Five brass bands played.

The years 1910 and 1911 saw a new Hollywood born, the Hollywood of today. In 1910 Hollywood was annexed to Los Angeles, the inevitable result of Hollywood's extended struggle for an adequate water supply. Colegrove was annexed at the same time and became known as South Hollywood.

WITH 1911 CAME the biggest factor that ever entered into the life of Hollywood. The motion picture industry had already several studios in Los Angeles proper. The Nestor Company leased the old Blondeau barn and tavern at the corner of Sunset and Gower and Hollywood came of age. One by one other companies followed, until the Hollywood area had the majority of the studios of the world. With the studios came their allied industries, such as film laboratories, costumers, booking offices, camera and film supply houses, electrical effect companies, film magazines, and the radio and television industries of today. Within a decade Hollywood grew from 7,000 souls to more than 100,000.

LAP merged into PE almost coincidentally with the coming of the movies to Hollywood. Hence the scope of this work accents the pre-1911 Hollywood. Hollywood, Colegrove and Beverly Hills were well served by the green cars, local and interurban. Lines on Hollywood Blvd. and Santa Monica Blvd. were the backbone of the rail system, with branches serving Franklin Ave., Beachwood-Brush Canyons, Highland Ave., Laurel Canyon, and the LAP Shops at Sherman (West Hollywood) provided the original impetus for that area. In most instances, the building of an LAP line resulted in the opening up of an entire new section; most of Hollywood can trace its origin to a nearby LAP line.

Pacific Electric, through an agreement with the Los Angeles Railway, enjoyed a monopoly in Hollywood for many years. The coming of bus lines in the Twenties brought an end to this, and one by one the rail lines succumbed to rubber-tired competition. The last line to go was the Hollywood Blvd. line which was abandoned on September 26, 1954. Since that date, all public transit in the Hollywood area has been supplied by buses.

COLEGROVE, 1905. The scene looks west on Santa Monica Blvd. from Western Ave.
(Security Pacific Bank)

BEVERLY, doubtless better known today as Beverly Hills, boasted this attractive depot, topped by a real electric sign.
(T.L. Wagenbach)

Beverly

AFTER THE GREAT BOOM waned in 1888, the townsite of Morocco faded and disappeared back into the soil. The *Pasadena & Pacific* electric line in 1896 had little reason to stop for passengers at what later became Wilshire & Santa Monica Boulevards. But by 1897 when the Santa Monica Short Line's cutoff to Los Angeles via W. 16th St. branched off at this point, some renewed stirrings of activity were noted.

The Amalgamated Oil Company secured title to the area and began drilling for oil. This brought about much business activity for a short time, but when oil proved elusive and the company withdrew, once again it seemed that fate had dealt a hard blow to Morocco.

However, in 1906 the Rodeo Land & Water Company bought the Amalgamated holdings and planned a city of homes, with large lots, parks and wide streets to be lined with all kinds of trees. Wilbur Cook, a landscape architect from New York, worked out plans for the townsite which was named "Beverly" after the Massachusetts home of President Burton E. Green of the Rodeo company.

On November 14, 1906, the subdivision known as Beverly was recorded. It covered the level land bounded by Wilshire and Santa Monica Boulevards. Such famous streets as Beverly, Rodeo, Canon, Crescent, Roxbury and Bedford then first appeared.

A few months later the subdivision of Beverly Hills was recorded (January 23, 1907) which covered the land that sloped up from Santa Monica Blvd. toward the hills. The first house was built by Henry C. Clarke in 1908. The panic of 1907-8 slowed the growth of the community but by 1910 lot selling revived and modern Beverly Hills began to take shape.

One of the first substantial buildings in Beverly was the stucco station erected by LAP in association with the Rodeo company.

To serve the Beverly Hills Hotel which was planned for Beverly (now Sunset) Blvd. and Rodeo Drive, LAP in 1907 built the Rodeo line which was a single track, 1.378 miles long, branching off from the Santa Monica line at Rodeo Drive. However, the hotel was not constructed until 1912, so LAP's Rodeo line insofar as that company was concerned enjoyed only light patronage.

Sawtelle

WHEN, IN 1896, Sherman & Clark acquired the old LAP right-of-way and proposed to build an electric line to the beach, they asked the citizens of Santa Monica and the Jones and Baker interests for a cash subsidy to aid them in their work. Instead of cash, Jones and Baker donated a tract of 225 acres now included in the Sawtelle townsite. Sherman soon offered to sell the land for cash, as he said he couldn't build a railroad with land. Jones and R.C. Gillis of Santa Monica purchased the tract which lay just south of the Soldiers' Home. Up to then, there had been no settlers on the land—only a shack at the railroad crossing known as Castle Garden.

In 1896, the Rev. Stephen H. Taft, who was 72 years of age and who had founded Humboldt, Iowa, and the Humboldt College, was invited to inspect the site. Taft was enthusiastic, and took charge of selling the lots.

Fourth Street was laid out from the Soldiers' Home to the LAP tracks and a tract office was opened May 1, 1897. The town was first named "Barrett," after General A.W. Barrett, for many years head of the Soldiers' Home. However, postal authorities objected to this name because of its similarity to Bassett, California, and a prominent local banker, W.E. Sawtelle, consented to the use of his name; so, on July 4, 1899, the town became "Sawtelle."

The town experienced a steady growth, especially after veterans were permitted to purchase lots, erect homes, and live off post. LAP erected a neat depot, many attractive business blocks followed, and on November 16, 1906, voters approved the proposition which made Sawtelle officially an incorporated city. It was a mile each way, and directly joined the northerly limits of Santa Monica.

In July, 1922, Sawtelle, in need of major improvements which by itself could not be gained, voted to annex itself to Los Angeles. In 1929 its name was again changed—this time to "West Los Angeles."

Sawtelle was a busy spot for LAP cars. Not only did the Main Line go down the main street, but two branch lines added to the liveliness of the community. One was the Westgate line which branched north and west, making a great loop through property controlled by interests friendly to Sherman and Clark. The Westgate line served that section and Brentwood, returning to the Main Line via Ocean Ave. in Santa Monica. The Soldiers' Home line branched off the Main Line at Sepulveda Blvd., then ran via the old SP tracks into the grounds of the Soldiers' Home where it followed the great loop once used to turn steam trains. Add to these passenger cars the express, mail and freight trains and one can readily see

SAWTELLE ABOUT 1901; view looks toward Hollywood with a part of Soldiers' Home grounds visible at upper left.
(Rudolph Brandt)

TOP
THE LAP depot at Soldiers'
Home. This building survives as
the newsstand at the home.
(T.L. Wagenbach)

BOTTOM
SANTA MONICA BLVD. in
Sawtelle about 1900.
(Security Pacific Bank)

that Sawtelle was indeed a fine spot to watch LAP cars at work.

Sawtelle streets running north and south were originally numbered. At the east city limits was National Military Boulevard, now Sepulveda; then in order came First, Second and through to Ninth Streets. Thus Fourth St., the main north and south street, later became Sawtelle Blvd., and the other numbered streets also got names.

Soldiers' Home

THE "PACIFIC BRANCH of the National Home for Disabled Volunteer Soldiers & Sailors at Santa Monica," to use its full name, was established near Santa Monica in 1887 by the federal government.

When it became known that the government was seeking a site for a branch of its Soldiers' Home, many California towns outdid themselves in spreading their charms before the commission encharged with selecting the site. Various San Francisco Bay communities pushed themselves forward, as did settlements in the southern part of the state. The final choice lay between Santa Monica and San Bernardino and again Sen. John P. Jones performed an important service for Santa Monica. Jones' prominence in the United States Senate, coupled with his prestige and great wealth brought the prize home to Santa Monica. Not only did Jones introduce the Senate bill authorizing erection of the home near Santa Monica, but he and his partner, Col. R.J. Baker, along with the owners of the Wolfskill Rancho, gave 640 acres of land with ample water.

The government engaged the noted architect, Stanford White, to draw the plans; to assure himself that the great wooden buildings were erected just as he envisioned them, White lived on the grounds during the greater part of the construction period.

Only a small part of the 640 acres was originally used. Attractive two-story barracks were spread out among the newly planted trees, and a handsome dining hall with a fine flight of impressive steps was the most prominent building.

In December, 1888, the Soldiers' Home opened. Some 2,000 veterans were brought out from the Midwest to be its first residents.

To provide rail connection with the outer world, the Southern Pacific built a branch line from its Santa Monica line; this branch culminated in a sweeping loop to permit the turning of entire trains.

LAP served the home first by means of the horse car line up Wilshire Blvd. from Santa Monica. This line entered the property of the home, terminating a short distance from the dining hall. When the Westgate Line was built it received the bulk of LAP patrons, and finally, in 1908, the SP branch was leased by LAP and electrified; it became the LAP Soldiers' Home Line and local service was provided between the home and downtown Sawtelle. The Balloon Route cars entered the home over this trackage and made a photo stop at the dining hall.

Santa Monica and especially Sawtelle derived great benefit from their proximity to the Soldiers' Home.

Santa Monica

SANTA MONICA, Queen of the Bay Cities, was founded in 1875 by Sen. John P. Jones of Nevada, a multimillionaire and an extraordinary man. A paragraph on Jones is certainly pertinent.

Jones was born in Wales in 1829 and in 1849 came around the Horn with the gold seekers; the ship became becalmed and the overbearing captain refused to break out foodstuffs to feed his starving passengers. The youthful Jones organized the suffering passengers, put the captain in irons, and sailed the ship to San Francisco; there he was tried for mutiny and acquitted. Jones went to the gold fields, struck it rich and ultimately became sheriff of Trinity County in its roughest, toughest days. A man of unusual power of mind and physique, Jones was at home wherever he went. His greatest bonanza was the Panamint Mine, near Independence, California. To get his ore to tidewater, Jones came to Los Angeles in 1874, rich and powerful, and decided on Santa Monica Bay as his logical port.

In January 1875, Jones bought a 66% interest in the San Vicente Rancho and in the same month organized his railroad, to be called the *Los Angeles & Independence*. Jones proposed to build this railroad from Santa Monica to Independence via Los Angeles and Cajon Pass, and perhaps continue it on to Salt Lake City. In April work began on a wharf at the foot of Colorado Ave. which was extended out to sea some 1,700 feet. Under Jones, a townsite was surveyed on a grand scale; the city limits were Montana Ave. on the north, Fremont Ave. (Pico) on the south, and 26th Street on the east.

On July 15, 1875, Santa Monica lots went on sale. The first train to Los Angeles ran on October 17, 1875, and was composed of flat cars as the coaches had not yet been delivered. The LA&I Wharf was ready for business; it reached out to 30-foot water and was substantially built with a depot and warehouses at its outer end; it cost Jones $45,000. Steamers at once began to put in, and the LA&I delivered passengers to Los Angeles twelve hours ahead of those who continued on to San Pedro. SP had to strike back, for it enjoyed a monopoly of San Pedro business. It dropped fares from San Pedro to Los Angeles to 50 cents and hauled freight at a dollar per ton. This forced the LA&I to drop its fares, with the result that it began its operations with losing rates. The people of Los Angeles, grateful for the loosening of the SP's monopoly, declared they would stand by the LA&I. Jones' wharf and railroad brought a brief period of commercial importance to Santa Monica which it was never again to enjoy.

The construction of the LA&I on to Independence was never to take place. Jones' Panamint Mine turned out to be a disappointment and without ore shipments a railroad to Independence would have no economic justification. Thus the LA&I had to depend on local business to survive and the SP's rate war was ruinous. Senator Jones announced he was tired of footing the bill and would sell the LA&I to the county; efforts by the citizens to take him up on his offer failed and so he sold out to the SP. SP took control of the LA&I on July 4, 1877, and at once increased fares and rates. Business dropped off but not fast enough to suit SP. So the depot was removed from the wharf and set up in the arroyo on shore. SP engineers inspected the wharf and declared it to be badly infested with teredos, making it a hazard to operate. On September 9 the "Senator" made its last landing at Santa Monica; business fell off badly and people moved away. Mortgages were foreclosed and all in all it was a crushing blow to the hopes of Santa Monicans. Early in 1879 SP ordered the wharf removed, but it proved to be so strong that the pilings resisted all efforts of a donkey engine to remove them. They were finally chopped off at low tide; only a very mild infestation of teredos was discovered. However, Santa Monica's dream of becoming a major ocean port was effectively shattered.

Santa Monica then entered upon a long period of economic slumber. Efforts were made to attract new capital (with the idea of obtaining a new wharf) but SP always prevented anything from maturing, threatening boycott. The LA&I, now SP, ran a minimum number of trains except on weekends and holidays, when Santa Monica was crowded with excursionists.

THE COMING of the Santa Fe in 1885 and the resultant rate war and big boom brought Santa Monica back to life. On November 30, 1886, Santa Monica was incorporated. The great Hotel Arcadia was built that year on the oceanfront between Railroad and Front Streets, today the Seaside Terrace area.

In 1888 the Los Angeles County Railroad built into Santa Monica from Hollywood and offered a little competition.

The boom broke in 1889 but Santa Monica withstood the reaction and proved to be well founded. It weathered the storm with the aid of Senator Jones, who remained a part-time

Santa Monica Wanted Ships, But Got Tourists Instead

resident of the community, although Virginia City was his legal residence.

Frederick H. Rindge became a pillar of the little city in 1890 and proved to be almost as much of an influence in its development as Jones. Rindge led the fight to make Santa Monica "dry." After a most bitter campaign, his side was victorious at the polls. Rindge then learned that one of his chief opponents had everything he owned tied up in liquor interests.

ONE OF THE FIRST large buildings in Santa Monica was this, the Bank of Santa Monica.   (Interurbans)

and was facing ruin; Rindge at once made a fair offer to his opponent for his holdings—a most unusual and fair act. Rindge brought about the establishment of some of Santa Monica's first churches by giving lots for them if the congregation would guarantee the pastor's salary.

The year 1891 saw Santa Monica's first public transportation established; a horse car line was opened in that year with a great banquet at the Arcadia. It ran along Ocean Ave. from the railroad bridge (Colorado) to Utah to Third to Nevada to Soldiers' Home (see *Santa Monica & Soldiers' Home Railroad Company*, Unit 42).

Eighteen ninety saw the first activity in regards to the Long Wharf. Santa Monicans rejoiced when SP President Huntington announced in that year that the SP would spend a million dollars building a mile-long wharf just north of Santa Monica Canyon. Huntington figured that a wharf at Santa Monica would short-haul the Santa Fe at Redondo and protect SP from Santa Fe's possible invasion of Ocean Park.

The Santa Fe reached South Santa Monica (Ocean Park) on June 18, 1892, and at once the southern part of town sprang to life.

The rebirth of Santa Monica and its new business boom brought about a couple of transportation schemes which should be mentioned. An electric line was proposed by a C.W. Stewart which would have run via Washington St. in Los Ange-les to the National Blvd. in Palms, thence over that old thoroughfare into Santa Monica. A more spectacular scheme would have been the so-called "bicycle railway" which would have transported passengers at a mile a minute on a single rail with a guide rail above; such a road was actually built on Long Island but ended in disaster.

In June, 1895, Gen. Sherman asked the Santa Monica city fathers for a franchise for his electric line which would be a rebuilding of the Los Angeles & Pacific (L.A. County) steam dummy line from Hollywood; the good General was turned down cold, due to ill feeling toward the dummy line which had ceased operations in December, 1889. Later, the franchise, amended, was granted him.

THE COMPLETION of the P&P (LAP) and its opening on April 1, 1896, was declared a half holiday in Santa Monica. Trolley parties thereupon became a new entertainment. In 1897 the local Third St. trolley line was opened, and the new route out of Los Angeles via W. 16th St. followed that same year; this cut the distance to Los Angeles by two miles and the so-called "Santa Monica Short Line" became so popular that SP and Santa Fe were compelled to take off almost all of their trains due to lack of patronage.

The LAP line on Ocean Ave. to Montana opened on December 28, 1899. That year the SP reduced its schedule from three to one train daily; as it carried the mails, this aroused great indignation and caused much inconvenience to business men. Vigorous protests were made and resulted in the mail contract being given to LAP.

In 1900 LAP put on the mail car which made three trips daily over the system and also carried express matter. The Hollywood line was opened on Feb. 21, giving Santa Monicans three trolley routes into Los Angeles. The SP and the Santa Fe, in a desperate attempt to recover their traffic, issued a ten-trip ticket for $1.50 good for one month; LAP met this with a ten-ride ticket, good until used and transferable, for $2.00. The railroads gained little.

Santa Monica, by 1901, was growing like a weed. LAP built a new powerhouse at Ocean Park which cost $25,000. President William McKinley visited the Soldiers' Home, arriving in General Sherman's private car, the "Mermaid." The Santa Fe asked permission to abandon its Inglewood-Ocean Park line and got it.

The Venice Short Line opened in 1902, giving a new and considerably shorter line to Los Angeles. LAP bought the Inglewood Line and electrified it, giving a rather desultory service to Inglewood.

In September, 1902, Los Angeles Traction Company asked for a franchise in Santa Monica and after opposition waned, got it for $3,500. After considerable agitation, the threat of trolley competition was ended by the purchase of the LAT by SP. (See *Los Angeles, Ocean Park & Santa Monica Railway Company*, Unit 24).

In 1902 LAP built the Lagoon line which ran down the Trolleyway from Santa Monica to Venice, giving improved service to Ocean Park. Two years previous to this the North Loop was built in Santa Monica; its route: from Ocean & Oregon, on Oregon to Third, north on Third to Montana Ave., west to Ocean Ave. and south on private way on Ocean Ave. to Oregon Ave.

The Westgate (Brentwood) line was built in late 1906 and opened up a vast area of desirable land along the south rim of Santa Monica Canyon. Sherman & Clark had an interest in the tract and saw to it that ample car service was provided.

This terminated LAP's construction period in Santa Monica except for the Eighth St. line; this line was proposed by LAP but was built by PE after the Great Merger. LAP's part consisted of installing the switch at 8th St. & Santa Monica Blvd.

LAP opened its Linda Vista Station sometime in 1906. This attractive little stucco building was located in Palisades Park on Ocean Ave. at the junction of Utah Avenue. It remained as the terminus of the Venice Short Line until abandonment on September 17, 1950 and was razed in November, 1955. The park itself, stretching for miles along the palisades on Ocean Ave., was given to the city by Sen. Jones and the Santa Monica Land & Water Company.

ABOVE
NORTH BEACH DEPOT,
Santa Monica, stood on the
palisades at the foot of
Santa Monica Blvd.

LEFT
PALMS DEPOT was
inherited from Southern
Pacific; today it is pre-
served as a historical
monument–threatened in
1975 by plans for removal.
(Both: T.L. Wagenbach)

Palms

LOCATED ABOUT five miles east of Santa Monica is the town of Palms. After the building of the Los Angeles & Independence Railroad in 1875, a section house was located here; it was known as "Grasshopper Station." A store was established, known as "Half Way House," where dusty travelers slaked their thirst midway in their trip from Los Angeles to Santa Monica.

With the great boom, the townsite of Palms was laid out in 1887; the name was inspired by two lonely palm trees which grew adjacent to the store. A very lively real estate campaign followed. An abundant supply of good water was struck and the soil was fertile. A school and hotel, the latter known as "Palms Villa," were built. The Southern Pacific erected a neat little depot.

Although the collapse of the boom retarded the growth of Palms, it did not cease to exist like many communities. In 1895 its spirited growth resumed.

In 1902 the Venice Short Line was built and this spurred the growth of the eastern part of Palms. Since then, Palms' growth has been steady.

Westgate-Brentwood

THE WIDE EXPANSE of gently sloping land located between Santa Monica Blvd. and the south rim of Santa Monica Canyon and between the Soldiers' Home and Santa Monica was soon recognized as being one of the most desirable residential tracts of land available in Southern California. Sherman and Clark obtained an interest in various tracts and to stimulate sales of lots had their Westgate Line constructed in 1906.

Leaving the Santa Monica Line in Sawtelle, the Westgate Line—double track, narrow gauge, went north to what is today Wilshire Blvd., then followed a broad divided avenue with tracks in a reserved center strip, continued in a wide sweep to the edge of the cliffs overlooking the canyon at Ocean Ave.; the line then went along the Linda Vista Park boundary to a junction with the Montana Ave. and Santa Monica Main Line.

The Westgate Line served its purpose: lots sold rapidly and some beautiful new residences rapidly replaced the old bean fields.

An unusual feature of the Westgate Line was the ornamental brackets on the arms of the poles, a deluxe treatment indeed.

Rancho Malibu

LAP SPENT CONSIDERABLE money and effort in some attempts to extend its coastline railway north of the Long Wharf (see *Santa Monica & Northern Railway Company,* Unit 58 and *Los Angeles Pacific Company,* Unit 66). This could only have been realized with the consent of Frederick H. Rindge and/or his wife, May K. Rindge, owners of the Rancho Topanga Malibu Sequit.

Rancho Malibu was the last of the great Spanish land grants. It was purchased by Rindge in 1890 for $10 an acre, a not inconsiderable price when it is realized that Rancho Malibu then consisted of 13,000 acres, extending 22 miles up the coast from Las Flores Canyon, just north of the Long Wharf. Rindge added to the Rancho Malibu by subsequent purchases until it covered 24,000 acres.

Frederick Rindge had spent some time in the French Riviera and envisioned his own American Riviera. While he projected his ideas for a resort center in Malibu which would surpass anything found along the shores of the Mediterranean, he did not neglect business; Rindge was one of the founders of the Union Oil Company, helped set up the Southern California Edison Company, and was partly responsible for the Pacific Mutual Life Insurance Company, all preeminent today.

Rindge died in 1905, but exhorted his wife on his deathbed to push through his plans for Malibu—in the meantime keeping Rancho Malibu intact and inviolate. Thus began the epic but ruinous contest with the forces of progress which lasted for years.

Barbed wire fences surrounded the great ranch. Armed riders patroled its borders and forcibly ejected any bold enough to venture inside. Highways and railroads stopped at its boundaries. Even the omnipresent Southern Pacific was thwarted; the Rindge forces built their own railroad, the Hueneme, Malibu and Port Los Angeles Railway.

May Rindge fought every effort of the state to cut the coast highway through her holdings. Bitter court fights raged all the way up to the United States Supreme Court (which rendered two decisions) and to the California Supreme Court (which handed down four decisions). In 1923 she was forced to allow the highway to pass through. Much of her great wealth was spent in legal battles and oil property which could have kept the Rindge side in opposition in the courts indefinitely was denied her by zoning ordinances. The 1929 depression further added to her woes, and in 1936 she went into bankruptcy. In 1940 all unsold property on Rancho Malibu went on the market and 17,000 acres were then subdivided. Thus ended the last of the ranchos, and May Rindge survived it by but a year.

Perhaps had LAP succeeded in obtaining its much desired line up the coast to the county line its parent, SP, would have taken over the valuable property; only SP would have been in a position to utilize such a line profitably.

Pacific Palisades

SINCE THE DAYS of Abbot Kinney (1886) the level land lying on the north side of Santa Monica Canyon exerted an unusual fascination insofar as railroad builders were concerned. Kinney's projected line from the entrance to the canyon proper up offshoot Rustic Canyon to the plateau on top was but the first of several similar dream lines. Kinney eventually sold out to the Southern Pacific, but SP's interest was confined to the shore at the foot of the cliffs; the fine land on top remained undeveloped for many years. After SP and LAP became affiliated, the Palisades saw renewed real estate activity. Spurring these efforts were repeated announcements of projected electric railway lines which would crisscross the Palisades.

Despite the fact that none of these projected lines was built, lots sold anyway and the Pacific Palisades section became a truly fine residential area.

Ocean Park

SANTA MONICA'S "South Beach," or South Santa Monica as it was better known, finally resolved into Ocean Park, a pleasant name which won public favor and prevailed.

In the spring of 1889 the Kenilworth Ostrich Farm (see *Los Angeles Ostrich Farm Railway,* Unit 36) moved to South Santa Monica in an effort to attract more patronage. The few

TYPICAL of the major buildings which comprised Ocean Park in LAP's day are the hotel, left, and the ornate plunge, right, taken in 1905. (Title Insurance)

beach cottages were joined by others, and slowly the little beach settlement grew. In 1892 the Santa Fe built into the community, relocating its Port Ballona line; the first Santa Fe train ran on June 18, 1892.

The year before Abbot Kinney and his partner, F.G. Ryan, bought more than two miles of beach frontage from about where Bicknell St. is today down to a point south of Venice. They influenced the Los Angeles County YMCA to locate its summer camp on their beach, and many other picnic parties and summer camps began using the beach area adjacent to today's Hill Street in Ocean Park. The park idea and the proximity to the beach were given expression in the name "Ocean Park." It caught the public fancy and proved profitable.

The coming of the Santa Fe brought new money into Ocean Park. The railroad built a depot near Front Street and lively real estate activity followed. In September, 1895, Santa Fe built a 500-foot wharf about 300 feet south of Hill Street. Kinney and Ryan next built a 1,250-foot pleasure pier. Some major buildings appeared and Ocean Park was well on its way.

The *Santa Monica & Soldiers' Home Railroad Company* (Unit 42) built a horsecar line connecting Ocean Park with Santa Monica in 1891 and this brought about heavy real estate activity along its route: Main Street, 4th Street, Hill Street and Fremont Ave. (Pico).

Ocean Park was separated from Santa Monica by a mile of soft sand, arroyos and railroad reservations. This disconnected physical status brought about resentment on the part of Southsiders, who felt they were neglected while Santa Monica proper prospered. Several attempts were made to separate the two centers, but each time the secessionists lost in the election.

Ocean Park included the area that later became Venice. In 1900 the Country Club was opened near Venice; it had one of the first golf links in Southern California.

In 1904 Kinney and Ryan split. Ryan kept that portion of Ocean Park lying inside Santa Monica, while Kinney took all of Ocean Park lying south of Marine St. In 1904 Kinney's Ocean Park was incorporated as an independent city with a city hall being constructed at what is today Venice Blvd. and Shell Ave. Thus for a time there were two Ocean Parks—Santa

Monica's and Kinney's. Kinney's became Venice a few months later, ending most of the confusion.

Santa Monica's Ocean Park continued to prosper, getting one of the coast's most elaborate plunges as well as excellent hotels. In 1910 Fraser's million-dollar pier was built, only to be destroyed in the great conflagration of September, 1912, which burned most of the area adjacent to the waterfront, causing damage estimated at $2,500,000. In 1913 a new pier was built, along with new fireproof buildings along the strand; new Ocean Park cost in excess of seven million dollars and hurt Venice and Playa del Rey. The new pier burned in January, 1924, and was replaced by another pier which finally was razed in 1975.

Although Ocean Park will probably never have Santa Monica's residential appeal, it has kept in the front rank insofar as popularity of amusements is concerned. After the Venice pier was removed in 1947, Ocean Park's only serious rival as a Coney Island type of resort was Long Beach, sufficiently far away to take the edge off direct competition.

LAP's first headquarters in Ocean Park was located at the northwest corner of 2nd (Main) and Hill Streets. Cars coming down Hill from 4th on the South Loop (all L.A. cars made this loop originally) made a sharp right turn into company property at this corner. A pit enabled cars to be oiled and inspected and a small structure at the extreme corner served as a station. Cars then pulled out into 2nd St. and returned to Santa Monica and Los Angeles.

Many new cars were first unloaded at 2nd and Hill Streets. LAP brought its new cars in via Santa Fe from Inglewood. They were delivered to LAP at the switch at 2nd and Hill where LAP and Santa Fe had combination gauge trackage. Cars which were thus unloaded from their flat cars included 156-159, 48-55, 180-189 and 190-199.

A landmark in the Ocean Park area in the early days was the Santa Fe Depot, near Front (Pico) and Ocean. On March 9, 1903, this structure burned to the ground. The fire was discovered at 1:20 AM by the conductor of an LAP car. The old depot was built in 1892 and was used as a passenger station until LAP purchased the Inglewood Line. LAP then used the building only for storage.

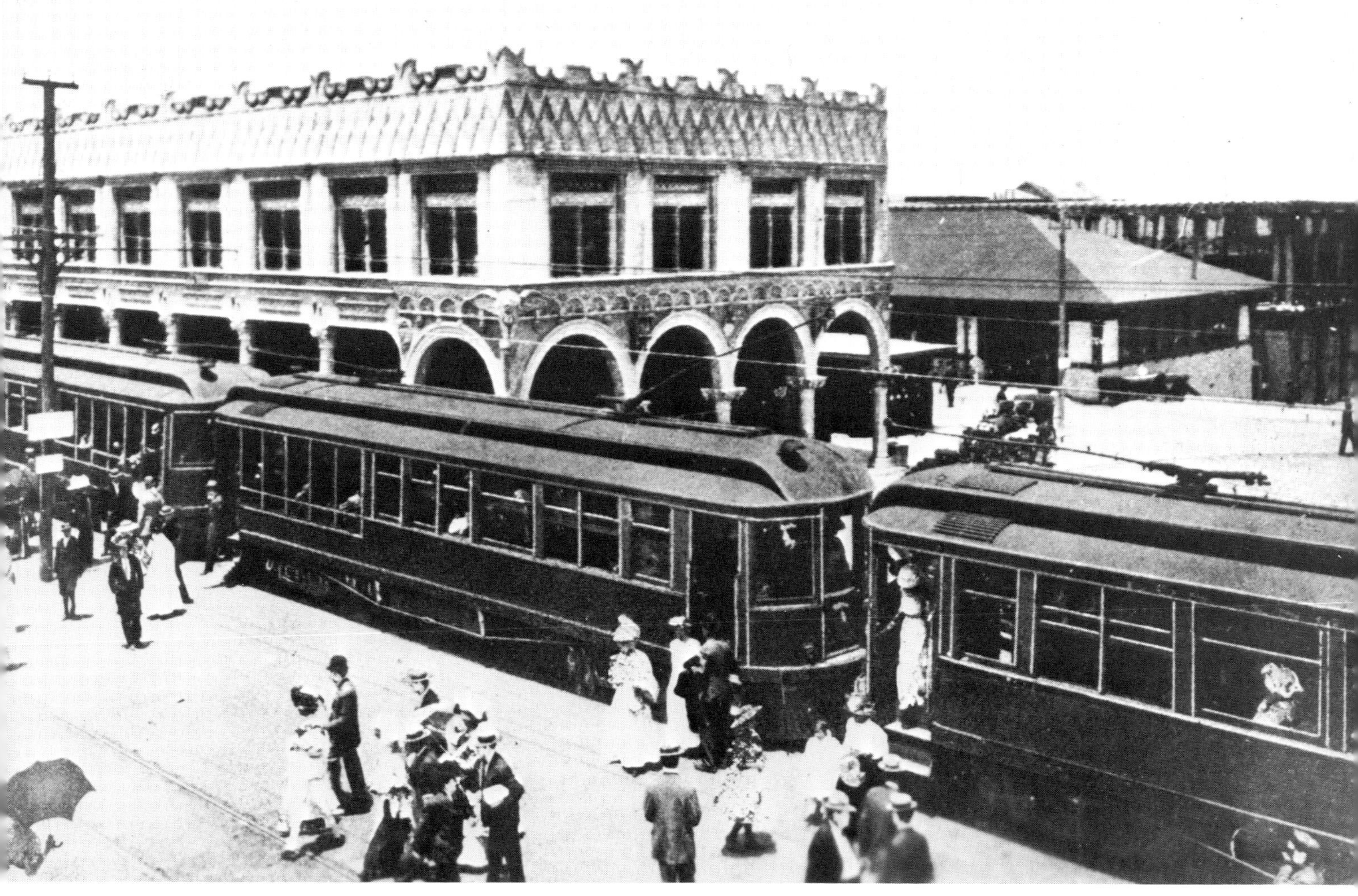

LAP ELECTRIC TRAINS brought most visitors to Venice.   *(Stephen D. Maguire)*

Venice

FABULOUS VENICE—"A Place of Perpetual Carnival," "The Paradise of America," "Joy From January to January," to quote but briefly from publicity handouts of the early years of this century—was beyond doubt the most captivating amusement park Los Angeles has yet had (and we have seen Disneyland).

Venice was founded in 1904 by Abbot Kinney, a remarkable man of many arts and skills. To know Venice, one must know its founder. Born in 1851 in Brookside, New Jersey, Kinney spent his formative years in Washington, D.C.; his uncle was Senator James Dixon of Connecticut. Kinney had all the advantages of education and of contact with many prominent men. He completed his education at Heidelberg and in France and Switzerland. In 1877 he began a three-year tour of the world. Kinney arrived in San Francisco in 1880 and finding the Sierras blocked by snow, detoured via Los Angeles. He was delighted with the climate here and bought a large tract of land near Sierra Madre which he planted to citrus and named "Kinneloa." He became widely known for his methods of citrus culture.

In 1883 Kinney displayed another facet of his versatile nature. With Helen Hunt Jackson he served as a commissioner in the investigation of the condition of the Mission Indians of Southern California. He recommended breaking up the reservations, while she obtained material for her famous book, *Ramona.*

In 1886 Kinney moved to Santa Monica and purchased a large parcel on the north side of Santa Monica Canyon; there he laid out streets and sidewalks, planted trees and planned a railroad. Later this tract was transferred to the Southern Pacific Company which used the land along the bottom of the bluffs for the right of way of its line to the Long Wharf.

Kinney then purchased a large tract of land in South Santa Monica which had more than two miles of beach frontage, extending south of what is today Venice. Kinney and his partner, F.G. Ryan, founded Ocean Park on a portion of this tract in 1891 and it became the most popular resort of its day.

Kinney and Ryan split in January, 1904, with Ryan keeping what is today the Ocean Park area and Kinney taking sole ownership of the stretch of seemingly worthless swamp land extending from today's Marine Court through present day Venice about to where Washington Blvd. reaches the ocean. On this desolate tract Kinney envisioned a "Venice of America," a city that should equal in beauty and picturesqueness the Venice of his youthful enthusiasm. With the unfettered confidence of the progressive American in the power of mind

THE "CABRILLO" Ship Cafe was the most unique structure on the Venice Pier (above), from an old postcard. Another postcard (below) extolled the serenity of a boat ride on the Venice canals.   *(Both, Interurbans)*

BOATING ON THE CANAL. VENICE, CALIF.

and money over material obstacles, he began creating an ideal city upon his salt marsh. The public was distinctly skeptical at his plans for a city with canals for streets. "Kinney's Dream" was heard on all sides.

On May 10, 1904, Kinney presented his plans for "The Venice View Tract," containing 67 lots. On June 21 the first contract was let, that for the Grand Canal which was 70 feet wide, four feet deep and a half mile long. Other branch canals extended from this one, each lined with concrete. An army of men and teams started work on the canals on August 15. The system was completed by extending a canal from Venice to the Playa del Rey lagoon.

Other major improvements followed rapidly. On September 5 work began on the famous Venice Pier—1,700 feet long, thirty feet wide—and on December 5 ground was broken for the St. Mark's Hotel. A complete electric system was installed, along with a fire-fighting pipeline using salt water at high pressure. By this time the public was fully alive to the fact that something was happening and interest mounted as plans and expenditures moved steadily upward. In but fourteen days in November, $386,000 worth of lots were sold.

THEN CAME THE HEAVIEST seas known for a generation. The Venice Pier was wrecked, the pavilion and other buildings damaged. At a low estimate, losses were set at about $50,000 and the public declared that buildings over the water, as planned, would never be safe. But Kinney was not daunted. He got permission from the government to build a breakwater at his own expense to protect his property. This, the only private breakwater in the United States, was built as soon as it was possible; it was 500 feet long, circular in form, and extended sixty feet from shore. In all, it cost Kinney $100,000.

The rebuilding of the pier and wrecked buildings was carried on at top speed. The auditorium, seating 3,600 and built in just 28 days, opened on July 2, 1905. On June 30, the water was turned into the canals and as the waterways and lagoon were filled for the first time, the true magnificence of Kinney's dream dawned upon the onlookers. On the evening of July 2, the electric lights for illumination were turned on, some 17,000 lamps being used. The effect was magical. During the day the great pipe organ in the auditorium was dedicated by Clarence Eddy. On July 4, Venice was the scene of the greatest celebration yet known in Southern California as more than 40,000 people visited the new dream city. On the program were listed band concerts, speeches, swimming contests and fireworks.

It was Kinney's hope to make Venice a center of education and culture. He secured Joaquin Miller, Dr. Josiah Strong and Ellery's Band, along with other equally famous names, in his auditorium. However, the public wanted to be amused, not educated. The Midway Plaisance contract was let in November, consisting of eleven buildings devoted to the pursuit of pleasure.

Nineteen hundred and six brought progress almost as great as the two previous years. The Midway opened in January. In May Sarah Bernhardt played in the auditorium for three days, drawing capacity crowds. As was her custom, she lived in her private car which Kinney accommodated on the pier trackage he had built to haul rock for his breakwater. The incomparable Sarah, with all the fervor of her ardent nature, declared herself to be delighted with this playhouse over the waves. During 1906 the bath house on the Lagoon and the dance pavilion on the pier were opened, both beautiful buildings and complete in all details.

Rapidly Venice built up. Each canal was lined with cottages, many striving to capture the atmosphere deemed appropriate by dint of stucco domes, stained glass windows and other questionable architectural whims and fancies. Each cottage had its rowboat or canoe which vied with Kinney's gondolas for space in the shallow watery boulevards. A dozen narrow, arching concrete bridges permitted wheeled vehicles access to the numerous islands; once there, they were confined to narrow alleyways from which they served the rear of the various properties.

In pre-automobile days, Venice was the LAP's most lucrative area. Summer weekends and holidays saw most of the LAP executive family make its headquarters at the "dog house" in the Trolleyway just off Windward Ave. From this shack, trains up to five cars in length were dispatched to Los Angeles as rapidly as required over as many as five different routes. Such trains were staffed by but two men: motorman and conductor. It is recalled by Harry Marler that a good conductor was one who could get all the fares collected by the time his five-car train got to Vineyard! Actually this was not as bad as it seems, for the rear four cars were filled at Venice using the prepayment system, leaving the conductor in the head car to care for local business.

STEADILY THE CULTURAL Venice of Kinney's dreams lost ground to the carnival Venice desired by the average city dweller. Tom Prior, the man mountain, built his "Race Through the Clouds," the world's largest roller coaster, on the site of the Midway; a scenic railroad wound its way among the canals from Windward and Trolleyway to what is today Washington and Venice Blvd. via a loop—serving not only as an amusement ride par excellence but also as the most practicable local transportation for residents; shows of all kinds took over the pier: The Titanic Disaster, Noah's Ark, Race for Life, Bump the Bumps, Racing Autos, Japanese Tea Parlor, Folies Bergere, and the most unique restaurant, The Ship Cafe—Ward McFadden's fabulously successful three-masted ship far above the waves. The people came in droves to be amused and Venice assumed its unique role as chief amusement purveyor to the City of the Angels. The Venice Plunge was the largest salt

They Came to Venice To Be Entertained, Not Educated

water swimming pool anywhere at the time of its opening. The Dancing Pavilion was advertised as "the west's finest, ten musicians." The Race Through the Clouds afforded its delighted patrons a double-tracked, high-speed coaster ride ballyhooed as the "fastest, safest, longest"—and counted it a dull Sunday when less than 20,000 passed through its turnstiles; the record was set on July 4, 1910, when 33,000 riders screamed delightedly as their twin coasters raced high in the skies, dropped and plummeted close to earth. Yes, Venice turned out to be the poor man's resort and remained the west's Coney Island for four decades.

Kinney's canals ran into trouble as early as 1912, when the State Board of Health pronounced them unsanitary; the free circulation of water was prevented by a dam. Too, folks found it convenient to use the canals as public dumps—it was easy to throw bottles out the window into the nearby canal. The years were hard on the stucco and lath buildings; they cracked and sagged and even the arches over the canals were condemned. The rise of the automobile caused the Kinney Company (on November 4, 1920 Abbot Kinney died) to ask permission to fill the canals and pave them over in 1924. A great hue and cry arose and not until June 10, 1929, was the final legal decision rendered which sounded the doom of the waterways. The canals were then filled and Venice lost much of its character.

The remainder was lost in 1947 when the Venice Pier was demolished, due to the refusal of the city of Los Angeles (to which Venice had annexed itself in 1925) to renew its lease on tidelands. Beach redevelopment followed and today a sandy beach extends all the way out to Kinney's old breakwater. Gone are all buildings on the ocean side of the concourse, and gone, too, are the interurbans which made their last run on September 17, 1950. Their Trolleyway is now paved over, becoming Pacific Avenue in Venice, and Neilson Way in Ocean Park. The Venice of 1976 is barely recognizable as Kinney's "Venice of America," and presents a notable instance of civic decadence. However, efforts were underway in the mid-1970s by many of Venice's latter-day residents to restore some of the grace and splendor of old.

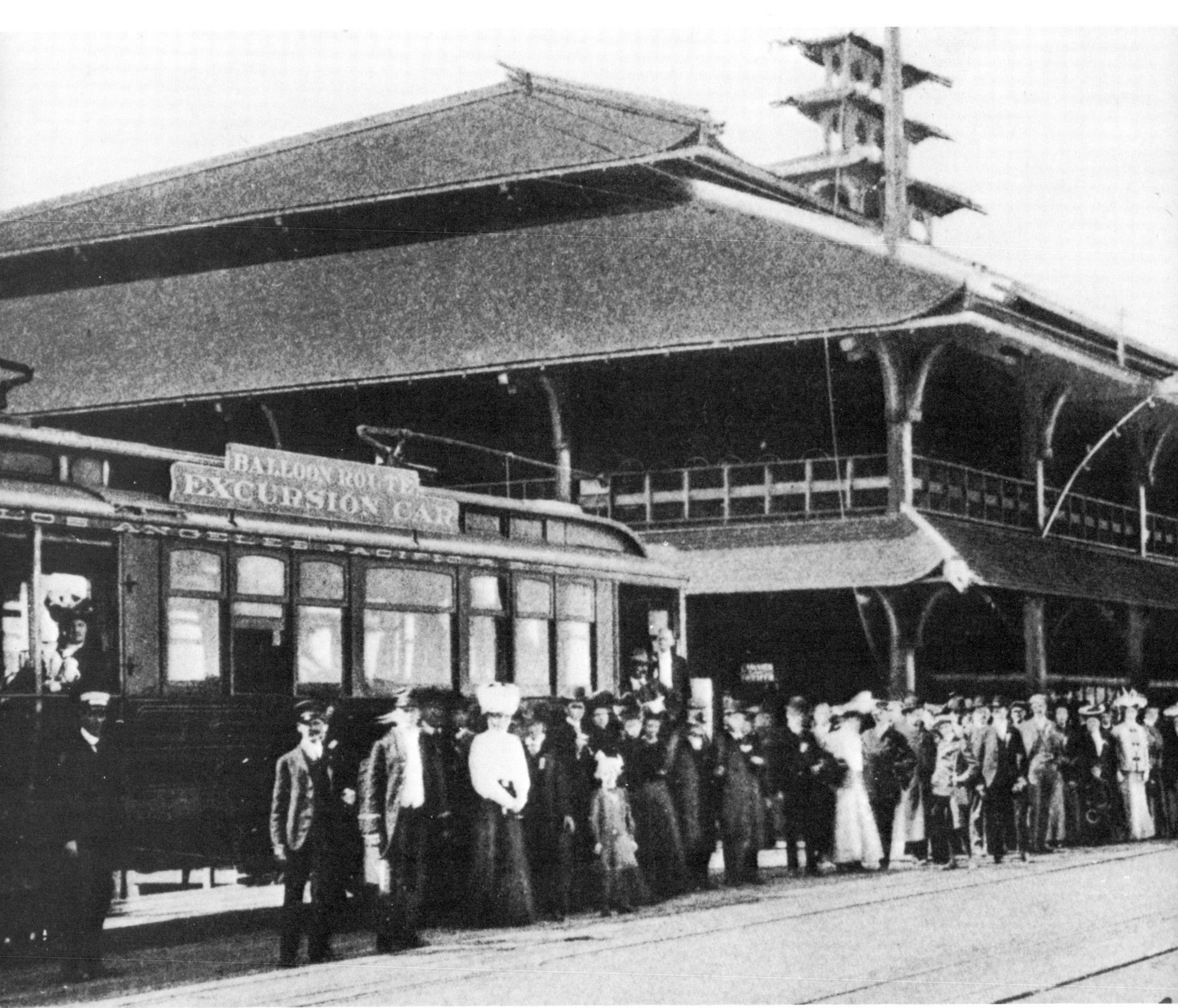

TOURISTS SUCH AS THESE, at Playa del Rey in 1908, came to see, and often decided to settle down. (C.M. Pierce)

Playa del Rey

THE EXTENSIVE Ballona Slough, composed of marshy fields broken by sand dunes, ponds and salt water lagoons, was considered to be utterly worthless. About 1870 Will Tell built a shack on the spot later occupied by the Del Rey Hotel and called it "Tell's Lookout." For several years he kept up this establishment, selling wines, brandies, etc., and renting boats, guns and fishing tackle to sportsmen.

About 1885 the approach of the Santa Fe and the first rumblings of the approaching boom brought many hitherto undreamed of projects to the surface. One of these was the scheme of creating a harbor out of the lagoons of La Ballona Slough.

In the spring of 1886 the Ballona Harbor & Improvement Company was organized by capitalists of Los Angeles, M.L. Wicks being the leading spirit. It was proposed to excavate a channel 200 feet long by 300 feet wide which would let the tide into the lagoon where Ballona Creek entered the sea. This would create an inner harbor two miles long and from 300 feet to 600 feet wide with depth varying from six to twenty feet. It was declared that this harbor would float the fleets of the world. This harbor was to be the terminus of the Santa Fe and was said to be 800 miles nearer Hawaii than San Francisco!

The Santa Fe built its line from Los Angeles to Inglewood, then headed straight for Port Ballona, as the new harbor had been named. The line was opened for use on August 21, 1887.

A large amount of dredging was done and a great deal of money—nearly $300,000—was spent during the three years in which work was carried on (more or less spasmodically) upon the proposed harbor.

By July 4, 1888, work had come to a standstill and only a watchman was left to guard the dredger and other property. A storm in 1890 carried away the greater portion of the wharf and deposited it along the shore at Santa Monica, where it was welcomed as firewood. The dredge was then taken away and Port Ballona became a thing of the past. Many causes operated to make the scheme impracticable: the blue clay formation underneath the sand, the currents which brought sand back faster than it could be dredged out, and the failure of the Santa Fe to cooperate. In 1892 Santa Fe took up its tracks from Port Ballona and relaid them to South Santa Monica (Ocean Park) where it built an iron wharf.

For fifteen years the lagoons and dunes remained a sportsmen's paradise, and then came a new era of life for Ballona Slough. In June, 1902, it was announced that a group of capitalists had incorporated as "The Beach Land Company" and had purchased a thousand acres of land, including more than two miles of beach frontage including the old Port Ballona. Among the incorporators were Sherman, Clark, Gillis and other prominent LAP men. The plans of this company were most elaborate. The new resort was to be named "Playa del Rey" ("Beach of the King"). LAP would at once build to the harbor, which was to be improved. A hotel costing $200,000 was proposed.

The first sale of lots, held on July 6, 1902, was a large one. Work began at once on grading and improvements. By October 19, LAP had cars running to Playa del Rey and a large number of excursionists visited the place.

Work continued steadily during the next year. The lagoon, two miles long, of still water for boating and bathing, proved to be popular; forty boats and launches were in use. During the year the LAP's Redondo line was completed, opening up a new district.

The year 1904 saw many major developments. Work on the three-story pavilion was rushed; it contained a restaurant,

dining room, dance floor, bowling alley, skating rink, bath house, banquet and picnic facilities. The pavilion opened on November 25 with a grand celebration, including boat races, dancing contests, etc. The Hotel del Rey, a handsome structure of fifty rooms, and a bandstand, grandstand and boat houses were completed. A two-story bank building was erected and many handsome cottages were erected along the lagoon and on the bluff. The LAP Lagoon line to Santa Monica was completed, giving a much improved car service, as the fare to Santa Monica was only five cents.

It is estimated that the Beach Land Co. and the LAP spent at least $200,000 on this resort. Six hundred acres of sand beach, rolling dunes and lofty bluffs were graded. Sidewalks, sewer, water and electricity were provided. Two suspension bridges were thrown across the lagoon and an incline railway was constructed to the top of Mt. Ballona, as the bluff is known.

C.M. Pierce, entrepreneur of the Balloon Route Trolley Trip, took over the management of the Playa del Rey project, paying LAP 10% of the proceeds of the various enterprises. All Balloon Route cars made their lunch stop at the pavilion, and even after Venice took undisputed first place among beach resorts, del Rey had its share of patronage.

Obsolescence and fire brought about the downfall of del Rey. Both the pavilion and the hotel were destroyed by fires which took lives. Discovery of oil along the lagoon in 1930 temporarily ended most of del Rey's attractiveness. Today Playa del Rey is once again a high-class area indeed, with a multimillion-dollar marina for pleasure boats nearby along with a huge apartment and shopping complex.

Redondo

REDONDO WAS STARTED during the boom of 1887 by the firm of Vail & Freeman. The site was on a gently curving bay where a deep ocean chasm came almost to shore; it was thus possible to provide ample depth for ships by constructing a wharf of modest length.

Redondo's name may have come from the shape of the shoreline ("round"), or it may have been taken from the street plan which saw streets laid out on gentle curves with an oval in the center of town, or the name of the old Spanish grant, "El Sausal Redondo" ("The Round Clump of Willows") may have been the inspiration. East and west streets were named alphabetically for precious stones (Agate, Beryl, Carnelian, Diamond, etc.) and north and south streets were named by the Dominguez family after its women folks: Alameda (now Pacific), Benita, Catalina, Dominguez (Broadway), Elena, Francisca, etc.

The earliest industry was the old salt works which worked the salt lake lying between Beryl St. and the present Edison power plant.

Vail & Freeman sold out to Thompson & Ainsworth, capitalists from Oregon. The new proprietors organized three companies which played a large role in developing the city: the Redondo Improvement Company, the Redondo Hotel Company, and the Los Angeles & Redondo Railway Company. They constructed three wharves and Redondo began to attract ocean commerce.

The Santa Fe, discouraged in attempts to get a Pacific harbor at Port Ballona, came to Redondo in March, 1888. A real estate boom started at once; great banners over Los Angeles streets announced the opening of a beautiful subdivision with a free barbecue dinner. Papers were filled with ads for Redondo. People came, saw great construction activity and the boom got off to a good start. Real estate turned over rapidly; some lots were sold several times in a day. Prices paid then have not been equaled since. That first summer everyone got water from a well in the center of town and carried it home in buckets; the next year a water delivery system was started.

In 1889 the Hotel Redondo was started; it was one of the finest on the coast and many noted persons from all over the world were guests. Adjoining the rambling wood structure were fine tennis courts and a golf course. The hotel was built where today stands the library; from its high vantage point, guests could look down on the busy wharves and watch the ebb and flow of ocean and commerce.

In 1889, also, the *Los Angeles & Redondo Railway* was built, a 3'-gauge steam line. Its Los Angeles terminus was at the corner of Jefferson and Grand Ave., and in Redondo it built a round brick building in front of the Hotel Redondo.

REDONDO BEACH from an old postcard; LAP 700-class car is discharging passengers.
                                               (Interurbans)

The LA&R roundhouse and shops were located just across the street. The LA&R operated as a steam line until 1903 when it was converted to electricity. This was done to enable it to compete with the LAP, which was building down the coast to Redondo from Playa del Rey.

In July, 1905, Henry E. Huntington purchased all holdings of the Ainsworth-Thompson Syndicate. Huntington announced he was going to spend millions improving Redondo. At once a boom started which eclipsed that of 1887. Business went wild. More than a hundred real estate offices set themselves up in business on the front street, many having only tents. Buying went on in a frenzied manner, speculators paying more for lots than they could ever be worth. It is recalled that the railroad conductors bought lots in Redondo, then sold them to passengers on the next trip. Huntington built a string of amusement buildings along the waterfront, including the Plunge, the largest indoor salt water plunge anywhere; it was 218 feet long by 70 feet wide and contained 561,000 gallons, of which 60,000 were changed hourly. It could accommodate 5,800 people daily, and was open every day in the year. Other buildings included a restaurant, dance hall and theater.

Thus LAP found itself more or less in the camp of the enemy when it attempted to get into Redondo. It stopped at the foot of Diamond Street where its station was located, and Balloon Route passengers who wanted to visit the Hotel Redondo had to walk several blocks (LA&R deposited its passengers at the door). Thus LAP never did much to push Redondo, preferring the exclusively LAP beaches to the north.

A few figures on the growth of Redondo: in 1890 there were 668 residents; by 1900 this figure had increased to 855; in 1910 the population had soared to 2,935—and to 4,900 in 1920 and to 9,375 in 1930. In 1892 Redondo incorporated as a city of the sixth class. As a seaport, Redondo imported in 1900 some fifteen million feet of lumber and 500,000 pounds of fish; by 1905 this had increased to 100,000,000 feet of lumber and 1,400,000 pounds of fish. As many as fifteen ships waited offshore in those busy days to unload. Pacific Steamship Company boats called at Redondo regularly, as did such famous coastwise passenger ships as the "Santa Rosa," "President," "Governor," and "Queen." The electric trains of the LA&R ran out on the wharves, allowing the passengers to make convenient connections.

In the great harbor fight of the Nineties between Santa Monica and San Pedro, Redondo abided by the first decision of governmental committees favoring San Pedro and did not press its own claims further. When San Pedro was built up to become the one port for Los Angeles County, Redondo gradually lost its maritime importance. Wharves 1 and 2 were removed and #1 was replaced by a pleasure pier. Wharf 3 was used until it, too, was torn down in 1926.

PE took over the amusement zone in 1914 and operated it until 1940, when it abandoned rail operation into Redondo. The amusement buildings were torn down after World War II, including the plunge. Today Redondo has lost much of the distinction it once enjoyed, although many parts of the seaside city retain a certain residential charm.

REDONDO LINE track and overhead construction. View looks north from Manhattan Beach.　　　(T.L. Wagenbach)

Shakespeare Beach

IN AUGUST, 1903, Clark and Sherman purchased a 200-acre tract between Manhattan Beach and Hermosa. This they proceeded to subdivide and named it "Shakespeare Beach." Several times previously there had been attempts to establish literary colonies in the Los Angeles area; one notable failure was at the Ostrich Farm (now Griffith Park) which did not work out because of transportation difficulties. Sherman and Clark believed there was a need for a center for writers and so Shakespeare Beach evolved.

Streets in this unique beach community bore rich and significant names: Othello, Romeo, Juliet, Stratford, Desdemona; other streets were named Burns, Tennyson, Longfellow and Hawthorne. Convenient electric service to Los Angeles was at the door and high hopes were visualized for this tract.

On August 15, 1903, the tract was put on the market. Extensive publicity campaigns were put on, and the name "Shakespeare Beach" loomed large on all LAP maps of the period.

The tract eventually sold, but the dream of making it a literary center did not come to pass. Shakespeare Beach took its place as just one more beach community and eventually became a part of Hermosa.

Hermosa

HERMOSA BEACH WAS originally part of the ten-mile ocean frontage of Rancho Sausal Redondo. In early days, Hermosa Beach (like Inglewood, Lawndale and Torrance) was one vast sweep of rolling hills covered with grain, mostly barley. During certain seasons of the year vast flocks of sheep grazed over this land, and large corrals and barns were located between Hermosa and Inglewood.

In 1900 Sherman and Clark bought 1,500 acres at $35 per acre and organized the Hermosa Beach Land & Water Company to develop this land. The first official survey was made in 1901, and that same year saw a well and storage tank constructed by Sherman and Clark.

Hermosa's original transportation came from the Santa Fe Railway, whose line to Redondo passed inland through a valley back of the sand dunes, some seven blocks back from the beach. The broad curving street leading from Hermosa to the Santa Fe was first called Santa Fe Avenue, but later was renamed Pier Avenue. This street and the main north-south street, Hermosa Ave. (on which ran LAP's del Rey-Redondo line) were paved in 1904 using asphalt which probably came from Ventura.

LAP built in to Hermosa in 1902-03 and located its passenger and freight station on the northeast corner of Pier and Hermosa Avenues. A substation was constructed at the north city limits. Both buildings were constructed of stucco and followed LAP's usual conception of Mission architecture.

In 1904 the first pier was built, and a two-mile boardwalk followed immediately. Sherman and Clark refused to allow cheap amusement devices, keeping Hermosa free to develop as a family seashore community.

OVERVIEW OF Hermosa Beach looking south toward Redondo; although taken in 1917 photo shows double track unchanged from LAP days. (Security Pacific Bank)

On January 14, 1907, Hermosa Beach was incorporated as a city of the sixth class. At this time the city obtained ownership of its two-mile stretch of ocean frontage, being included in the deed from the Hermosa Beach Land & Water Company (Sherman and Clark).

This company built the first public building, the Hermosa Pavilion, at the south corner of Pier Ave. and the Strand. The company's offices were in the building and the first post office was located there.

Hermosa Beach attracted an excellent type of permanent resident, and its calm bathing beach, its equable year-round climate, and its proximity to Los Angeles brought it steady growth. Among its earliest boosters was famed William Jennings Bryan, who frequently could be seen on the Hermosa Pier trying his luck with the fish, and dressed informally in overalls and an old straw hat.

Manhattan Beach

MANHATTAN BEACH was passed by in the settlement of Santa Monica Bay. Not until 1902 did it get a name and not until 1912 did it get a charter. The town was incorporated in 1910 and received its charter from the Secretary of State on September 12, 1912.

Manhattan is located on the coastline of the LAP between Playa del Rey and Hermosa Beach. It is about twenty miles from Los Angeles and has an ocean frontage of about 2¼ miles. Its area is approximately 2,300 acres—about two miles square. The townsite is bisected by a high sand ridge; that part along the shore is known as the "sand" section, while that part inland is called the "soil" section.

Manhattan Beach was originally called "Shore Acres," which name was used by the Santa Fe for its station on Center St. just east of the business district. George Peck, who owned the north section of town, liked this name and wished to continue it. Stewart Merrill, who came in 1902 and owned the south portion, called his section "Manhattan" after his old home, New York City. Peck and Merrill decided to settle the matter by flipping a coin; the toss was won by Merrill and the town thereafter bore the Manhattan name. It later became Manhattan "Beach" when the postmaster petitioned postal authorities to change it to avoid mail confusion with fourteen other Manhattans in the country.

The first settlement of the area took place in 1900 when Frank S. Daugherty and five Los Angeles businessmen incorporated the Highland Beach Company and bought 20 acres in the area from Marian to 15th and Highland and east to the Santa Fe tracks. They subdivided, laid sidewalks in the middle of blocks and put water pipes in alleys. They then chartered a Santa Fe train and brought 500 people down to the opening sale of lots.

Merrill and Peck laid out the south and north sections of city respectively. The south part developed much faster. Boardwalks were laid on the sand and civic-minded citizens, out for a walk, took along a hammer and nails to keep the walks repaired.

The shifting of sand by high winds was a serious problem; finally the women solved it by organizing themselves into planting brigades, planting a mosslike succulent which finally laid the sand permanently.

Two wooden piers were built in 1902, one at Center St. and one at Marine Ave. The Center St. pier supported a wave motor to generate electricity from waves. It was able to generate enough power for a short time for the Strand lighting system.

In 1903 Sherman and Clark built the LAP south along the coast from Playa del Rey to Redondo, giving Manhattan Beach its first good transportation service and bringing a wave of settlers. The 1905 Redondo boom was also felt by Manhattan and lots sold at fabulous prices for a short time. The LAP dou-

Lights Dimmed Along the Beach When the LAP Cars Came By

ble tracks were on a shelf above the beach but considerably below the level of Manhattan Beach, whose terrain rises quite sharply from the shore. In the early days the railway sold electric power to illuminate homes and businesses; power was so weak that the Strand lights and those in homes along the way always dimmed as the interurban cars passed by.

Manhattan Beach was not spectacular insofar as speedy growth was concerned. As late as 1920 it had less than a thousand permanent residents, although its summer population, of course, rose considerably. It has a splendid bathing beach and this was its main attraction in LAP's time.

From Hill Street

Chapter Three

LAP 235 visits the Long Wharf, circa 1909. (Jeff Moreau)

to the Long Wharf

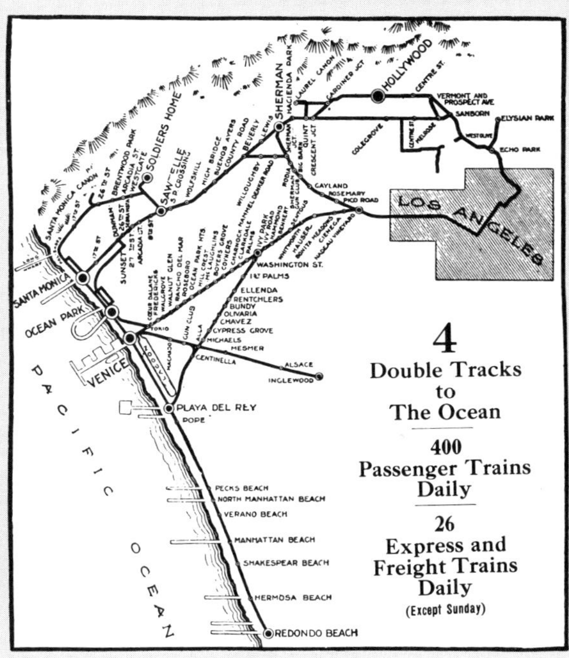

LAP's Rails Provided

Fine Rapid Transit.

An Earlier Generation

Appreciated It.

ON SEPTEMBER 1, 1911, all LAP lines were turned over to the Pacific Electric Railway Company, LAP's successor by consolidation. As of that date, lines owned by LAP totaled 103.6 route miles, of which 77.97 miles were double track and 25.63 miles were single track. This was equivalent to 204.67 miles of single track, including 23.10 miles of spurs and unused track. All of this track was 4'8½" gauge. In addition, LAP turned over 13.49 miles of leased line, equivalent to 26.2 miles single track, including 12.71 miles of spurs and sidings. This was that portion of the Southern Pacific's Santa Monica line extending from Sentous to the outer end of the Long Wharf and the Soldiers' Home branch of this line. All of this trackage turned over to PE was operated by overhead electric trolley except that portion of the Cahuenga Valley line on Beverly Blvd. from Alexandria Ave. to the oil spur behind Bimini Baths, near Vermont and Third, which was operated by steam.

LAP operated many lines, but four were outstanding: The Main Line, the Hollywood Line, the Venice Short Line and the Hermosa-Redondo Line. Other important lines were: Colegrove Line, Franklin Ave. Line, and the Westgate Line. Then there were the small lines, chiefly performing local service: Lagoon Line, Melrose Cutoff, Brush Canyon Line, Highland Ave. Line, Elysian Park Line, Rodeo Line, North Loop, South Loop, SP Air Line and Inglewood Line. Each of these lines is taken up in detail in this chapter.

Before standard gauging, lines were built with light rail, from 40 to 70 pounds per yard; this light rail was laid on ties 6"x8"x6'. After standard gauging the rail weight averaged considerably more—most was 70 or 75 pounds, laid on 6"x8"x8' ties.

W. 16th DIVISION

THE W. 16th DIVISION extended from Hill St. Station to Beverly Hills Station, a distance of 10.19 miles, all double track. It was built in 1897 by *Pasadena & Pacific Ry. Co. of California* (Unit 44). The route was as follows: on Hill from 4th to 16th, on 16th or closely adjacent thereto from Hill to the west city limits at Arlington Ave., then via private right of way across country to Beverly where it joined the old P&P line to Santa Monica. This new line was somewhat shorter than the route via Colegrove and soon got most of the beach traffic. It was known then as the "Santa Monica Short Line."

A part of this route ran over tracks belonging to the *L.A. Traction Company;* on Hill between 4th and 8th Sts., and on 16th from Georgia to Bush St. (Burlington Ave.). In return, LAP gave LAT trackage rights over a portion of this line: 4th between Broadway and Hill, Hill between 8th and 16th Sts., and 16th between Hill and Georgia. Thus the entire line city-ward from 16th & Rush was joint operation; this coexistence

Lines covered in this chapter will be considered to have had the following terminals:

LINE	FROM	TO
Brush Canyon	Franklin Ave.	Quarry
Cahuenga Valley	S.M. & Western	Alexandria
Colegrove	Sanborn Jct.	Crescent Jct.
Del Rey–Redondo	Ivy Park	Redondo
Elysian Park	Sunset Blvd.	Cerro Gordo
Franklin Ave.	S.M. & Western	Holly-Vine
Hollywood	4th & Hill	Beverly Hills
Highland Ave.	S.M. & Highland	Cahuenga Pass
Inglewood	5th St., S.M.	Inglewood
Lagoon	Oregon & Ocean	Del Rey Jct.
Laurel Canyon	Gardner Jct.	Laurel Canyon
Melrose Cutoff	S.M. & Virgil	Holly-Vermont
Rodeo	Beverly Hills	Coldwater Cyn.
Southern Pacific	Sentous	S.M. SP Depot
Sawtelle	Beverly Hills	North Beach
North Loop	North Beach	3rd & Montana
South Loop	Ocean & Oregon	2nd & Hill
Port Los Angeles	S.M. SP Depot	Port L.A.
Venice Short Line	Vineyard	Venice
W. 16th St.	4th & Hill	Beverly Hills
Westgate	S.M. Blvd.	North Beach
Soldiers' Home	S.M. Blvd.	S.H. Loop

lasted until June 30, 1946 when the narrow gauge "A" line of *Los Angeles Transit Lines* was abandoned.

Between Vermont Ave. and Western Ave. this line crossed Rosedale Cemetery. To avoid disturbing graves, the line originally described a circuitous arc around the cemetery, bringing it onto Cambridge St. (a block north of 16th) for a distance and entailing sharp curves which cut down the speed of cars seriously. In late 1901 the company arranged with Rosedale Cemetery to move some graves and open up a new private way through the cemetery property; this W. 16th Cutoff was constructed at a cost of $40,000 in late 1902.

In 1907, cars left L.A. at 6:05 AM and every 30 minutes to 12:05 AM, then one at 1:15 AM; returning, cars left Ocean Park at 5:35 AM and every half hour to 1:05 AM. Extra service was operated as traffic demanded.

The 1911 schedule saw cars running through to Venice. First car left L.A. at 4:45 AM, then 6:15 and half hourly to 12:45 AM, then one at 1:00 AM. Returning, cars left Windward Ave. at 5:32 AM, then half hourly to 12:02 and finally one at 12:49. These cars made the run to Hill St. Station in 66 minutes, to Windward Ave. in 64 minutes. At this time this line was known as the Sawtelle Line. Passengers to or from Colegrove and Hollywood transferred at Beverly.

In addition to the beach service, local service was provided on W. 16th St., terminating at Vineyard. In 1907 there were four morning trips at 30-minute intervals starting at 7:15 AM, and four evening runs at half hour intervals starting at 4:45 from Fourth St. Station; inbound, there were six morning trips at 30-minute intervals from 6:45, and only two evening runs at 5:15 and 5:45. No local service ran on Sundays. In 1911 the local service had increased markedly; five minute headway in rush hours and 15 minute service in the off peak periods was given, much of it by through beach cars.

PE operated through service over this line as its Santa Monica via Sawtelle Line until abandoned on July 7, 1940. Service as far as Olympic Blvd. ran until October 1, 1950.

PALMS DIVISION

THE PALMS DIVISION, later known as the Venice Short Line, extended from a junction with the W. 16th St. Division at Vineyard to a junction with the Lagoon Division at Center St., Venice. This line was nine miles long, was entirely double track and was standard gauged in 1908.

In an interview published in the Santa Monica *Outlook* on August 31, 1901, Gen. Sherman stated, "Already we have 90% of the right of way for our new cutoff via Palms. We will run a direct line from the Ocean Park Powerhouse to the L.A. city

BUSINESS END of the Long Wharf in steam days, when triple-masted sailing schooners came to call.   (Security Pacific Bank)

THIS WAS SPRING STREET, Los Angeles, in 1905, with car 229. LAP's Hollywood and Colegrove lines used this tortuous entrance until the Hill St. tunnels were opened in 1909.
(Rudolph Brandt)

limits at a junction with the W. 16th St. line. We had to pay as much as $1,500 per acre for the right of way. The line will be practically level, no curves, and will reduce time to 20 minutes from the city limits to Ocean Park."

Work began shortly thereafter and continued until fall, when a recess was called to allow farmers time to harvest their crops on the right of way. Grading was completed late in February and laying of rails began. By the end of March, 1902, rails were in place from Ocean Park to Ivy (now Culver City). By July, this line was about ready, with some tamping to be done. On Saturday, August 2, a great celebration was held at the Ocean Park Casino commemorating the opening of this line; included in the program, which was attended by the elite including Mayor Snyder of L.A. and the L.A. City Council (brought down over this line on four special cars), was a polo match, a dinner, and dancing on the tennis courts. However, this was premature. There was much work yet to be done and the Palms Division did not open to the public until August 22; its new cars, good roadbed and heavy rails brought it immediate public favor.

According to the *Outlook,* LAP began a loop operation which was continued off and on throughout the history of this line and the Sawtelle Division: cars leaving L.A. by one route returned via the other, eliminating deadhead mileage and increasing convenience to passengers. Said the *Outlook* on

August 26, 1902: "The new line is running satisfactorily. Cars running south on Oregon Ave. go to L.A. via Ocean Park; those running north on Oregon Ave. go to L.A. via Sawtelle. There is but little difference in time. LAP offers 15-minute service via either Palms or Sawtelle."

In those days the route curved at the site of the Venice City Hall and entered Ocean Park via Electric Ave., now Inglewood Line. In June, 1903, work began on a new connection between the Palms Line at Tokio (City Hall) and the Lagoon Line at Center St.; when this connection was completed, Palms Division cars gave up Electric Avenue and thereafter ran on the Lagoon Line and its Trolleyway from Center St. to Santa Monica.

According to oldtimers, there was a grade separation at Ivy between this line and the SP Santa Monica Line; LAP cars went under the steam track in a plank-lined underpass. No date has been found for the elimination of this underpass but it is probable that it was changed to a grade level crossing with interchange switches at the time the Palms Division was standard gauged in 1908.

Ivy was also the location of a large and ornamental substation. This was built in 1903 and was in a triangular park between the Palms Division and the Redondo Division which diverged at that point.

This line rapidly took its undisputed place as LAP's heaviest

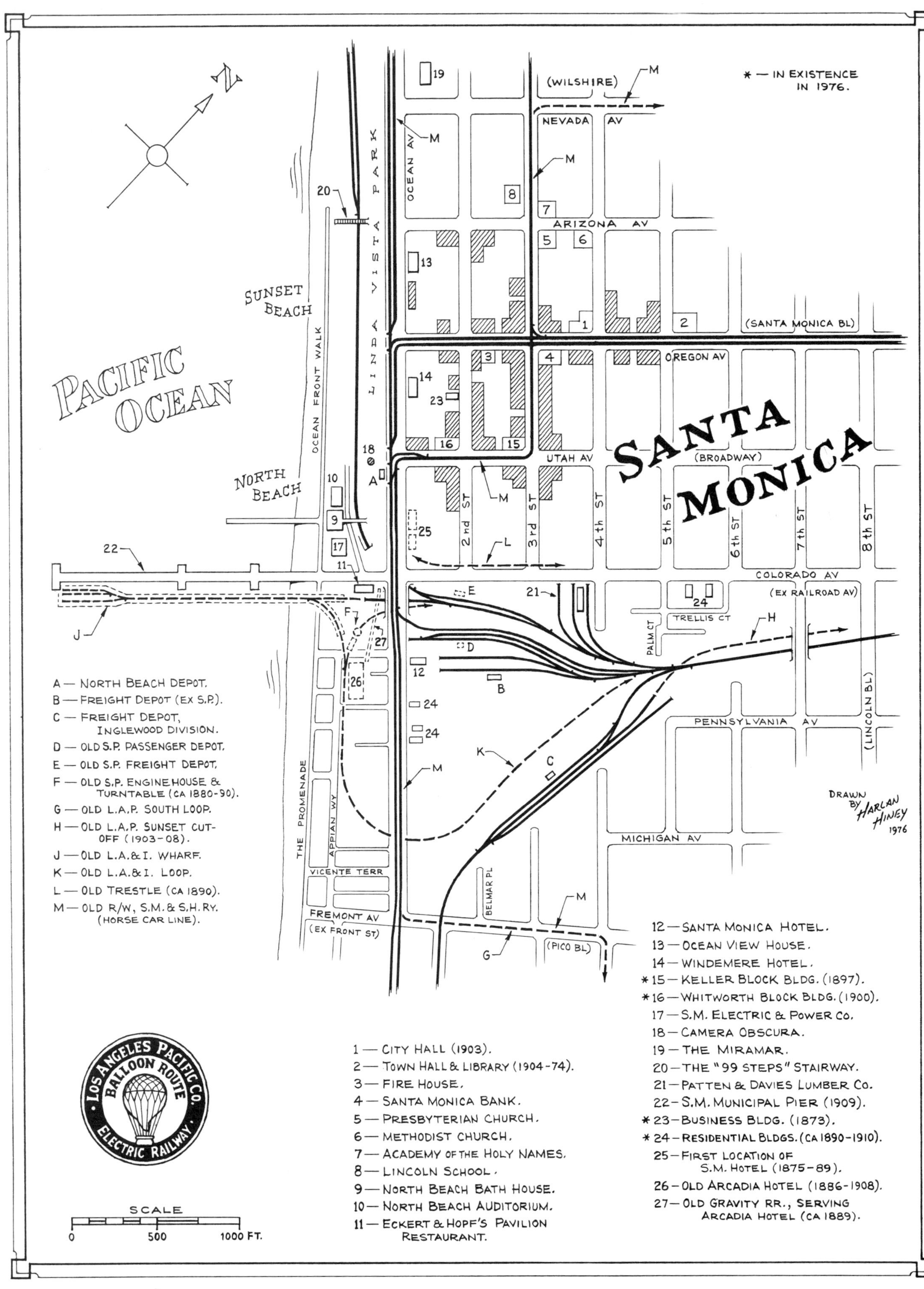
* — IN EXISTENCE IN 1976.
(WILSHIRE)
NEVADA AV
M
M
M
OCEAN AV
ARIZONA AV
LINDA VISTA PARK
SUNSET BEACH
OCEAN FRONT WALK
PACIFIC OCEAN
(SANTA MONICA BL)
OREGON AV
SANTA MONICA
(BROADWAY)
NORTH BEACH
UTAH AV
2nd ST
3rd ST
4th ST
5th ST
6th ST
7th ST
8th ST
M
L
COLORADO AV
(EX RAILROAD AV)
(LINCOLN BL)
PALM CT
TRELLIS CT
H
E
D
B
PENNSYLVANIA AV
K
C
THE PROMENADE
APPIAN WY
M
DRAWN BY HARLAN HINEY 1976
MICHIGAN AV
VICENTE TERR
BELMAR PL
M
FREMONT AV
(EX FRONT ST)
G
(PICO BL)
A — NORTH BEACH DEPOT.
B — FREIGHT DEPOT (EX S.P.).
C — FREIGHT DEPOT, INGLEWOOD DIVISION.
D — OLD S.P. PASSENGER DEPOT.
E — OLD S.P. FREIGHT DEPOT.
F — OLD S.P. ENGINE HOUSE & TURNTABLE (CA 1880-90).
G — OLD L.A.P. SOUTH LOOP.
H — OLD L.A.P. SUNSET CUT-OFF (1903-08).
J — OLD L.A. & I. WHARF.
K — OLD L.A. & I. LOOP.
L — OLD TRESTLE (CA 1890).
M — OLD R/W, S.M. & S.H. RY. (HORSE CAR LINE).
LOS ANGELES PACIFIC CO.
BALLOON ROUTE
ELECTRIC RAILWAY
SCALE
0   500   1000 FT.
1 — CITY HALL (1903).
2 — TOWN HALL & LIBRARY (1904-74).
3 — FIRE HOUSE.
4 — SANTA MONICA BANK.
5 — PRESBYTERIAN CHURCH.
6 — METHODIST CHURCH.
7 — ACADEMY OF THE HOLY NAMES.
8 — LINCOLN SCHOOL.
9 — NORTH BEACH BATH HOUSE.
10 — NORTH BEACH AUDITORIUM.
11 — ECKERT & HOPF'S PAVILION RESTAURANT.
12 — SANTA MONICA HOTEL.
13 — OCEAN VIEW HOUSE.
14 — WINDEMERE HOTEL.
* 15 — KELLER BLOCK BLDG. (1897).
* 16 — WHITWORTH BLOCK BLDG. (1900).
17 — S.M. ELECTRIC & POWER CO.
18 — CAMERA OBSCURA.
19 — THE MIRAMAR.
20 — THE "99 STEPS" STAIRWAY.
21 — PATTEN & DAVIES LUMBER CO.
22 — S.M. MUNICIPAL PIER (1909).
* 23 — BUSINESS BLDG. (1873).
* 24 — RESIDENTIAL BLDGS. (CA 1890-1910).
25 — FIRST LOCATION OF S.M. HOTEL (1875-89).
26 — OLD ARCADIA HOTEL (1886-1908).
27 — OLD GRAVITY RR., SERVING ARCADIA HOTEL (CA 1889).

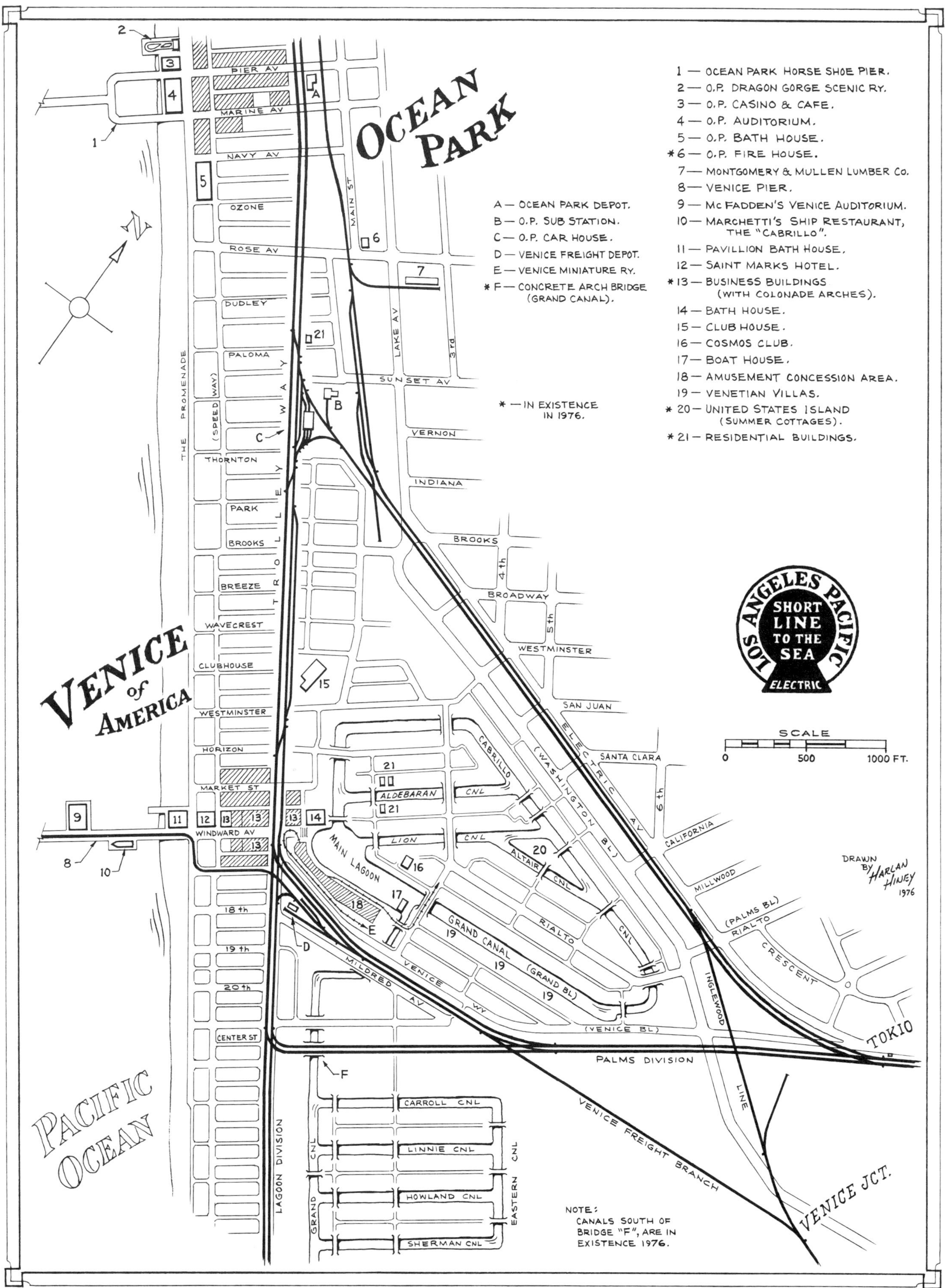

OCEAN PARK
VENICE of AMERICA
PACIFIC OCEAN

1 — OCEAN PARK HORSE SHOE PIER.
2 — O.P. DRAGON GORGE SCENIC RY.
3 — O.P. CASINO & CAFE.
4 — O.P. AUDITORIUM.
5 — O.P. BATH HOUSE.
* 6 — O.P. FIRE HOUSE.
7 — MONTGOMERY & MULLEN LUMBER CO.
8 — VENICE PIER.
9 — Mc FADDEN'S VENICE AUDITORIUM.
10 — MARCHETTI'S SHIP RESTAURANT, THE "CABRILLO".
11 — PAVILLION BATH HOUSE.
12 — SAINT MARKS HOTEL.
* 13 — BUSINESS BUILDINGS (WITH COLONADE ARCHES).
14 — BATH HOUSE.
15 — CLUB HOUSE.
16 — COSMOS CLUB.
17 — BOAT HOUSE.
18 — AMUSEMENT CONCESSION AREA.
19 — VENETIAN VILLAS.
* 20 — UNITED STATES ISLAND (SUMMER COTTAGES).
* 21 — RESIDENTIAL BUILDINGS.

A — OCEAN PARK DEPOT.
B — O.P. SUB STATION.
C — O.P. CAR HOUSE.
D — VENICE FREIGHT DEPOT.
E — VENICE MINIATURE RY.
* F — CONCRETE ARCH BRIDGE (GRAND CANAL).

* — IN EXISTENCE IN 1976.

LOS ANGELES PACIFIC
SHORT LINE TO THE SEA
ELECTRIC

SCALE
0   500   1000 FT.

DRAWN BY HARLAN HINEY 1976

PIER AV
MARINE AV
NAVY AV
OZONE
ROSE AV
DUDLEY
PALOMA
THORNTON
PARK
BROOKS
BREEZE
WAVECREST
CLUBHOUSE
WESTMINSTER
HORIZON
MARKET ST
WINDWARD AV
18 th
19 th
20 th
CENTER ST
THE PROMENADE
(SPEED WAY)
TROLLEY WAY
MAIN ST
LAKE AV
3 rd
SUNSET AV
VERNON
INDIANA
BROOKS
Broadway
4 th
5 th
WESTMINSTER
SAN JUAN
SANTA CLARA
6 th
CALIFORNIA
MILLWOOD
ELECTRIC AV
(WASHINGTON BL)
(PALMS BL)
RIALTO
CRESCENT
INGLEWOOD
CABRILLO
ALDEBARAN
LION
ALTAIR
RIALTO
CNL
MAIN LAGOON
GRAND CANAL
(GRAND BL)
VENICE WY
MILDRED AV
LAGOON DIVISION
GRAND CNL
CARROLL CNL
LINNIE CNL
HOWLAND CNL
SHERMAN CNL
EASTERN CNL
PALMS DIVISION
VENICE FREIGHT BRANCH
VENICE JCT.
TOKIO
LINE
(VENICE BL)

NOTE:
CANALS SOUTH OF BRIDGE "F", ARE IN EXISTENCE 1976.

beach line. In 1907, alternate 10 and 20-minute service was provided until 6:50 PM when half hourly service continued to 11:50 PM, then a 12:45 car; returning, cars left Ocean Park on similar schedules with alternate cars leaving from North Beach. Mornings from Ocean Park and evenings from L.A. Flyers were operated.

In 1911, 20-minute service was provided from 6:20 AM to 7:00 PM, then half hourly till the last car at 12:30 AM. Of these trips, those leaving L.A. at 20 and 40 minutes after the hour ran as Flyers, making limited stops. Similar service was offered leaving North Beach Station. Running time was 50 minutes outbound and 52 minutes inbound. Cars did no local work east of Ivy Park until 7:00 PM.

In October, 1906, plans were revealed by LAP to four-track this line from Vineyard to Venice. Right of way for the two additional tracks was secured and certain preliminary work was done, such as making cuts, widening banks, and excavating.

At about the same time the so-called Vineyard Subway was announced. This line would have run in a double track tunnel from Hill St. Station to 4th and Vermont, then proceed via a cut and tunnel under Wilshire to surface operation to Vineyard. The complete story of this subway project is found under "4th St. Subway."

First the 1907 business depression and then the Great Merger delayed both the four-tracking and the subway. Although both were talked about for years after the Merger, changing times eventually caught up with both and neither materialized.

PE operated the Venice Short Line until September 17, 1950, when it was abandoned and rails removed its entire length except for a very short stretch adjacent to the Culver City freight station.

SOUTH LOOP

THE SOUTH LOOP was built by *Pasadena & Pacific Ry. Co. of Arizona* (Unit 43) in 1896. Its route was as follows: from Oregon and Ocean Avenues on Ocean to Front (Pico), to 4th, to Hill, to 2nd, to Main St., to Front. That part of the above routes on 2nd, Main, Front and Ocean had previously been operated as a horse car line by the *Santa Monica & Soldiers' Home Railroad Co.* (Unit 42) which built it in 1891. The South Loop was built under a time bonus clause and P&P crews barely completed it in time to earn the bonus for Sherman and Clark.

The South Loop opened on July 1, 1896, and became on that date a part of the P&P's main line to L.A. with all cars making this loop. The company opened an office at the corner of 2nd and Hill Sts., and the single track curved into this small yard where a pit enabled cars to be inspected and oiled. All information available points to the fact that cars made this loop always in a clockwise direction.

It was this South Loop entry into Ocean Park which took away the Santa Fe's passenger business to such an extent that the Santa Fe abandoned its Inglewood Line in 1901; LAP (Unit 49) purchased the Inglewood Line on March 21, 1902, and converted it at once to electric operation. However, as it was standard gauge and the South Loop then was narrow (3'6") gauge, there was no common operation possible.

LAP LINE VIEWS: Narrow-gauge tracks on W. 16th St., 1905 (top) and standard-gauge tracks on the Venice Short Line near the old Ivy Substation.   (Top: Security Pacific Bank; Bottom: T.L. Wagenbach)

IVY (later Culver City).   (T.L. Wagenbach)

Freight was transshipped at 2nd and Hill Sts. and a combination gauge interchange track was constructed. In February, 1901, work was begun on the first trackage to use the Trolleyway; this left the South Loop at Azure and 2nd and ran up into the Trolleyway, continuing southward to the Club House where Venice later was built. A connection was made at Rose Ave. (Sunset) to the Inglewood Line and combination gauge trackage was constructed on the latter line as far as the new Palms Division. When the Palms line to L.A. (Venice Short Line) opened on August 16, 1902, the importance of the South Loop decreased greatly; after that date, through cars used the Trolleyway line through Ocean Park and the South Loop provided only local service to and from Santa Monica.

The South Loop dwindled so markedly in importance after through cars were transferred to the Trolleyway that its schedule was not even printed in LAP timetables.

In 1910 the South Loop was abandoned; it is probable that passenger service on this line terminated even earlier.

NORTH LOOP

THE NORTH LOOP operated in Santa Monica from Ocean and Utah via Utah, 3rd, Montana, and Ocean back to Utah. Its early history is clouded, for the PE official history declares it to have been built in its entirety "in 1899 and early in 1900." However, the Santa Monica *Outlook* reports it to have been built in at least two segments; quoting from the *Outlook*: "December 28, 1899—The first car ran over the Ocean Ave. Extension this morning. The local car makes the loop every half hour and meets all L.A. cars at Ocean Ave." However, we read on February 25, 1902: "The horse car line on 3rd and Utah will soon be electrified." Again on March 6th of that year: "LAP broke ground today for the electrification of the horse car line on 3rd St." And on May 7, 1902: "A large force is at work taking up the old horse car rails on 3rd and Utah Ave." It is probable that the original North Loop operation was via Oregon Ave. instead of via Utah Ave. The *Outlook* states that the North Loop was double tracked in October, 1902, but the official PE records show it to have been a single

track line; photos unanimously show it to have been single track. It was standard gauged in 1908.

On July 20, 1903, the North Loop began being used by Flyers from L.A.; cars coming in from L.A. via Palms ran around the loop all day and extra cars left Montana Ave. every half hour via Palms to L.A. Santa Monicans evidently were well pleased, for on July 31, 1903, the *Outlook* reported: "LAP's new Montana loop service by the Los Angeles cars is very well liked."

Evidently business of a strictly local nature was poor on the North Loop for in September, 1908, in connection with being granted a franchise for a new line on Montana Ave. from 7th St. to San Vicente Blvd., LAP promised to resume operations on 3rd St. at once.

In 1910 an extension was built on Montana Ave. from 3rd to 7th Sts.; it was a single track standard gauge line. The plan to build east on Montana to San Vicente Blvd. to hook up with the Westgate Line never materialized.

In 1910 the North Loop operation as such was discontinued. The only track abandoned was on Montana Ave. between Ocean Ave. and 3rd St. Thereafter, Lagoon cars ran via Ocean, Utah, 3rd, and Montana to 7th St.

PE abandoned this line December 13, 1929.

8th STREET LINE

LAP DID THE preliminary work on this line, but did not construct it except to place the switch at the intersection of Oregon Ave. and 8th St. PE completed this line in January, 1912, and opened it on January 30th. The 8th St. Line ran south on that street from Oregon Ave. to Garfield Ave., about a mile. It served the Santa Monica High School and the Garfield School. The line was abandoned by PE on January 22, 1927.

SOLDIERS' HOME HORSE CAR LINE

THIS WAS SANTA MONICA'S first rail transit operation. The line started in South Santa Monica at the old Santa Fe Station at Hill and 2nd Sts., then ran north on 2nd and Main Sts. to Front St. (Pico), west to Ocean Ave., up Ocean across two bridges over the ravines in which SP's railroad tracks ran and to the intersection with Utah Ave., east on Utah to 3rd, through the business district on 3rd to Nevada (Wilshire) and on Nevada to Soldiers' Home—a total distance of about six miles. The barn was located near 7th and Arizona Ave. and was connected to the Nevada Ave. line by a track along 7th St. At the Soldiers' Home the line actually entered the grounds and terminated near the big dining hall. This line was built by the *Santa Monica & Soldiers' Home Railroad Company* (Unit 42) and opened in 1891. It did a good business carrying veterans to and from Santa Monica, and with the growth of South Santa Monica, that end, too, provided good business.

On June 17, 1895, this company, controlled by W.S. Vawter and E.J. Vawter, prominent businessmen of Santa Monica for many years, agreed to sell out to Clark and Sherman who paid for it in bonds of the *Pasadena & Pacific Railway Company of Arizona* (Unit 43).

Clark and Sherman rebuilt the South Santa Monica end of this line into an electric railway (the South Loop), opening on July 1, 1896. It appears that previous to this date the horse car operation was cut back to Utah and Ocean. At the time of the sale to Clark and Sherman, the horse car company owned four cars, sixteen horses, two bridges, a depot at the Home, various sheds and buildings, about six miles of track, and several valuable franchises.

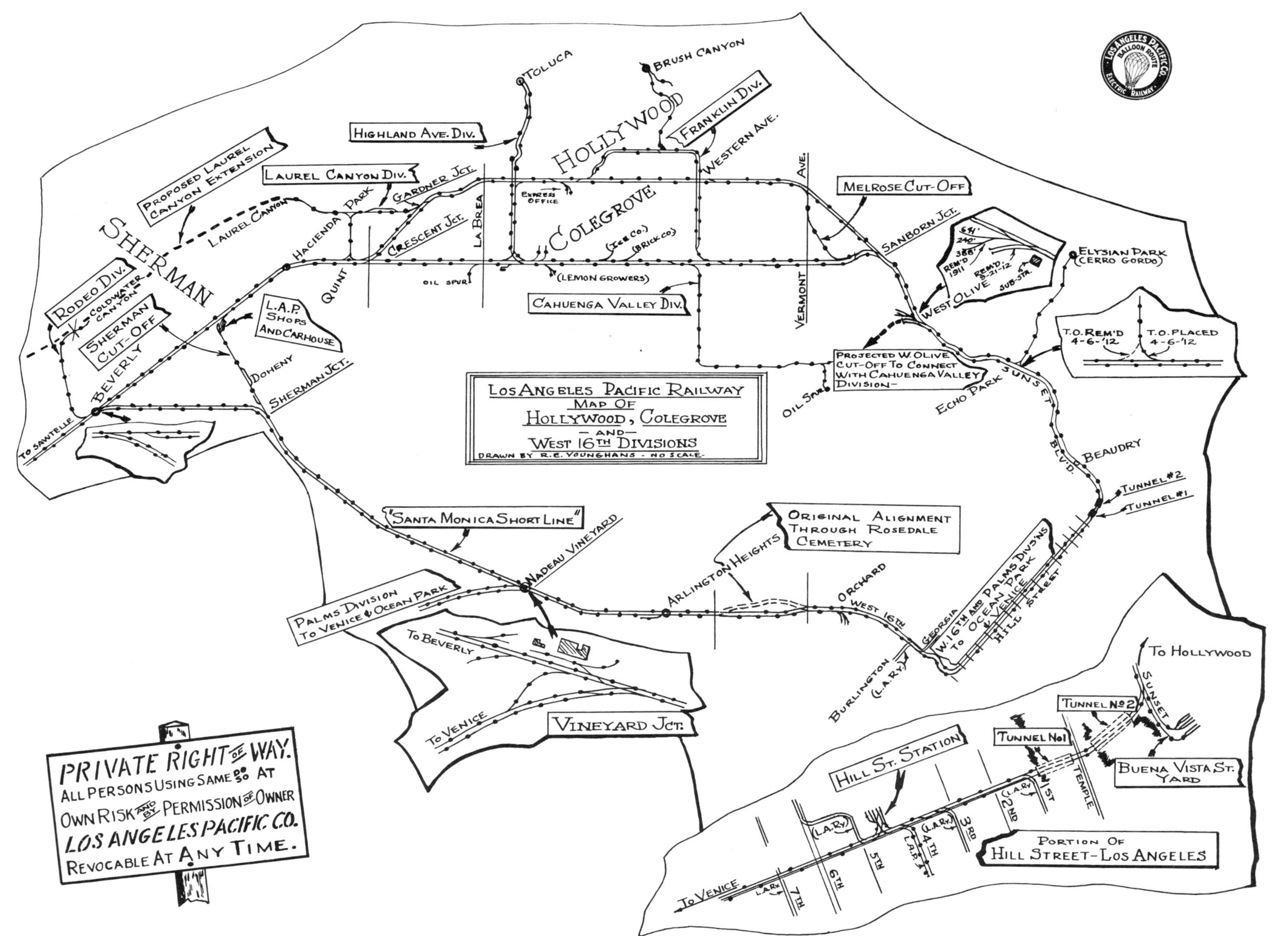

LOS ANGELES PACIFIC CO.
BALLOON ROUTE
ELECTRIC RAILWAY
TOLUCA
BRUSH CANYON
HOLLYWOOD
FRANKLIN DIV.
HIGHLAND AVE. DIV.
WESTERN AVE.
MELROSE CUT-OFF
PROPOSED LAUREL CANYON EXTENSION
LAUREL CANYON DIV.
EXPRESS OFFICE
COLEGROVE
SANBORN JCT.
SHERMAN
LAUREL CANYON
HACIENDA PARK
GARDNER JCT.
CRESCENT JCT.
LA BREA
(ICE CO.)
(BRICK CO.)
VERMONT AVE.
S.H. 240' 386' REM'D 1911
REM'D 3-31-12
SUB-STA.
ELYSIAN PARK (CERRO GORDO)
RODEO DIV.
COLDWATER CANYON
SHERMAN CUT-OFF
BEVERLY
QUINT
OIL SPUR
(LEMON GROWERS)
CAHUENGA VALLEY DIV.
WEST OLIVE
T.O. REM'D 4-6-'12
T.O. PLACED 4-6-'12
L.A.P. SHOPS AND CARHOUSE
DOHENY
SHERMAN JCT.
PROJECTED W. OLIVE CUT-OFF TO CONNECT WITH CAHUENGA VALLEY DIVISION—
OIL SPUR
ECHO PARK
SUNSET BLVD.
BEAUDRY
TUNNEL #2
TUNNEL #1
TO SAWTELLE
LOS ANGELES PACIFIC RAILWAY
MAP OF
HOLLYWOOD, COLEGROVE
—AND—
WEST 16TH DIVISIONS
DRAWN BY R.E. YOUNGHANS - NO SCALE-
"SANTA MONICA SHORT LINE"
NADEAU VINEYARD
ORIGINAL ALIGNMENT THROUGH ROSEDALE CEMETERY
ARLINGTON HEIGHTS
ORCHARD
WEST 16TH
GEORGIA
W. 16TH AND PALMS DIVN'S TO OCEAN PARK
TO VENICE
HILL STREET
PALMS DIVISION TO VENICE & OCEAN PARK
TO BEVERLY
TO VENICE
VINEYARD JCT.
BURLINGTON (L.A.Ry.)
TO HOLLYWOOD
SUNSET
TUNNEL Nº 2
TUNNEL Nº 1
BUENA VISTA ST. YARD
HILL ST. STATION
TEMPLE
1 ST
2 ND
3 RD
4 TH
5 TH
6 TH
7 TH
(L.A.Ry.)
L.A.Ry.
TO VENICE
PORTION OF HILL STREET—LOS ANGELES
PRIVATE RIGHT OF WAY.
ALL PERSONS USING SAME DO SO AT
OWN RISK AND BY PERMISSION OF OWNER
LOS ANGELES PACIFIC CO.
REVOCABLE AT ANY TIME.

LAP CAR 32 in local Pacific Electric service, Pt. Fermin, just after the 1911 Great Merger.   *(Interurbans)*

Santa Monicans were proud of the Nevada Ave. horse car operation even after the electric cars began running; in the Santa Monica *Outlook* on January 5, 1898, there appeared this item: "The Soldiers' Home horse car line has the reputation of being the fastest horse car line in Southern California."

On October 17, 1899, an ad in the *Outlook* carried the horse car line's schedule: three round trips were made daily, one in the morning, one in the early afternoon and one in the late afternoon; running time was 35 minutes down to Santa Monica, 45 minutes back to the Home. Rails were only 20 pounds to the yard and the line was narrow gauge.

The North Loop was built in 1899 and a part of the horse car line was used in it, 3rd St. from Nevada to Oregon Ave. This resulted in the abandonment of the horse car track on 3rd from Oregon to Utah and on Utah from 3rd to Ocean Ave. Thereafter, horse cars turned back at 3rd and Nevada. The old horsecar barn at 7th and Oregon was removed in November, 1899, and "taken to Sherman," as the *Outlook* put it. However, some sort of horse car operating center took its place for the Nevada Ave. horse car line continued for some years thereafter.

In March, 1902, the former horse car line on Utah and on 3rd was removed and a new single track electric line built. This then was incorporated in the North Loop.

Mention is made continuously in the *Outlook* in 1902, 1903 and after of the running of the Nevada Ave. horse car line. There can thus be no doubt that the PE official history errs in saying the line was abandoned in 1899. In its October 20, 1906, issue the *Electric Railway Journal* states: "Only a short time remains now until all that is left of the old horse car line to the Soldiers' Home will be but a memory. LAP has abandoned its franchise and the rails are being torn away to

make room for a magnificent boulevard. Since the construction of the trolley line to the Home by way of Brentwood and Westgate, the necessity for the Nevada Ave. route has passed."

COLEGROVE DIVISION

THE COLEGROVE DIVISION extended from Sanborn Jct. to Crescent Jct., 4.71 miles, all of which were double track and on Santa Monica Blvd. Spurs aggregated 0.5 mile, making its total equivalent single track mileage 9.92.

It was built as a double track narrow gauge electric line in 1896 from Sanborn Jct. to Hoover St., and as a narrow gauge single track electric line from Hoover St. to Crescent Jct. (Fairfax Ave.) the same year. In 1905 a second track was built from Hoover St. to Crescent Jct. Both tracks were standard gauged in 1908.

For portions of this route the line followed the old steam railroad built in 1888 by the *Los Angeles County Railroad Company* (Unit 37).

This line was opened on April 1, 1896, as a part of the through line to Santa Monica. It lost ground in 1897 when the so-called "Santa Monica Short Line" was built via Vineyard, and was permanently eclipsed in 1900 when the Hollywood Blvd. line was constructed.

LAP operated this line in 1911 as its "Colegrove-Sherman Line" and made it from 4th and Hill to Sherman in 39 minutes. Ten-minute base service was provided during the day at this same period with extra cars morning and evening as traffic demanded. Certain cars ran from 4th and Hill as far as Western Ave., then switched to the Franklin Ave. line to terminate at Vine and Hollywood Blvd.

PE operated this line as its West Hollywood Line and abandoned passenger service on same on June 1, 1953. Freight service was provided from West Hollywood (Sherman) to Seward St. until 1972.

FRANKLIN AVE.

THIS LINE RAN from Santa Monica Blvd. and Western on Western to Franklin Ave., west on Franklin to Argyle, south to Yucca, west to Vine and south to Hollywood Blvd.

This line was originally known as the Brush Canyon Line. It was built in early 1908 as a narrow gauge line; it was single track from Santa Monica Blvd. and Western to Franklin and Western, and double track from there to Hollywood and Vine. It was standard gauged a month after it was built. A second track (standard gauge) was built on Western from Santa Monica Blvd. to Franklin Ave. in early 1910. The entire line amounted to 2.18 miles of double track, all in streets.

As of March, 1911, through cars were run over this line to downtown Los Angeles from 6:05 AM to 5:35 PM at half-hourly intervals. A similar service was operated in opposite direction from 6:49 AM to 6:19 PM. This service was listed in timetables as integral with that of the Colegrove Line, of which it was considered to be a branch. After the hours noted, half-hourly service operated to and from Santa Monica Blvd. and Western Ave. until 11:06 PM.

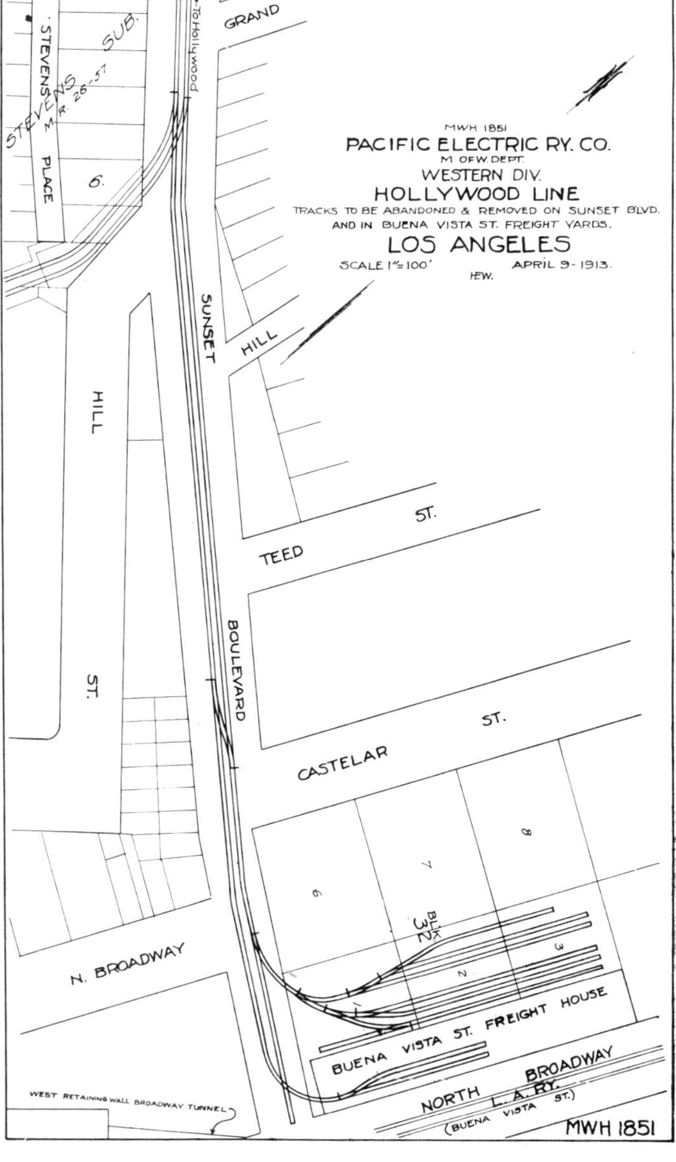

After the Merger, PE for the most part ran this line as a shuttle, with morning and evening through service.

This line was abandoned on March 17, 1940.

BRUSH CANYON

THE BRUSH CANYON LINE was constructed to reach a quarry in the hills at its northerly extreme. It ran from a junction with the Franklin Ave. Line at Franklin and Bronson, north on Bronson to private right of way and into the quarry. Its length was 1.56 miles, all single track, although 0.95 miles of spurs (in the quarry) raised its total to 2.51 miles.

The line was constructed in early 1908 as a narrow gauge line, but was standard gauged during May and June, 1908.

A single car was operated, connecting at half-hourly intervals with the through cars to L.A. and Hollywood on Franklin Ave.

PE abandoned this line on August 6, 1918.

BUENA VISTA LINE

THE BUENA VISTA LINE was a relic of LAP operation via Spring St. to its Fourth St. Station. This line extended from Sunset and a junction with the Hill St. line east to Sunset and Buena Vista (N. Broadway), 0.188 miles.

The line was placed in service on April 1, 1896, and formed a part of the old Main Line to Colegrove, Hollywood, Beverly and Santa Monica until the Hill St. tunnels were completed and that cutoff placed in service on September 15, 1909. After that date, the Buena Vista stub was used chiefly by freight trains and express motors to reach the Buena Vista Freight House. One passenger round trip daily was made to preserve the franchise.

This line was standard gauged in mid-1908. In 1911 the city decided to open and widen Sunset Blvd. to a hundred feet between Marion St. and the Plaza and LAP was assessed $7,500. The following year the Freight House ceased operations as the Merger and electrification of the airline made it possible for ex-LAP line freight to be handled at the PE Freight House.

Effective July 10, 1913, trackage of this line was abandoned; at that time there was only a morning and afternoon franchise car and one mail car delivering mail to the post office. The trackage remained in place until mid-1914, when the city began work on Sunset Blvd. and pulled the rails.

ELYSIAN PARK LINE

THE ELYSIAN PARK LINE was known in later years as the Echo Park Ave. line. It was built by the *Elysian Park St. Ry. Co.* (Unit 39) in 1889 from Temple St. to about 600 feet north of Sunset on Echo Park Ave. In the fall of 1890 that portion between Temple St. and Sunset was abandoned and the rails removed. In late 1890 the line was extended about a mile up Echo Park Ave. to Cerro Gordo St. All the above operation was by horse car. The *Elysian Park St. Ry. Co.* was purchased by the *Pasadena & Pacific Co.* (Unit 43) on November 15, 1895. P&P and its successor companies continued operation of this line by horse car until 1902; in September, October and November of that year the line was rebuilt into a single track, narrow gauge electric line and was opened for service on November 20, 1902. It was the intention of LAP's directors to extend this line to Glendale but such never happened. In 1909 the 1:26 miles of this line was standard gauged.

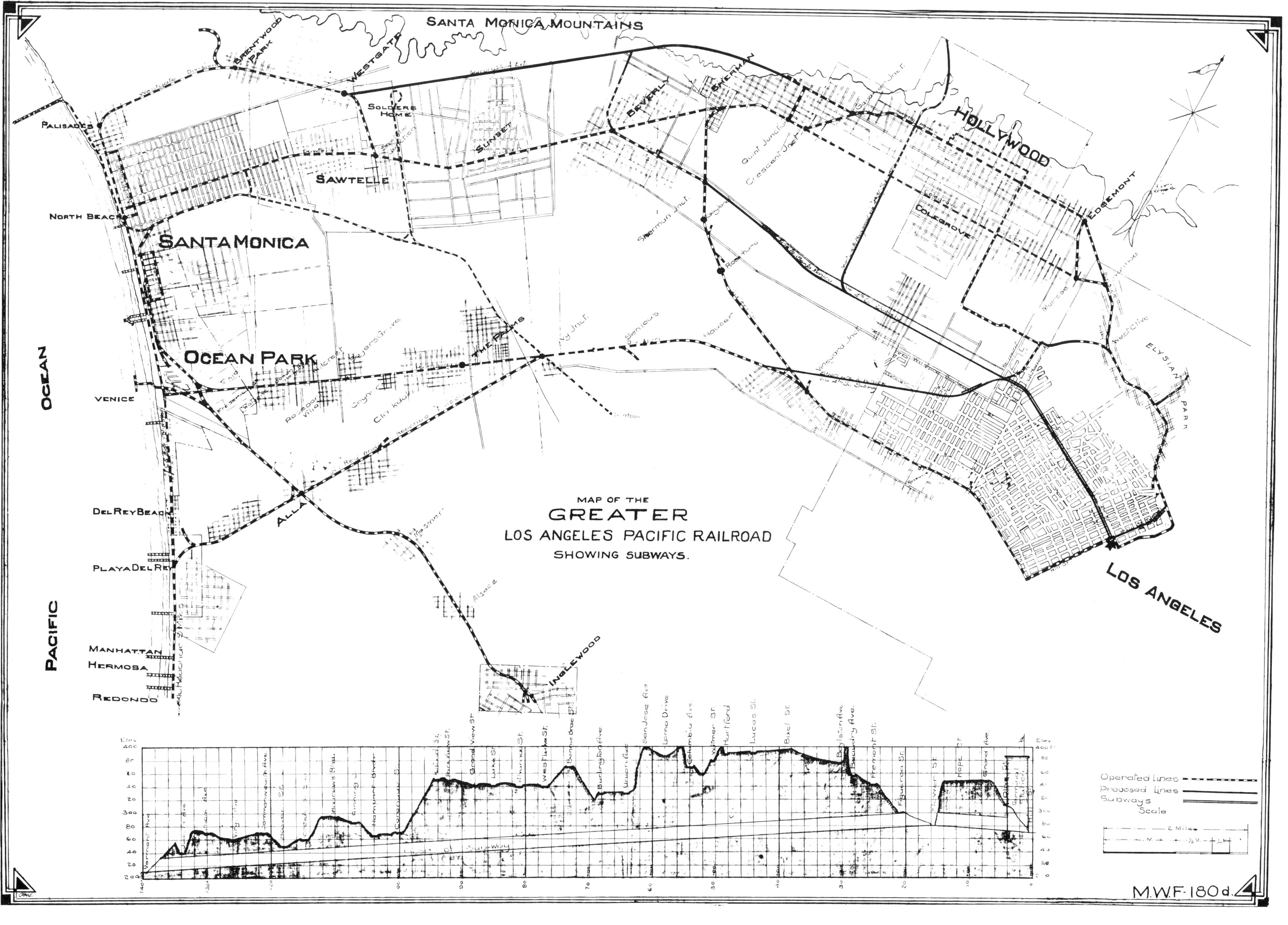

SANTA MONICA MOUNTAINS
BRENTWOOD PARK
WESTGATE
PALISADES
SOLDERS HOME
NORTH BEACH
SANTA MONICA
SAWTELLE
SUNSET
OCEAN PARK
THE PALMS
VENICE
OCEAN
PACIFIC
DEL REY BEACH
PLAYA DEL REY
MANHATTAN
HERMOSA
REDONDO
BEVERLY
SHERMAN
HOLLYWOOD
COLEGROVE
EDGEMONT
Quint Junc R
Crescent Junc
Sherman Junc
Vineyard Junc
ELYSIAN PARK
LOS ANGELES
INGLEWOOD
MAP OF THE
GREATER
LOS ANGELES PACIFIC RAILROAD
SHOWING SUBWAYS.
Operated Lines
Proposed Lines
Subways
Scale
Miles
M.W.F. 180 d.

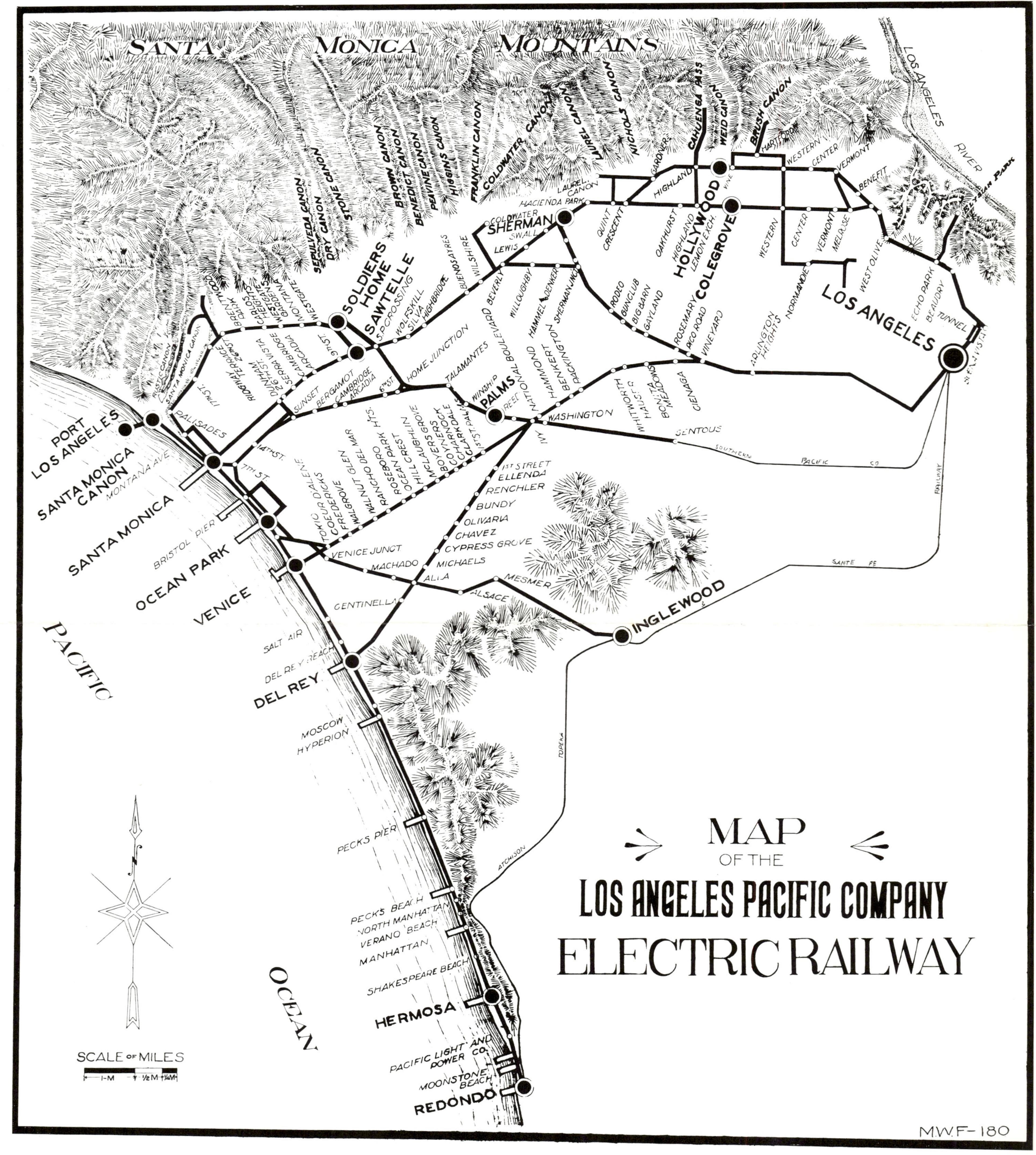

SANTA MONICA MOUNTAINS
LOS ANGELES RIVER
SANTA MONICA MOUNTAINS
SEPULVEDA CANON
DRY CANON
STONE CANON
BROWN CANON
BENEDICT CANON
BEANE CANON
HIGGINS CANON
FRANKLIN CANON
COLDWATER CANON
LAUREL CANON
NICHOLS CANON
CAHUENGA PASS
WEID CANON
BRUSH CANON
HARTSOOK
GARDNER
HIGHLAND
LAUREL CANON
HACIENDA PARK
WESTERN
CENTER
VERMONT
BENEFIT
QUINT
CRESCENT
OAKHURST
HIGHLAND
LEMON EXCH
VINE
HOLLYWOOD
COLEGROVE
WESTERN
CENTER
VERMONT
MELROSE
WEST OLIVE
ECHO PARK
BEAUDRY
TUNNEL
LOS ANGELES
BEL AIR VISTA
SHERMAN
SWALL
LEWIS
WILSHIRE
BEVERLY
BUENOSAYRES
WILLOUGHBY
HAMMEL
BENKERT
SHERMAN JUNC
RODEO
BUNCLUB
BIGBARN
GAYLAND
ROSEMARY
PICO ROAD
VINEYARD
ARLINGTON HEIGHTS
NORMANDIE
SOLDIERS HOME
SAWTELLE
SPCROSSING
WOLFSKILL
SILVA
HIGHBRIDGE
BROCK
CARLOS HEIGHTS
WESTERN
WESTGATE
MONTANA
RIDGWAY
26TH ST
DUNHAM
SERRA BRIDGE
ARCADIA
CAMBRIDGE
SUNSET
BERGAMOT
HOME JUNCTION
TALAMANTES
WINSHIP
PALMS
9TH ST
14TH ST
6TH ST
1ST PALMS
CLARKDALE
CHARNOCK
BOYERS
McLAUGHLIN
OCEAN PARK HTS
HILLCREST
RANCHO DEL MAR
WALNUT GLEN
ROSEBORO
WASHINGTON
IVY
NATIONAL BOULEVARD
HAMMOND
BACKINGTON
WHITWORTH
HAUSER
BONITA MEADOWS
CIENAGA
GENTOUS
SOUTHERN PACIFIC CO
RAILWAY
SANTE FE
1ST STREET
ELLENDA
RENCHLER
BUNDY
OLIVARIA
CHAVEZ
CYPRESS GROVE
MICHAELS
MACHADO
ALLA
MESMER
ALSACE
PORT LOS ANGELES
SANTA MONICA CANON
PALISADES
1ST ST
MONTANA AVE
7TH ST
SANTA MONICA CANON
I SWLL
SANTA MONICA
BRISTOL PIER
OCEAN PARK
VENICE
TOKIO DALENE
COEUR D'ALENE
FREDERICKS
WALGROVE
VENICE JUNCT
GENTINELLA
SALT AIR
DEL REY BEACH
DEL REY
MOSCOW
HYPERION
INGLEWOOD
TOPEKA
ATCHISON
PACIFIC
PECKS PIER
PECKS BEACH
NORTH MANHATTAN
VERANO BEACH
MANHATTAN
SHAKESPEARE BEACH
OCEAN
HERMOSA
PACIFIC LIGHT AND POWER CO.
MOONSTONE BEACH
REDONDO
SCALE OF MILES
1-M
1/2 M
1/4 M
MAP
OF THE
LOS ANGELES PACIFIC COMPANY
ELECTRIC RAILWAY
MWF-180

SUNSET BLVD., end of line at Laurel Canyon, 1909.

(Interurbans)

LAP did not operate through service on this line. All cars connected with Hollywood-Colegrove cars at Sunset Blvd. PE reversed the switch at Sunset Blvd. in 1912 and began sending the Echo Park Ave. cars downtown. This line was abandoned by PE on October 1, 1950.

MELROSE CUTOFF

THE MELROSE CUTOFF was built in the early part of 1900 as a part of the Hollywood line. Its function was to get Hollywood cars from the Colegrove line at Santa Monica Blvd. and Virgil to the Hollywood line proper at Hollywood Blvd. and Vermont Ave. It was a single track line, 0.84 miles long, which ran diagonally to a point on Vermont Ave. about 600 feet south of Hollywood Blvd., thence following Vermont due north and making a sweeping curve westward into Hollywood Blvd. This curve exists yet in the unusual highway junction at the intersection.

In 1905 the Hollywood Cutoff was constructed, entailing some very heavy construction. This opened Hollywood Blvd. through in a straight line to Sanborn Jct. and a double track line was built thereon. This relegated the Melrose Cutoff to standby operation; in rush hours a few cars were sent over it as far as Hollywood and Vermont, returning thence to L.A. In 1908 the Melrose Cutoff was standard gauged but remained single track. PE removed it in 1915.

HIGHLAND DIVISION

THE HIGHLAND AVE. LINE was built in 1908 from the Santa Monica Blvd. line on Highland Ave. in a northerly direction to the south city limits of Hollywood (Fountain Ave.). It was a single track standard gauge line. That same year a double track standard gauge extension was constructed from Fountain Ave. to the north city limits of Hollywood, approximately the entrance to Cahuenga Pass where today is the entrance to Hollywood Bowl. In 1909 the original portion was double tracked.

This line did not operate through to Los Angeles. It was served by one car (usually one of the 70 Class) which gave half-hourly service from 5:55 AM until 11:07 PM (as of 1911).

LAP was in the process of extending this line to Hanna in the San Fernando Valley when the Great Merger occurred. The line was completed by PE to Lankershim, Van Nuys, Owensmouth and San Fernando. All of this line was abandoned on December 28, 1952, except one block off Santa Monica Blvd. which was in use for freight only until the early 1960s.

LAUREL CANYON LINE

THE LAUREL CANYON LINE ran on Sunset Blvd. from Gardner Jct. on the Hollywood Line to Laurel Canyon Blvd., 0.96 miles, single track with one turnout midway. The line was built in 1894 as a single track, narrow gauge steam line by the *Cahuenga Valley Railroad Co.* (Unit 41) which built a pavilion at the terminus.

In 1905 the line was electrified by LAP (Unit 55) and through service to Los Angeles was started, the run being made in 40 minutes as of 1911. In 1908 this line was made standard gauge but was never double tracked.

LAP operated it as of 1907 as a through line to downtown L.A. via Hollywood Blvd.; 10-minute headway was provided morning and evening, alternate 10 and 20-minute service during midday. In 1911 LAP operated alternate 10 and 20-minute service through to the Canyon.

PE ultimately made this line a shuttle from Gardner Jct. using a Birney. It was abandoned on April 10, 1924. Trackage was removed in 1930.

ONE OF THE LAP's biggest projects was the big cut on Sunset Blvd. near Coronado St. Old line followed line of poles at left of center, while new line comes at camera from right of center.
(C.M. Pierce)

LAP LINESCAPES: North portal of the north Hill Street Tunnel, at Sunset Blvd. (top); Hollywood Blvd. in narrow-gauge days, looking east from about Bronson in 1905. Note center poles and pepper trees.

(Top: T.L. Wagenbach; bottom, Security Pacific Bank)

HOLLYWOOD BLVD. at Gower, shortly before 1901 double-tracking.

(Security Pacific Bank)

HOLLYWOOD DIVISION

THIS MAJOR LINE ran from 4th and Hill Sts. to Beverly, a distance of 12.23 miles, all double track. From 4th and Hill Sts. to La Brea Ave. (except for the short stretch in the Hill St. Tunnels) this line was in city streets; from La Brea to Santa Monica Blvd. it ran on private way with the exception of a short two-block stretch on Hawthorn Ave.; from Santa Monica Blvd. and Fairfax Ave. to Santa Monica Blvd. and Croft Ave. it was on city street, and from Croft Ave. to Beverly it was on private way.

The history of the various components of this line is too complex to repeat here. It will suffice to say that the Hollywood Line opened Feb. 21, 1900, when LAP built the loop line from its original line on Santa Monica Blvd.; this loop started at Melrose Cutoff, ran northwest to Hollywood Blvd., west to La Brea, southwest to Crescent Jct. where it rejoined the Santa Monica Blvd. line. As this line soon developed traffic far in excess of that originated by the old line on Santa Monica Blvd., it replaced that line as LAP's main line to Beverly.

This line was standard gauged in 1909 and its downtown route changed from Sunset and N. Broadway via Sunset, Main, Spring, and 4th to the 4th St. Station—to Sunset, Hill St. to the Hill St. Station.

In 1907 10-minute base service was provided from 6:20 AM to 8:00 PM, then 30-minute service until 12:30 AM; all this service operated through to Laurel Canyon. In addition, 30-minute service to the Santa Monica-Ocean Park-Venice beaches passed through Hollywood, the first beach car leaving 4th St. Station at 7:15 AM and the last leaving at 6:15 PM.

In 1911 very frequent service was provided along this route by these lines: (1) Hollywood-Venice Line, 30-minute head-way; (2) Hollywood-Gardner Jct., 30-minute headway; (3) Hollywood-Laurel Canyon, alternate 10 and 20-minute headway. Extra service was operated as required. Running time from Hill St. Station to Laurel Canyon was 40 minutes.

This line was abandoned on September 26, 1954, by *Metropolitan Coach Lines,* successor to PE.

QUINT CUTOFF

THE QUINT CUTOFF was built in 1900 on Crescent Heights Blvd. from Santa Monica Blvd. to Sunset Blvd. At Sunset Blvd. it connected with the old steam line which was serving a quarry a block or two west of Laurel Canyon Blvd. Thus steam trains were enabled to reach the quarry without having to traverse Hollywood Blvd. or the Laurel Canyon Line. Both at Sunset Blvd. and at Santa Monica Blvd. wyes were constructed to turn the steam locomotives; these wyes are perpetuated today in the street arrangements.

The Quint Cutoff was 0.553 miles long and was originally narrow gauge; it was standard gauged in 1908 (apparently) and was electrified (apparently) in 1905. The official history is vague on both these points. It is fairly certain, however, that the Quint Cutoff was built primarily for the gravel trains and not for passenger service; the only use of this trackage by passenger cars that oldtimers recall was to get to and from Sherman.

There is no mention of the abandonment of this line in PE records as such; however, it was usually considered to be a part of the Cahuenga Valley Line, and said line was abandoned in 1915.

CAHUENGA VALLEY

THE CAHUENGA VALLEY LINE was the old steam dummy line to Hollywood. It opened in 1887 from what is today Beverly and Belmont to Western and Santa Monica; in 1888 it was extended to Hollywood Blvd. and Wilcox, and in 1894 was built through to Sunset and Laurel Canyon. The line was about seven miles long, narrow gauge.

Sherman and Clark obtained control of this road in 1895 and subsequently incorporated a part of it in the Hollywood Line, another part in the Laurel Canyon Line, a part in the Western Ave. Line. The Oil Spur was built from this line in 1900. A connection was made to the Colegrove Line at Western and Santa Monica Blvd. in 1900 and thereafter this line's terminals were at that intersection and at the terminus of the Oil Spur, a distance of about two miles, via Western, private way just south of Beverly Blvd. to Alexandria, then out onto Beverly Blvd., to Virgil, then south on private way to approximately Fourth St., a total distance of about two miles.

Apparently only a single car was operated over this line, more to preserve the franchise than to convenience the public. The main use of this line was to get oil from the wells at Bimini to the LAP power houses and to other users.

Certain interesting points regarding this line deserve mention. On Western, the line ran close to the eastern curb of the street. On Beverly, from Heliotrope to New Hampshire, it had the center of the street while Los Angeles Railway's Heliotrope line hugged the southern curb (double track). Behind Bimini Baths, this line went underneath LARY's Heliotrope Line, the latter being carried over on a pile trestle built on an angle—one of the few bridges on LARY private way.

This line was always single track. It was electrified from Santa Monica and Western to Beverly and Alexandria (1.654 miles) in 1905, and was standard gauged in 1908. That portion from Beverly and Alexandria to the end of the Oil Spur apparently was never electrified.

PE abandoned this line in 1915.

OIL SPUR

THE OIL SPUR was built in 1900 from a connection with the Cahuenga Valley Line at a point near what is today Beverly and Virgil south on private right of way to approximately Fourth St. It was a single track narrow gauge line as built, and was always operated by steam. The line was 0.544 miles in length.

This spur gave LAP access to cheap oil which was used in its power houses in the early days, later sold to other users.

Inasmuch as the yield from this field was comparatively light, service over the Oil Spur was desultory.

The Oil Spur was standard gauged 1908 but apparently never was electrified.

PE abandoned it in 1915.

4th ST. SUBWAY

LAP'S FOURTH STREET SUBWAY would have been the greatest rapid transit system west of Chicago. It would have superimposed a network of cutoff lines on the heart of the LAP system, and almost every passenger would have benefited thereby.

The Subway proper would have run from the rear of the Hill Street Station west under Fourth St. to Vermont Ave.; only at Flower St. would there have been a station at grade.

At the Vermont portal, a system of cutoff lines would have permitted subway trains easy access to all major lines.

At its deepest point, the subway would have been 120 feet below San Jose Ave., near Union. It would have sloped in a westerly direction; at Hill St. Station it would have had an elevation of 265 feet; at Vermont Ave. this would have decreased to 210 feet.

The Fourth St. Subway and attendant cutoffs were the outcome of the purchase of control of LAP in March, 1906, by the Southern Pacific through its president, E.H. Harriman. The following summer witnessed the first public announcement of the great subway plan. In January, 1907, the Los Angeles City Council by a unanimous vote granted LAP the necessary permits for the 4th St. Subway. At that time some of the details of the plan were revealed.

The Harriman plan called for two parallel tunnels from Hill St. to Vermont Ave.; each would have contained two tracks, thus creating a four-track subway. At first only one subway would be built and this one would be started before March 1, 1907, and completed by January 1, 1909. By use of this subway, trains would reach the western city limits at Vineyard in but six minutes. Mayor Harper of L.A. exclaimed: "Subway building is comparatively a new undertaking in the west. Such a system of underground railways as that proposed by the LAP Company is unprecedented in a city the size of Los Angeles." The two Hill St. Tunnels were tied in with the Vineyard (4th St.) Subway as a package. LAP bought all the land between Hill St. Station and Vineyard under which its subway would have run; some of this land was held by PE until the 1950s and finally sold for residential use. Actually, the breaking up of this right-of-way began around 1920, when the site of the Ambassador Hotel was sold. Other segments were retained for some years afterward.

VENICE SHORT LINE CUTOFF: Most important cutoff line from the Vermont portal would have been the straight line to Vineyard, accommodating trains of the Venice, Redondo and Santa Monica via SP Division. This cutoff would have run in a ravine extending from Vermont Ave. southwest to a point about 200 feet northwest of 6th St., then would have entered a tunnel about 1,700 feet long, 17 feet high and 70 feet wide which would have taken it under Wilshire and the site of the Ambassador Hotel. It then would have run on the surface as a double track private right of way line to Vineyard. It would have been double track at first but sufficient land was purchased to enable four-tracking later. From Vineyard to Venice the Venice Short Line was to have been four-tracked in order to permit express service and local service.

FIFTH STREET CUTOFF: Extending due west from the Vermont portal would have been a double track line entirely on private way on the line of W. 5th St. extended (vacant land in those days). This cutoff would have connected at Sherman Jct. and would have given Santa Monica via Sawtelle trains a straight run to Beverly. It would have been 5.09 miles in length, double tracked.

From this cutoff would have branched two other cutoffs: (1) The Hollywood Cutoff, running north on Highland Ave. into Hollywood, and (2) the Western Ave. Cutoff, running north on Western to connect at Beverly Blvd. with the Cahuenga Valley-Franklin Ave.-Brush Canyon lines. Each of these cutoffs would have been 2.41 miles long.

Also, a cutoff would have left the Vermont portal in a northeasterly direction along what is now Silver Lake Blvd. to

A DUO OF DEPOTS: At top is the Hermosa Beach LAP depot, which was also a combination post office, telephone and water service business office. Bottom, Playa del Rey depot.   *(Both: T.L. Wagenbach)*

*A 90-CLASS CAR plies
the deserted streets of
Redondo, circa 1906.
(Interurbans)*

connect with the Hollywood Line at Sunset and Occidental. This, 1.77 miles long.

LAUREL CANYON EXTENSION: A scenic line from the Laurel Canyon Line west along the foothills through Beverly Hills to a connection with the Westgate Line was another 1907 project. It was this line which was to have connected with the Rindge railroad in Malibu, although to do it, it would have had to be built through Santa Monica Canyon and up the coast. It would have been 6.95 miles long to Montana Ave. and San Vicente Blvd.

REDONDO DIVISION

THE LINE DOWN THE COAST from Del Rey to Redondo constituted the most spectacular bit of LAP trackage. It was a high speed line as well, for the sand gave it good, quiet foundation. This line ran from Ivy Junction on the Palms Division to Diamond St., Redondo Beach, a distance of 14.40 miles, all double track and all on private right of way.

That part of the line from Ivy to del Rey was built in 1902 as a double track, narrow gauge electric railway. The part from Manhattan to Redondo was built early in 1903, and the three-mile gap was built later in 1903, the delay being caused by the heavy construction (grading) entailed in getting past the bluffs near El Segundo. This line was standard gauged in 1908.

In 1907 LAP offered half-hourly service leaving 4th St. Station, L.A., at 6:30 AM through to 7:30 PM, then hourly to 11:30 PM. Returning, cars left Diamond St. at 5:45 AM and every 30 minutes till 8:15, then at hourly intervals until 11:15 PM.

In 1911 the service was half hourly from 6:30 AM to 6:30 PM, then hourly to 11:30 PM from Hill St. Station; from Redondo, cars left at 6:15 AM and every 30 minutes to 6:15 PM, then 7:15, 8:30 and hourly until 11:30 PM. Unusual note: the 7:00 AM car from Los Angeles connected at Ivy with the car to the Long Wharf and Port Los Angeles, giving fishermen their choice of two favorite angling locations. Outbound cars made the trip in 63 minutes, inbound 66 minutes.

It is possible that LAP in 1911 operated through to Hotel Redondo using tracks of the L.A. & Redondo Ry. LAP Distance Table No. 2 indicates that this line operated 0.32 miles beyond Diamond St., its original terminus.

The Redondo Line had two substations: one at Del Rey and one at Hermosa Beach. Both were built in 1903 and were of LAP's usual Mission style.

PE abandoned this line on May 12, 1940.

MOTORDROME SPUR

THE MOTORDROME SPUR was built in 1910 to serve an auto racetrack constructed adjacent to the Redondo Line 1.12 miles from Playa del Rey. The spur was 0.736 miles in length and was single track. It was a joint project with the racetrack promoter, a man from the east who assured LAP such an undertaking would be prosperous for all concerned.

The track was built and races were held featuring such famous drivers as Barney Oldfield and Teddy Tetzlaff. H.O. Marler recalls being sent out there on race days to help fill holes in the dirt track.

LAP operated special service to this racetrack from Los Angeles and Santa Monica and evidently the track did attract crowds for a time. When the novelty wore off, it was a different matter.

PE removed the line a piece at a time; records state that the Motordrome Spur was removed in 1916, 1918, 1932 and 1934.

PIER AVE. LINE

THE PIER AVE. LINE was in Hermosa Beach and extended back up the widely curving avenue leading back to the Santa Fe tracks. Records show it to have been 0.461 miles in length, single track, and all on private way. The latter is confusing, for everyone the editor has interviewed states this line was in the center of Pier Ave. and ran on said thoroughfare to the Santa Fe tracks.

The Pier Ave. Line was built in 1910 but apparently it was

a real estate promoter's undertaking for no record exists in any LAP or PE history of LAP's building the line. History does record the fact that Hermosa residents wanted a cross-country connection with the Los Angeles & Redondo's line which ran back from the beach and parallel thereto at a distance of roughly four miles. In fact, a company was incorporated to build such a line in October, 1910; this company, *The Los Angeles-Western Railway Company,* was formed to build an electric railway to Culler, on the LA&R, from Hermosa. None of the incorporators were previously known in the electric railway field. Apparently this company did build this line as far as the Santa Fe tracks and then turned it over to LAP. However, there is no record of LAP operating regular service over it.

PE removed the trackage in 1928, but it seems improbable that service existed on this line to anywhere near that date.

INGLEWOOD LINE

THE INGLEWOOD DIVISION officially began at 5th St., Santa Monica, and ended at the Santa Fe Depot in Inglewood, a distance of 9.056 miles. The line was single track and always was standard gauge.

This line was originally the Santa Fe's line to Santa Monica from Los Angeles. It was built in 1887, opening in June of that year from Inglewood to Port Ballona. Five years later it was changed in route: Port Ballona was given up, South Santa Monica was added. Service to South Santa Monica, later Ocean Park, was inaugurated on June 18, 1892, with seven trains daily.

After LAP took away all passenger business, Santa Fe received permission to abandon this line, such permission being received on April 10, 1901. However, LAP acted quickly to purchase the line and got it on March 21, 1902.

After buying the line from the Santa Fe's subsidiary, the *Southern California Railway,* on March 21, 1902, the LAP commenced standard-gauge steam operation over the line. The March 25 *Outlook* reported, "In taking over the Santa Fe branch from Inglewood to this place, the Electric Railroad Company has procured a locomotive and combination passenger and freight car to be used on the road until it can be electrocized. The bob-tailed train will connect with Santa Fe trains at Inglewood."

On July 10, the *Outlook* reported that poles had been set for the electrification and wire was being strung. On October 1, the *Outlook* blared a headline, "FREIGHT BY ELECTRICITY," over a story reporting that the Ocean Park Lumber Co. was now receiving all its lumber by electric motor. (Presumably, carload shipments were received from the Santa Fe at Inglewood.) Finally, on October 18, reporting a development of that day or perhaps a few days earlier, the *Outlook* said,

LAGOON LINE CAR leaves the Playa del Rey Pavilion about 1907, showing grandstand where spectators watched boat races.

"The old Santa Fe railroad . . . to Inglewood . . . has been electrocized all the way. . . ."

One car a day met all traffic demands in 1902; it left the old Santa Fe Depot near Front (Pico) St. at 11:00 AM and returned immediately, leaving Inglewood at 12:15 PM. Note that this was LAP's only standard gauge operation for the next five years.

In 1907, the timetable listed but one car daily; it left Front St. at 8:00 AM and left Inglewood at 9:00 AM.

In 1911 the one daily run remained; it was listed as a mixed passenger and freight and left 2nd and Hill, Ocean Park, at 3:00 PM and left Inglewood at 4:30 PM.

PE abandoned passenger service in 1928 but retained the line in its entirety for freight service.

LAGOON DIVISION

THE LAGOON DIVISION got its name from the long lagoon whose shore it followed from Venice to Playa del Rey. This line was a minor line during the week, but when vacationing crowds descended upon beaches, it carried as many people as the cars were able to hold.

At its greatest extent, the Lagoon Line extended from 7th and Montana, Santa Monica, to Playa del Rey, a distance of 6.10 miles. This was after the North Loop had been abandoned (1910) and the extension on Montana from 3rd to 7th added that same year.

In February, 1901, LAP began work on an extension from Ocean Park to Venice via a private way about 300 feet from the ocean. This apparently was the first use of the Trolleyway; LAP built the line from 2nd and Azure Sts. to the Club House, about four blocks from what later became Windward Ave. This extension was opened on Sunday, April 29, 1901, with cars every half hour. Alternate L.A. cars were routed over this line throughout the summer; on September 14, this line got all the through cars and the South Loop thereafter had local service only. In July and August, 1902, LAP double tracked this line.

In October, 1902, the line was straightened: from Ocean and Front (Pico) over private right of way to a point on Trolleyway between Strand and Hollister where above line entered Trolleyway; when this was completed, old connection from 2nd and Azure to Hollister and Trolleyway was removed. At about this same time Ocean Ave. was double tracked from Colorado Ave. to Front except across the two bridges—and down at Short Line Beach (Venice) some double track was constructed toward Playa del Rey. However, right of way trouble prevented this extension from being linked with the Club House terminus until August, 1903, when the gap (1400 feet long) was closed.

The acquisition of the *Traction* track along the Trolleyway in 1904 enabled LAP to eliminate competition forever from the Trolleyway by spreading its tracks to the extreme width of the Trolleyway.

On Aug. 26, 1904, the final extension was made, down the coast to connect with the Redondo Line at "A" St. Jct. in Playa del Rey. This enabled LAP to offer passengers an oceanside trolley journey from Port Los Angeles to Diamond St. in Redondo, approximately 16½ miles.

In 1907 Lagoon cars made the North Loop in Santa Monica, connecting with L.A. via Sawtelle cars at 3rd and Oregon. The first car left North Beach Bath House (Oregon and Ocean) at 6:15 AM, then every half hour until 11:54 PM. Returning, the car left Playa del Rey at 6:12 AM, then every 20 minutes until 11:42 PM. Connections were made at Playa del Rey with trains to and from L.A. and Redondo.

In 1911 the northern terminus was 7th and Montana; cars left at 6:10 AM and every 30 minutes until 9:38 PM; then 10:40 and 11:40 PM; then 12:40 AM to Ocean Park barn. Returning, cars left Playa del Rey at 6:14 AM and every 30 minutes until 10:14 PM; then 11:14 PM and 12:14 AM. As in 1907, connections were made at del Rey with trains to and from L.A. and Redondo, but only until 8:14 PM; thereafter, these connections were "irregular."

Also in 1911 through service to L.A. was offered over almost the entire route of the Lagoon Line by two different lines; the Venice Short Line ran on this line between Center St., Venice, and North Beach, while hourly service ran from Playa del Rey to L.A. via Venice and Palms daily except Sunday—leaving Playa del Rey at 6:30 AM through to 5:30 PM and leaving the Hill St. Station at 7:30 AM through until 6:30 PM.

PE continued to operate this line until July 13, 1936, when it was abandoned.

WESTGATE DIVISION

THE WESTGATE LINE was built in the form of a great loop, reaching from the Main Line at Sawtelle north and west into the flat and beautiful countryside abutting on Santa Monica Canyon and the Pacific Ocean and coming back into the

(Interurbans)

SANTA MONICA CANYON looking south about 1907. Port of Los Angeles line at right. (Title Insurance)

Main Line at Oregon and Ocean in Santa Monica after traversing the Ocean Ave. tracks of the North Loop from Montana Ave. This line was built to serve subdivisions in which Sherman and Clark had heavy investments; it helped sell lots admirably.

The Westgate Line was built in 1906 as a double track, narrow gauge electric line; it was standard gauged in 1908. It was 5.81 miles in length, all on private right of way.

In 1907 LAP operated through service over this line from downtown L.A. to Ocean Park; hourly service was given, leaving L.A. from 7:25 AM to 7:25 PM and leaving Ocean Park from 5:55 AM to 7:50 PM; thereafter, a car ran hourly to and from Sawtelle and North Beach Station until 11:50 PM.

In 1911 the through service left L.A. at 7:25 AM and hourly to 6:25 PM arriving at North Beach Station 56 minutes later; cars left North Beach for L.A. at 6:25 AM and hourly to 5:25 PM with identical running time. Interspersed were cars from North Beach to Sawtelle; these left North Beach at 5:55 AM hourly until 3:55 PM, then 7:30 PM and every half hour until 11:00 PM with the last car at midnight; these connected at 6th St., Sawtelle, for cars to and from L.A. Cars left Sawtelle for North Beach at 5:32 AM and hourly until 3:32 PM, then 6:45 PM, then 7:56 PM and every half hour until 10:26 PM, then 11:26 and 12:26 AM.

PE continued the through service at rush hours, with a shuttle the rest of the day. This line was abandoned June 30, 1940.

SOUTHERN PACIFIC DIVISION

THE SOUTHERN PACIFIC DIVISION was better known by its modern name, "Santa Monica Air Line," so called because once free of Los Angeles, it made almost a straight line to the beach city. In the heyday of the Long Wharf and Port Los Angeles, the Air Line was a passenger and freight hauler of prime importance. Passenger trains hauled by engines of SP's 1200 Class regularly made the run to the Arcadia Hotel from Arcade Depot in about 25 minutes. Why not? There was nothing but farmland between the settled areas.

LAP leased the Air Line from SP from Port Los Angeles to Sentous, 10.880 miles, on July 1, 1908; LAP was itself by that time controlled by SP, so the Air Line remained within the family. This lease also included the Soldiers' Home Branch, 2.610 miles long. LAP proceeded to electrify the Air Line and the Soldiers' Home Branch in the summer of 1908 and placed same in service as electric lines.

The remainder of the Air Line, from Sentous to Clement Jct. (7.866 miles) was not leased by LAP but by its successor, Pacific Electric; the effective date of this lease was January 28, 1912. However, LAP acting without a lease had electrified this portion between December 1, 1910 and July 31, 1911; about the time this portion was ready for operation by electricity, all LAP property was acquired by consolidation by the new Pacific Electric Railway Company.

The early history of the Air Line is exceptionally interesting. The line was built by the *Los Angeles & Independence Railroad Company* in 1875. Its leading director was the fabulous Sen. John P. Jones of Nevada who desired a railroad from his mines near Independence, California, to tidewater. He built a 1700-foot wharf at the foot of Railroad (Colorado) Ave. in Santa Monica and a townsite was surveyed adjacent to the terminus. Santa Monica was thus born, and the first LA&I train ran on October 17, 1875. Jones' mines proved less valuable than he thought, and with fierce competition from SP's line to tidewater at San Pedro, Jones found his railroad losing money. So, in 1877 he sold out to SP. SP relegated the road to the status of a passenger line, quit the wharf and eventually

SOUTHERN PACIFIC Tunnel, Santa Monica, on line to Long Wharf. (T.L. Wagenbach)

LOOKING ALONG the Westgate line right-of-way in the center of San Vicente Blvd., at 23rd St., Santa Monica. Ornate iron scroll-work on the center poles gave this line a bit of extra distinction. (T.L. Wagenbach)

tore it down. But in 1891 SP returned with a vengeance and built the Long Wharf just north of Santa Monica Canyon. For about 10 years Santa Monica again saw ships anchored offshore, but San Pedro eventually won out in the great harbor fight. By 1908 the Long Wharf and the Air Line were of so little importance that SP was happy to turn them over to LAP.

LAP made little effort to develop the Air Line as an important line for passengers. In 1911, only one trip daily ran through to Santa Monica from Los Angeles; this operated via W. 16th St., Vineyard, Ivy to Ocean and Montana Ave., Santa Monica, leaving L.A. at 5:25 PM and returning at 8:05 AM. Between Santa Monica and Ivy there were two regular trips daily; the car left S.M. at 6:55 AM and 6:00 PM and left Ivy at 7:20 AM and 6:20 PM. However, good service was given all day between Santa Monica (Colorado) and Port Los Angeles, the car running every 30 minutes. Extra service was provided on Sundays and holidays as required.

Balloon Route cars operated over portions of this line; into the Soldiers' Home via the Soldiers' Home Branch from Sawtelle, and up the coast to the Long Wharf from Santa Monica.

Connections with other LAP lines were as follows: (1) Ivy, where originally the Palms Division went underneath the Air Line in a plank-lined tunnel; (2) Sawtelle, where the Soldiers' Home Branch connected with the Main Line at Santa Monica Blvd. and Sepulveda; (3) 26th St., Santa Monica, where a brick yard spur was extended to Santa Monica Blvd.; (4) Railroad and Ocean, Santa Monica, where a ramp got cars up out of the SP arroyo; and (5) 2nd and Fremont (Pico) where the SP tracks joined those of the old Santa Fe Inglewood Branch and later those of the South Loop.

The Air Line and the Soldiers' Home line were always standard gauge, and were single track. Trains were turned on a loop at the Home and on a wye at Santa Monica.

High hopes were entertained for the future of the Air Line as a passenger carrier after LAP electrified it, for in October, 1909, the *Electric Railway Journal* stated: "The Los Angeles Pacific, through the Southern Pacific, will purchase 84 all-steel passenger motor cars for use on the Santa Monica branch of the SP which is electrically operated." Of course, the cars went to SP's Oakland-Alameda-Berkeley electrification.

After the 1911 Merger, PE continued to operate the Air Line; through it, the LAP lines were tied to the PE freight house and the Buena Vista Freight House was abandoned. Through the years PE operated the once-daily franchise car for passengers; this was finally abandoned in 1953, after which the Air Line was converted to diesel operation, freight only.

RODEO LINE

THE RODEO LINE ran from Santa Monica Blvd. and Rodeo Drive on Rodeo north to Sunset and east on Sunset to Beverly Drive; 1.38 miles, all single track. It was built in 1907 as a narrow gauge line and was standard gauged in 1908.

The Rodeo Line is not listed in timetables of 1911, hence we are unable to state definitely the type of service it rendered. Probably its single car met the through cars at Beverly and ran as often as the traffic demanded.

This line was considered to be a rather high class line as its primary function was to serve the Beverly Hills Hotel. LAP kept a clean, attractive car on the run, while PE early assigned a 170 Class steel center entrance car to this run, later a one-man single trucker. The line was abandoned January 15, 1923.

SOLDIERS' HOME LINE

THIS BRANCH of the *L.A. & Independence Railroad* (later SP) was built in 1875 as a single track, standard gauge steam line. It was leased to LAP in 1908 and electrified that year. It was 2.61 miles long from its junction with the SP Santa Monica Line.

LAP operated passenger service over this line from its Sawtelle Station at Santa Monica Blvd. and Sawtelle Blvd. via Santa Monica Blvd., Sepulveda Blvd. to the loop inside the Home.

As of 1911, LAP operated half-hourly service from 6:55 AM to 6:55 PM from Sawtelle; 7:15 AM to 7:15 PM from Sol-

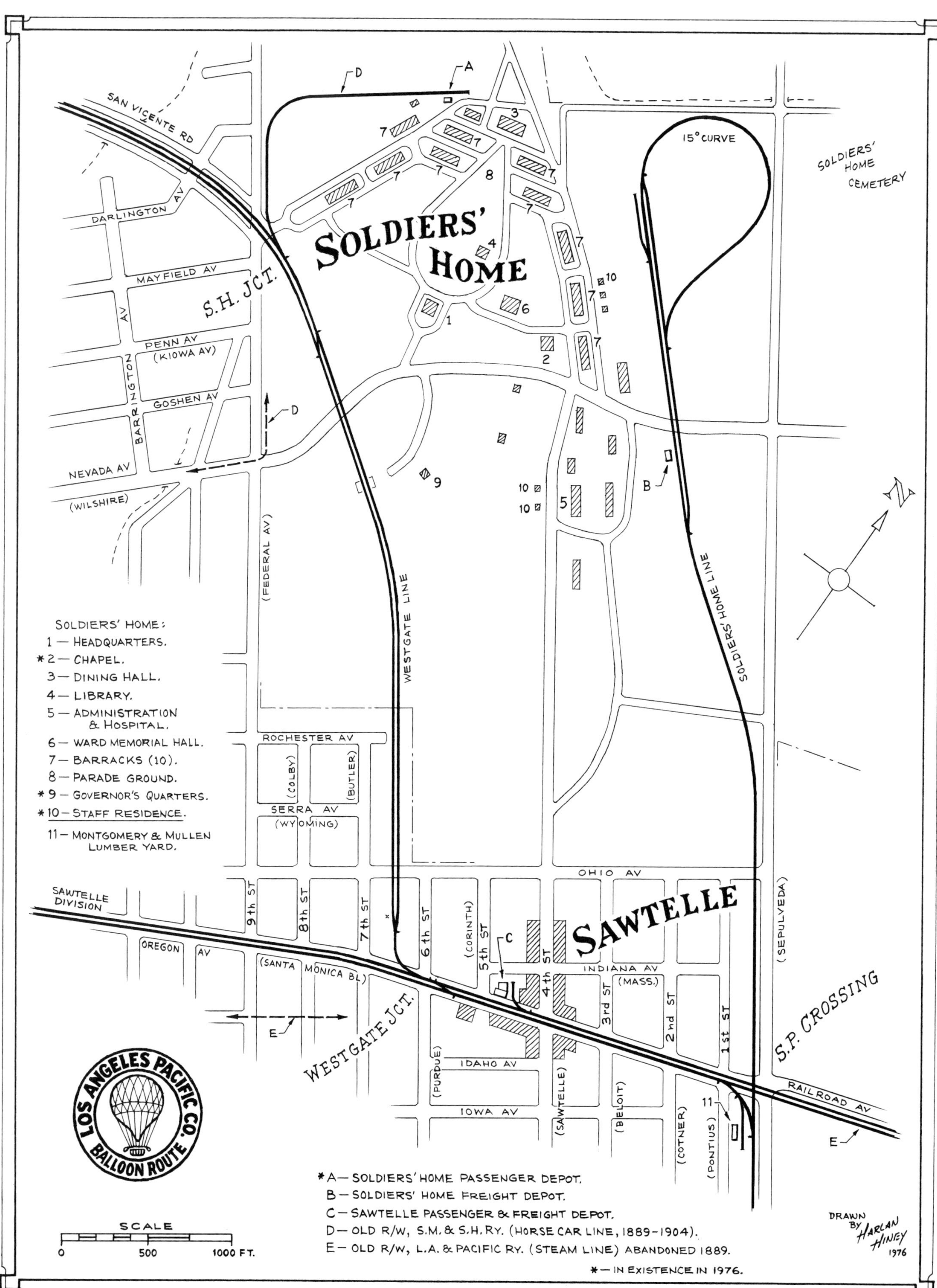

SOLDIERS' HOME
SAWTELLE
San Vicente Rd
Darlington Av
Mayfield Av
S.H. Jct.
Penn Av (Kiowa Av)
Goshen Av
Nevada Av
(Wilshire)
Barrington Av
Zook Av
15° Curve
Soldiers' Home Cemetery
Westgate Line
(Federal Av)
Soldiers' Home Line
Rochester Av
(Colby)
(Butler)
Serra Av
(Wyoming)
A
B
Ohio Av
Sawtelle Division
Oregon Av
(Santa Monica Bl)
Westgate Jct.
9th St
8th St
7th St
6th St
5th St
4th St
3rd St
2nd St
1st St
(Corinth)
Indiana Av
(Mass.)
(Sepulveda)
S.P. Crossing
(Purdue)
Idaho Av
(Sawtelle)
(Beloit)
(Cotner)
(Pontius)
Iowa Av
Railroad Av
C
E
11
Soldiers' Home:
1 — Headquarters.
*2 — Chapel.
3 — Dining Hall.
4 — Library.
5 — Administration & Hospital.
6 — Ward Memorial Hall.
7 — Barracks (10).
8 — Parade Ground.
*9 — Governor's Quarters.
*10 — Staff Residence.
11 — Montgomery & Mullen Lumber Yard.
*A — Soldiers' Home Passenger Depot.
B — Soldiers' Home Freight Depot.
C — Sawtelle Passenger & Freight Depot.
D — Old R/W, S.M. & S.H. Ry. (Horse Car Line, 1889-1904).
E — Old R/W, L.A. & Pacific Ry. (Steam Line) Abandoned 1889.
* — In Existence in 1976.
Los Angeles Pacific Co. Balloon Route
Scale
0   500   1000 FT.
Drawn by Harlan Hiney 1976

A BRACE OF 700-series MU cars ready to leave from Sherman. White-capped attendants in open section of 748 are Balloon Route barkers.
(Interurbans)

diers' Home. At later hours, Soldiers' Home passengers used Westgate cars.

PE abandoned passenger service on this line after July, 1920.

SAWTELLE DIVISION

THIS LINE WAS the Main Line from Beverly to North Beach Station (Ocean and Oregon). It was originally a narrow gauge steam line but was rebuilt and electrified in 1896, opening for service from L.A. to Santa Monica on the first of April, 1896. A second track was built in 1898. Both were standard gauged in 1907. The length of this line was 6.95 miles.

As this particular stretch of trackage was used by the Main Line and the service to L.A. via Hollywood and Colegrove, it had very frequent service.

As built, this part of the Main Line was almost entirely on private right of way until Santa Monica was reached. It then proceeded along Oregon Ave. to Ocean Ave. The cars rapidly brought settlers and little by little the private way gave way to street running. At the end, only that portion from Beverly to Sepulveda was on private way. PE abandoned this line on August 24, 1941.

A major spur led from this line at 26th St., Santa Monica, to the Air Line. The spur was built in 1903 to serve the brickyard then being built at this location. The kiln could thus send out its products by standard gauge steam line to distant points, and by narrow gauge electric line to nearby towns.

The Cars that

Chapter Four

Carried the Crowds

LOS ANGELES Pacific's cars reflect the development of the company from that of a frail and primitive country trolley line into a high-speed, heavy-duty electric railroad. The transformation may be said to have taken place in three stages: the original, light equipment dating from 1896 until 1901; the middle period when heavier single-unit cars replaced the original equipment on main lines, 1901-1908; and finally the multiple unit, standard gauge trains which took over in March, 1908.

In this chapter we will examine each class of car in detail. With each car class is the official LAP plan and data sheet.

SINGLE TRUCK PASSENGER CARS
40-42

The photo in this chapter of the flower-carrying matron boarding early LAP single-truck car 42 shows one of the three single truck closed passenger motors LAP operated in its earliest years. From the little information uncovered, it appears the cars were built by Pullman in 1896 and were used in Santa Monica local service on the South Loop and on the Third St. line. They were retired by 1900 and then entered Cholo service—transporting track gangs. One was wrecked near Sherman and rebuilt into shop switcher 11; another became a line car, probably tower car 4; a third was sold to a cement concern at Acton, California, and ran there for years.

These cars resembled the 40-class trailers and the 70-class motors, all built by Pullman.

DOUBLE TRUCK PASSENGER CARS
30-39

By 1902 LAP's system had increased to a size which demanded differentiation in the matter of rolling stock. Hence 10 streetcars were purchased from American Car Co. in that year for use on the lighter lines such as Echo Park Ave.

These streetcars, numbered 30-39, were true California cars —LAP's first—and were quite symmetrical and attractive. Of interest are the omission of the curved corner vestibule windows and steam hood roof; streetcars of the Los Angeles area used deck roofs to distinguish them from interurbans—but not the 30s!

The following four pages are devoted to reproductions of official LAP rosters
of rolling stock as of April, 1911–immediately prior to the Great Merger.

CAR No. (Old Series)	OWNED BY	CONTROL	MOTORS	GEAR RATIO	STYLE TRUCK	AXLE	TYPE OF BRAKE	SEATING CAPACITY	LENGTH	WEIGHT	NOTES
OBSERVATION CARS.											
900-901	L.A.P	G.E Type M	4.GE #73	21:54	CLASS A.4 6'5	5×9	W.A.5½ & Hand	56	49'2"	74800	
902	L.A.P	K6	4-38^{A}W	26:60	CLASS A.3 5'10"	4'×8"	W.S.2 & hand	56	46'0"	54200	
903	L.A.P	G.E Type M	4.GE #73	21:54	CLASS A.4 6'5"	5'×9'	W.A.5½ & Hand	46	49'2"	74800	Private car "El Viento"
904	L.A.P	K 6	4.38B.N.G	24:58	MAGUIRE 5'6"	3½×9	W.S.2	34	40'6'	38910	" " "Mermaid"
PASSENGER CARS.											
32-33	L.A.P	K 11	2.38 B N.G	22:60	MAGUIRE 5'2"	4×8	C.S.2 & Hand	36	35'0"	30800	
35	L.A.P	K2	2.38 B N G	22:60	MAGUIRE 5'2"	4×8	C.S.2 & Hand	36	35'0"	30800	
42	L.A.P	———	———	———	MAGUIRE 5'6"	4×8	Hand & N.Y. air	44	35'0"	18850	Trailers
45 To 47	L.A.P	———	———	———	MAGUIRE 4'6'	3½×6½	Hand & N.Y air	44	35'0	18850	"
48 To 54	L.A.P	———	———	———	MAGUIRE 5'4	3½×6⅝	Hand & N.Y air	40	33'1	21300	" car 49 have W.A. Brake
55	L.A.P				PECKAM 5'3"	3½×8½	Hand & N.Y.air	40	33'1	18850	"
60 & 62	L.A.P	K 11	2-38A Basterd	22:64	MAGUIRE 5'2"	collarless 4×8	C.S.2 & hand	40	36'0	33100	
65 & 66	L.A.P	K 11	2.38A Basterd	22:64	MAGUIRE 5'2"	collarless 4×8	C.S.2 & hand	40	36'0	33100	
63 & 67	L.A.P	K.11	2-38A Basterd	26:60	MAGUIRE 5'2"	collarless 4×8	C.S.2 & hand	40	36'0	33100	
64, 68, 69	L.A.P	K.11	2.38B.N.G	22:60	MAGUIRE 5'2"	Collarless 4×8	C.S.2 & hand	40	36'0	33100	
70	L.A.P	K.11	2.38B.N.G	22:60	MAGUIRE 5'4"	3½×6⅝	C.S.2 & hand	48	39'2"		
71	L.A.P	K.11	———	———	Pullman 5'3"	3½×9	———	48	39'2'		No Motors
72	L.A.P	K.11	———	———	Pullman 5'3	3½×9		48	40'2"		No Motors
73	L.A.P	K.11	———	———	———	———		46	39'2'		Trucks removed
76	L.A.P	K.11	———	———	———	———		48	39'2"		" " Partly Wrecked
156	L.A.P	K.11^H	4.W. #69	14:68	MAGUIRE TYPE 5'6"	4×8	W.A.4 & hand	44	38'0	39100	has 4 H.P. Chris. National Compr.
157 To 159	L.A.P	K.11^H	2.W. #89	22:64	MAGUIRE TYPE 5'6'	4×8	C.S.2 & hand	44	38'0	39100	
180 To 182	L.A.P	K.11^H aux.contact	2 W #89	22:64	MAGUIRE TYPE 5'6'	4×8	C.S.2 & hand	48	39'6'	39800	
184 To 189	L.A.P	K.11^H aux.contact	2 W.#89	22:64	MAGUIRE TYPE 5'6'	4×8	C.S.2 & hand	48	39'6"	39800	
191 To 194	L.A.P	K.28F aux.Contact	4.38A	26:60	class A.3 5'10"	4×8	W.S.2 & hand	48	39'6"	45000	
195 To 199	L.A.P	K.28F aux.contact	4-#89	26:60	class A3 5'10"	4×8	W.S.2 & hand	48	39'6"	50700	
190	L.A.P	K.28F aux.Contact	2.W.89	22:64	MAGUIRE 5'6'	4×8	W.S.2 & hand	48	39'6"	45000	
200 To 249	L.A.P	K.11 28.BF 28F	2.W.89	22:64 18:68 26:60	MAGUIRE 5'6'	4×8	W.S.2. W.A.2 & hand	48	41'2'	40400 43200	See Note #
400	L.A.P	K-11	2.38B BASTERD	22:60	MAGUIRE 5'2"	5×9	C.S.2 & hand		39'9'	-	10 seats on platforms other seats removed.
700 To 746	L.A.P	G.E.Type M	4 GE.#73	21:54	class A.4 6'5'	5×9	W.A 5½ & hand	56	49'2"	74800 56400	Contr. Cars 700 to 715 & 725 — no motors

Cars # 212. 228, 240 to 244 have 18:68 G.R.

✠ Cars.210, 217, 230, 23+, 248 have W.A.2 air

" 200 To 202, 204 to 209, 211, 234, 239, 247 have 22:64 G.R.

" 210, 211, 212, 214, 217, and 224, 229, 230 To 234, 239 To 244 & 246 have 5" I Beam — 219 have 8" I Beam

All cars without I Beam have 2. K.11 controllers

" " With " " 2-28 BF " except

210 & 217 " 2-28 F "

" " With I Beams — Weights 43200

" " Without " " 40400

No 1 Car 203 has Peckam 5'4 Truck — 2-38A Bast. Motors — 26:60 G.R.

CAR No (Old Series)	OWNED BY	CONTROL	MOTORS	GEAR RATIO	STYLE TRUCK	AXLE	TYPE BRAKE	CAPACITY	LENGTH	WEIGHT	NOTES
COMBINATION U.S. MAIL & EXPRESS CARS.											
98 – 99	L.A.P	K.11 K.6	2 & 4. 38A. std	26:60	Peckam 5:3" 5:10. A3	$3\frac{1}{2} \times 8\frac{1}{2}$ 4 + 8	W.A.2 C.S.2		39:0		Car 98 has 2 motors _ C.S.2 " 99 " 4 " _ W.A.2
EXPRESS CARS											
1505 – 1506	L.A.P				5:6"	4' × 7"	AUTO & Hand		39:1"	25250	Trailers
1507	L.A.P				5:6'	4' × 7'	AUTO & Hand		45:0"	27200	Trailer
1509 To 1511	L.A.P				5:6"	4' × 7'	AUTO & Hand		32:0'		Trailers
1550	L.A.P	K6	4. 38B N.G	22:60	Class B1 5:3"	$3\frac{1}{2}" \times 6\frac{5}{8}"$	W.A 5$\frac{1}{2}$ & Hand		41:5"		
1551	L.A.P	K6	4. 38B N.G	22:60	Class B1 5:3"	$3\frac{1}{2} \times 6\frac{5}{8}"$	W.A 5$\frac{1}{2}$ & Hand		36:8"	40,000	
1553	L.A.P	K6	4. 38A. NG	18:64	Class B1 5:3"	$3\frac{1}{2} \times 6\frac{5}{8}"$	W.A. 5$\frac{1}{2}$ & Hand		41:5"		
1554 1556.1559	L.A.P	K6	4. 38B N.G 4. 38A Bstd	18.64 26:60	5:3"	$3\frac{1}{2} \times 6\frac{5}{8}"$ $3\frac{1}{2} \times 8$	W.A 5$\frac{1}{2}$ & Hand		39:0"	42000	1554. 1556 have B1 Truck 1555 _ Peck. Truck _ 1554 has 4. 38 B N.G
1555 – 1558	L.A.P	K6	4. 38A Bstd	18:68	5:3"	$3\frac{1}{2} \times 6\frac{5}{8}"$	W.A 5$\frac{1}{2}$ & Hand		36:7"		Car 1558 is stripped of all equipment
WRECKER CAR											
1557	L.A.P.	K6	4. 38A Bstd	26:60	Peckam 5:3'	$3\frac{1}{2} \times 8$	C.S.2 & Hand		39:0	42000	
TOWER CARS											
1	L.A.P	K.11 K 8	2. 38B. Bstd	14.68	Class B1 5:3"	$3\frac{1}{2} \times 6\frac{5}{8}$	C.S.2 & Hand		35:9"	31000	
2	L.A.P.	K8B	2. 38B. N.G	22:60	Class B1 5:3"	$3\frac{1}{2} \times 6\frac{5}{8}"$	W.S.2 & Hand		35:2"	31000	
3	L.A.P	K6	2. 38A Bstd	22:60	Peckam 5:3"	$3\frac{1}{2} \times 6\frac{5}{8}"$	W.A 5$\frac{1}{2}$ & Hand		34:0"		
5	L.A.P	K2	2. 38B	22:60	Class B1 5:3'	$3\frac{1}{2}" \times 6\frac{5}{8}"$	C.S.2 & Hand		36:0		
WORK MOTOR CARS											
11	L.A.P	K8B	2. 38B & Bstd.	14:68	Pullman 6:6	$3\frac{1}{2} \times 6\frac{5}{8}"$	C.S.2 & Hand		18:2"		yard Motor
1575. 1577. 1578	L.A.P	K6	See Note	22:60 14:68 18:68	class B1 5:3"	$3\frac{1}{2} \times 6\frac{5}{8}"$	W.A 5$\frac{1}{2}$ & Hand		34:0"	39900	1575 has 22:60 G.R & 2. 38B Mot. 1577 " 18:68 " " 4. 89 " 1578 " 14:68 " " 4. 38B "
1579	L.A.P	K6	4. 38B N.G	14:68	Class B1 5:3"	$3\frac{1}{2} \times 6\frac{5}{8}"$	W.A 5$\frac{1}{2}$ & Hand	172. HP	36:0"		
1581 To 1584	L.A.P	K6	4. 38A bstd 4. 38B N.G.	14:68 18:68	Class B1 5:3"	$3\frac{1}{2} \times 6\frac{5}{8}"$	W.A. 7$\frac{1}{2}$" & Hand	172-HP	30:0"	44000 48700	Car 1584 has 4. 38A M. & 18:68. G.R " 1581 " E.L 10 Air " 1582 to 1584 has E.L.12 Air
ELECTRIC LOCOMOTIVES											
1580	L.A.P	K6	4. 38B N.G	14:68	5:3"	$3\frac{1}{2} \times 6\frac{5}{8}"$	W.A 7$\frac{1}{2}$	172. H.P	30:0"	52000	E.L. equip't.
1585. 1586	L.A.P	K34B	4. GE. 73	17:73	6:5"	5' × 9"	W.A 7$\frac{1}{2}$	300 H.P	30:0"	84800 74000	← Car 1585 ← " 1586 E.L. equip't.
1587	L.A.P	K34D	4. GE. 73	17:73	6:5"	5" × 9"	W.A. 7$\frac{1}{2}$	300. HP	30:0"	83350	E.L equip't.
ELECTRIC SHOVELS											
62	L.A.P	K8B	1. 89. W.	18:68	4:8"	4 × 7	Hand	32. cub ft	52:6"		
63											data. Not yet available
PORTABLE VACUUM CLEANER											
12	L.A.P	W.11812P	W. 7. H.P		4:10	$3\frac{3}{4}" \times 7"$	Hand		39:10"		
BONDING CARS											
2 Cars No numbers	L.A.P.	Cars equipped with necessary controlling devices									

CAR No (old series)	OWNED BY	STYLE TRUCK	AXLE	TYPE BRAKE	CAPACITY	LENGTH	WEIGHT	NOTES
FLAT CARS								
500 to 524	L.A.P.	5:2"	5" × 9"	Auto & Hand	80,000	36:0"	25500	
533 to 535	L.A.P	5:6"	4' × 7'	N.Y. Auto & Hand	50 000	34:0"	21500	
537, 539	L.A.P	5:6"	4" × 7"	N.Y. Auto & Hand	50 000	34:0"	21500	
543 to 548	L.A.P	4:10"	4" × 7'	Auto & Hand	50 000	36:0"	20,500	
550 to 562	L.A.P	4:10	4" × 7"	Auto & Hand	50 000	36:0"	20,500	
564	L.A.P	4:10"	4" × 7"	Auto & Hand	50 000	36:0"	20,500	
566 to 579	L.A.P	4:10"	4" × 7"	Auto & Hand	50000	36:0"	20,500	
305 & 317	L.A.P	4:10	4 × 7	Hand	24 000	26:0	10,000	
BOX CARS								
401 – 402	L.A.P	4:10"	3¾" × 7"	Auto & Hand	30 000	26:2"	17900	
403	L.A.P	4:10"	4 × 7"	Auto & Hand	50 000	36:2'	25400	
404 to 413	L.A.P	4:10" 5:6"	4" × 7"	Auto & Hand	60 000	34:2"	28 000	Cars 404, 405, 407, 410 have 4:10" Truck " 406, 408, 409, 411, 412, 413 – 5:3" Truck
DUMP CARS								
350 to 353	L.A.P	4:11"	4¼ × 8'	Auto & Hand	60000	30:0"	27 900	Hart convertible cars
360 to 379	L.A.P	4:10 Single	4 × 7	" "	50.000	34:2"	30 000	12 Sect. Dump cars - 376 & 377 have 5:00 W. Base
1132 to 1206	L.A.P	5:7"	3½ × 7	Hand	124.5 cub.ft	14:2"	10 260	Side Dump cars
GONDOLA								
13	L.A.P	Single 8:7'		Hand	196 cub.ft	18:0		For Rubbish
OIL CARS								
1004	L.A.P	4:10"	4 × 7	Auto & Hand	5665 Gall	29:10½"		
1005	L.A.P	5:0	4 × 7	Auto - Hand	5665 Gall	34:2"		
1006	L.A.P	5:0	4 × 7	Auto - Hand	6780 "	31:0		
1007 to 1018	L.A.P	5:0	4" × 7"	Auto & Hand	6500 Gall.	34:0"		
SPRINKLING CAR								
1003	L.A.P	4:10"	4" × 7"	Auto & Hand	6900 Gall.	36:0	32700	From Oil car
PORTABLE SUB-STATION								
15	L.A.P	4:10"	4 × 7	Auto - Hand	W. 400 k.w.	37:7½"		
WEEDS BURNER								
20	L.A.P.	4:10"	4 × 7	Auto - Hand	50.000	36:0 49:7"	19200 car only	

No. 3

RECAPITULATION
Showing Brake & Electrical Equipment of Motors and Motors Control Cars.

PASSENGER CARS

CAR No (Old Series)	NO. CARS	MOTORS	CONTROL	BRAKES
32.33	2	2 38B.N.G.	K.11	C.S.2 ✗ / Hand
35	1	2 38B N.G.	K.2	C.S.2 ✗ / Hand
~~36~~	1	2 38A	1-K7 / 1-K7C	C.S.2 ✗ / Hand
~~38~~	1	2 38A	2-K7C	C.S.2 ✗ / Hand
~~39~~	1	2 38A	1-K8 / 1-K8B	C.S.2 ✗ / Hand
42	1	—	—	Hand & N.Y.Air
45 to 55	11	—	—	Hand & N.Y Air
60	1	2 38A bstd	K.11	CS2 ✗ / Hand
62.63.65.66.67 64.68.69	8	2-38.A / 2 38B N.G.	K 11	CS2 ✗ / Hand
70	1	2 38B.N.G.	K 11	CS2 ✗ / Hand
71	1	—	K.11	
72	1	—	K 11	—
73	1	—	K 11	—
76	1	—	—	—
156 / 157 to 159	1 / 3	4 W.69 / 2 W.89	K 11^H	W.A.4 / CS2 ✗ Hand
180 to 182	3	2 W.89	K 11^H aux. contact.	CS2 ✗ Hand
184 to 189	6	2 W.89	K.11^H aux. contact.	CS2 ✗ Hand
190 / 191 to 194	1 / 4	4²-89 / 38A	K.28F aux contact	W.S2 ✗ Hand
195 to 199	5	4 W 89	K 28F aux contact	W.S2 ✗
200 to 249	50	2 W.89	K.11 see Note	W.S.2 - WA2 See Note
400	1	2 38B bstd	K-11	CS2 ✗ Hand
700 to 746	47	4 GE.73	GE Type M	WA5½ ✗ Hand

COMBINATION CARS

CAR No (Old Series)	NO. CARS	MOTORS	CONTROL	BRAKES
98	1	2 38A	K 11	C 52
99	1	4 38A	K 6	WA2

EXPRESS CARS

CAR No (Old Series)	NO. CARS	MOTORS	CONTROL	BRAKES
1505 to 1507	3	—	—	W. Auto ✗ / Hand
1509 to 1511	3	4 38B. N.G.	K6	W. Auto ✗ / Hand
1550 ,, 1551	2	4 38B N.G.	K6	W.A 5½ ✗ / Hand
1553	1	4 38A N.G.	K6	W.A 5½ ✗ / Hand
1554.	1	4 38B N.G.	K6	W.A 5½ ✗ / Hand
1555. 1556.1559	3	4 38A bstd	K6	W.A 5½ ✗ / Hand

Cars with I beam have K.11 Controllers

Note. Cars 210, 217, 230, 231, 248 have W.A 2 Air — All cars with
I Beam have 2-28 BF Contr. except 210 & 217 — 2-28F Contr.
Hand Br. all cars

WRECKER CAR

CAR No	NO. CARS	MOTORS	CONTROL	BRAKES
1557	1	4 38A bstd	2-K6	C.S.2 ✗ / Hand

TOWER CARS

CAR No	NO. CARS	MOTORS	CONTROL	BRAKES
1	1	2 38B bstd	K.11 / K.8	CS2 ✗ / Hand
2	1	2 38B N.G.	K.8B	W.S.2 ✗ / Hand
3	1	2 38A bstd.	K6	WA 5½ ✗ / Hand
5	1	2 38B.	K2	CS2 ✗ / Hand

WORK MOTOR CARS

CAR No	NO. CARS	MOTORS	CONTROL	BRAKES
11	1	2 38B bstd	K.8B	C.S.2 ✗ / Hand
1575	1	2 38B	K6	W.A 5½ ✗ / Hand
1577	1	4 89	K6	W.A 5½ ✗ / Hand
1578 - 1579	2	4 38B std N.G	K6	W.A 5½ ✗ / Hand
1581	1	4 38B N.G	K6	W.A 7½ - E.L.10.A ✗ Hand
1582 - 1583	2	4 38B N.G	K6	W.A 7½ - E.L.12 A ✗ Hand
1584.	1	4 38A bstd	K6	W.A 7½ - E.L.12 A ✗ Hand

ELECTRIC LOCOMOTIVES

CAR No	NO. CARS	MOTORS	CONTROL	BRAKES
1580	1	4 38B N.G	K6	W.A 7½
1585 - 1586	2	4 G.E.73	K 34B	W.A 7½
1587	1	4 G.E.73	K 34D	W.A 7½

ELECTRIC SHOVELS

CAR No	NO. CARS	MOTORS	CONTROL	BRAKES
62	1	1 W.89	K8B	HAND

OBSERVATION CARS

CAR No	NO. CARS	MOTORS	CONTROL	BRAKES
900 - 901	2	4. GE.73	GE. Type M	W.A.5½ - Hand
902	1	4. 38A. W	K.6	W.S.2 "
903	1	4. GE.73	G.E Type M	W.A.5½ "
904	1	4 38B. N.G	K.6	W.S.2 "

No 4.

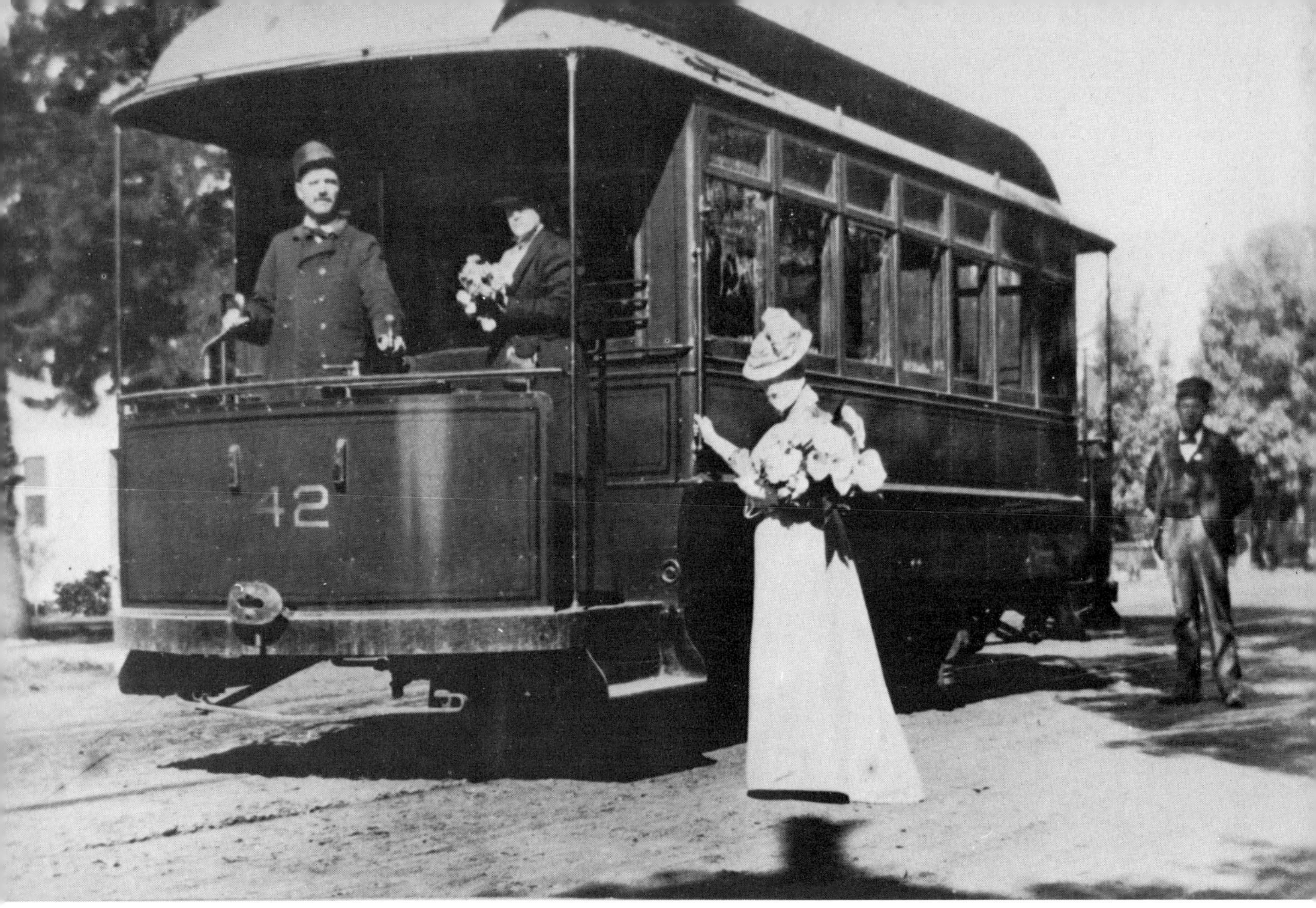

WEIGHTED DOWN WITH FLOWERS, Santa Monica matron prepares to board single-trucker 42, one of three such closed cars built by Pullman.
(Magna Collection)

ROSTER NOTES — FREIGHT CARS
See Page 82

350-353	Hart Convertible cars built by Rogers Ballast Car Co. For each car there was an LAP-made contrivance, by the use of which the car could be converted to 12 section side dump car. When so equipped each section had a capacity of 2 cubic yards.
360-379	Apparently built as flatcars and dump bodies added.
401-402	Originally narrow gauge.
404-413	Built by LAP at Sherman, 1906.
526	Not listed in roster but shows up in an old photo.
533-535, 537,539	Evidently the survivors of a larger class as dimensions the same for all 5 cars. 530-539?
540-579	Cars 540, 541, 542, 549, 563 unaccounted for. Car 565 to weed burner 20 about 1909. The 1909 valuation survey pictures show this car as a weed burner with the number 565; either operated as a weed burner for a time with this number or was just finished at time photo was taken.
1003	Sprinkling car. What it sprinkled is unknown but it was required to have a headlight..
1132-1206	Built by Western Dump Car.

LAP Car 33, at Sherman.

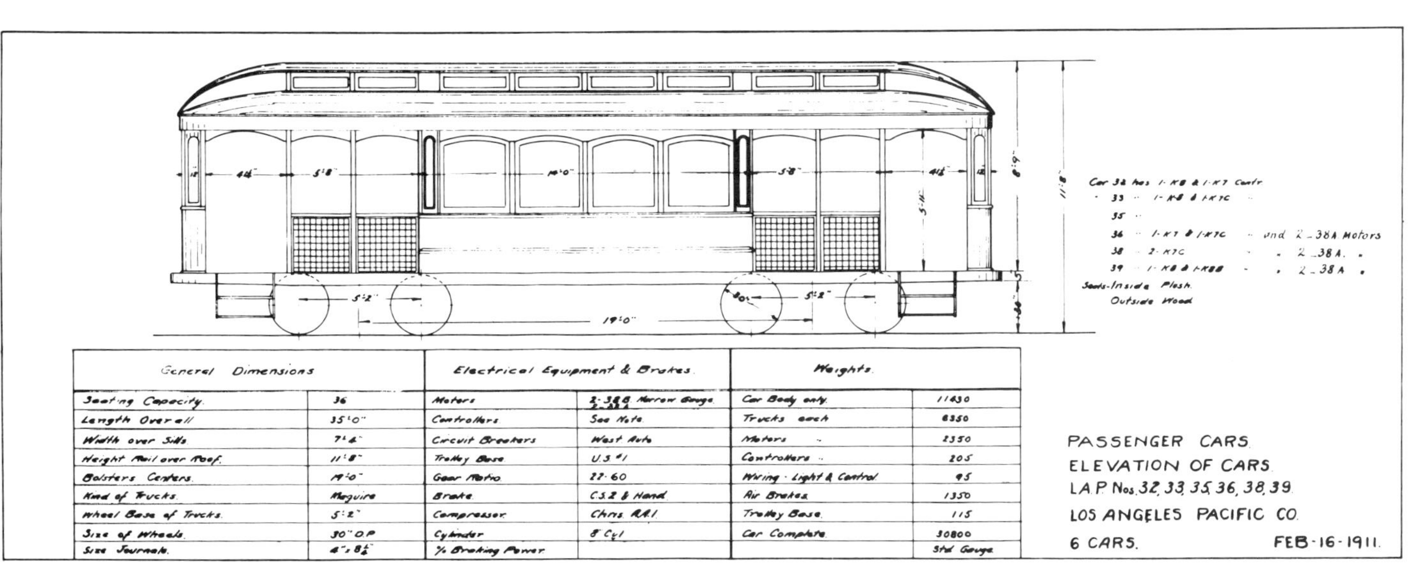

General Dimensions		Electrical Equipment & Brakes.		Weights.	
Seating Capacity.	36	Motors	2-38B Narrow Gauge. 2-38A	Car Body only.	11430
Length Over all	35'0"	Controllers.	See Note.	Trucks each	8350
Width over Sills	7'4"	Circuit Breakers	West Auto	Motors "	2350
Height Rail over Roof.	11'8"	Trolley Base.	U.S.#1	Controllers "	205
Bolsters Centers.	19'0"	Gear Ratio.	22-60	Wiring - Light & Control	95
Kind of Trucks.	Maguire	Brake.	C.S.2 & Hand.	Air Brakes	1350
Wheel Base of Trucks.	5'2"	Compressor.	Chris. RA1.	Trolley Base.	115
Size of Wheels.	30" O.P	Cylinder	8 Cyl	Car Complete.	30800
Size Journals.	4"x8½"	% Braking Power.			Std. Gauge.

PASSENGER CARS.
ELEVATION OF CARS.
LAP Nos. 32, 33, 35, 36, 38, 39
LOS ANGELES PACIFIC CO.
6 CARS.   FEB-16-1911.

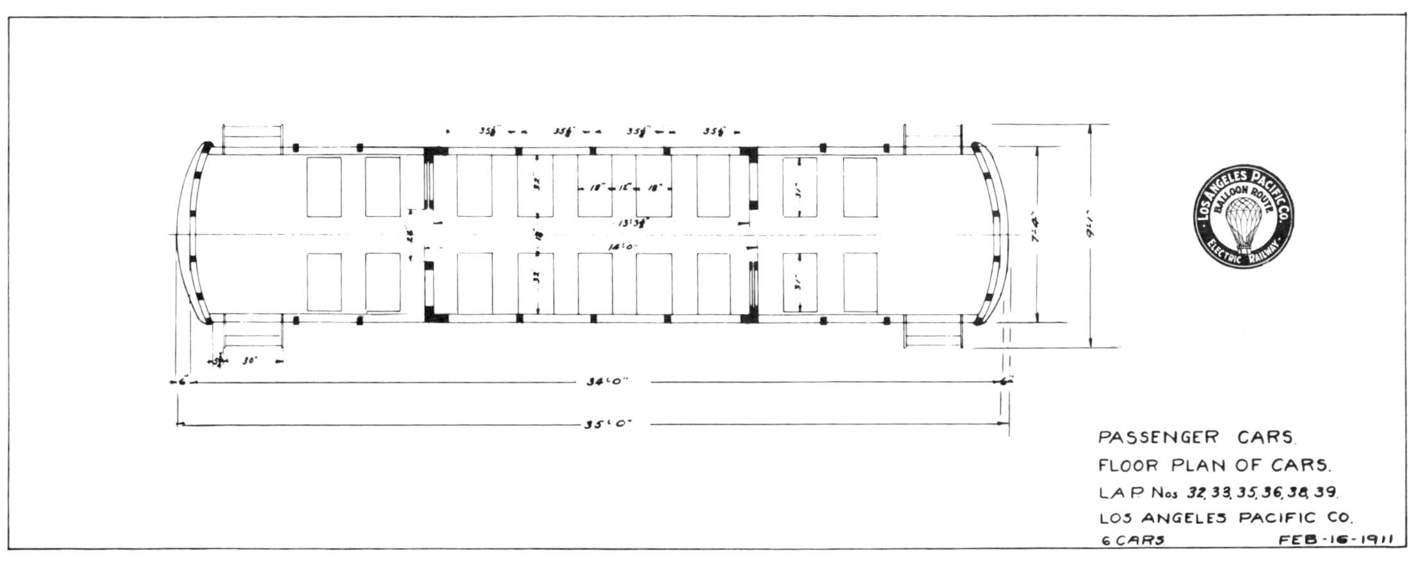

PASSENGER CARS.
FLOOR PLAN OF CARS.
LAP Nos. 32, 33, 35, 36, 38, 39.
LOS ANGELES PACIFIC CO.
6 CARS   FEB-16-1911

THE GRANDSTAND, Grand Lagoon, Venice, with 40-class trailers.   *(Interurbans)*

The 30s had McGuire trucks of only a 5'2" wheelbase; wheels were 30" and the cars were driven by two Westinghouse 38 motors which were rated at 50 hp. A low gear ratio of 22:60 made these cars unhappily slow.

By 1911 only three were left on LAP; 32, 33 and 35; the others had been disposed of: 30, 31, 34 and 37 before 1911 and 36, 38 and 39 during 1911. Of the cars retired before 1911, two went to the *South Park & East Side* in San Diego where they became the 10 and 11. In 1909 the SP&ES was absorbed by the *San Diego Electric Railway* and the 10 became SDER's second 12 while 11 became second 11. Car 12 was converted to wrecker 54 in 1913 and scrapped as 054 in 1940. Car 11 was retired in 1920, replaced by Birneys.

Cars 32, 33 and 35 became PE 110-112 and were operated without rebuilding into the early 1920s. Car 110 was sold to the *Peninsular Railway* in 1923 and operated as the Bascom local car for many years. Car 111 was sold for non-railway use in 1923. Car 112 was severely damaged in a collision with a sand truck in Hermosa Beach on March 20, 1922, and was scrapped on October 25 after being stored at Sherman.

40-47

These trailers were among LAP's first interurban rolling stock. The exact number of cars of this type is not known for records are contradictory; official corporate history records show *Pasadena & Pacific Railway Co.* owning "14 Pullman coaches" on January 1, 1897, costing $2,000 each. It would appear that these eight cars were LAP's share of the class.

After they were received from Pullman in 1896 as many as three were hauled to the seashore behind the 70-class motor cars. As received, they were open trailers. At an undetermined date they were completely enclosed.

Cars 40, 41, 43 and 44 were motorized at Sherman about 1906 and sent to Phoenix, Ariz., about 1907 where an affiliated company operated the city's street railway system. Apparently they became Phoenix cars 30, 32, 33 and possibly line car 31. Cars 30 and 32 had been rebuilt to combines with enclosed ends by the 1920s while 33 had its ends similarly enclosed but remained a straight passenger motor.

The four cars remaining on the LAP saw little use after 1907, and only 42 was standard gauged. They retained their original numbers after the merger with 3'6" gauge cars 45, 46 and 47 stored at Sherman. These three cars were scrapped in the housecleaning of 1913 while standard gauge car 42 lasted until 1927.

47-49

These three cars are the LAP's share of the 40-49 group built by Pullman in 1896 for the *Pasadena & Los Angeles.* When the P&LA and the LAP were separated in 1898 the cars, which had been pooled, were split between the two companies.

In the case of the 40-class, 40-46 went to P&LA while LAP got 47-49. These cars were superseded in passenger service early and assumed roles as work cars. Car 47 was converted to line car 4 and 49 was sold to a cement company at Acton,

DERELICT BODY of LAP 42-47 class trailer at Sherman, Dec. 8, 1940.

(Interurbans—Gillespie)

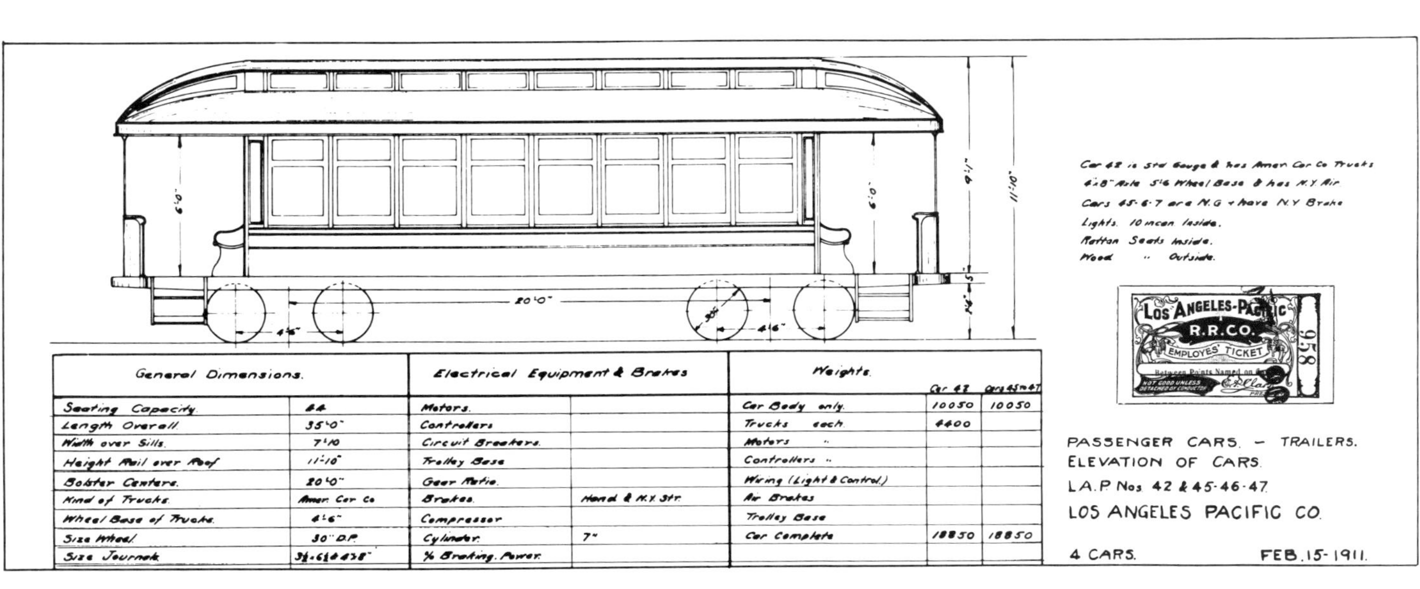

Car 42 is Std Gauge & has Amer. Car Co Trucks
4x8" Axle 5'6 Wheel Base & has N.Y. Air.
Cars 45-6-7 are N.G. & have N.Y. Brake
Lights. 10 incan Inside.
Rattan Seats Inside.
Wood   "   Outside.

General Dimensions.		Electrical Equipment & Brakes		Weights	Car 42	Cars 45 & 46 47
Seating Capacity.	64	Motors.		Car Body only.	10050	10050
Length Overall.	35'0"	Controllers		Trucks each.	4400	
Width over Sills.	7'10	Circuit Breakers.		Motors "		
Height Rail over Roof	11'-10"	Trolley Base		Controllers "		
Bolster Centers.	20'0"	Gear Ratio.		Wiring (Light & Control.)		
Kind of Trucks.	Amer. Car Co	Brakes.	Hand & N.Y. Str.	Air Brakes		
Wheel Base of Trucks.	4'-6"	Compressor		Trolley Base		
Size Wheel.	30" D.P.	Cylinder.	7"	Car Complete	18850	18850
Size Journals	3¾·6⅛·4¾8"	% Braking Power.				

PASSENGER CARS. — TRAILERS.
ELEVATION OF CARS.
L.A.P. Nos 42 & 45·46·47
LOS ANGELES PACIFIC CO.

4 CARS.   FEB. 15-1911.

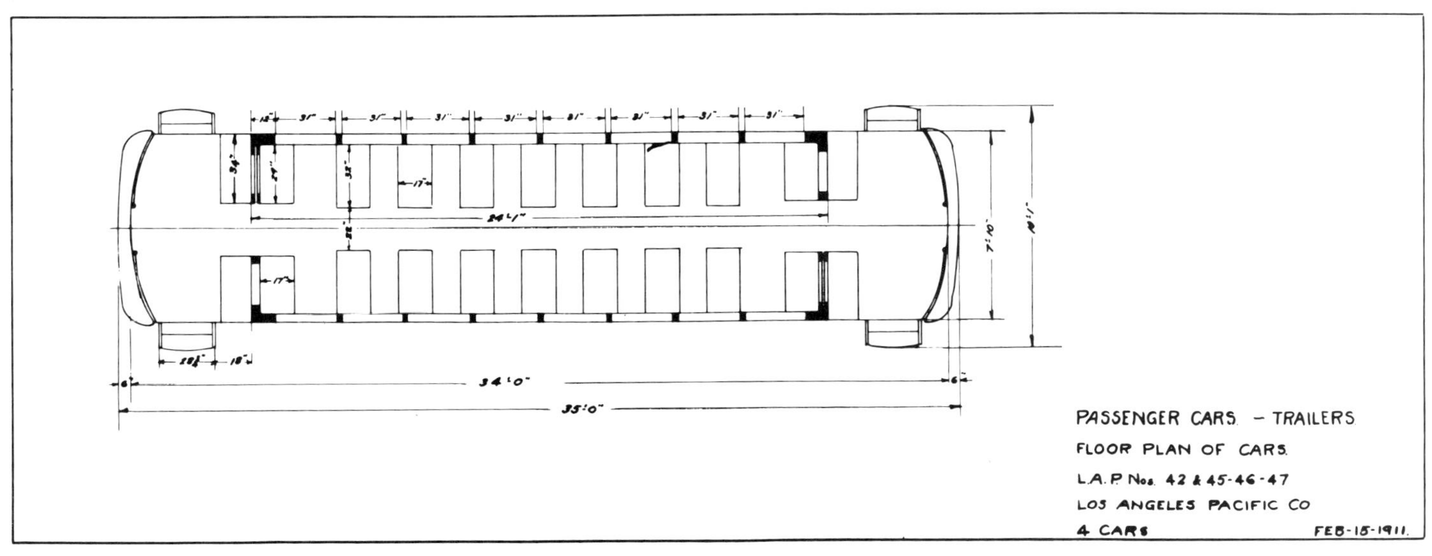

PASSENGER CARS. — TRAILERS
FLOOR PLAN OF CARS.
L.A.P. Nos. 42 & 45·46·47
LOS ANGELES PACIFIC CO
4 CARS   FEB·15·1911.

CARS 49 (Top) and 64 (Bottom) at Sherman.

(Magna Collection)

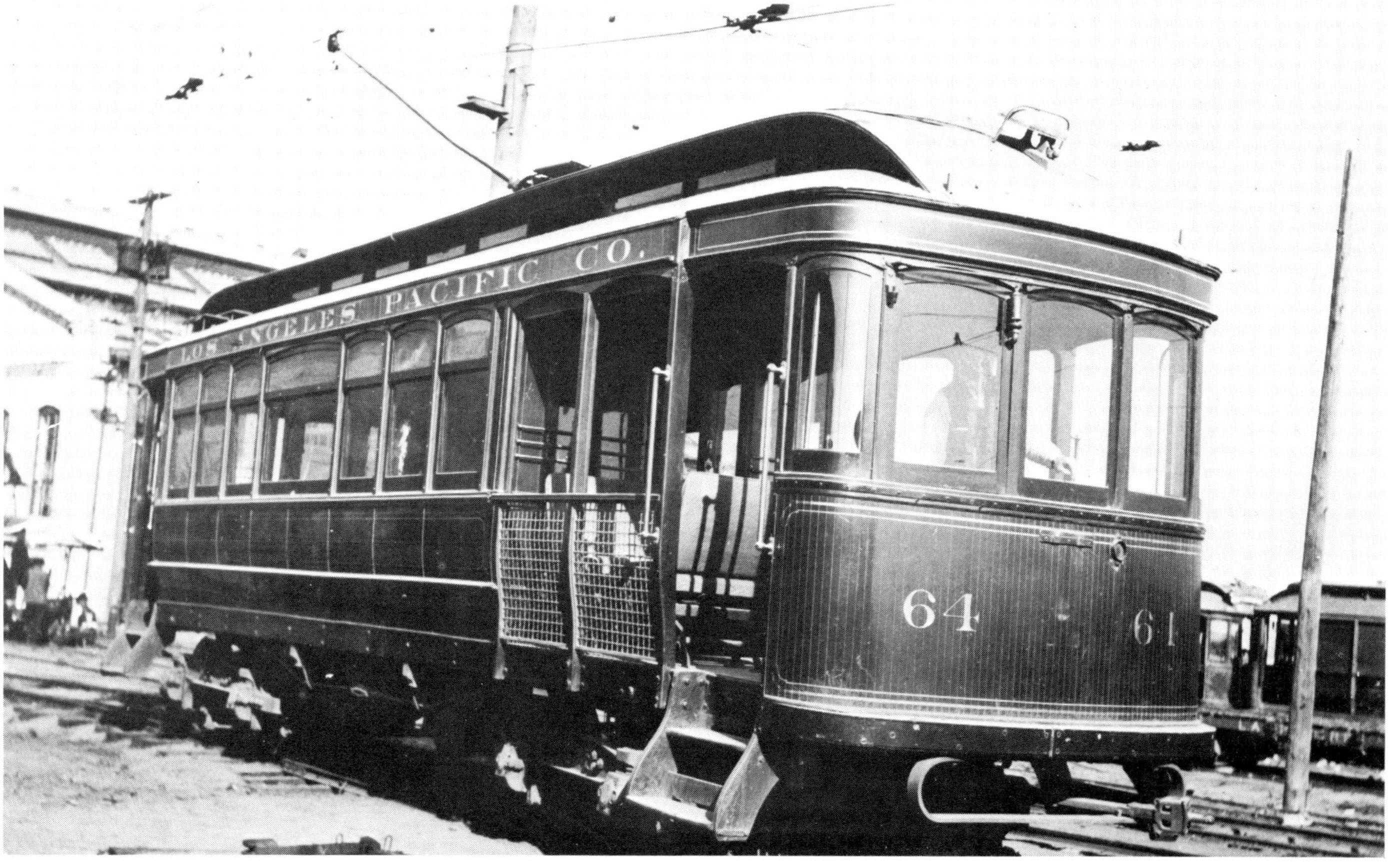

Calif. Car 48 was used as a Cholo car. On October 11, 1901, this car was involved in a disastrous wreck with one of the "lemon trains," consisting of an express motor and trailer, in the fog near Sherman. Four men were killed in the mishap and five more badly injured. Subsequently, 48 was rebuilt to a shop switcher (#11) for Sherman Shops.

48-55

These eight cars were built in 1902 by American to run with the 180 class, also built that year. They seated 40 as against 44 for the older trailers, but had a heavier, better built body.

Car 55 had Peckham rigid bolster 5'3" trucks while the others had the American 5'4" swing bolster type which was a close copy of McGuire's 35 type (see also cars 70-76). All had 30" cast iron wheels.

LAP trailers depended on the motor car for lights, a wire jumper running beneath cars. Oldtimers recall with what glee gay young blades pulled out the jumpers, leaving themselves and their lady friends in darkness on the way home from the beach.

The trailers (both types) used New York straight air brakes which made them hard to stop quickly. Later car 49 received the Westinghouse automatic brake which greatly increased its braking power.

In 1901 cars 56 and 57 were renumbered to 48 and 49 respectively. After the Great Merger they got their original numbers back. The class became PE 50-57. Cars 50, 51, 53, 54 and 56 were scrapped in 1913, 52 in 1919 and 55 in 1920. Car 57 was the only car to see much use on the PE, being used between Riverside and the Crestmore Cement Plant. It was renumbered 43 in 1921 and was finally scrapped in 1926.

60-69

The 60s were LAP's first cars. An attractive car, they were built by Brill in 1895-96 with an unusually wide letterboard which was continued around the ends, giving the body a strong and integrated appearance. They were, of course, closely similar to the *Pasadena & Los Angeles* 80 class for Sherman and Clark controlled both companies.

The end window arrangement continued the five-window front incorporating curved end windows at corners. This feature, first introduced by P&LA a year previously, was continued by Sherman and Clark in their subsequent LAP car purchases (the 700s were bought under SP auspices) and was adopted by Henry E. Huntington for his PE and Los Angeles

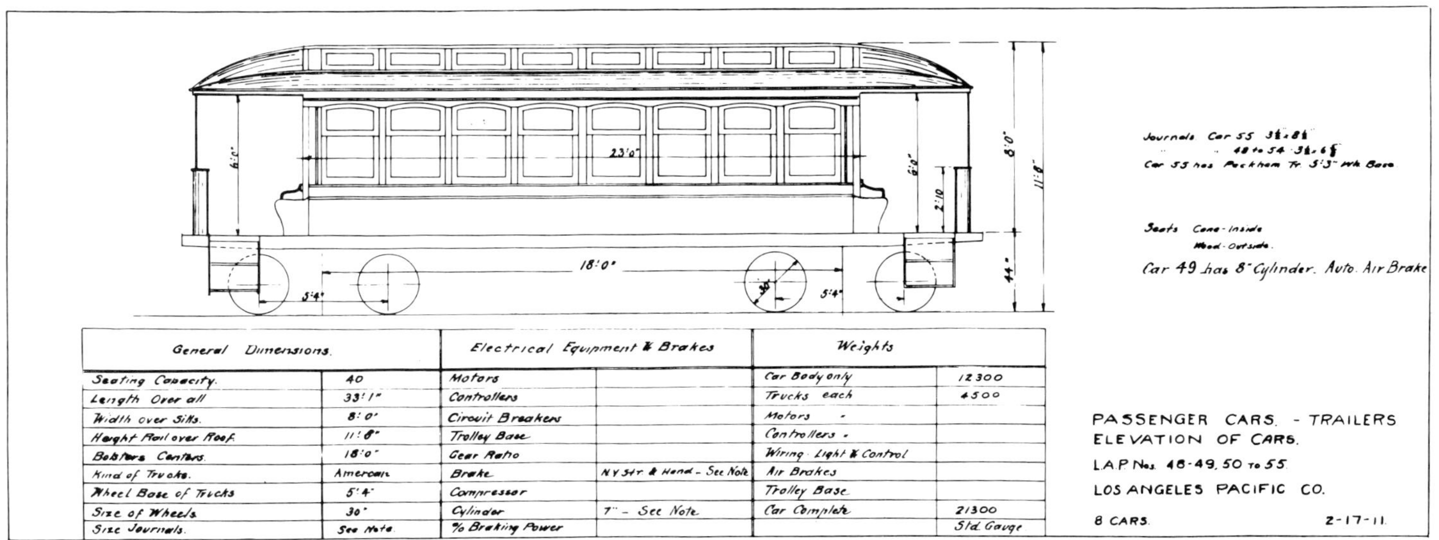

General Dimensions.		Electrical Equipment & Brakes		Weights	
Seating Capacity.	40	Motors		Car Body only	12300
Length Over all	33'1"	Controllers		Trucks each	4500
Width over Sills.	8'0"	Circuit Breakers		Motors ·	
Height Rail over Roof.	11'8"	Trolley Base		Controllers ·	
Bolsters Centers.	18'0"	Gear Ratio		Wiring · Light & Control	
Kind of Trucks.	American	Brake	N.Y. Str. & Hand – See Note	Air Brakes	
Wheel Base of Trucks	5'4"	Compressor		Trolley Base	
Size of Wheels	30"	Cylinder	7" – See Note	Car Complete	21300
Size Journals.	See Note.	% Braking Power			Std. Gauge

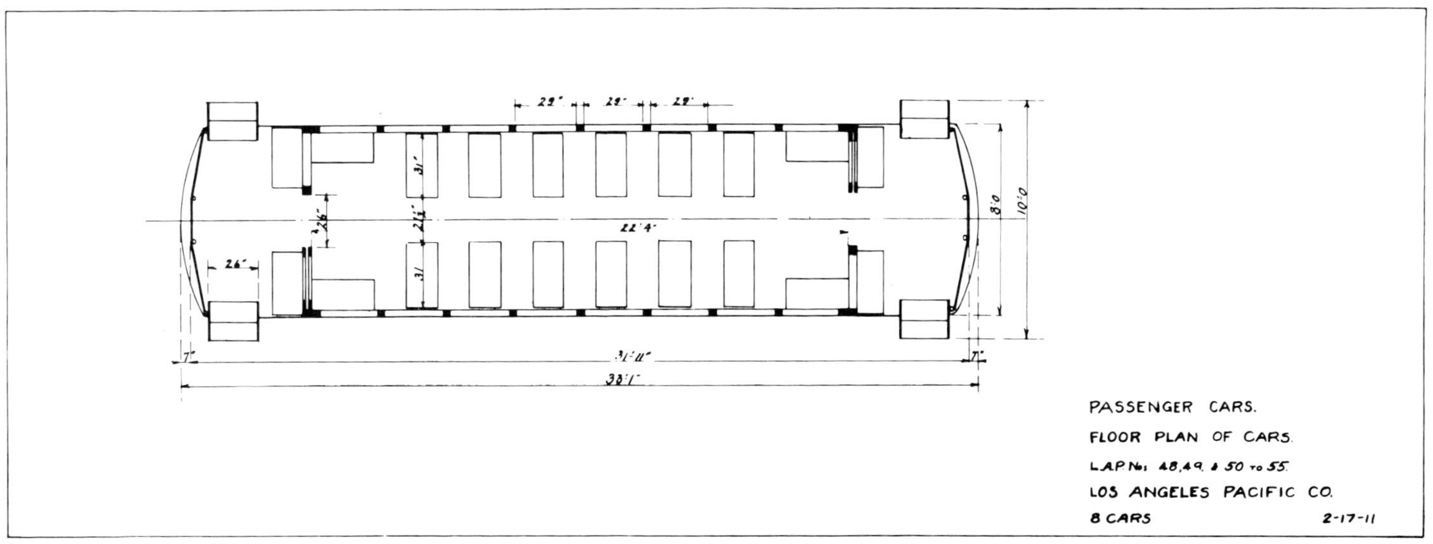

FOUR OF THE 40-class trailers were motorized at Sherman and sold to Phoenix; here is one of these heavy-roofed cars in the Arizona capital.   (A.E. Barker)

Railway cars; it became perhaps the most famous characteristic of all early Los Angeles streetcars.

The 60s also continued the double width window in the closed section, flanked by single width windows, and this feature was carried out on all wooden suburban and interurban cars built by Sherman and Clark, Huntington and SP.

As originally built these cars had outward facing longitudinal seats in the open sections and running boards. At an unknown date, LAP rebuilt the open sections with cross seats and mesh siding.

Car 61 was sold to San Jose Railroads before 1911. The rest of the class went to PE, which rebuilt the cars giving them opposite open ends and deck roofs. The cars were renumbered PE 136-144 and ran as city cars until scrapped in 1926 and 1927.

70-76

This class was built by Pullman in 1896 as *Pasadena & Los Angeles* 70-79. When P&LA and LAP were separated in 1898, cars 70-76 became the property of LAP while 77-79 went to P&LA. As built, the cars were fully closed but at some later date a short open section was added, although not to all cars. The diagrams reproduced here show the cars as rebuilt with the open section.

These cars either were on hand for the opening of the line to Santa Monica on April 1, 1896 or were delivered shortly thereafter. By 1904 their day had passed and they were assigned unimportant runs or were in dead storage. By 1911 only car 70 was still operable; 71 and 72, still on narrow gauge trucks were in storage, 73 and 76 (partially wrecked) had no trucks at all and were stored in the old Sherman car house. The disposition of cars 74 and 75 remains unknown.

PE renumbered the five remaining cars 403-407 in order. Cars 404, 405, 406 and 407 were burned in the Sherman car house fire of 1913; 403 remained in service until scrapped in 1923.

90-99

The 90 class cars seem not to have been very highly thought of by LAP. They left passenger service early and few photos or records of these cars can be found.

These cars were built in 1898 or 1899 for New York's *Third Avenue Railway* by St. Louis Car Co. The 10 cars which became LAP 90-99 were purchased by Clark in 1902. They were unloaded at Ocean Park on July 10, 1902 and entered passenger service late that summer. Two remained standard gauge for use on the Inglewood line while the remaining eight were narrow-gauged for use on the balance of the LAP.

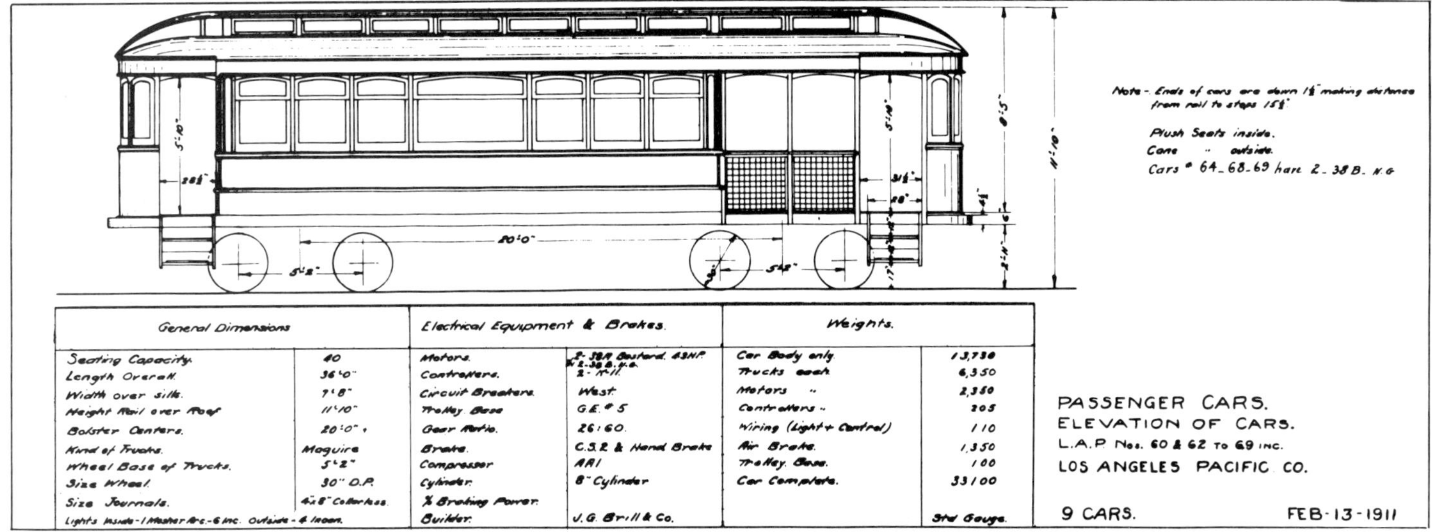

General Dimensions		Electrical Equipment & Brakes.		Weights.	
Seating Capacity.	40	Motors.	2-38R Bastard. 43HP. 2-38B.H.a.	Car Body only.	13,730
Length Overall.	36'0"	Controllers.	2-K-11.	Trucks each.	6,350
Width over sills.	7'8"	Circuit Breakers.	West.	Motors "	2,350
Height Rail over Roof	11'10"	Trolley Base	G.E. #5	Controllers "	205
Bolster Centers.	20'0" +	Gear Ratio.	26:60.	Wiring (Light + Control)	110
Kind of Trucks.	Maguire	Brake.	C.S.2 & Hand Brake	Air Brake.	1,350
Wheel Base of Trucks.	5'2"	Compressor	ARI	Trolley. Base.	100
Size Wheel.	30" O.P.	Cylinder.	8" Cylinder	Car Complete.	33100
Size Journals.	4x8" Collarless	% Braking Power.			
Lights Inside-1 Master Arc-6 Inc. Outside-4 Incan.		Builder.	J.G. Brill & Co.		Std Gauge.

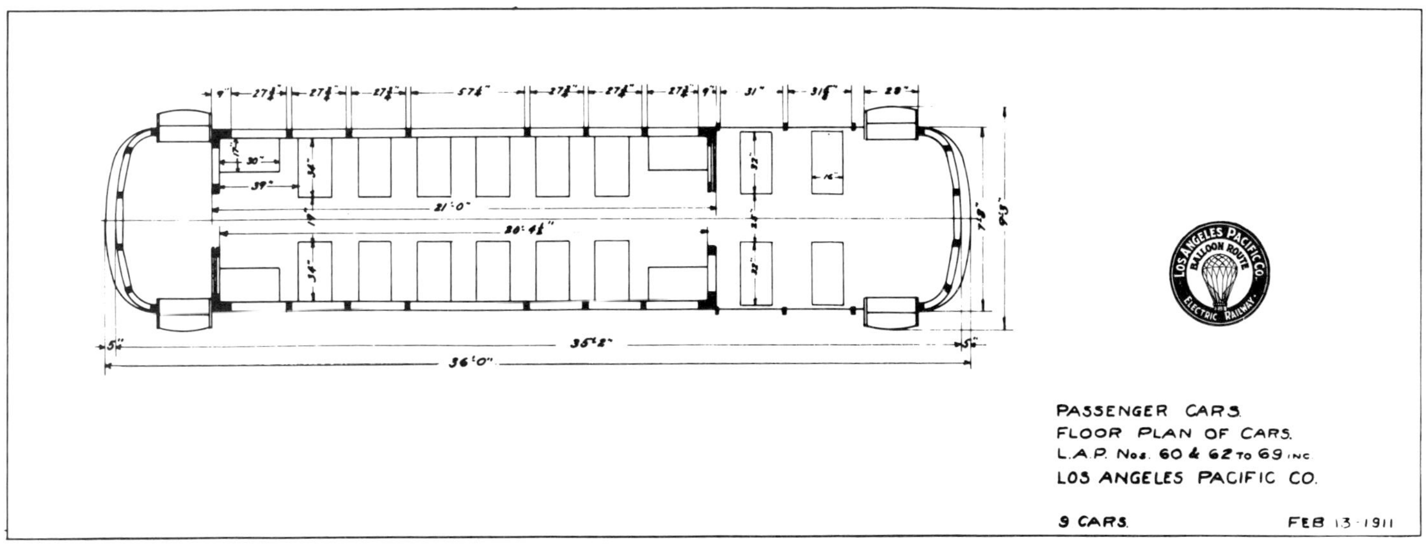

A MEMBER of the 70-76 class, at Sherman.

(Interurbans)

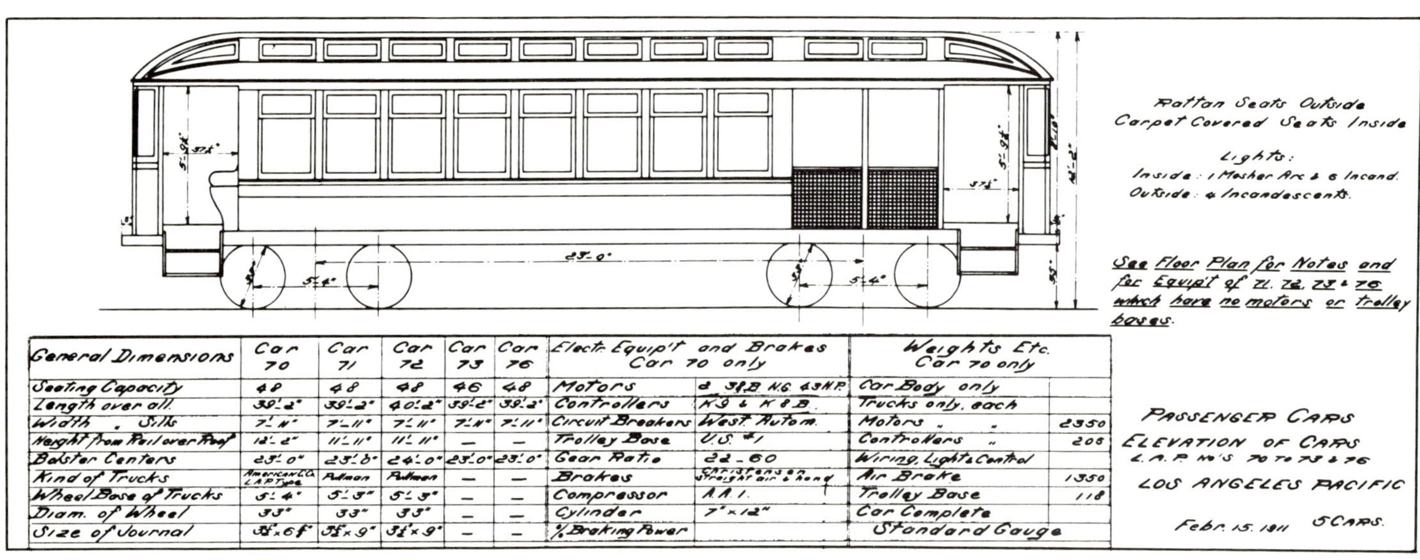

General Dimensions	Car 70	Car 71	Car 72	Car 73	Car 76	Electr. Equip't and Brakes Car 70 only		Weights Etc. Car 70 only	
Seating Capacity	48	48	48	46	48	Motors	2 38.B N.G. 43H.P.	Car Body only	
Length over all.	39'.2"	39'.2"	40'.2"	39'.2"	39'.2"	Controllers	K9 & K8B.	Trucks only, each	
Width „ Sills	7'.11"	7'.11"	7'.11"	7'.11"	7'.11"	Circuit Breakers	West. Autom.	Motors „ „	2350
Height from Rail over Roof	12'.2"	11'.11"	11'.11"	—	—	Trolley Base	U.S. #1	Controllers „	208
Bolster Centers	23'.0"	23'.6"	24'.0"	23'.0"	23'.0"	Gear Ratio	22-60	Wiring, Lights & Control	
Kind of Trucks	American Co. L.A.P. Type	Pullman	Pullman	—	—	Brakes	S.A.F. Suspension Straight air & hand	Air Brake	1350
Wheel Base of Trucks	5'.4"	5'.3"	5'.3"	—	—	Compressor	A.A.1.	Trolley Base	118
Diam. of Wheel	33"	33"	33"	—	—	Cylinder	7"×12"	Car Complete	
Size of Journal	3⅝"×6⅝"	3⅝"×9"	3¼"×9"	—	—	% Braking Power		Standard Gauge	

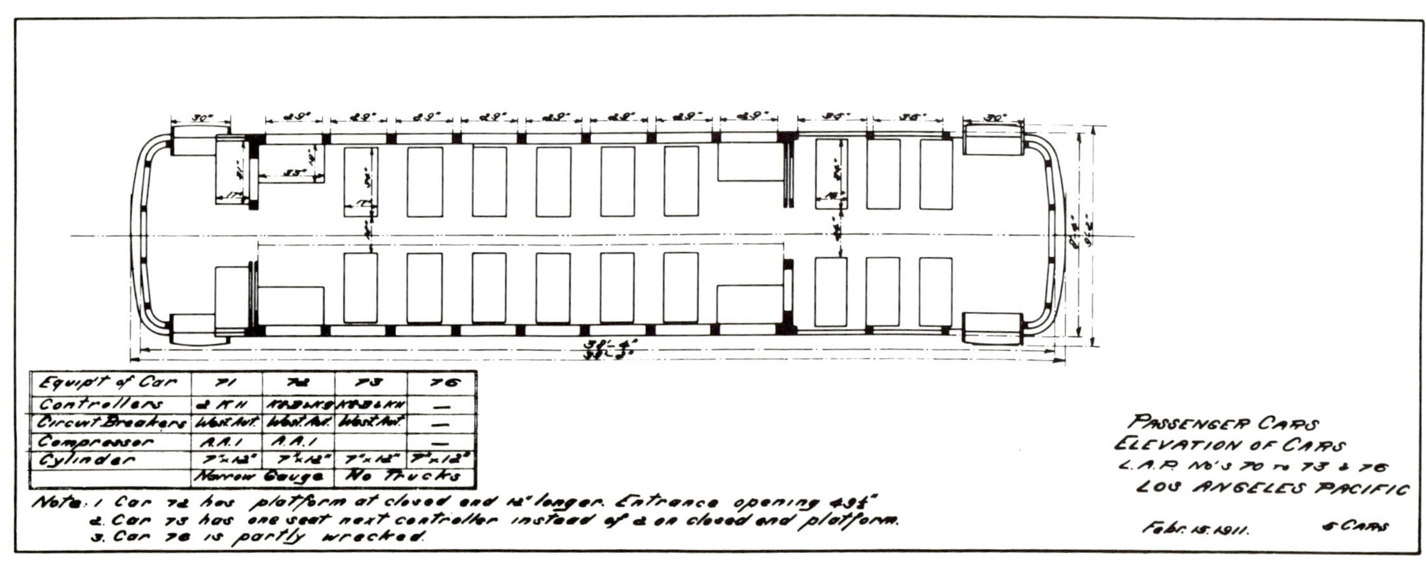

Equip't of Car	71	72	73	76
Controllers	2 K11	K9.B.N9.B.K11	K9.B.&.K11	—
Circuit Breakers	West. Aut.	West. Aut.	West. Aut.	—
Compressor	A.A.1	A.A.1		—
Cylinder	7"×12"	7"×12"	7"×12"	7"×12"
	Narrow Gauge		No Trucks	

Note: 1. Car 72 has platform at closed end 12" longer. Entrance opening 43½"
      2. Car 73 has one seat next controller instead of 2 on closed end platform.
      3. Car 76 is partly wrecked.

Car 159, at Sherman.   *(Interurbans)*

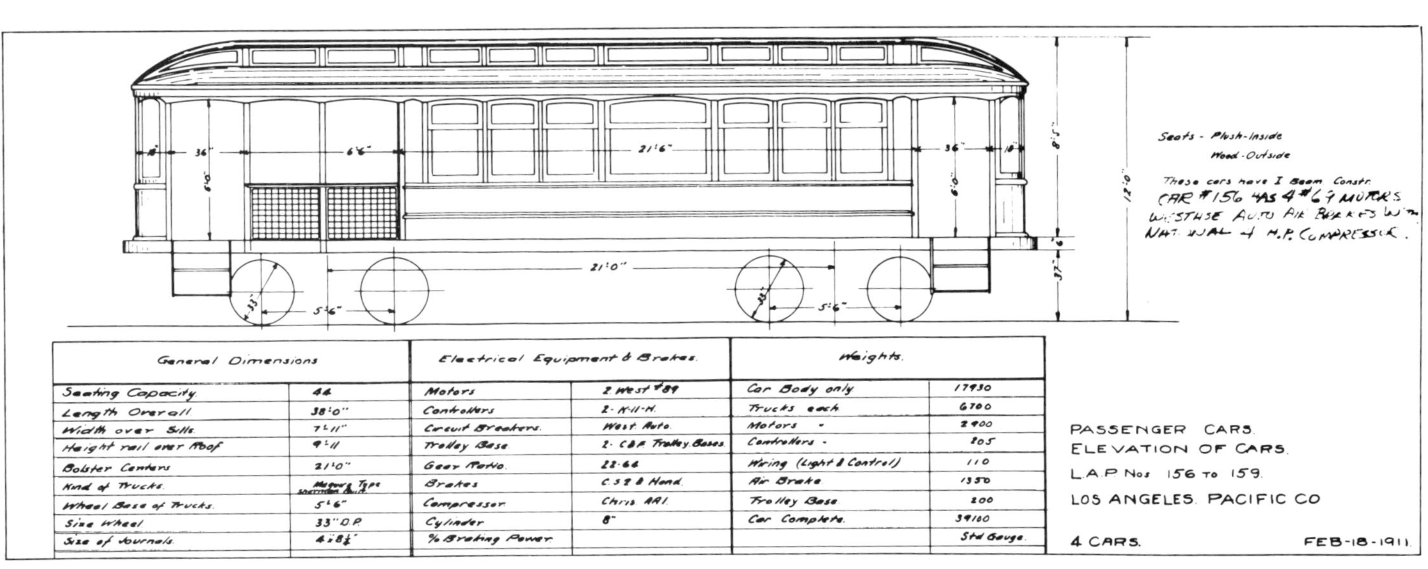

General Dimensions		Electrical Equipment & Brakes.		Weights.	
Seating Capacity.	44	Motors	2 West #89	Car Body only	17930
Length Over all	38'0"	Controllers	2 - K-11-H.	Trucks each	6700
Width over Sills	7'11"	Circuit Breakers.	West. Auto.	Motors "	2400
Height rail over Roof	9'11	Trolley Base.	2 - C.B.F. Trolley Bases.	Controllers -	205
Bolster Centers	21'0"	Gear Ratio.	22-66	Wiring (Light & Control)	110
Kind of Trucks.	Magure Type Sherman Built.	Brakes	C.S.2 B Hand.	Air Brake	1350
Wheel Base of Trucks.	5'6"	Compressor.	Chris. AA1.	Trolley Base.	200
Size Wheel	33" O.P.	Cylinder	8"	Car Complete.	39100
Size of Journals.	4 x 8½"	% Braking Power.			Std Gauge.

PASSENGER CARS.

ELEVATION OF CARS.

L.A.P Nos 156 to 159.

LOS ANGELES. PACIFIC CO

4 CARS.   FEB - 18 - 1911.

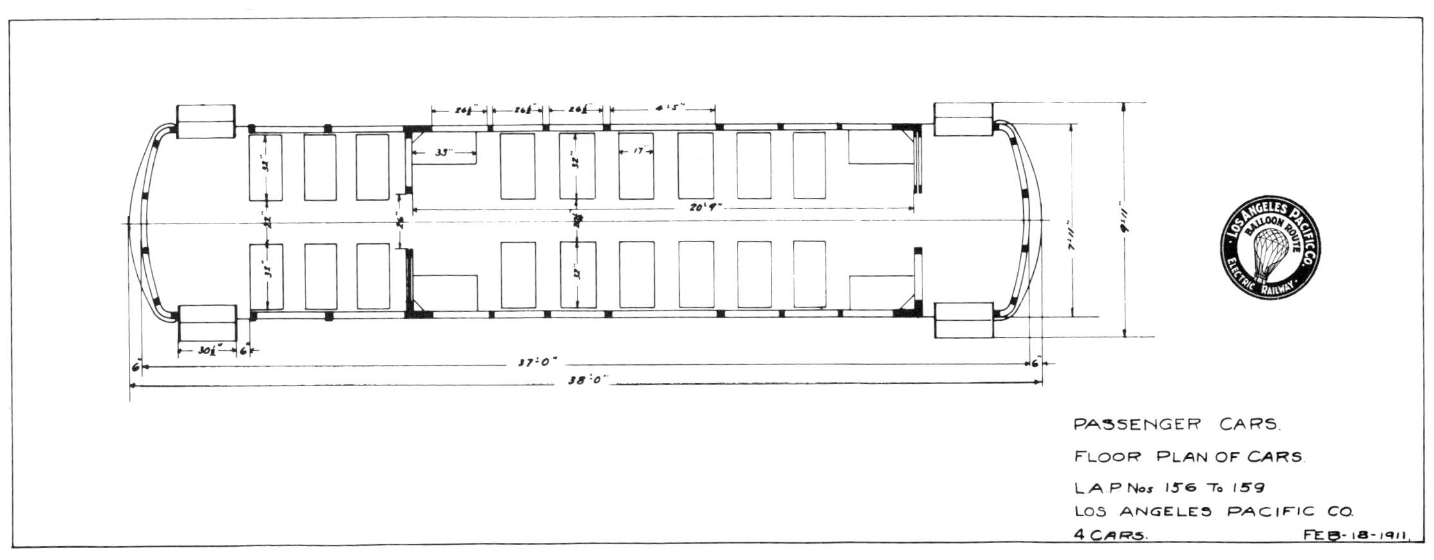

PASSENGER CARS.

FLOOR PLAN OF CARS.

L.A.P Nos 156 To 159

LOS ANGELES PACIFIC CO.

4 CARS.   FEB - 18 - 1911.

AMERICAN CAR CO. builders photo of Car 186.   (Interurbans)

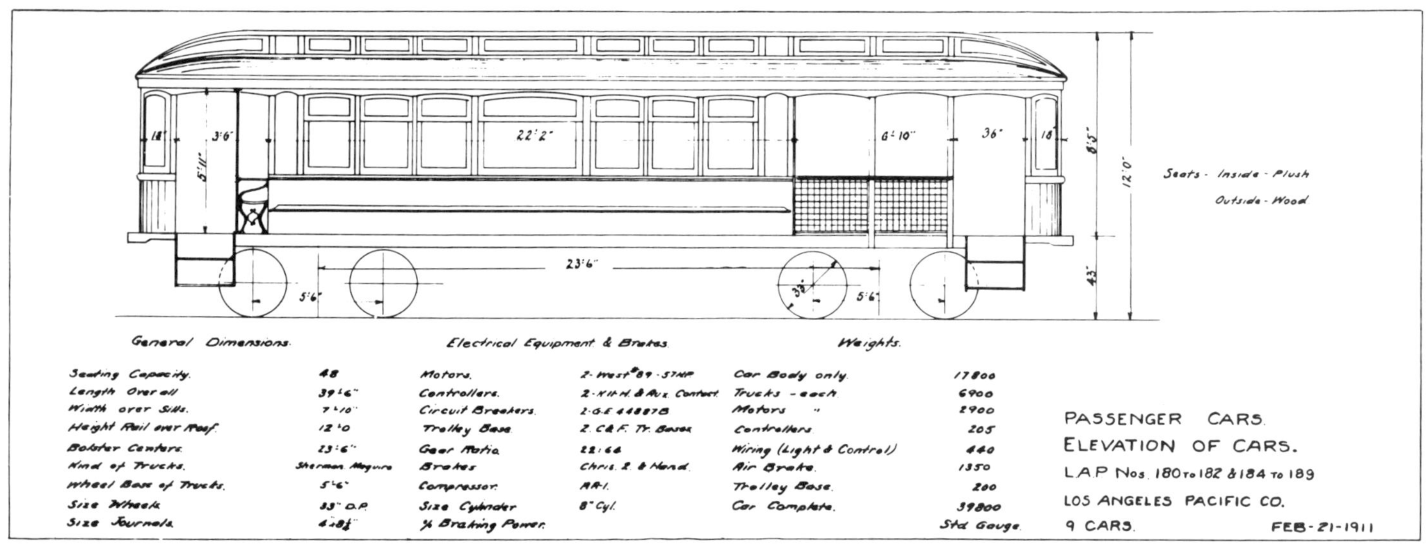

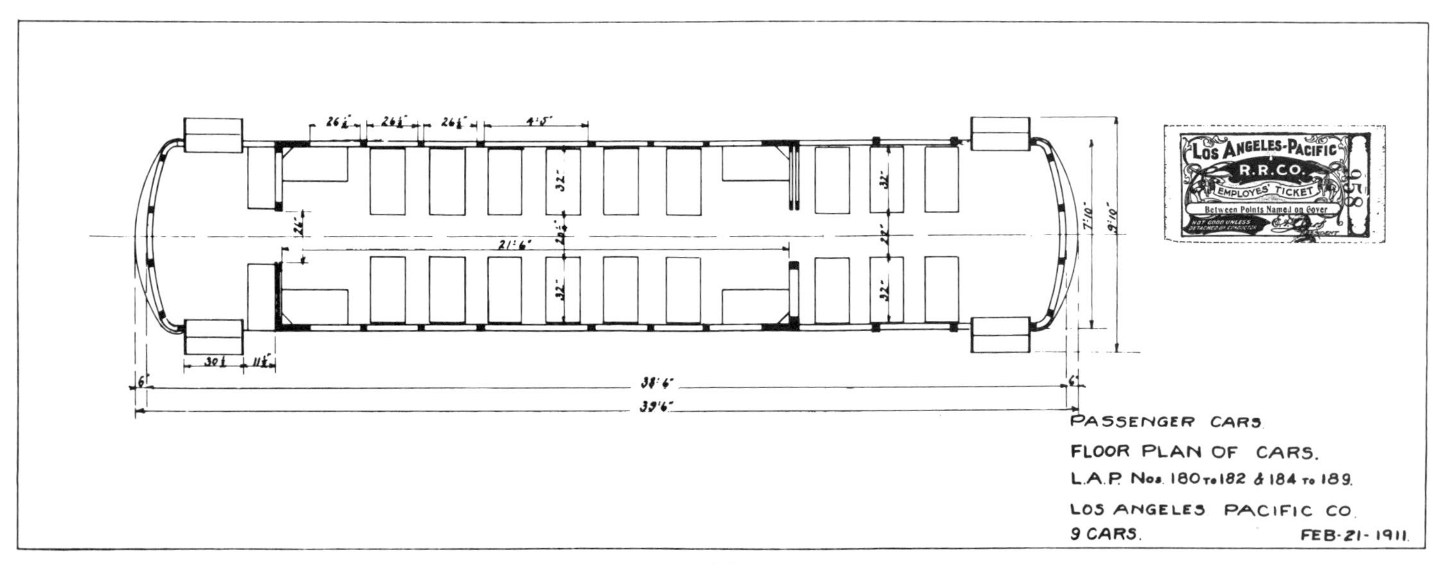

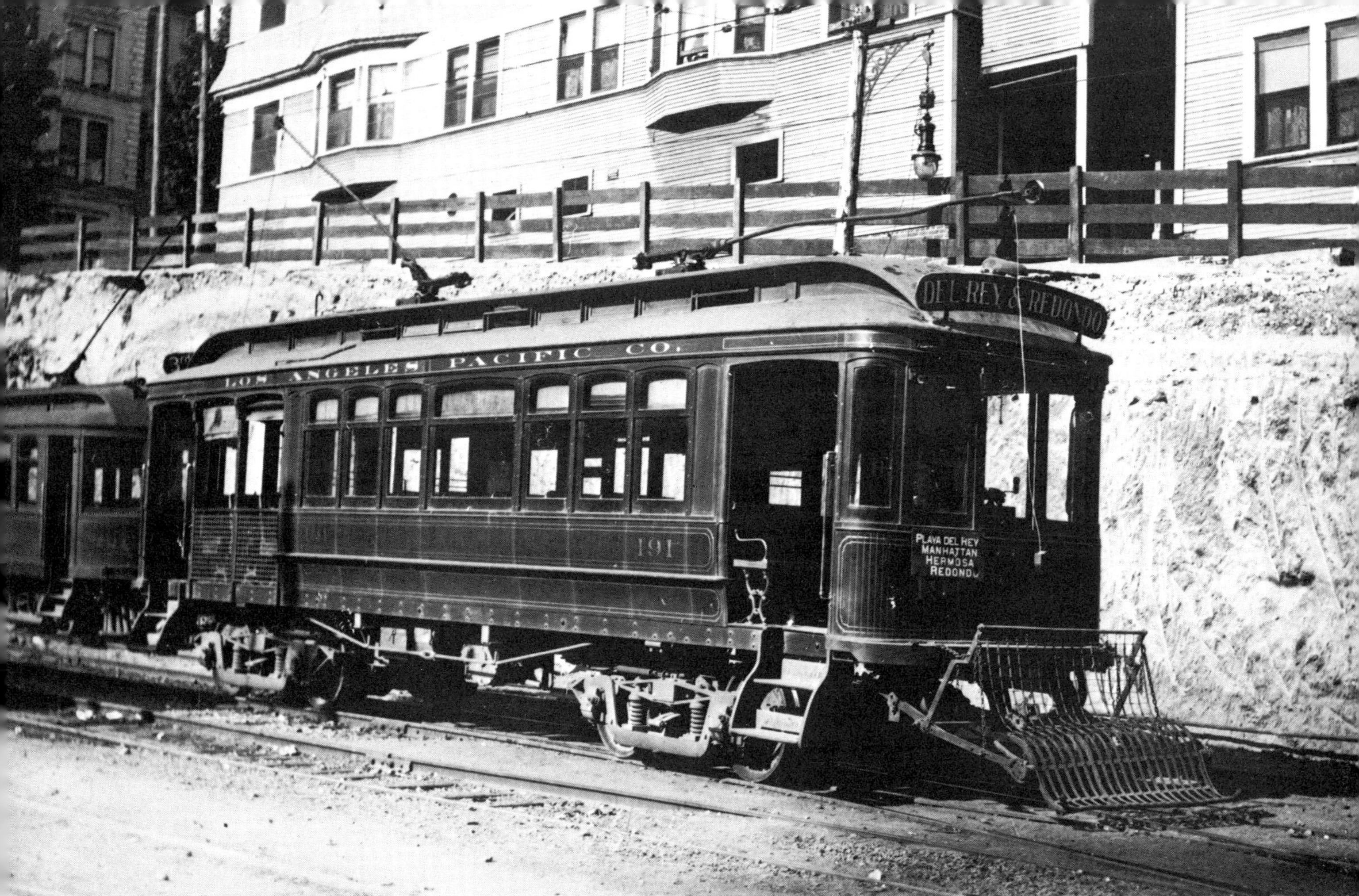

CAR 191 AT HILL ST. Station ready for the Redondo run.   *(Magna Collection)*

Evidently the drop platforms sagged badly enough by 1905 to require repairs, but by then large numbers of new cars built to LAP's own specifications had been delivered and the 90s were no longer needed in passenger service, except for the two standard gauge cars on the Inglewood line. Thus, when the 90s emerged from the shops they had been rebuilt as follows: two cars had the platforms rebuilt for continued use on the Inglewood line, car 92 was completely rebuilt to excursion car "Hermosa," four cars had the platforms rebuilt and doors cut midway in the sides to become express cars 1554, 1556, 1557 and 1559, and three cars were de-motored and had the platforms removed entirely becoming express trailers 1509, 1510 and 1511. In 1907 the 1557 was equipped with bins, etc., and became the system wrecker.

By 1907 the growth of the standard gauge portion of the LAP system and the consequent increasing numbers of standard gauge cars made the assignment of the two 90s to the Inglewood line unnecessary and they were withdrawn from this service. It would appear that these two cars may have been 98 and 99, as 98 and 99 were rebuilt to mail and express combines in 1908 and in this latter service were quite dissimilar in appearance to the 90s converted to express service in 1905.

100-109

These 10 cars were combination open and closed motors with benches and running boards in the open sections. It is believed that they were purchased about the same time as 90-99, but they were retired before 1911 and left no trace of their existence in the company's records.

156-159

Cars 156-159 were originally numbered 56-59 and were larger versions of the 60 Class. Built in 1901 by the Hammond Car Company (San Francisco) they were the first new passenger interurban cars LAP purchased since its original equipment.

The 156-159 had 36" doors, unusually roomy for their time. They also had a two-window open section but with three seats, breaking away from the usual seat-per-window tradition.

It is not certain what type of trucks these cars used in narrow-gauge days; probably they had the LAP standard: McGuire swing bolster. After being standard gauged, we note on the data sheet below: "Kind of Trucks: McGuire Type, Sherman Built." As the photo shows, the trucks certainly were McGuires or an excellent copy.

Car 156 was experimentally given four motors to test it hauling trailers, ostensibly for Hollywood Blvd. use. It kept these four motors to the end, while the others remained two motor cars.

PE renumbered them 476-479 and used them until scrapped 1926-27. The body of 478 was around for years at Macy St., used as a lunch room.

180-189

Ten new cars, 180-189 (perhaps 80-89 originally) were ordered in 1902 from American and were delivered late that year and early in 1903. This class was an improved version of

156-159, slightly larger and heavier all around although similar mechanically.

There is reason to believe that 180-189 were ordered for the Venice Short Line which opened in August, 1902.

The 180 Class, although intended for interurban service, was too light and slow to remain in such demanding service long. They were soon relegated to lighter service by the 190s and 200s which came along very shortly.

The 180s remained unchanged in the years PE had them; only their numbers were changed: 481-489—car 183 burned on Oct. 15, 1907. The specifications reproduced here remained okay till all were scrapped in 1928.

190-199

LAP 190-199 were almost exact duplicates of 180-189 when delivered. Bodies were identical, as were trucks, motors and wheels. They were also by American and were delivered in mid-1903, probably intended for the Redondo Line where they saw most of their LAP service.

From *Street Railway Journal,* June 27, 1903: "The cars are strongly built for the fast heavy loads that are carried all the year. Side sills are 4"x6" yellow pine, plated on outside with ½"x6" steel. Bracketed to the steel sill plates are straight posts for the open portion, 2¾" thick, which, with the vestibule posts, make an excellent support for the roof at this end. The corner posts of closed compartment are double, 8" wide, and the side posts 2¼" and 3½". The curved glass in the vestibule corners adds to the bright and rich appearance, and particularly suitable since single seats are introduced in these corners. To obtain room for the corner seats the controllers and brake shafts are placed nearer together than usual. Protection from rain or wind for the open part is had by drawing the curtains to floor. The closed compartment has large comfortable reversible back seats. Woodwork is plainly finished mahogany with red brick ceilings stained to the same tone of the mahogany and neatly decorated. Large mirrors of beveled plate are placed in the corners and over the end windows to assist the light. The lower sashes of the windows are arranged to raise. The trucks are American Car Company's special trucks for this company; wheelbase, 5'4", 30" wheels. The weight of car body and trucks: 21,000."

LAP soon retrucked and remotored the 190s, giving them the A-3 swing bolster, truck (5'10"), manufactured by LAP, 33" wheels, and four 38A or 89 motors. This greatly increased

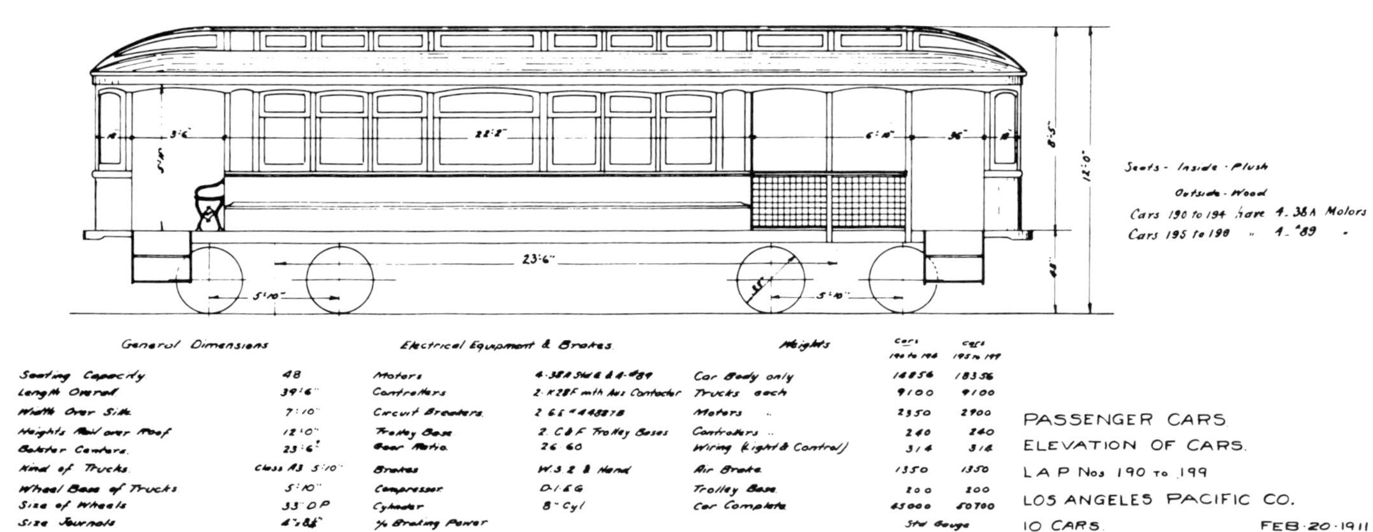

General Dimensions		Electrical Equipment & Brakes		Heights	Cars 190 to 194	Cars 195 to 199
Seating Capacity	48	Motors	4-38A Std & 4-89	Car Body only	14856	18356
Length Overall	39'6"	Controllers	2-K28F with Aux Contactor	Trucks each	9100	9100
Width Over Sills	7'10"	Circuit Breakers	2-65 #44887B	Motors	2350	2900
Heights Rail over Roof	12'0"	Trolley Base	2-C&F Trolley Bases	Controllers	240	240
Bolster Centers	23'6"	Gear Ratio	26-60	Wiring (Light & Control)	314	314
Kind of Trucks	Class A3 5'10"	Brakes	W.S.2 & Hand	Air Brake	1350	1350
Wheel Base of Trucks	5'10"	Compressor	D-1 EG	Trolley Base	200	200
Size of Wheels	33" OP	Cylinder	8" Cyl	Car Complete	45000	50700
Size Journals	4"x8½"	% Braking Power			Std Gauge	

PASSENGER CARS
ELEVATION OF CARS.
LAP Nos. 190 to 199
LOS ANGELES PACIFIC CO.
10 CARS.   FEB - 20 - 1911

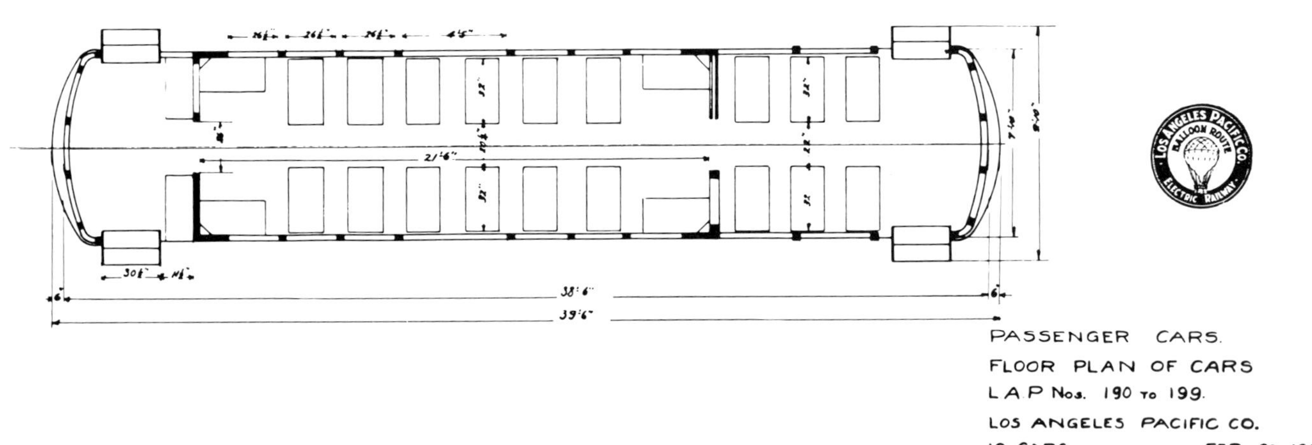

PASSENGER CARS.
FLOOR PLAN OF CARS
LAP Nos. 190 to 199.
LOS ANGELES PACIFIC CO.
10 CARS.   FEB - 20 - 1911.

CAR 242 on the Venice Freight Spur, 1910. Rollsign says: "L.A. via Hollywood."   (Interurbans)

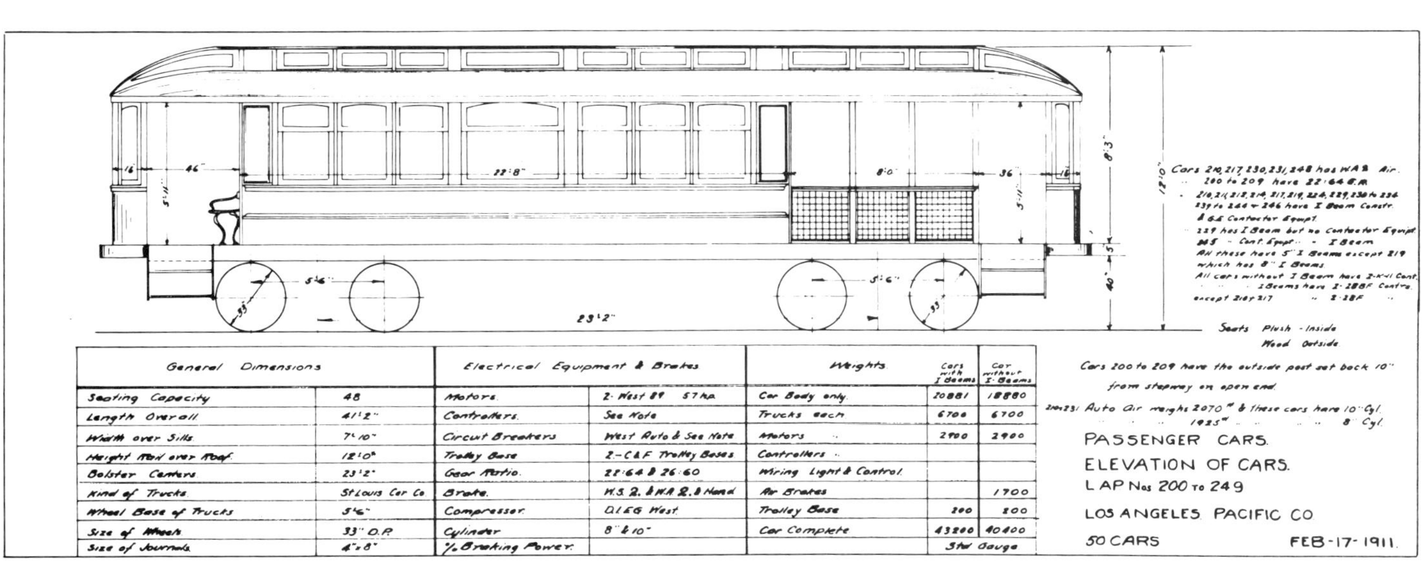

General Dimensions		Electrical Equipment & Brakes		Weights		Cars with I Beams	Car without I Beams
Seating Capacity	48	Motors	2-West 89 57 h.p.	Car Body only		20881	18880
Length Over all	41'2"	Controllers	See Note	Trucks each		6700	6700
Width over Sills	7'10"	Circuit Breakers	West Auto & See Note	Motors		2900	2900
Height Rail over Roof	12'0"	Trolley Base	2-C&F Trolley Bases	Controllers			
Bolster Centers	23'2"	Gear Ratio	22:64 & 26:60	Wiring Light & Control			
Kind of Trucks	St Louis Car Co	Brake	W.S. 2. & W.A. 2. & Hand	Air Brakes			1700
Wheel Base of Trucks	5'6"	Compressor	D.I.E.G West	Trolley Base		200	200
Size of Wheels	33" O.R.	Cylinder	8" & 10"	Car Complete		43200	40400
Size of Journals	4"x8"	% Braking Power			Std Gauge		

Cars 210, 217, 230, 231, 248 has WAB Air.
200 to 209 have 22-64 G.M.
210, 211, 212, 214, 217, 219, 224, 229, 230 to 234, 239 to 244 & 246 have I Beam Constr. & G.E. Contactor Equipt.
229 has I Beam but no Contactor Equipt.
245 — Cont. Equpt. — I Beam
All these have 5" I Beams except 219 which has 8" I Beams.
All cars without I Beam have 2-K-41 Cont.
I Beams have 1-28BF Contrs. except 216 & 217   2-28F

Seats Plush - Inside
Wood Outside.

Cars 200 to 209 have the outside post set back 10" from stepway on open end.

200-231 Auto Air weighs 2070" & these cars have 10" Cyl.
1925"   8" Cyl.

PASSENGER CARS.
ELEVATION OF CARS.
L A P Nos 200 to 249
LOS ANGELES PACIFIC CO
50 CARS   FEB-17-1911.

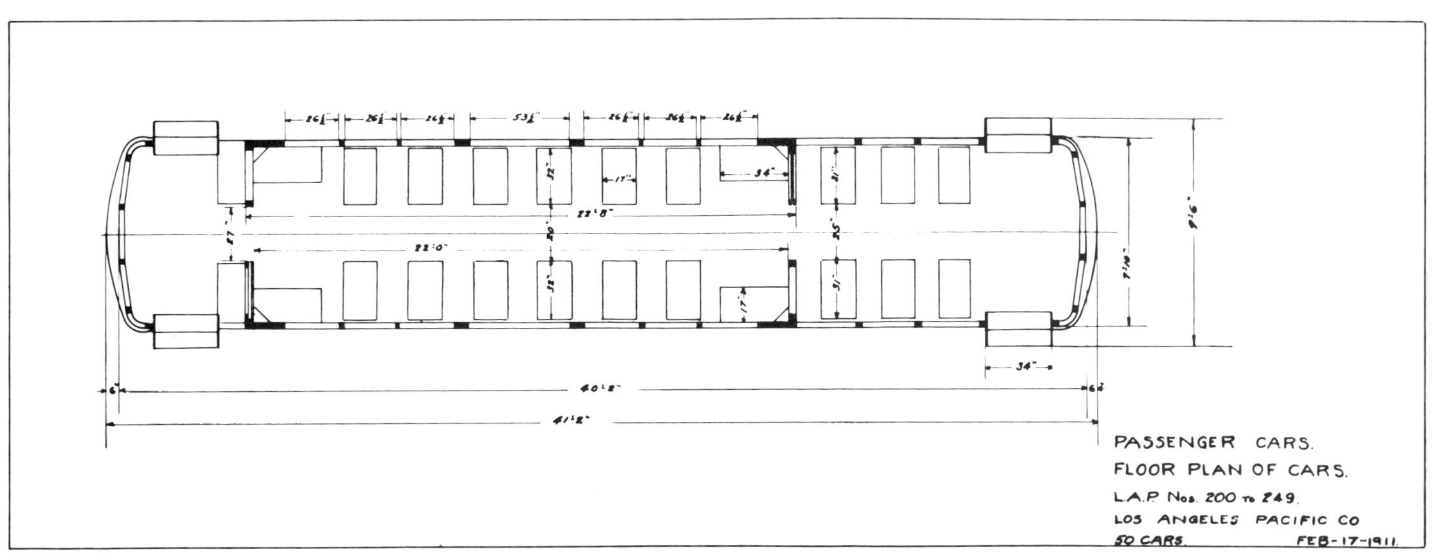

PASSENGER CARS.
FLOOR PLAN OF CARS.
L.A.P. Nos. 200 to 249.
LOS ANGELES PACIFIC CO
50 CARS.   FEB-17-1911.

PARLOR CAR 400 and car 219, Balloon Route Excursion.   *(Charles Smallwood)*

their speed and enabled them to haul trailers more effectively than any LAP type previously used.

PE renumbered them 490-499. The 491-494 were rebuilt into true California cars (twin open ends, center closed section) probably about 1918. The 490-494 scrapped in 1927; 495, 496, 497 and 499 went in 1934, and 498 was retired in 1927.

200-249

These 50 cars were built by the St. Louis Car Company in 1904-05 and were LAP's first by that builder.

The body type continued the trend toward greater size; the 200s were larger and better 190s—or at least were intended to be. But LAP early found that the cars were too weak in the underframe and began a program of rebuilding them with steel I-beams. This program was about 40 per cent complete when PE took over. Cars given 5" I-beam underframes by LAP were: 210-212, 214, 217, 219, 224, 229-234, 239-244 and 246. One car, 219, got 8" I-beam underframe. At the same time, these cars got G.E. 28BF contactor equipment; originally all had Westinghouse K-11 controllers.

Note that as LAP cars the 200s were all two-motor cars. They were simply a nice, comfortable car—not too fast and not what one would expect to find on important lines such as the Venice Short Line.

When PE got these cars, it renumbered them 550-599 and rebuilt them in such a thorough-going way that it was difficult to recognize the old cars. That part of the body above the belt rail was unchanged, but below the belt rail you had practically a new car. All got new steel underframes and width was increased to 8'5" over side sills. All got A-3 swing bolster trucks, 5'10" wheelbase. All got Janney radial couplers and G.E. Type M multiple unit control equipment. Four G.E. 210-F motors of 60 hp replaced the two Westinghouse 89s (57 hp). Weight was increased from 40,400 lbs. to 59,700 lbs. The cars ran until 1939 when they were scrapped.

(While the LAP data sheet reproduced here lists this car type as having St. Louis Car Co. trucks, it is in error. Cars 200-249 used McGuire 35 trucks.)

400

"Ride the luxurious parlor car 400," rhapsodized early Balloon Route barkers, and thousands did just that—getting their first glimpse of the wonders of Southern California from the windows of this odd car.

Its origin is unknown and it met its fiery fate early—but in between it had as spectacular a career as such famous cars as "Alabama" and "Mermaid."

Undoubtedly 400 began life as a steam coach—its every line suggests it. But its rebuilding, ostensibly at Sherman—brought into being a car utterly different from anything which has ever run in the Los Angeles area. 400 was a small car: 39'9" over-all and only 11'3" over top of roof. It had no fixed seats; it was furnished with folding chairs. Its windows were remarkable both for their small size and their large number. Its entries were deeply arched—another indication of its steam coach ancestry. Center end windows were also arched, completely unusual. To top it off, 400 was painted royal blue—suitable for this flagship of the Balloon Route cars.

In February, 1898, newspapers reported that LAP was building a funeral car for use to Rosedale Cemetery. Jesse Green says the 400 was that car; the casket was placed on board through a front window. By December, 1902, the car had been rebuilt into an excursion car for it took a party from Ocean Park to the L.A. Orpheum Theater December 10.

With its roof and "Parlor Car" end signs outlined by scores of electric lights, 400 led the daily Balloon Route Excursions from 1904 till 1909, when it was succeeded by 900 and 901. It then was stored at Sherman in the old car house. PE renumbered it 09 but it never turned a wheel as a PE car. In 1913 it burned in the old car house conflagration.

ANGELUS

Excursion car "Angelus" was apparently rebuilt from a steam road car. No record of the car survives; it had been disposed of by 1911.

700-749

Here we have LAP's largest passenger cars and its only interurbans. Undeniably influenced in design by old PE's 300 Class, the LAP 700s were sufficiently different to give them their own personality.

Built in 1907 and shipped to Los Angeles from St. Louis on their own wheels, the 700s introduced to Southern California the train door, the three-window end (for interurbans) and the short-lived open section with half-enclosed sides. A remarkably well-built car, the 700 type derived much of its sturdiness from a very heavy bottom framing. There were two center sills, each formed of an 8-inch 18-lb. I-beam sandwiched between wood fillers; the side sills were made up of a 7-inch, 15-lb. I-beam placed between a 5"x8" wood sill on the outside and a filler block inside. This wood sill was further reinforced by a ½"x8" steel plate bolted to the outside. The center sills ran the full length of the car.

Although built for double-end operation, the car was of the typical combination open and closed type; the closed end was vestibuled, while on the open end there was no partition between passengers and motorman. In this respect the 700s were similar to the PE 300s, and also followed the five-year-old de-

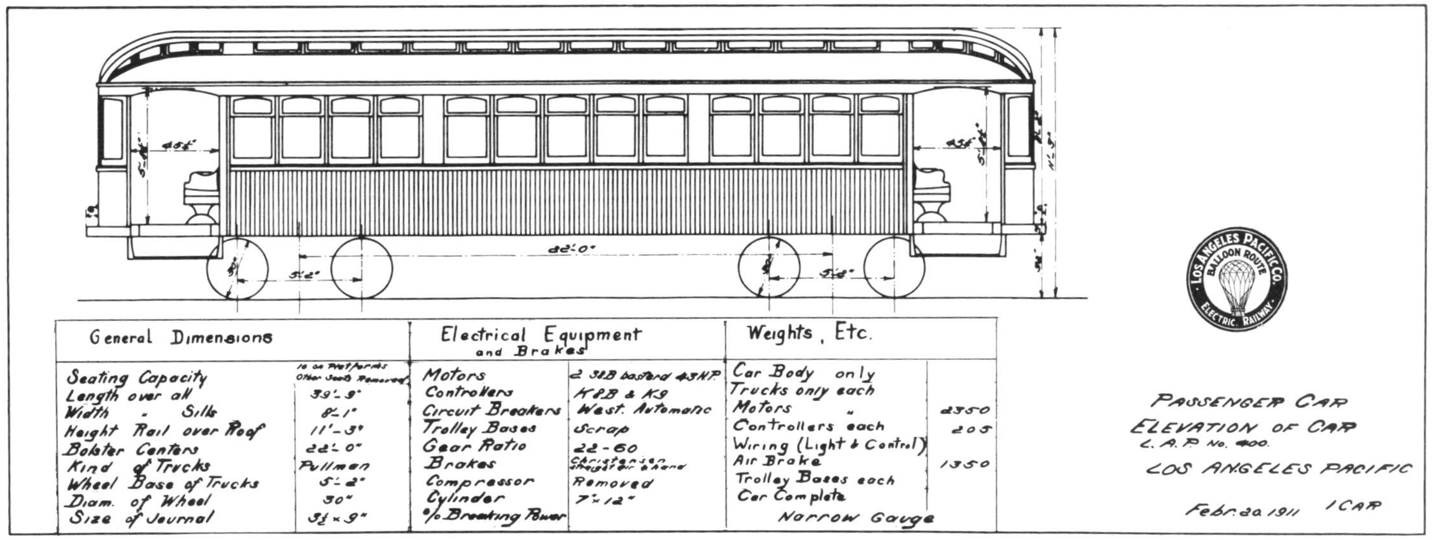

General Dimensions		Electrical Equipment and Brakes		Weights, Etc.	
Seating Capacity	10 on Platforms Other Seats Removed	Motors	2 32B Westg'se 43HP.	Car Body only	
Length over all	39'-9"	Controllers	K2B & K9	Trucks only each	
Width " Sills	8'-1"	Circuit Breakers	West. Automatic	Motors "	2350
Height Rail over Roof	11'-3"	Trolley Bases	Scrap	Controllers each	205
Bolster Centers	22'-0"	Gear Ratio	22-60	Wiring (Light & Control)	
Kind of Trucks	Pullman	Brakes	Christensen straight air & hand	Air Brake	1350
Wheel Base of Trucks	5'-2"	Compressor	Removed	Trolley Bases each	
Diam. of Wheel	30"	Cylinder	7"x12"	Car Complete	
Size of Journal	3¼"x9"	% Breaking Power		Narrow Gauge	

PASSENGER CAR
ELEVATION OF CAR
L.A.P. No. 400.
LOS ANGELES PACIFIC
Febr. 20 1911   1 CAR

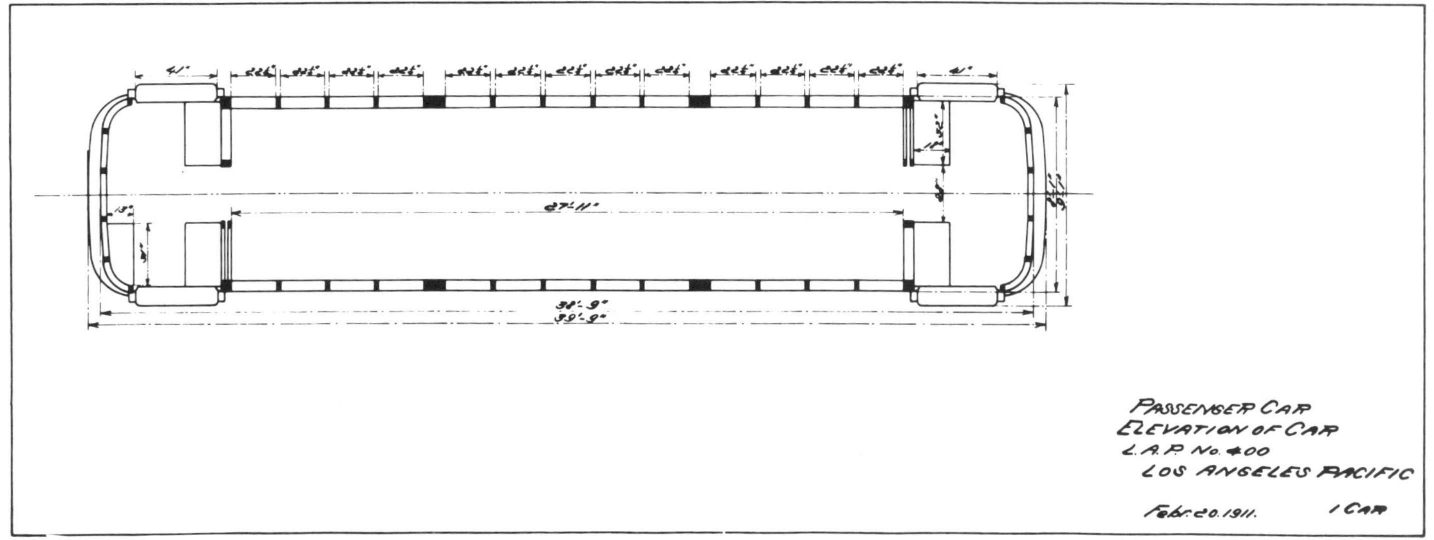

PASSENGER CAR
ELEVATION OF CAR
L.A.P. No. 400
LOS ANGELES PACIFIC
Febr. 20. 1911.   1 CAR

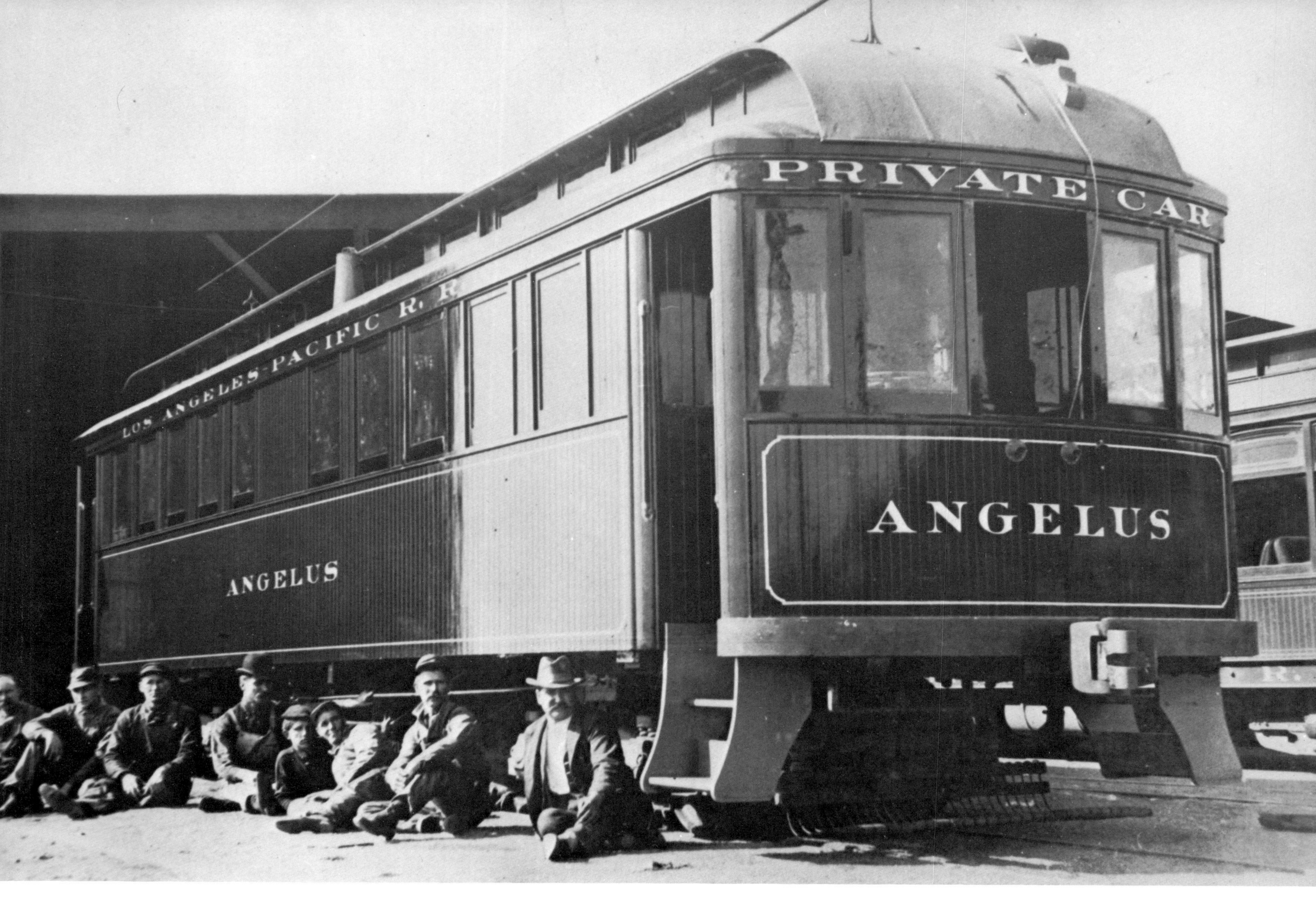

THE PRIVATE CAR "Angelus" at Sherman, c. 1901. Not much is known about this LAP mystery car.

(T.L. Wagenbach)

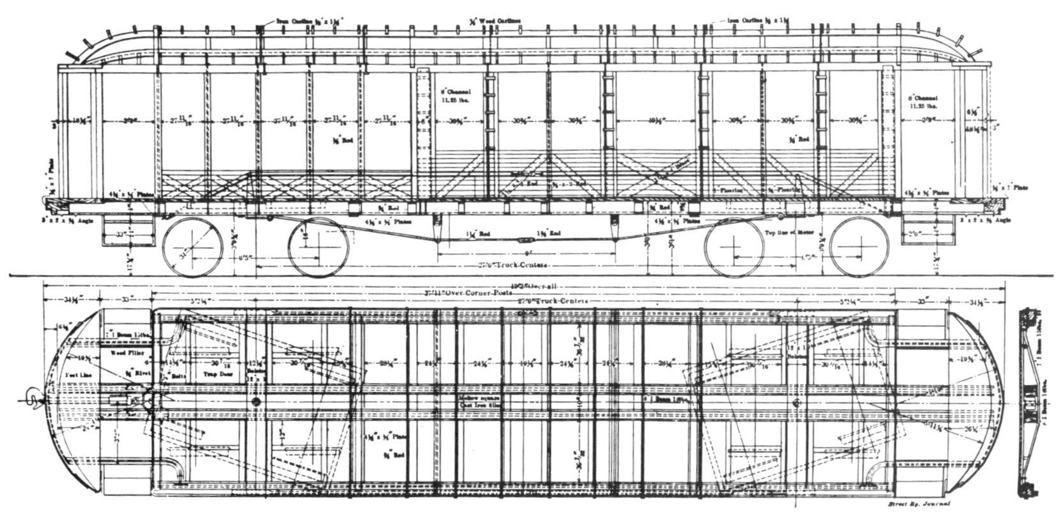

A PAIR OF LAP shopmen take their ease aboard platform of car 742.

(Southern California Edison)

sign of the 300s in having the same number of seats, the same number of windows in both open and closed sections, and wood seats outside, plush seats inside.

Four seats in the closed section were placed longitudinally, one at each corner of the closed section (as shown in plan). Above each of these seats, and placed diagonally across the corner formed by the car side and the partition, was a 10-inch mirror. These four longitudinal seats were somewhat shorter than the cross seats which were 37 inches long.

Adding to the solidarity of these cars was a double floor, made up of an underfloor of 1"x5¼" yellow pine laid diagonally, and an upper one of ¾"x3¼" flooring. The roof sheathing was also double, with felt paper between the two layers.

The interior was finished in inlaid mahogany and was noticeably free from metal fixtures. No registers were employed, and as a result no register brackets and rods were installed; no ventilator fittings were visible either. What metal trimmings there were had nickel plating.

Mechanically the 700s were not up to their excellent bodies. The St. Louis 61-A truck was used—a built-up truck which required reinforcement in later years. This truck was fitted with GE 73 motors which had a rating of 75 hp each, insufficient to give these 75,000-lb. cars sparkling performance. The wheels were spoked, of ¾" diameter, including their steel tires. The gear ratio was 21:54, giving the cars a balancing speed of approximately 48 mph.

SIDE ELEVATION AND PLAN OF LOS ANGELES COMBINATION CAR

These were LAP's first cars equipped for train operation. The GE Type M controller was used, along with Washburn radial couplers slotted to take a link. Jumper receptacles were located low on the dash, one on either side of the train door; later these were relocated higher on the dash.

The 700s were LAP's first and only cars built new for operation on standard gauge trackage. They arrived as the company was engaged in spreading its rails from 3'6" to 4'8½" and were delivered via the Air Line to the 26th St. brick yard spur in Santa Monica where their electrical equipment was installed. As soon as they were ready to operate, they were moved under their own power up Santa Monica Boulevard to Sherman Car Barn, the standard-gauging of said trackage having preceded them by but a few weeks.

All 50 entered service March 31, 1908 on the Venice Short Line and Santa Monica via Beverly Hills Line, running out of the city on West 16th Street. They remained on these lines until the Great Merger.

At the time the 700s were conceived, the Vineyard Subway was regarded as inevitable; the cars were therefore designed for steady running rather than for agility in traffic, which (so it was thought) they would never have to endure. Rather the opposite turned out to be true; the subway idea was permanently shelved and the 700s were sentenced to years of constantly increasing automobile traffic on relatively narrow streets.

LAP (SP) was so pleased with the 700 Class that a second order for 50 identical cars was in the works; the 1907 business panic resulted in the cancellation of this order. Of the second 50, half were to have been motors and half trailers.

Immediately after the Great Merger, PE placed the 700s on its Northern District; they ran to Pasadena, Sierra Madre and elsewhere (even while in LAP's green paint). The six special service cars (01, 021-025) were used anywhere on the 600-volt lines, but mostly the excursion cars remained on the Western District (Balloon Route); 01 was rebuilt into a passenger car and renumbered 999 in 1925. The 021-025 entered passenger service in 1927 with the numbers 994-998. The 700s were returned to the Western District in 1924, where they remained until scrapped.

SCRAPPING DATA

1940: 951, 953, 956, 961, 963, 964, 967, 968, 970, 974, 977, 978, 980, 987, 991, 992, 996, 997, 998.

1950: 950, 952, 954, 955, 957, 958, 959, 960, 962, 965, 966, 969, 971, 972, 973, 975, 976, 979, 981, 982, 983, 984, 985, 986, 988, 989, 990, 993, 994, 995, 999.

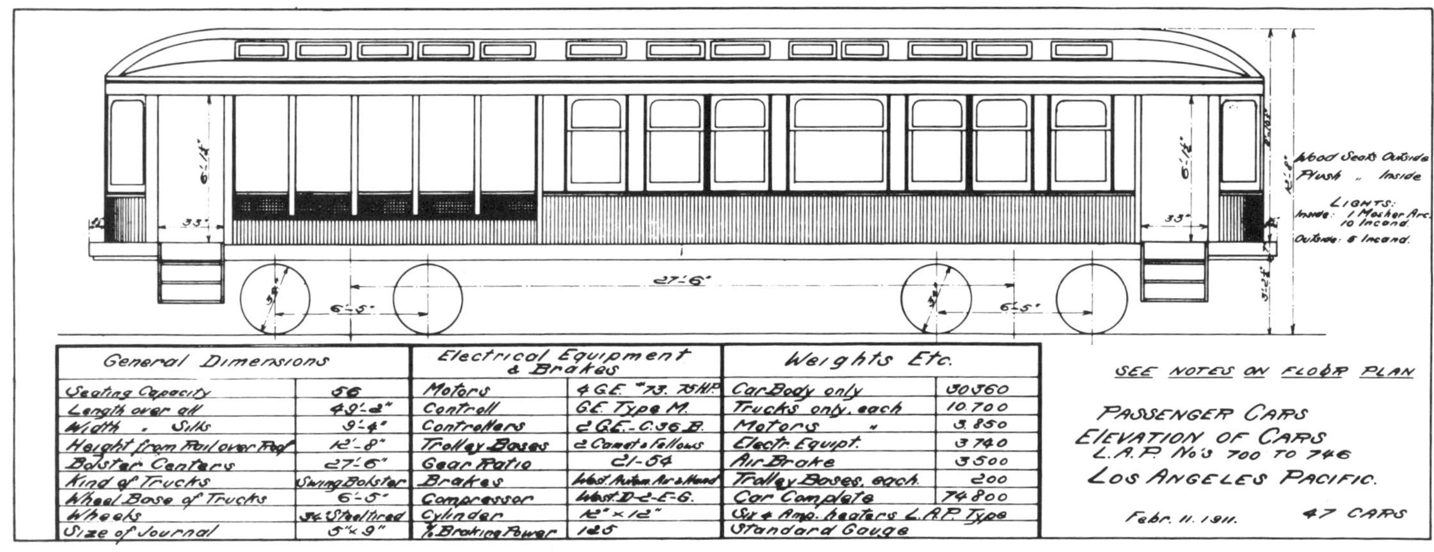

General Dimensions		Electrical Equipment & Brakes		Weights Etc.	
Seating Capacity	56	Motors	4 G.E. "73. 75HP.	Car Body only	30360
Length over all	49'-2"	Controll	G.E. Type M.	Trucks only. each	10.700
Width . Sills	9'-4"	Controllers	2 G.E.-C.36 B.	Motors "	3.850
Height from Rail over Roof	12'-8"	Trolley Bases	2 Canet & Fellows	Electr. Equipt.	3740
Bolster Centers	27'-6"	Gear Ratio	21-54	Air Brake	3500
Kind of Trucks	Swing Bolster	Brakes	West. Autom. Air & Hand	Trolley Bases. each.	200
Wheel Base of Trucks	6'-5"	Compressor	West. D-2-E-G.	Car Complete	74800
Wheels	34" Steel tired	Cylinder	12" × 12"	Six + Amp. heaters L.A.P. Type	
Size of Journal	5" × 9"	% Braking Power	125	Standard Gauge	

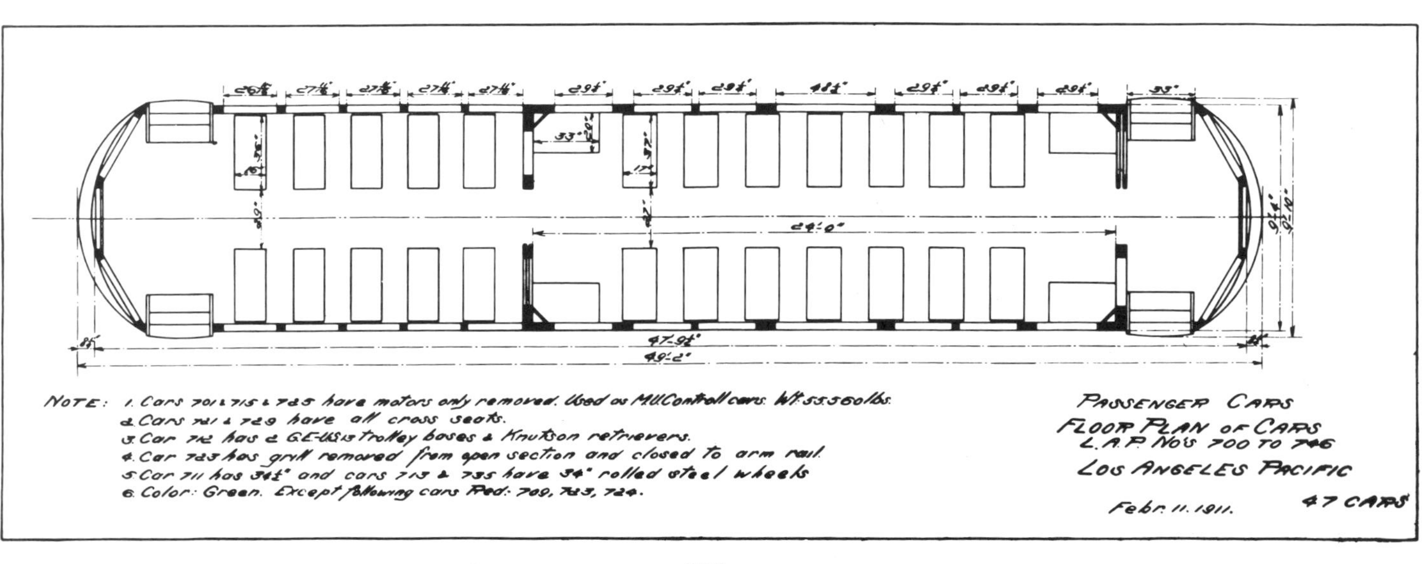

GENERAL SPECIFICATIONS, CARS 700-749

General Dimensions:

Seating Capacity:	56
Length over-all:	49'2
Width over sills:	9'4"
Height over roof:	12'8"
Bolster Centers:	27'6"
Kind of Trucks:	Swing Bolster
Truck Wheelbase:	6'5"
Wheels:	34" steel tired
Journals:	5" by 9"

Equipment:

Motors:	4 GE 73 (75 hp)
Control:	GE Type M
Controllers:	GE C36B
Trolley Bases:	2 Camet & Fellows
Gear Ratio:	21:54
Brakes:	West. Auto. Air, hand
Compressor:	West. D2-EG
Cylinder:	12" by 12"
% Braking Power:	125

Weights:

Car Body:	30,360 lbs.
Trucks, each:	10,700
Motors, each:	3,850
Electrical Eqpt.:	3,740
Air Brake:	3,500
Trolley Base:	200
Car Complete:	74,800

Miscellaneous:

Headlight:	One Mosher Arc
Lights:	10 Incandescent inside, 5 Incandescent outside

The following notes applied as of February 11, 1911:

1. Cars 701, 715 and 725 had motors removed and were used as control trailers; the weight was thus reduced to 55,560 lbs.

2. Cars 721 and 729 had all cross seats.

3. Car 712 had two GE-U.S.-13 trolley bases and Knutson retrievers.

4. Car 723 had grill removed from open section and was closed to arm rail.

5. Car 711 had 34½" and cars 713 and 735 had 34" rolled steel wheels.

6. Color: green, except following cars red: 709, 723, 724.

RENUMBERING DATA

(First column, LAP; second column, PE 1911 number; third column, PE 1924 number)

700-023-996	713-713-963	726-726-976	738-738-988
701-744-950	714-714-964	727-727-977	739-739-989
702-024-997	715-745-952	728-728-978	740-740-990
703-025-998	716-716-966	729-729-979	741-741-991
704-704-954	717-717-967	730-730-980	742-742-992
705-705-955	718-718-968	731-731-981	743-743-993
706-706-956	719-719-969	732-732-982	744-701-951
707-707-957	720-720-970	733-733-983	745-715-965
708-708-958	721-721-971	734-734-984	746-725-975
709-709-959	722-722-972	735-735-985	747- 01-999
710-710-960	723-723-973	736-736-986	748-021-994
711-711-961	724-724-974	737-737-987	749-022-995
712-712-962	725-746-953		

Note that the 700s were renumbered in 1911 in numerical order except for the three trailers and the three special service cars. The trailers became 744, 745 and 746 and were later re-motorized by PE. 747 was rebuilt into "El Viento" (903) in 1909. 748 and 749 were rebuilt in 1909 into excursion cars 900 and 901. PE rebuilt 700, 702 and 703 in 1911-12.

900-901

In 1909, Sherman Shops rebuilt cars 748 and 749 into deluxe observation cars for use as base equipment on the Balloon Route Trolley Trip.

Principal modification was enclosing the open section. This entailed closing in the open grill work to the belt rail and putting in windows. The work was done tastefully and with care; for instance, instead of installing all single width windows, Sherman Shops did it the hard way: a post was removed to permit a double width window, balancing the double width window already existing in the closed section. High back green plush seats similar to those in the closed section were installed in the former open section. Completing the transformation, the cars were renumbered 900 and 901 respectively and given an ornate paint job, inside and out. One of the few times Los Angeles interurban cars had painted-on destination signs occurred when "Balloon Route" was painted beneath each end window.

As Pacific Electric cars, 900 and 901 were renumbered in 1911 to 021 and 022; in 1927 they lost their deluxe status and became passenger coaches 994 and 995. They were retired in 1950.

902

902 was rebuilt in 1908 from the old excursion car "Hermosa," which was rebuilt from car 92 in 1905. "Hermosa's" first rebuilding was a thorough-going one for the body dimensions no longer resembled 92's. "Hermosa" had three six-foot windows, alternated with 34" windows. It was a single compartment car, entirely enclosed. Wicker furniture and elaborate silk drapes at windows made the old "Hermosa" quite luxurious. It used arc lights inside, which gave off a brilliant light but proved difficult to maintain.

The 1908 rebuild resulted in car 902, pictured here. The body was unchanged, but leather seats replaced the wicker furniture and the car got new trucks and two additional motors. The A-3 swing bolster 5'10" trucks replaced the old McGuires, while four 38-A motors of 43 hp each boosted the car's speed somewhat. 902 always was a single-unit car, having K-6 controllers.

PE renumbered her 020 in 1911 and used her on various trolley trips. In 1925 the car became a passenger-baggage combo, 1303, which was scrapped in 1933.

903

Car 903 was "El Viento"—The Wind—and it was the finest car ever to roll on the LAP. "El Viento" was rebuilt in 1909 from passenger motor 747. Sherman Shops did perhaps its finest rebuild job here; its expert cabinetmakers worked and reworked the car's beautiful mahogany woods until there resulted a veritable jewel box on wheels.

As can be seen from the plans, 903 was quite changed, inside and out. Outside, new vestibules were constructed incorporating the typical five-window front with curved glass in

CARS 900, 901 in front of Playa del Rey Pavilion, 1910.   (Interurbans)

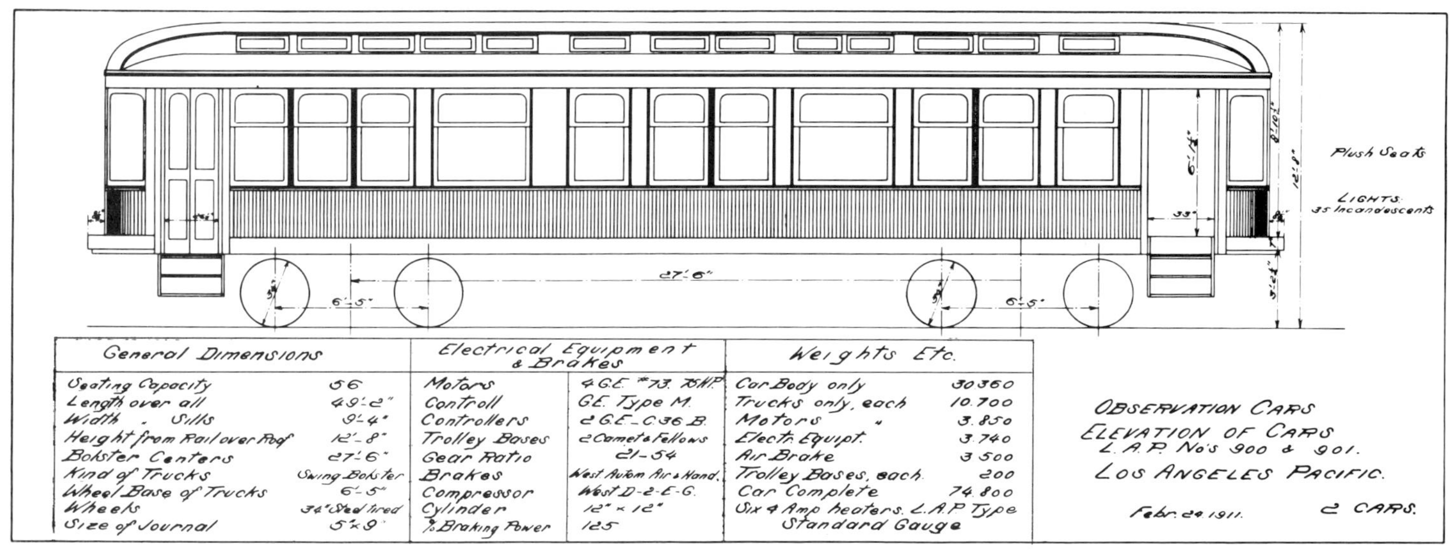

General Dimensions		Electrical Equipment & Brakes		Weights Etc.	
Seating Capacity	56	Motors	4 G.E. #73. 75 H.P.	Car Body only	30.360
Length over all	49'-2"	Controll	G.E. Type M.	Trucks only, each	10.700
Width . Sills	9'-4"	Controllers	2 G.E.-C.36 B.	Motors "	3.850
Height from Rail over Roof	12'-8"	Trolley Bases	2 Comet & Fellows	Electr. Equipt.	3.740
Bolster Centers	27'-6"	Gear Ratio	21-54	Air Brake	3.500
Kind of Trucks	Swing Bolster	Brakes	West. Autom Air & Hand.	Trolley Bases, each	200
Wheel Base of Trucks	6'-5"	Compressor	West D-2-E-G.	Car Complete	74.800
Wheels	34" Steel tired	Cylinder	12" x 12"	Six 4 Amp heaters. L.A.P Type	
Size of Journal	5" x 9"	% Braking Power	125	Standard Gauge	

OBSERVATION CARS
ELEVATION OF CARS
L.A.P. No's 900 & 901.
LOS ANGELES PACIFIC.

Febr. 24. 1911.   2 CARS.

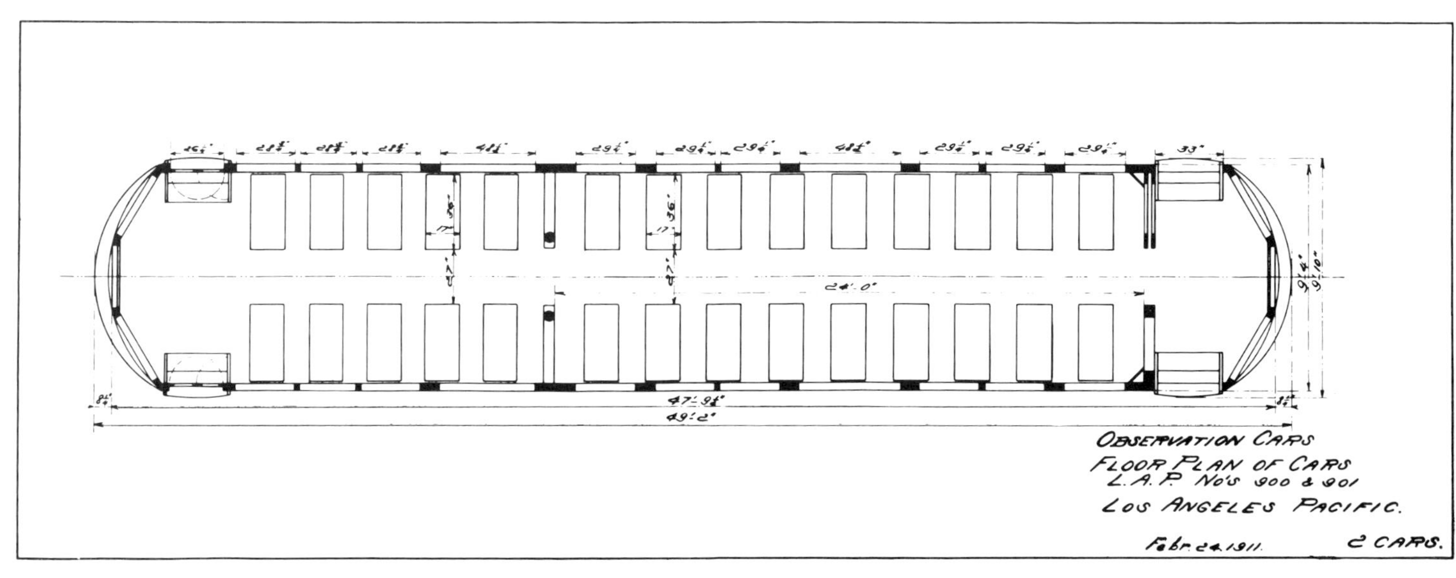

OBSERVATION CARS
FLOOR PLAN OF CARS
L.A.P. No's 900 & 901
LOS ANGELES PACIFIC.

Febr. 24. 1911.   2 CARS.

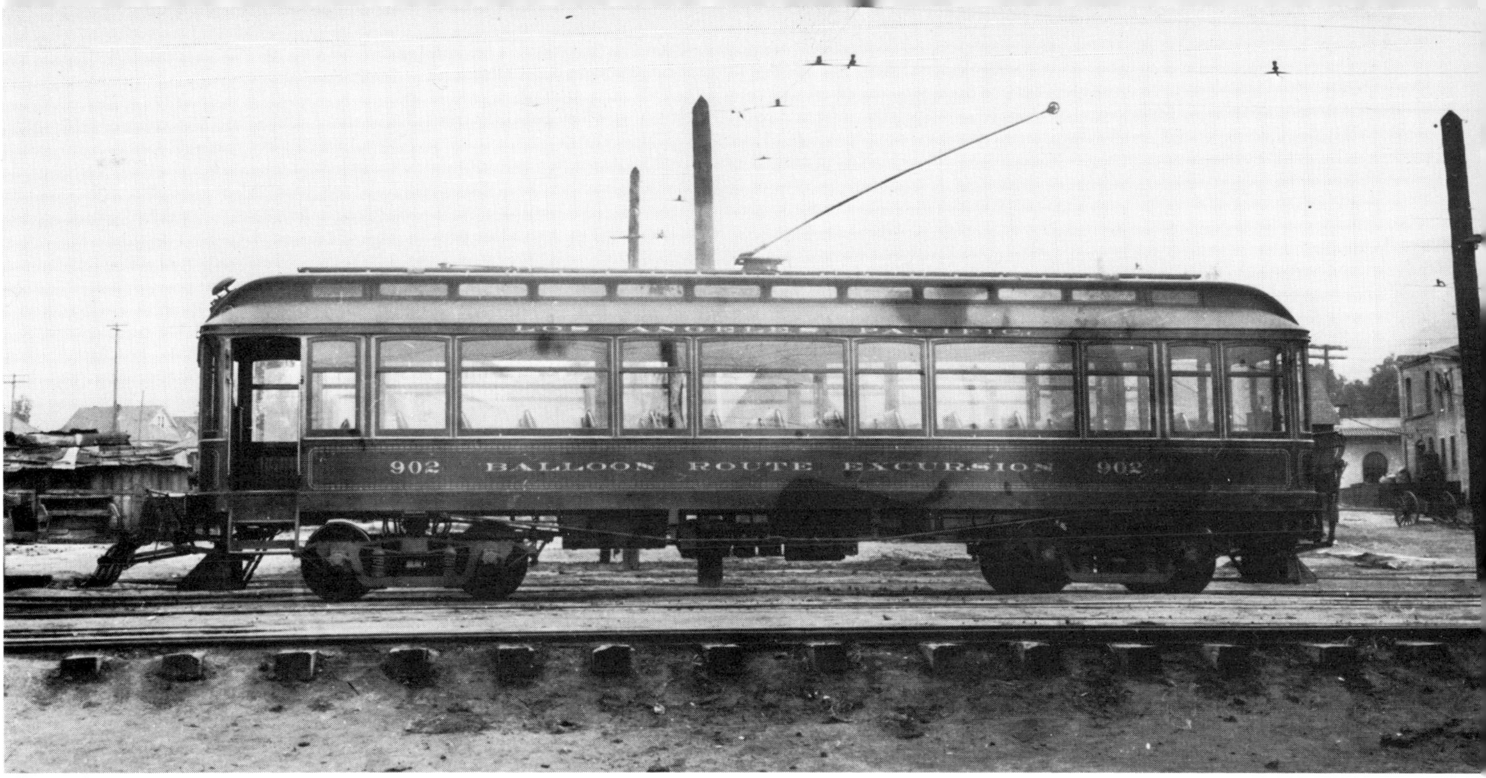

BALLOON ROUTE Excursion car 902, the ex-"Hermosa." *(Interurbans)*

General Dimensions		Electrical Equipment & Brakes		Weights	
Seating Capacity.	56	Motors.	4-38A West. 43hp.	Car Body only	
Length Over all.	46'0	Controllers.	2-K-6	Trucks-each.	8100
Width over Sills.	8'2"	Circuit Breakers.	West Auto	Motors "	2350
Height Rail over Roof.	12'0"	Trolley Base	2-C&F.	Controllers "	
Bolster Centers.	28'0"	Gear Ratio	26:60	Wiring (Light & Control)	
Kind of Trucks.	Class A3	Brakes.	WS2 & hand.	Air Brake.	1350
Wheel Base of Trucks.	5'10"	Compressor.	D-1-E.G.	Trolley Base. each.	200
Size Wheels.	33" D.P.	Cylinder.		Car Complete.	54200
Size Journals.	4"x8"	% Braking Power.			Std. Gauge.

Leather Seats & 4 Wood.
Rebuilt from Car "Hermosa"

OBSERVATION CAR #902.
ELEVATION OF CAR
LOS ANGELES PACIFIC CO.
1 CAR. FEB-24-1911.

OBSERVATION CAR #902.
FLOOR PLAN OF CARS.
LOS ANGELES PACIFIC CO.
1 CAR FEB-24-1911

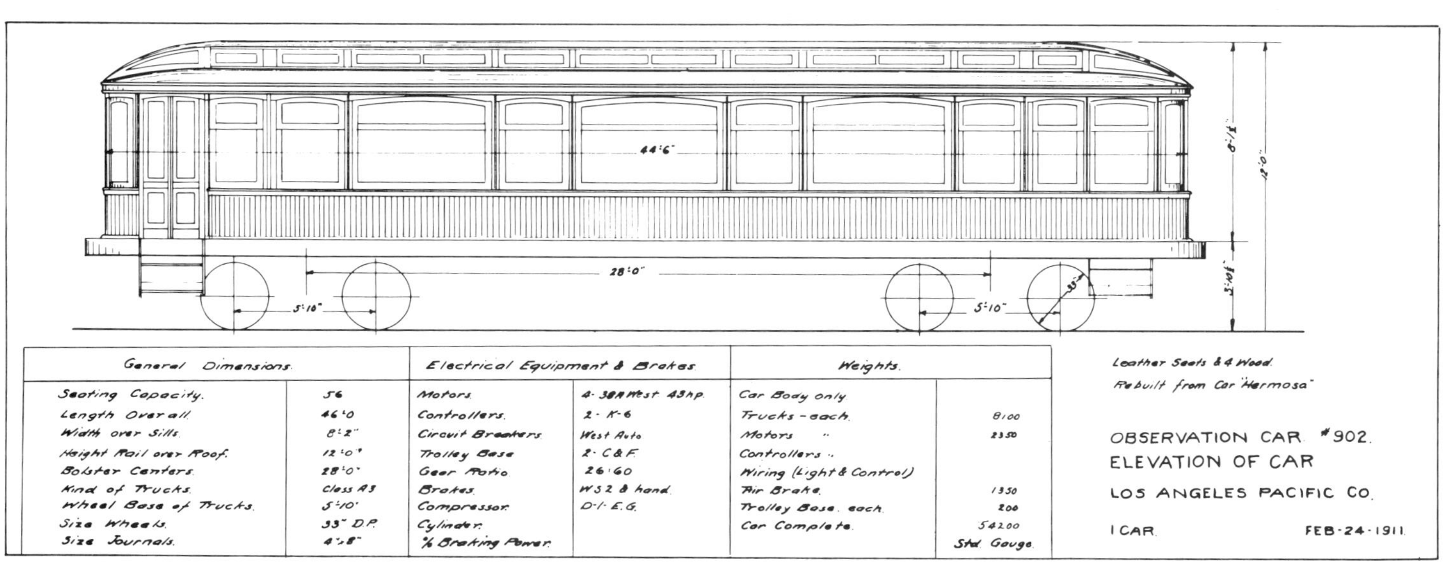

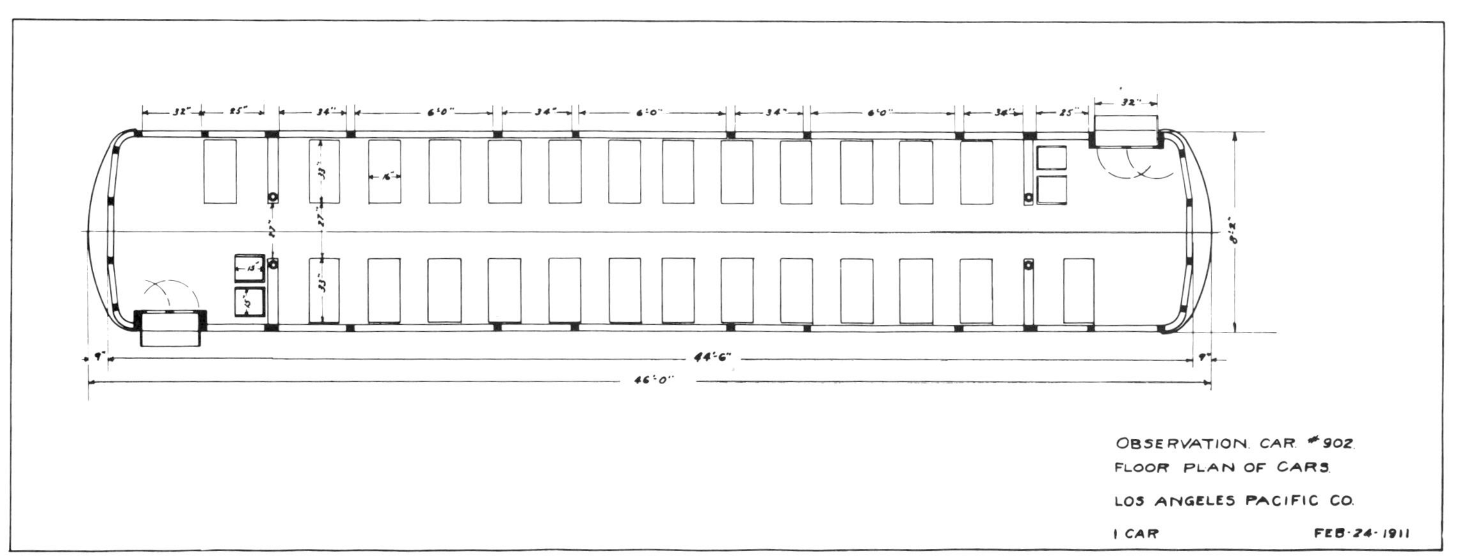

CAR 903—El Viento—ex 747, at Sherman.   *(Interurbans)*

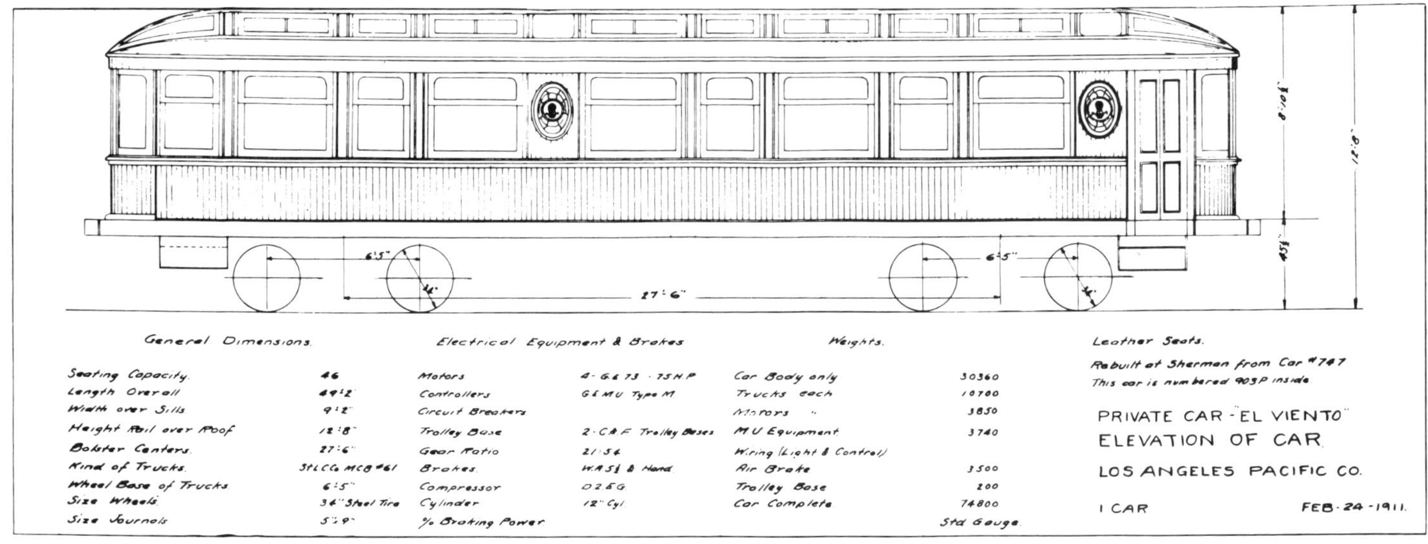

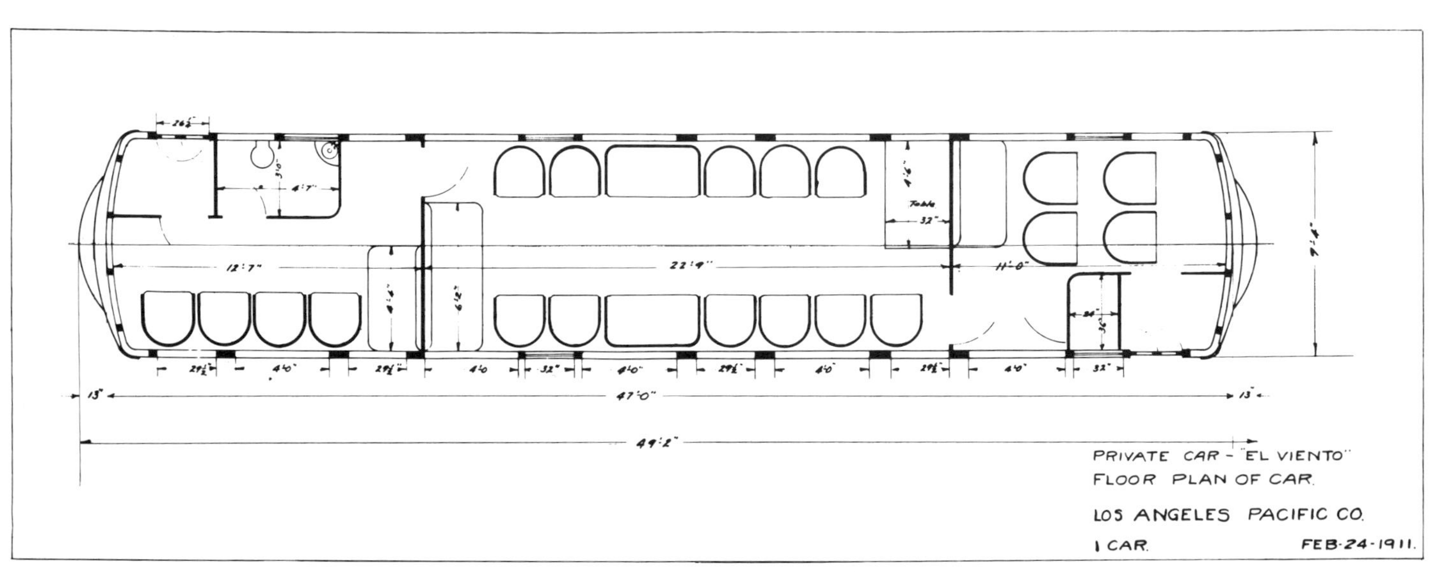

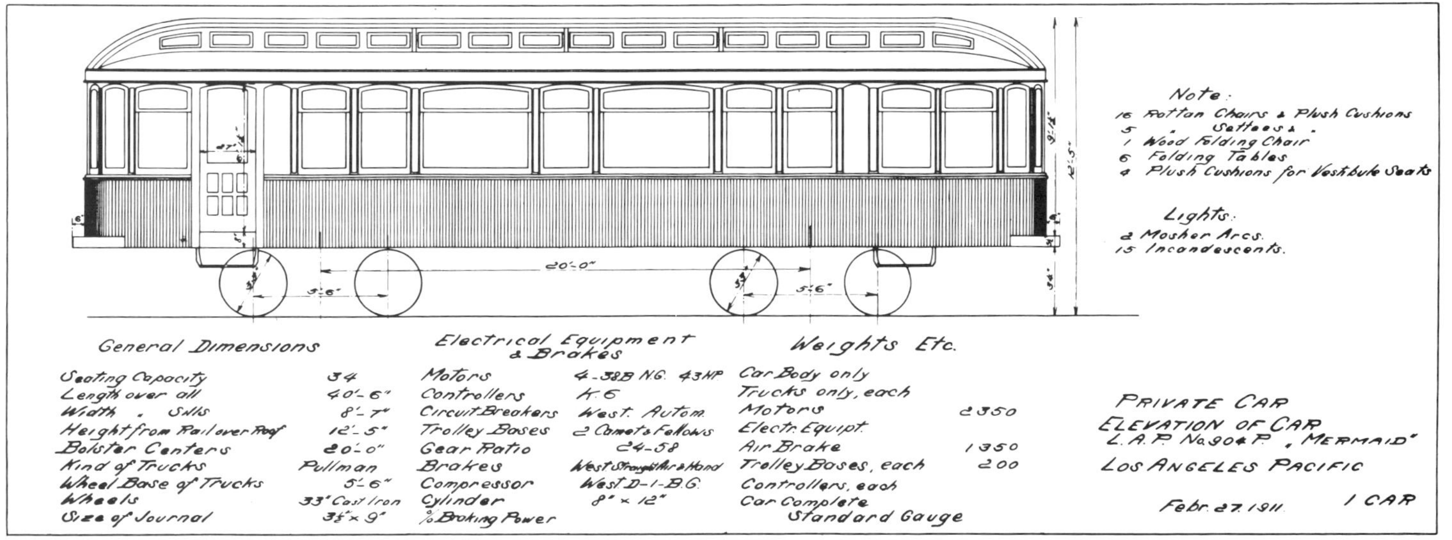

GENERAL SHERMAN's private car "Mermaid" just after the 1911 Merger.

(Interurbans)

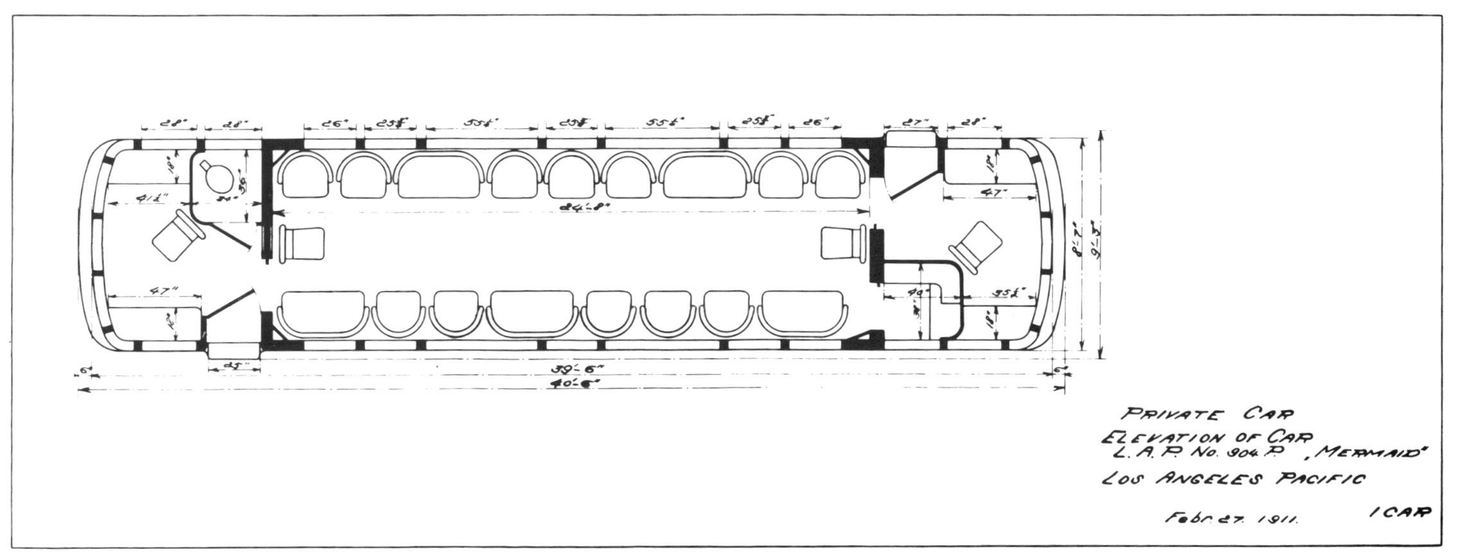

corner windows; this required certain changes in the buffers. The entire window arrangement was altered and a door at each end was closed. Even the ornamental oval windows were unusual: the LAP balloon emblem was reproduced in frosted glass. Wood signs proclaimed it to be a private car and a blue paint job further set "El Viento" apart.

The interior was fitted up with large leather chairs and divans; a toilet was installed at the #2 end; tables and built-in sofas completed the deluxe job. LAP's officers indeed traveled in style.

PE rebuilt the 903 into its 01. The end windows were cut lower, partitions created an office and separated vestibules from the car proper. 01 ran as an officers' car until 1925, when it was turned back to passenger service as car 999. 999 ran with the other 950s until 1950 when it was scrapped.

904

Gen. Sherman's private car sported the name "Mermaid," although no one can recall the General's explaining why this particular name was chosen. At any rate, the General ordered this car in 1900 and Sherman Shops turned it out—a rebuild of an older car, which one the records do not disclose. The "Mermaid" entered service in 1901 and ran far and wide; even PE narrow gauge rails felt the car's passing for there is mention of the General's taking the ball team from Belmont, San Francisco, to Mt. Lowe in this car back in October, 1902. Probably

the "Mermaid" had something to do with PE President Huntington's decision to build "Alabama."

Perhaps "Mermaid's" most glorious day was May 9, 1901, when it transported U.S. President McKinley to the Soldiers' Home.

In 1909 "Mermaid" became LAP 904 and two years later was renumbered PE 010.

PE immediately rebuilt 010 into an even more luxurious private car and it is reputed to have carried President Taft in 1911. 010 served out its years as a combo, renumbered 1302. Retired, 1937.

LINE CARS

LAP's line cars were a motley lot. None was built new for this important work; they were all makeshift adaptations of older, unimportant cars.

Tower Car 1 was originally a steam railroad combine acquired from a predecessor company. Sherman Shops rebuilt the car at an unknown date. It got rather a complete treatment; the windows were covered with tongue and groove siding, the old baggage door was covered, new windows were cut in one end, and a center tower operated by hand was cut into the roof with platforms extending nearly the full length of the roof on either side of the tower. Electrical equipment for this car was obtained from various cars; it had two 38-B motors, one K8 and one K11 controller; gear ratio was 14:68 and 33"

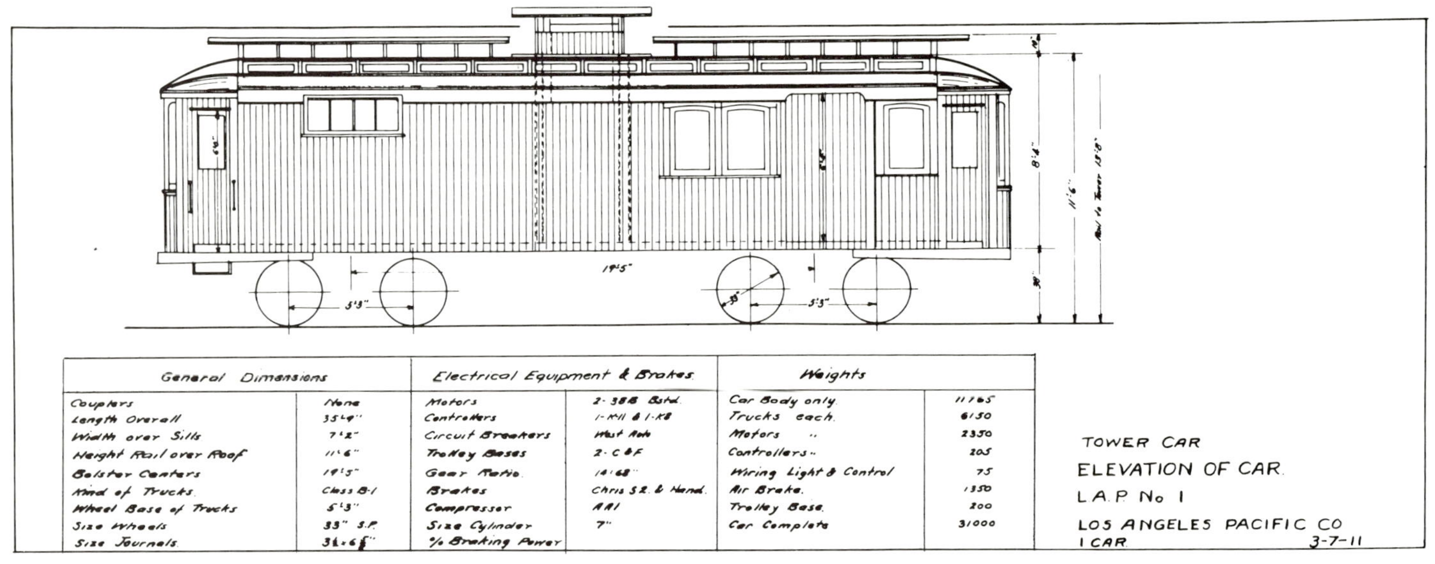

General Dimensions		Electrical Equipment & Brakes		Weights	
Couplers	None	Motors	2-38B Bstd.	Car Body only.	11165
Length Overall	35'4"	Controllers	1-K11 & 1-K8	Trucks each.	6150
Width over Sills	7'2"	Circuit Breakers	West Auto	Motors "	2350
Height Rail over Roof	11'6"	Trolley Bases	2-C&F	Controllers "	205
Bolster Centers	19'5"	Gear Ratio	14:68	Wiring Light & Control	75
Kind of Trucks.	Class B-1	Brakes	Chris S2. & Hand.	Air Brake.	1350
Wheel Base of Trucks	5'3"	Compressor	AA1	Trolley Base.	200
Size Wheels	33" S.P.	Size Cylinder	7"	Car Complete	31000
Size Journals.	3½×6⅝"	% Braking Power			

TOWER CAR
ELEVATION OF CAR.
L.A.P No 1
LOS ANGELES PACIFIC CO
1 CAR   3-7-11

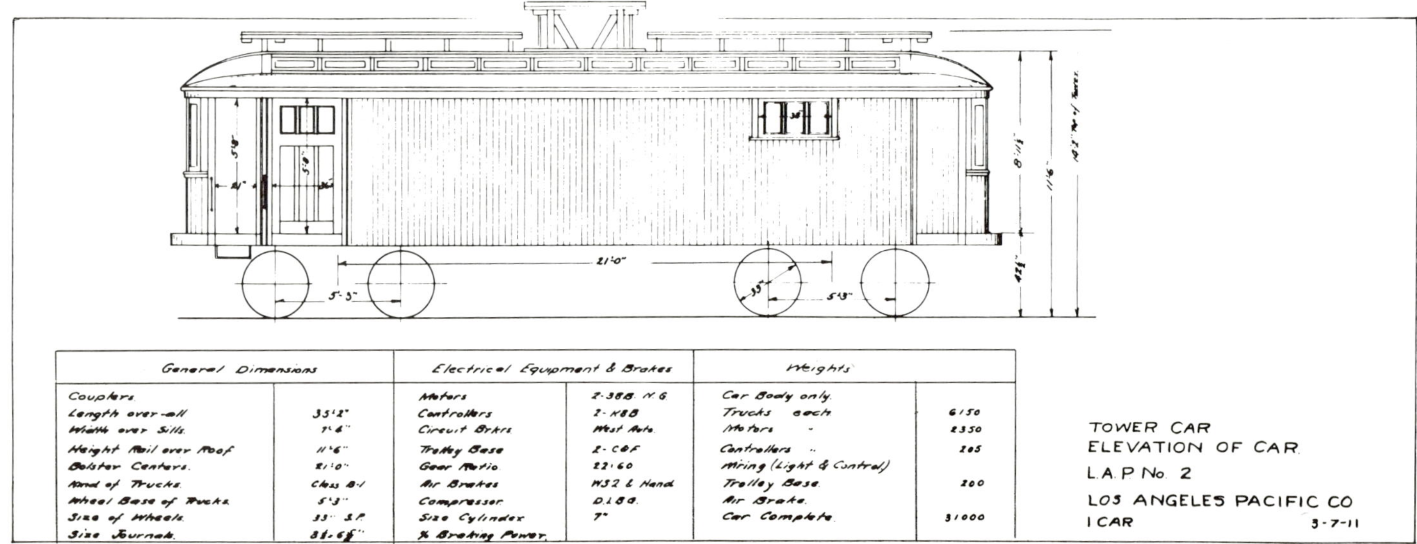

General Dimensions		Electrical Equipment & Brakes		Weights	
Couplers.		Motors	2-38B. N.G.	Car Body only.	
Length over-all	35'2"	Controllers	2-K8B	Trucks each.	6150
Width over Sills.	7'6"	Circuit Brkrs.	West Auto.	Motors -	2350
Height Rail over Roof	11'6"	Trolley Base	2-C&F	Controllers "	205
Bolster Centers.	21'0"	Gear Ratio.	22:60	Wiring (Light & Control)	
Kind of Trucks.	Class B-1	Air Brakes	WS2 & Hand	Trolley Base.	200
Wheel Base of Trucks.	5'3"	Compressor.	D.L.B0.	Air Brake.	
Size of Wheels.	33" S.P.	Size Cylinder	7"	Car Complete.	31000
Size Journals.	3½×6⅝"	% Braking Power.			

TOWER CAR
ELEVATION OF CAR.
L.A.P No. 2
LOS ANGELES PACIFIC CO
1 CAR   3-7-11

LINE CAR 1 (Above) and Tower Car 3. The 1-spot's steam road parentage is evident in the railroad roof. Car 3, undoubtedly LAP's homeliest piece of rolling stock (note it has one McGuire motor truck and one wood-beam arch bar freight car truck) survives in 1976!
(Top: Southern California Edison; bottom: Interurbans)

wheels were used in the rigid bolster trucks of the usual 5'3" wheelbase. Total weight of this car was 31,000 lbs. PE renumbered it 1728 and scrapped it in 1920.

Tower Car 2 was a steam baggage car originally and its modification at Sherman Shops was not nearly as big a job as was 1's. It, too, got a center tower, operated by hand; it also got the full-length platform on the roof. It bears a certain resemblance, insofar as body is concerned, to LAP cars 12 and 1551. There is doubt that this car ever got standard gauge trucks for oldtimers recall it virtually abandoned even before the Merger. It had two K8B controllers, B-1 rigid bolster trucks with 5'3" wheelbase, two 38B narrow gauge motors, and a 22:60 gear ratio. It weighed 31,000 lbs. ready to roll. PE renumbered it 1729 and scrapped it a year after the Merger, 1912.

3

Probably the car voted least likely to succeed on PE after the Merger would have been this sorry looking tower car. With its decrepit appearance heightened by a notably mismated pair of trucks, car 3 would have been understandably chosen to lead the long line of LAP veteran cars to PE's scrap track. However, this car was actually the last one of the hundreds of LAP cars to roll!

LAP 3 was built in 1899 at the Sherman Shops for service as a work motor. It was converted into a tower car at an undetermined date, possibly as early as 1902 when the LAP's newer work motors relieved it of its first duties. The rebuilding at that time was minor in nature; a hand operated tower was built on one end, and miscellaneous bins were added to storing line material.

Car 3 had a McGuire motor truck and a freight truck, the only car to have this unique combination insofar as LAP photos tell us. Later the car received two Peckham trucks, probably from one of the 90 class motor cars.

PE renumbered it 1710 in 1911 and 00150 in 1931. In 1953, it became MCL 00153, with the sale of PE's passenger business to Metropolitan Coach Lines. Even the demise of MCL's rail network as the Freeway Era took over failed to put an end to ex-No. 3's improbable career; in 1958 it was sold to the Orange Empire Trolley Museum for preservation; it can still be seen at work today at the OET museum near Perris, Calif., as a trolley greaser.

4

Line car 4 was rebuilt from single truck motor 47. This car disappeared early enough to leave no trace in the company's records by the 1911 Great Merger.

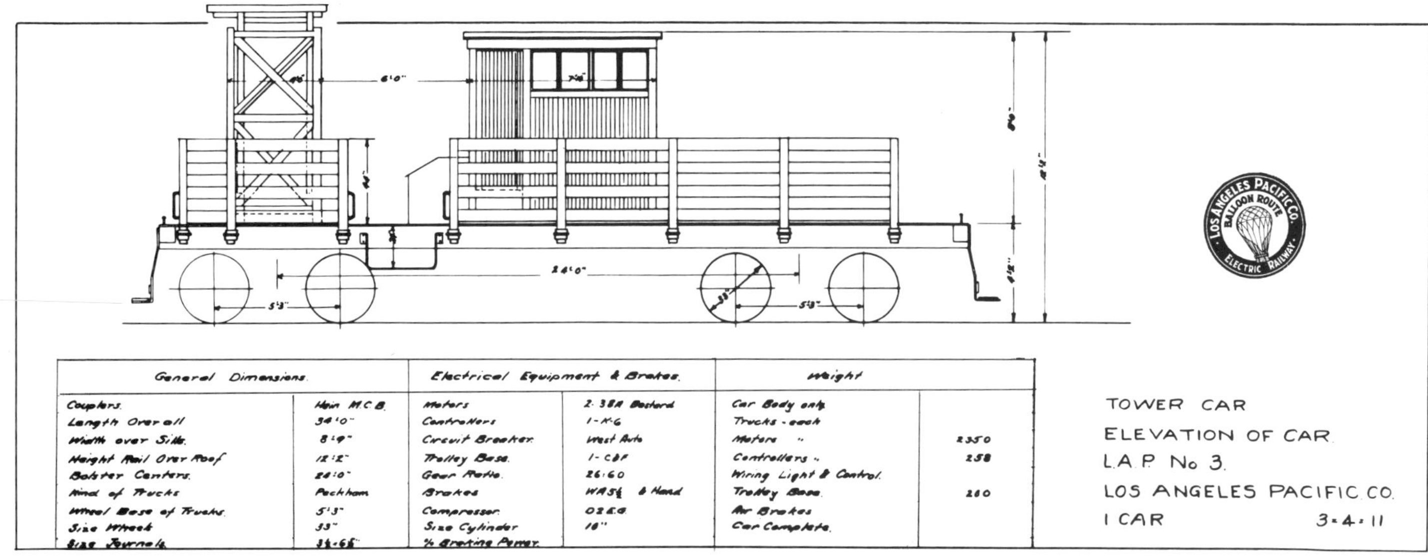

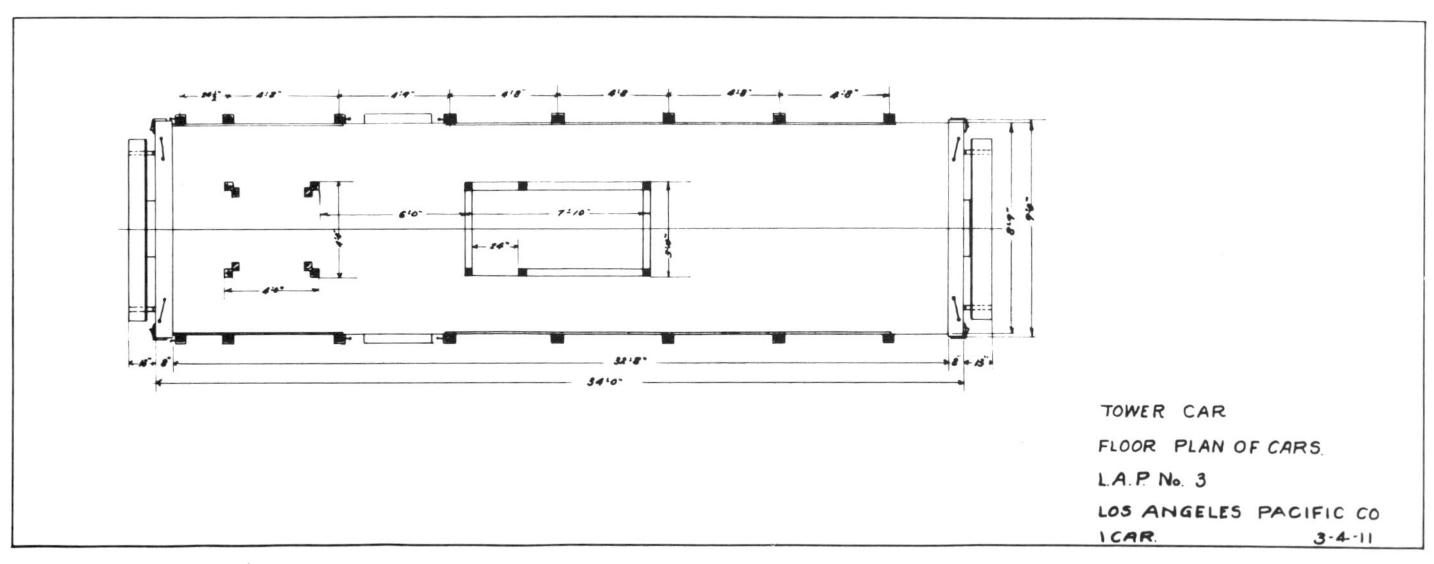

5

LAP 5 was the company's largest tower car, built at Sherman Shops in 1899. It closely resembled the work motors of the 1575 Class and may have been put in service as a work motor before being rebuilt.

Tower car 5 was kept busy; it was the LAP's number one tower car and did most of the work keeping overhead taut and serviceable.

Whether or not the 5 was ever in service as a work motor, it certainly could not have hauled much of a train in its later conversion; it had two 38B motors (50 hp) and an AA1 compressor. It used the rigid bolster B-1 type of truck, with the customary 5'3" wheelbase and 30" wheels. Gear ratio was 22:60, and one K2 controller served.

PE renumbered this car 1711 in 1911 and 00151 in 1931. It was scrapped in 1934.

11

Yard Motor 11 was built by LAP's Sherman Shops in 1902. It is definite (authority: Jesse B. Green) that the trucks, motors, controls and underframe of the 40 Class Cholo car wrecked in October, 1901, in a collision near Sherman were used in its construction.

The purpose of this car was, of course, to shift passenger cars undergoing repairs at the Shops; it also switched single freight cars as necessary.

PE records list its total weight at 16,000 lbs. As PE 1511, this car was in service until scrapped in 1923.

12

In common with a large number of electric railways, LAP used a vacuum cleaner car to facilitate the cleaning of cars.

This car, LAP 12, was built at Sherman Shops in 1898, using an old steam baggage car body and freight trucks.

The vacuum cleaner proper was mounted in approximately the center of the car. The cleaner was built by the Sanitary Devices Manufacturing Company of San Francisco and was driven by a 7-hp Westinghouse motor. The single trolley pole supplied current only to the cleaner, the car itself being a trailer.

In operation, the car was run along a track paralleling a string of passenger cars. The hose and nozzle were pulled through a window of the passenger car, and in no time it was clean.

LAP 12 became PE 1801 and was scrapped in 1930. On PE it weighed 35,000.

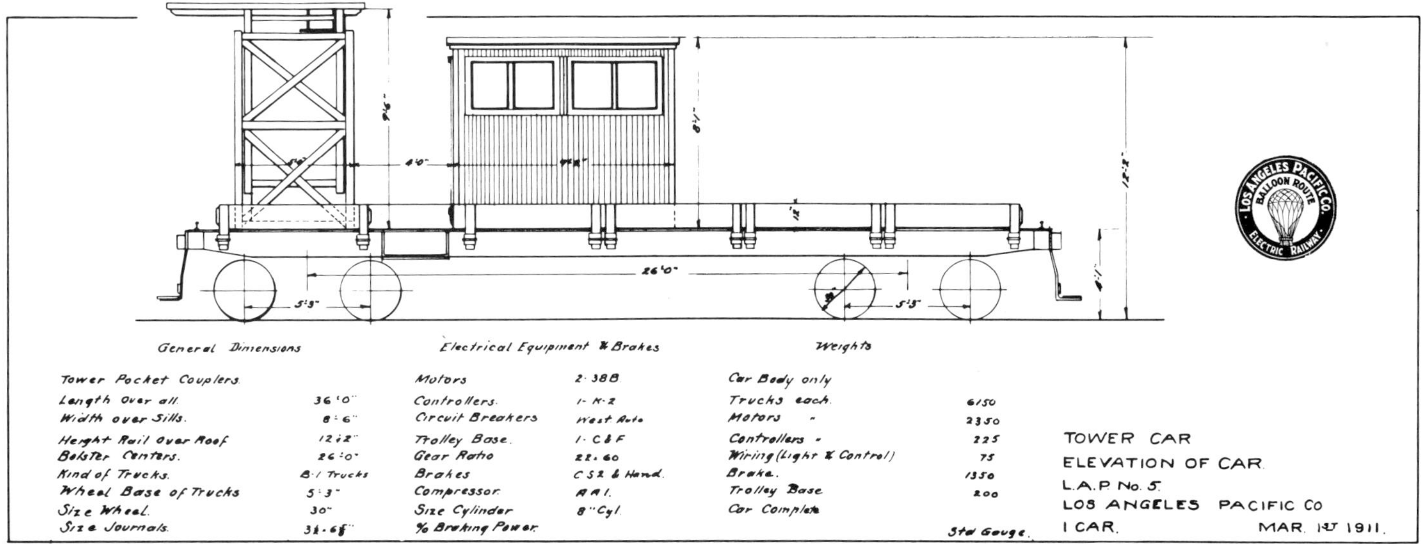

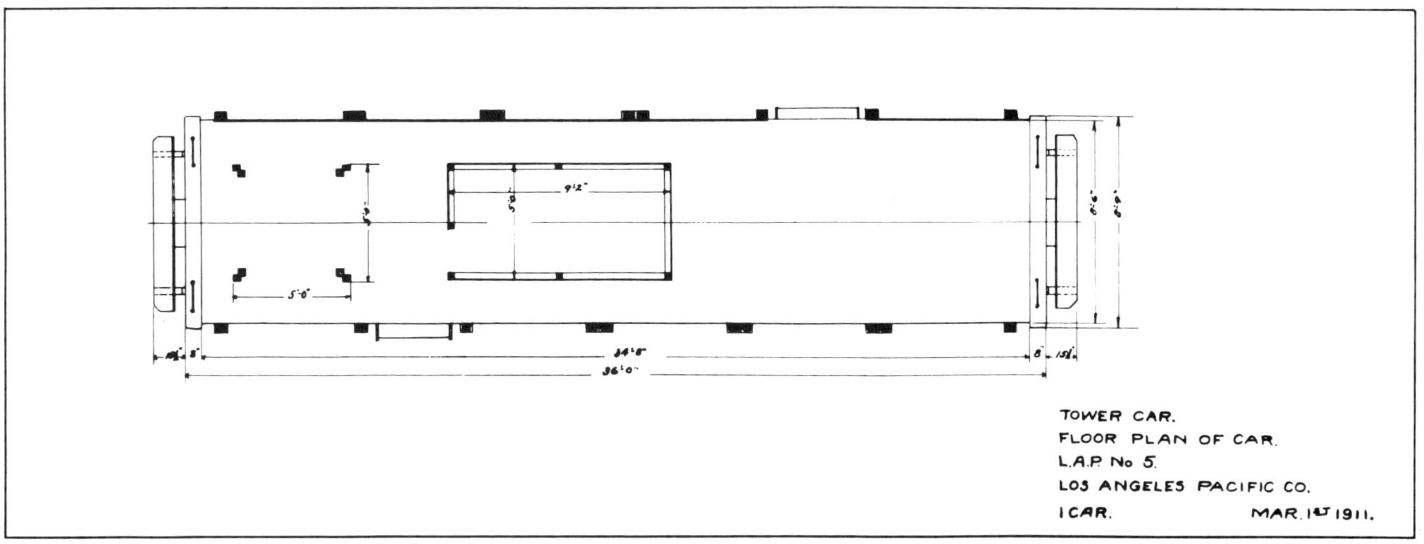

UTILITY CARS: Line car 5 (top photo) was the LAP's largest tower car and bore the brunt of the job of keeping LAP's overhead in repair. Yard motor 11 (photo above) was the Sherman Shop shifter. The portable substation (photo at right) was the only car of its type on the system. *(All: Interurbans)*

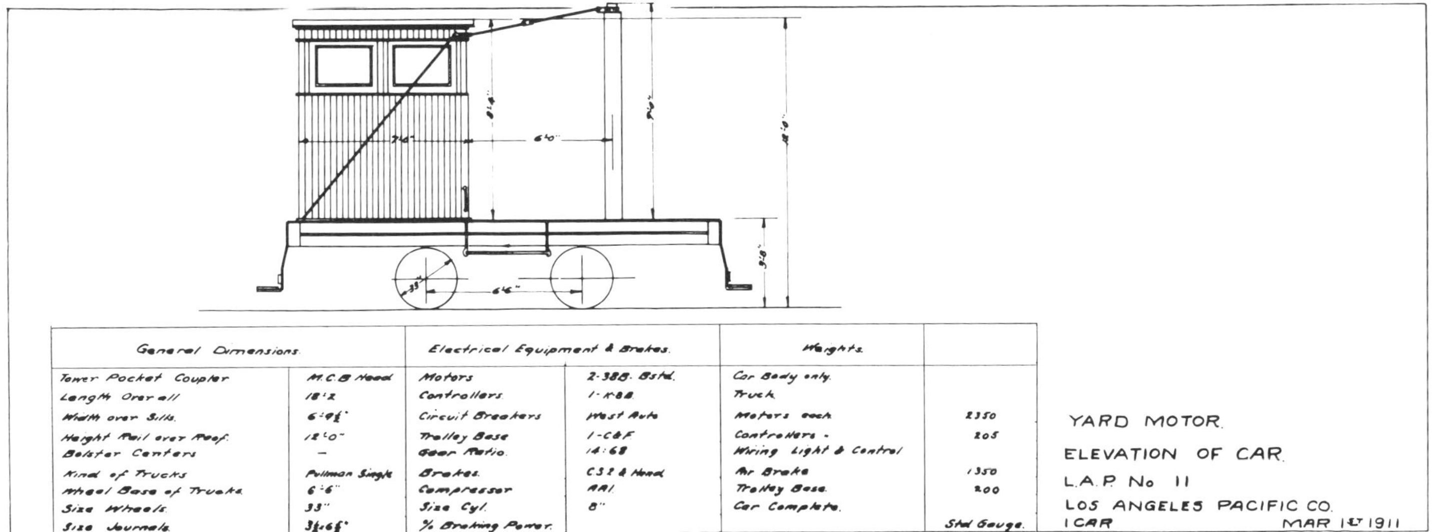

General Dimensions.		Electrical Equipment & Brakes.		Weights.	
Tower Pocket Coupler	M.C.B Head	Motors	2-388. Bstd.	Car Body only.	
Length Over all	18'2	Controllers.	1-K88.	Truck.	
Width over Sills.	6'-9½°	Circuit Breakers	West Auto	Motors each	2350
Height Rail over Roof.	12'-0"	Trolley Base	1-C&F.	Controllers -	205
Bolster Centers	—	Gear Ratio.	14:68	Wiring Light & Control	
Kind of Trucks	Pullman Single	Brakes.	C32 & Hand	Air Brake	1350
Wheel Base of Trucks.	6'-6"	Compressor	AA1	Trolley Base.	200
Size Wheels.	33"	Size Cyl.	8"	Car Complete.	
Size Journals.	3¾×6⅝°	% Braking Power.			Std Gauge.

YARD MOTOR.
ELEVATION OF CAR.
L.A.P. No 11
LOS ANGELES PACIFIC CO.
1 CAR   MAR 1st 1911

15

Portable Substation 15 was LAP's only car of this type. Built in 1909 by LAP, this portable sub was used at various points on the system; one apparently longtime hitch was spent on a spur at the corner of W. 16th St. & Orchard Ave., three blocks east of Vermont Ave.

Sherman Shops, in building this car, took an ordinary flat car and mounted thereon a 400-kw induction motor-generator set, boxed in on the sectional plan so that repairs or removals of equipment could be effected without affecting other parts.

PE renumbered this car 1750, and listed its total weight at 85,000 lbs. It lasted only about a year on PE, burning in 1912.

B-3

Bonding car B-3 was built in 1909 by the Electric Railway Improvement Company and was similar to two cars built by the same builder for Old PE that same year.

The car weighed 6,800 lbs., was 6'10" long, 6'0" wide and 6'11" high over the roof (9'2" over trolley base).

It was mounted on a single truck with 4'2½" wheelbase with 20" cast iron wheels.

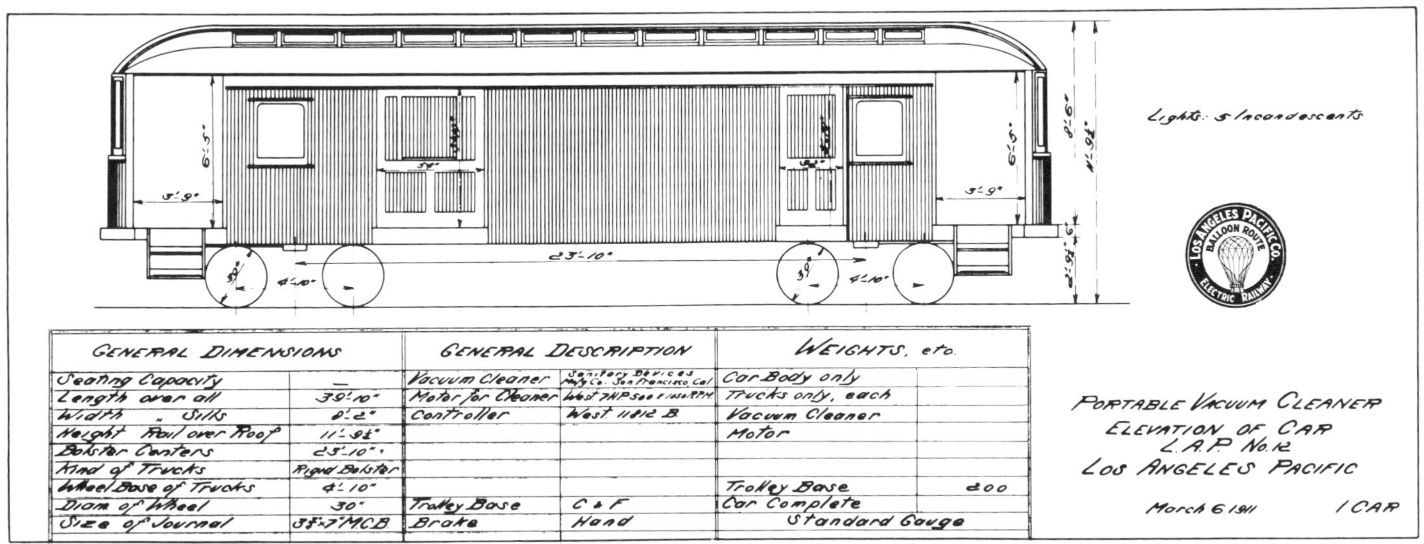

General Dimensions		General Description		Weights, etc.	
Seating Capacity	—	Vacuum Cleaner	Sanitary Devices Mfg Co. San Francisco, Cal	Car Body only	
Length over all	39'-10"	Motor for Cleaner	West 7HP 500 1/1150 RPM	Trucks only, each	
Width „ Sills	8'-2"	Controller	West 11012 B	Vacuum Cleaner	
Height Rail over Roof	11'-9½"			Motor	
Bolster Centers	23'-10"				
Kind of Trucks	Rigid Bolster				
Wheel Base of Trucks	4'-10"			Trolley Base	200
Diam of Wheel	30"	Trolley Base	C & F	Car Complete	
Size of Journal	3¾×7"MCB	Brake	Hand	Standard Gauge	

PORTABLE VACUUM CLEANER
ELEVATION OF CAR
L.A.P No 12
LOS ANGELES PACIFIC
March 6 1911   1 CAR

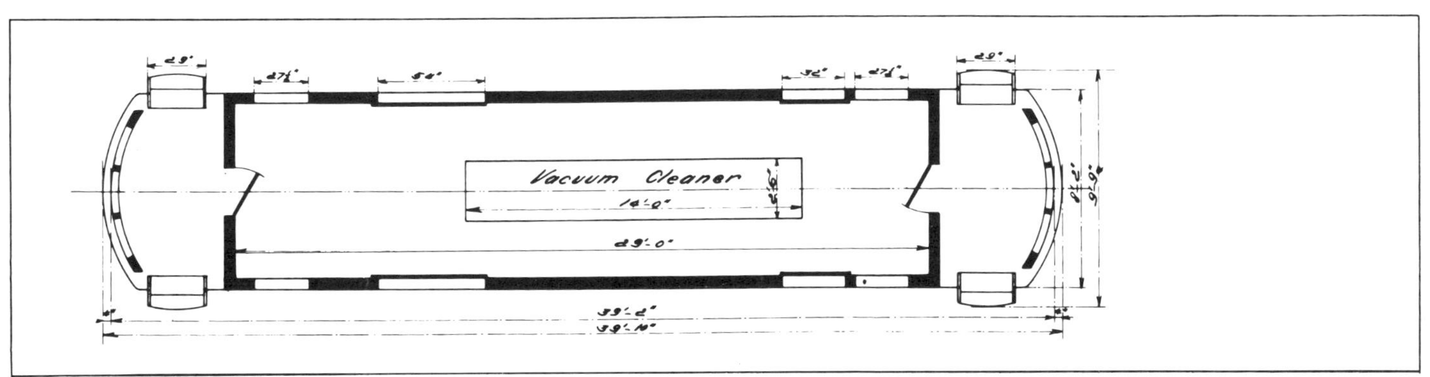

BONDING CAR B-3 at work at Sherman about 1909. Note the long bond on track beneath the closest wheel; these were unique in the Los Angeles area to the LAP. Note also the end of Express trailer 1510 on nearby track. (T.L. Wagenbach)

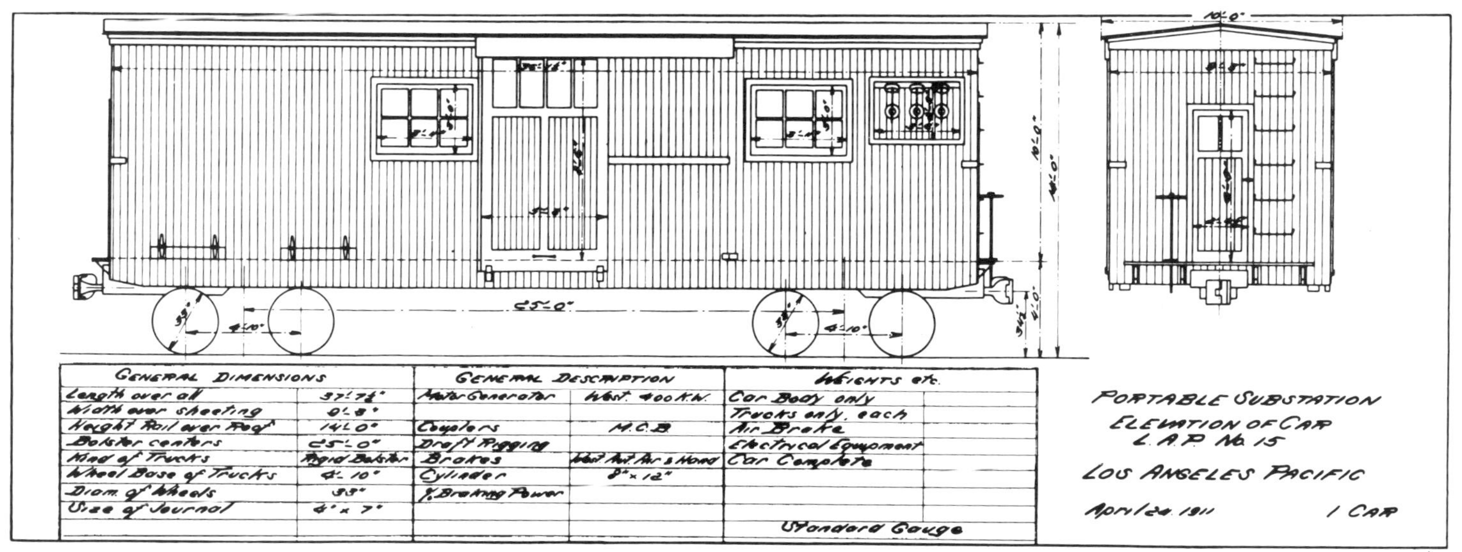

LAP's one Portable Substation is shown above in drawing.

WEED BURNER was little more than a flat car with pipes and tanks as drawing indicates. But it played an important role in tidying up the LAP right-of-way.

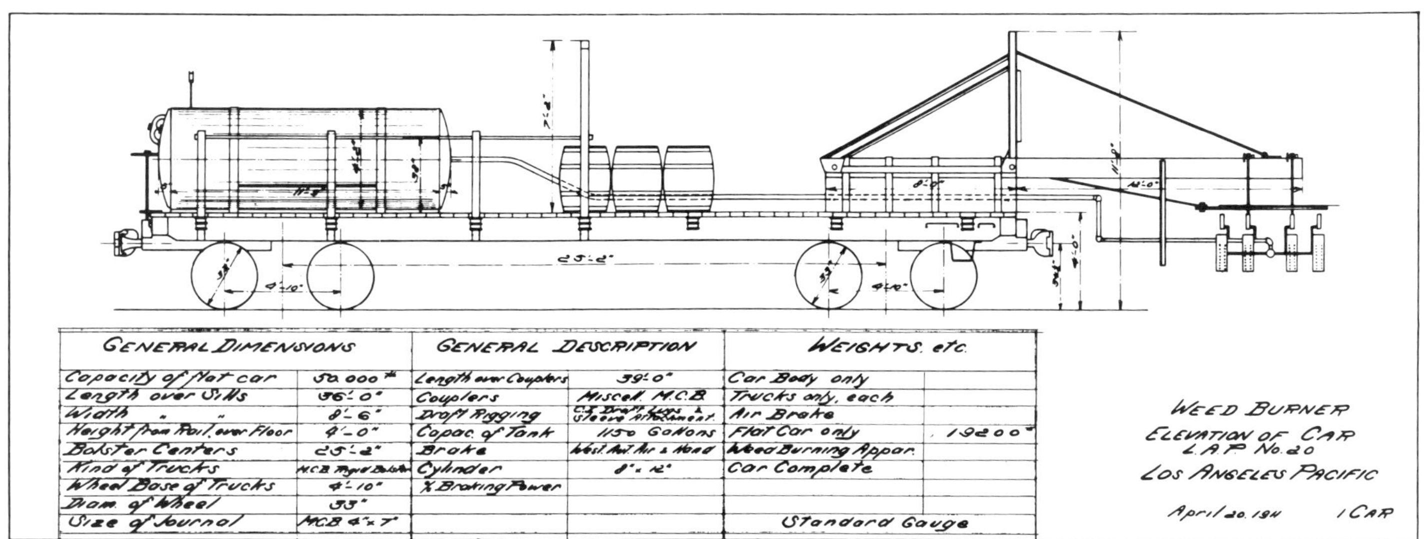

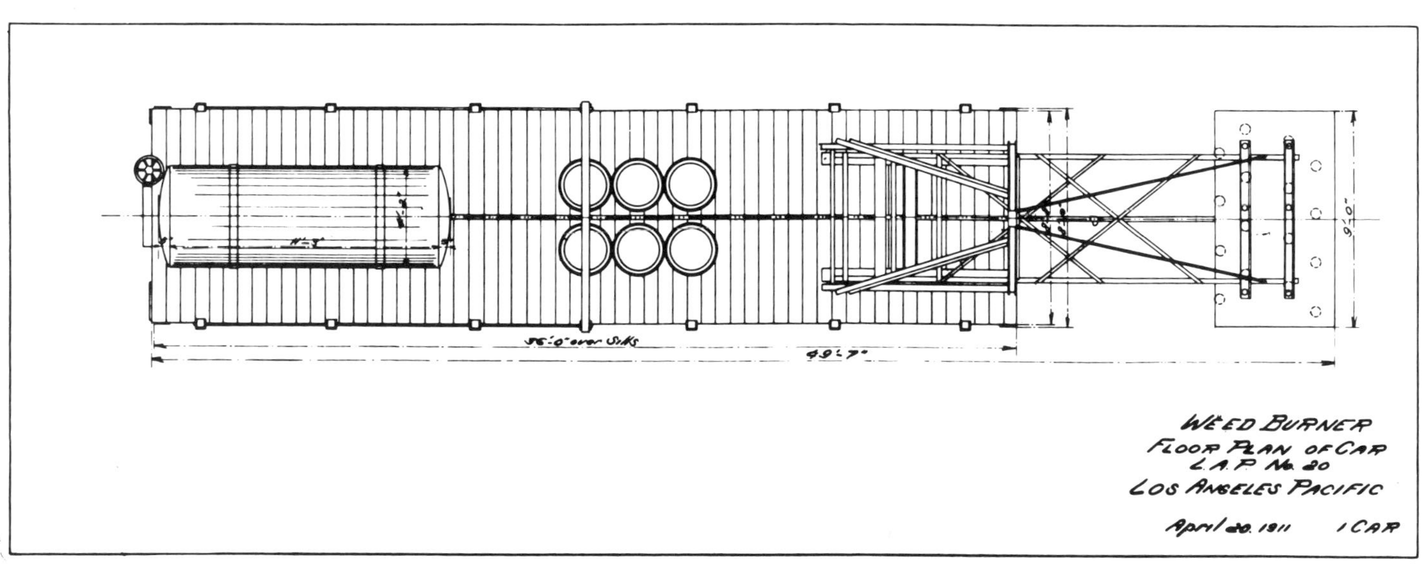

BIG ELECTRIC SHOVEL 62 was home-built at Sherman, 1903.

WEED BURNER 20 still bears flat car number 565 in this Sherman Shops view.   *(Both: Interurbans)*

Electrical equipment consisted of one rotary converter (Westinghouse Type S No. 5, 18½ KW) with rheostat control. Brakes were of the hand type.

The car was able to move itself by means of a mechanically operated clutch and chain drive from the rotary converter shaft to the axle.

PE renumbered the car 1792 and used it until 1930 when it was scrapped.

20

LAP's weed burner 20 was built in 1909 from flat car 565. In 1911 it became PE 1841, and it was scrapped in 1920.

The weed burning apparatus consisted of a flat car on which were mounted an 1,150-gallon tank for oil at one end; a three-inch pipe carried the oil to a 16-nozzle burner suspended over the other end. Six water barrels provided some degree of fire control; these were carried amidships.

Russell Westcott recalls the 20 at work on the Main Line beyond Beverly, also on the Sherman Cutoff, where the weeds especially flourished. After the consolidation he remembers seeing the 1841 parked on a siding at Sherman and cannot recall seeing it used again.

62

LAP's big electric shovel, car 62, was built at Sherman in 1903 and was a major factor in the rapid building of the company's lines. Perhaps its biggest job was the series of cuts on Sunset Blvd. circa 1905.

The 62 was not self-propelled. It used a Westinghouse #89 motor (60 hp) to power its 32 cubic foot scoop. A long jumper cable brought current from the nearest trolley wire. Originally, of course, the car was mounted on 3'6" gauge trucks.

PE rebuilt the 62 into an electric crane and renumbered it PE 1820; in 1931 it became PE 00191 and was retired in 1955.

63

LAP 63 apparently was not included in the 1911 Plan Book and little data has been found on it as an LAP car. 63 was an electric crane and became PE 1821 in 1911 and was rebuilt in 1916. In 1931 it was renumbered 00192 and was scrapped in 1948.

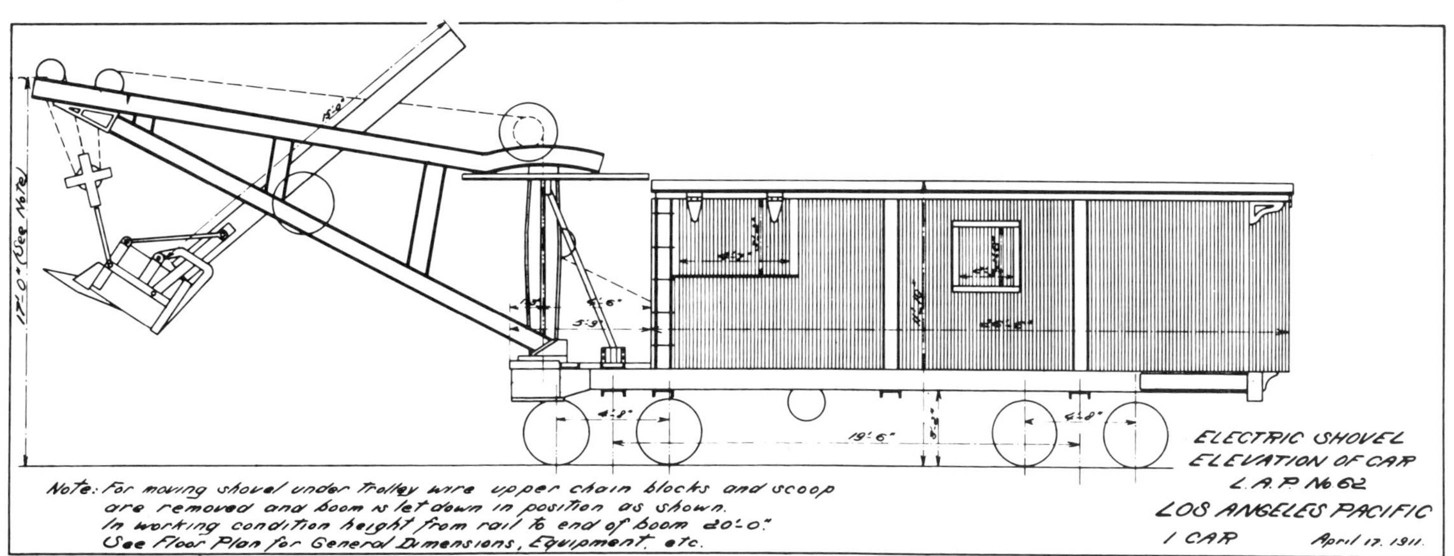

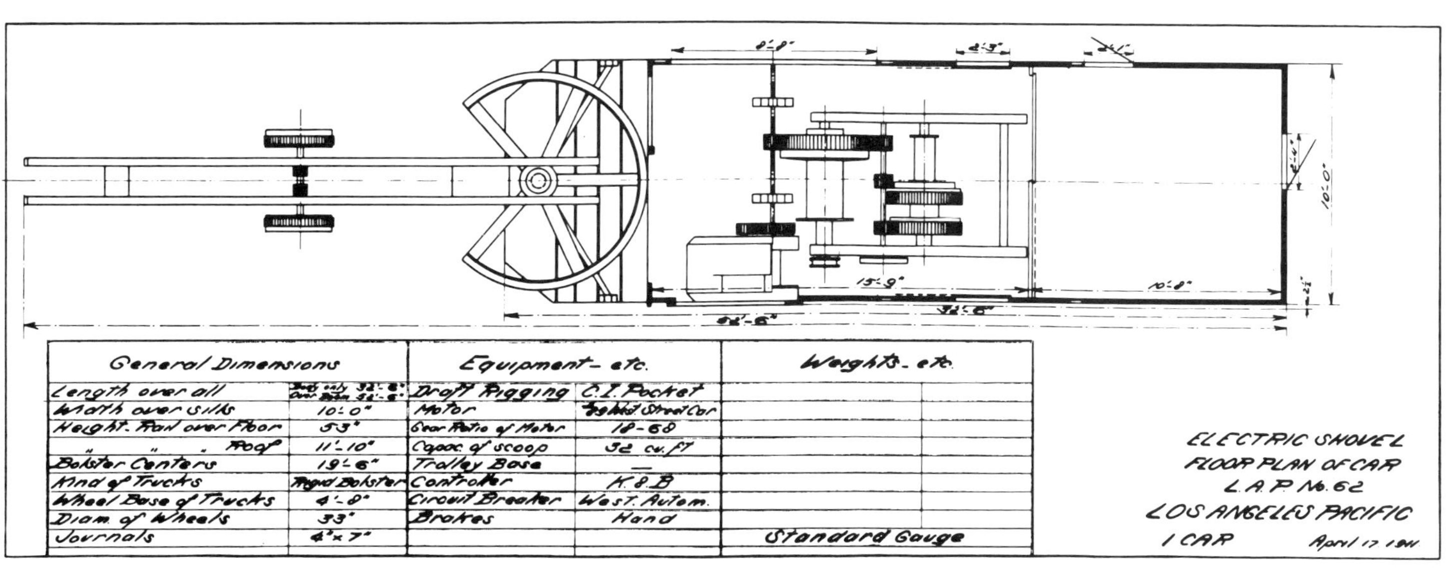

General Dimensions		Equipment - etc.		Weights - etc.	
Length over all	Body only 32'-8" over Beam 32'-8"	Draft Rigging	C.I. Pocket		
Width over sills	10'-0"	Motor	Typical Street Car		
Height. Rail over Floor	53"	Gear Ratio of Motor	18-68		
" " " Roof	11'-10"	Capac. of scoop	32 cu. ft		
Bolster Centers	19'-6"	Trolley Base	—		
Kind of Trucks	Rigid Bolster	Controller	K.8.B		
Wheel Base of Trucks	4'-8"	Circuit Breaker	West. Autom.		
Diam. of Wheels	33"	Brakes	Hand		
Journals	4"×7"			Standard Gauge	

98-99

Mail and express combos 98 and 99 were the sole remnants of the mysterious LAP 90 Class which kept their original numbers. Others of the 90s became express cars (see 1554, 1556 and 1559) and one was LAP's wrecker (see 1557). For theories as to origin of this class see the 90 Class.

The story of how LAP got into the hauling of the mail is an interesting one and goes back to 1899. Southern Pacific had always had the mail contract for Santa Monica. As the LAP cars took away most of SP's passenger business, it was forced to lop off trains. Finally, effective September 17, 1899, SP cut to one train a day to Santa Monica; this meant up to 24 hours delay to the mails and Santa Monicans were outraged. They crusaded for electric railway mail cars and got their way. LAP was awarded the mail contract in 1900 and began carrying sack mail on freight trains, as well as on passenger cars. About 1908 these two cars were rebuilt to do the job.

By 1907, LAP timetables listed two mail car runs per day; one left Los Angeles at 8:20 AM for Redondo via Hollywood and return, serving all intermediate points with the exception of Palms; the other left L.A. at 4:45 PM for Venice via Hollywood, serving all intermediate post offices except Palms.

It is probable that these two new cars were the first standard gauge electric cars on LAP, running from Ocean Park to Inglewood.

PE renumbered them 1380 and 1381 and kept them in the mail service. 1381 was burned in the old carhouse fire in 1913 at Sherman. 1380 became box motor 1400 in 1926, wrecker 008 in 1931 and was scrapped in 1937.

1505-1506

Originally steam coaches from a predecessor company, these two cars were never electrified. After the 1911 Merger these cars became PE 1850 and 1851, maintenance of way cars; both were retired in 1926. These cars were originally narrow-gauge cars with open platforms; LAP rebuilt them, removing the platforms and standard-gauging them.

1507

Former steam coach 1507 was rebuilt by Sherman Shops into an express trailer about 1900. LAP chopped end platforms off all express trailers, and the 1507 received this amputation with the others. In 1911 it was renumbered PE 1852, a maintenance of way car. It was scrapped in 1926.

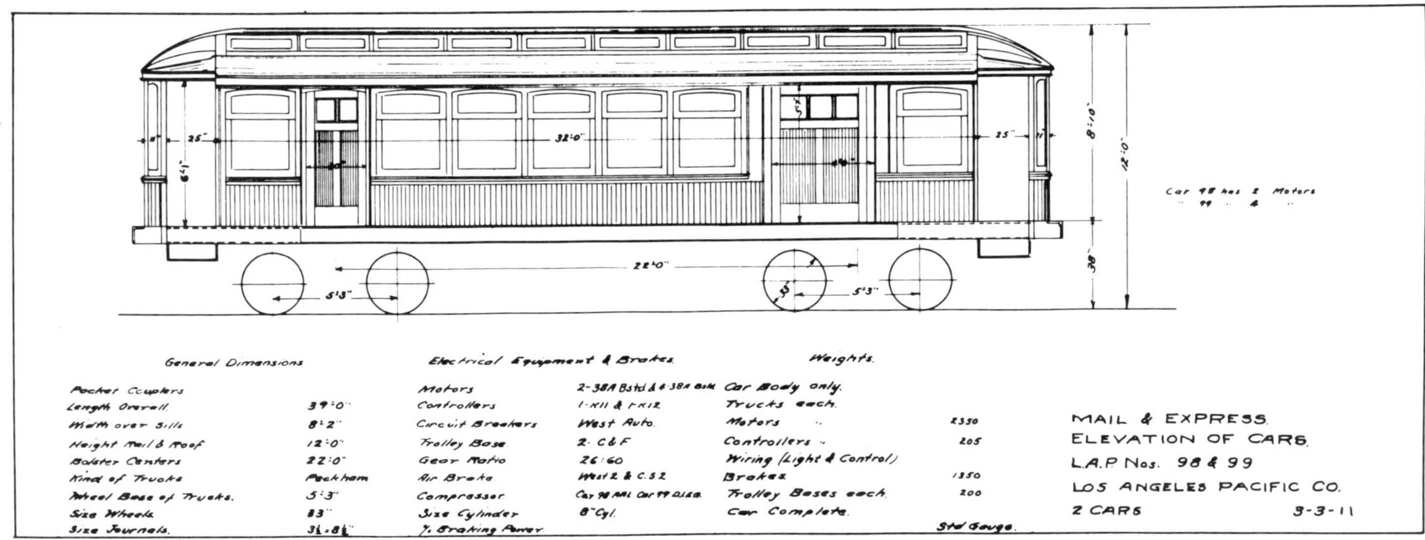

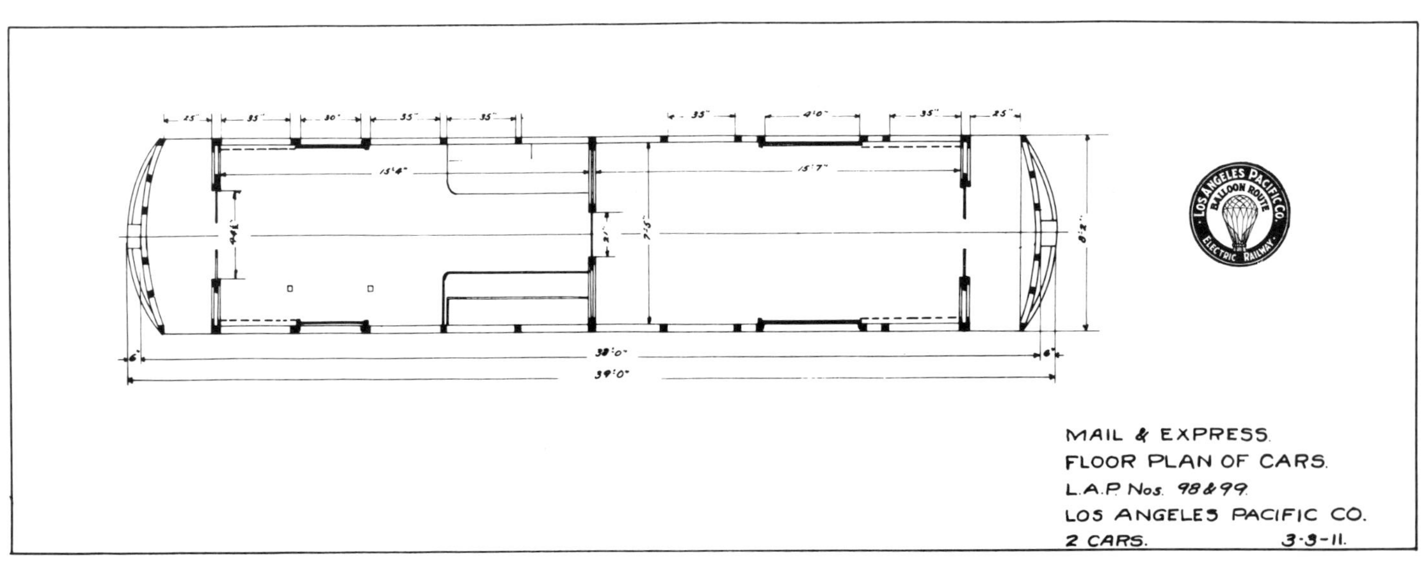

COMBO 99 at Hill St. (top); Motor 1554 most likely at Sherman (bottom). Note Peckham trucks on car 99.
(Both: Interurbans)

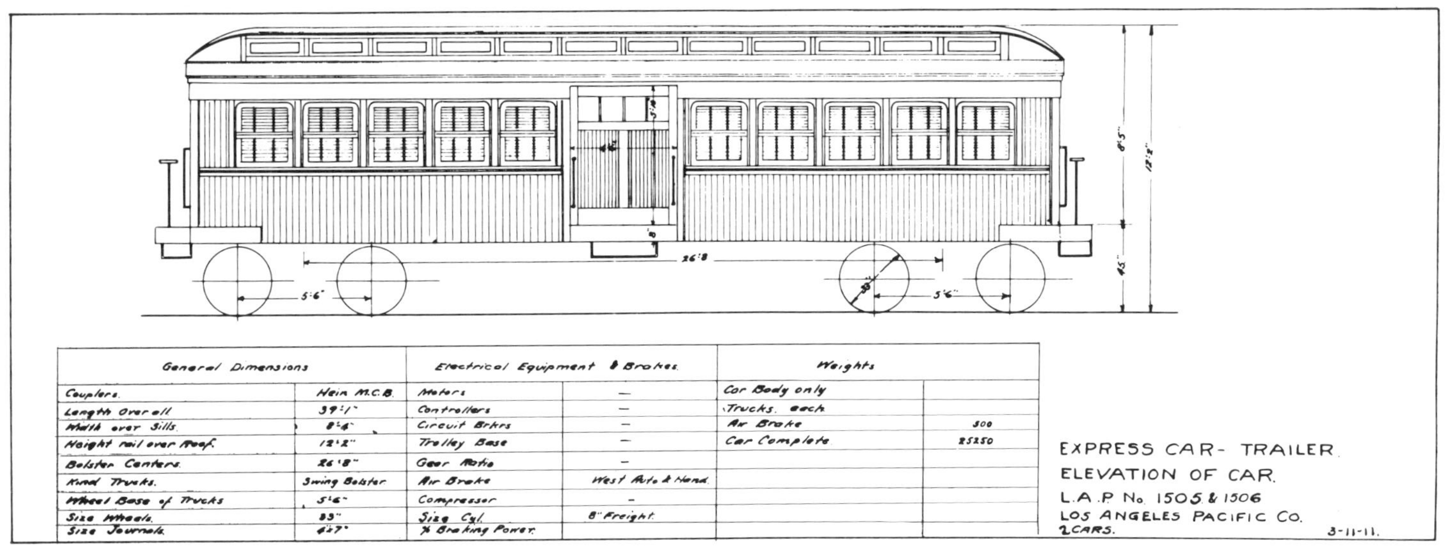

General Dimensions		Electrical Equipment & Brakes		Weights	
Couplers.	Hein M.C.B.	Motors	—	Car Body only	
Length Over all	39'1"	Controllers	—	Trucks. each.	
Width over Sills.	8'4"	Circuit Brkrs	—	Air Brake	500
Height rail over Roof.	12'2"	Trolley Base	—	Car Complete.	25250
Bolster Centers.	26'8"	Gear Ratio	—		
Kind Trucks.	Swing Bolster.	Air Brake	West Auto & Hand.		
Wheel Base of Trucks	5'6"	Compressor	—		
Size Wheels.	33"	Size Cyl.	8" Freight.		
Size Journals.	4⅛7"	% Braking Power.			

EXPRESS CAR- TRAILER.
ELEVATION OF CAR.
L.A.P No. 1505 & 1506
LOS ANGELES PACIFIC CO.
2 CARS.   3-11-11.

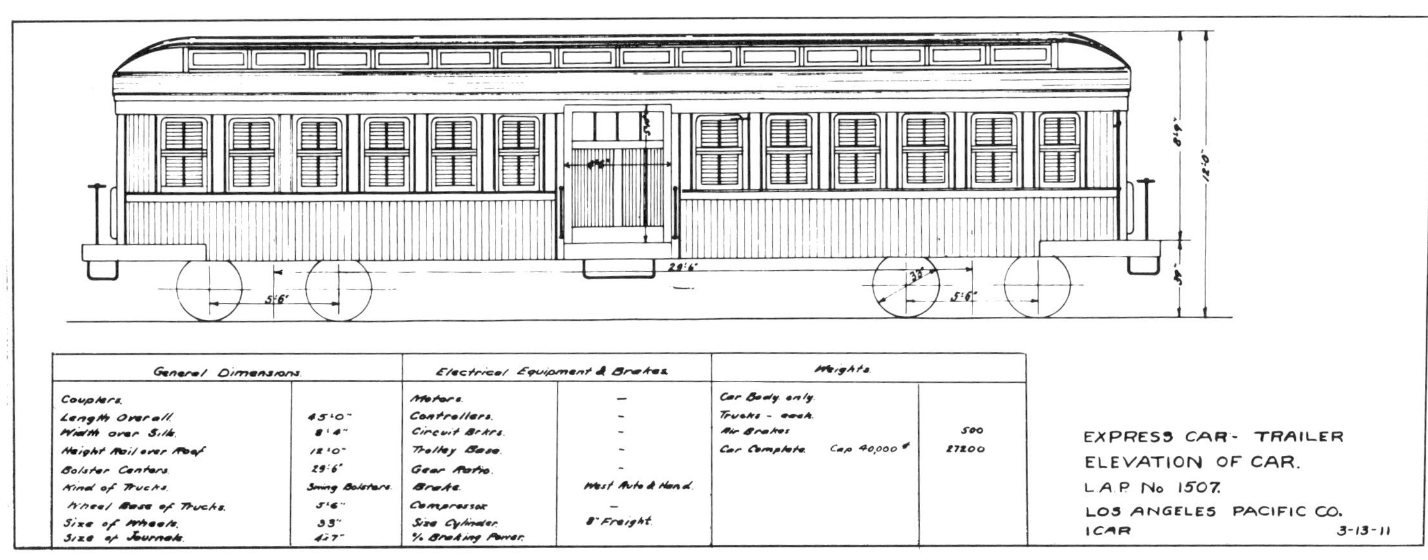

General Dimensions.		Electrical Equipment & Brakes.		Weights.	
Couplers.		Motors.	—	Car Body only.	
Length Overall.	45'0"	Controllers.	—	Trucks - each.	
Width over Sills.	8'4"	Circuit Brkrs.	—	Air Brakes	500
Height Rail over Roof	12'0"	Trolley Base.	—	Car Complete. Cap 40,000 #	27200
Bolster Centers.	29'6"	Gear Ratio.	—		
Kind of Trucks.	Swing Bolsters.	Brake.	West Auto & Hand.		
Wheel Base of Trucks.	5'6"	Compressor	—		
Size of Wheels.	33"	Size Cylinder.	8" Freight.		
Size of Journals.	4⅛7"	% Braking Power.			

EXPRESS CAR- TRAILER
ELEVATION OF CAR.
L.A.P No 1507.
LOS ANGELES PACIFIC CO.
1 CAR   3-13-11

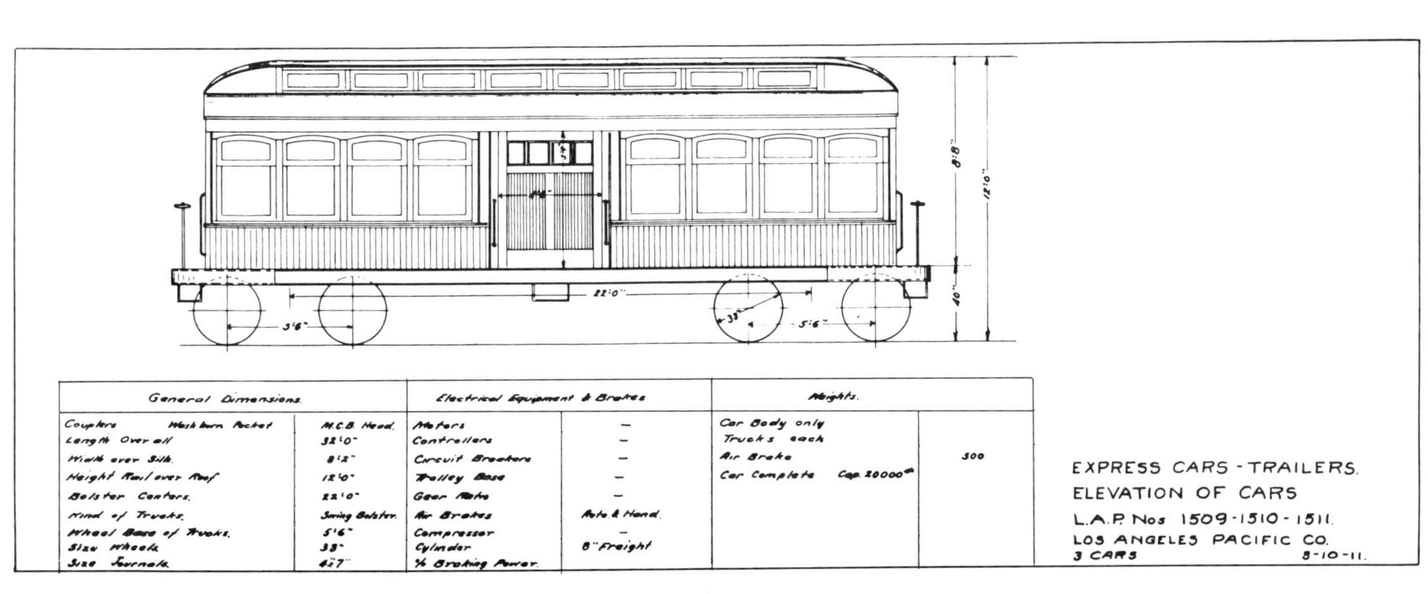

General Dimensions.			Electrical Equipment & Brakes		Weights.	
Couplers Washburn Pocket	M.C.B. Head.	Motors	—	Car Body only	
Length Over all	32'0"	Controllers	—	Trucks each	
Width over Sills.	8'2"	Circuit Breakers	—	Air Brake	500
Height Rail over Roof	12'0"	Trolley Base	—	Car Complete Cap. 20000 #	
Bolster Centers.	22'0"	Gear Ratio	—		
Kind of Trucks.	Swing Bolster.	Air Brakes	Auto & Hand.		
Wheel Base of Trucks.	5'6"	Compressor	—		
Size Wheels	33"	Cylinder	8" Freight		
Size Journals.	4⅛7"	% Braking Power.			

EXPRESS CARS - TRAILERS.
ELEVATION OF CARS
L.A.P Nos 1509-1510-1511.
LOS ANGELES PACIFIC CO.
3 CARS   8-10-11.

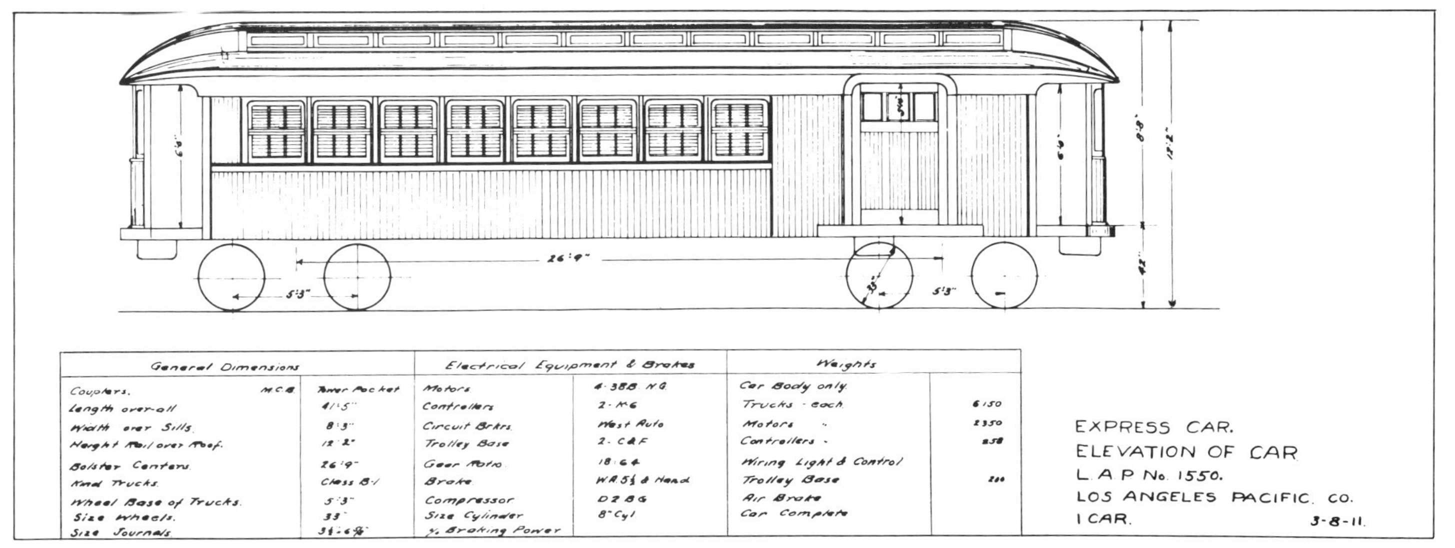

General Dimensions		Electrical Equipment & Brakes		Weights	
Couplers. M.C.B.	Tower Pocket	Motors	4-38B N.G.	Car Body only.	
Length over-all	41'-5"	Controllers	2-K6	Trucks - each.	6150
Width over Sills.	8'-3"	Circuit Brkrs.	West Auto	Motors "	2350
Height Rail over Roof.	12'-2"	Trolley Base	2-C&F	Controllers -	258
Bolster Centers.	26'-9"	Gear Ratio.	18-64	Wiring Light & Control	
Kind Trucks.	Class B-1	Brake.	W.A.5½ & Hand	Trolley Base	200
Wheel Base of Trucks.	5'-3"	Compressor	D2BG	Air Brake	
Size wheels.	33"	Size Cylinder	8" Cyl	Car Complete	
Size Journals	3¼-6⅞"	% Braking Power			

EXPRESS CAR.
ELEVATION OF CAR
L.A.P. No. 1550.
LOS ANGELES PACIFIC. CO.
1 CAR.   3-8-11.

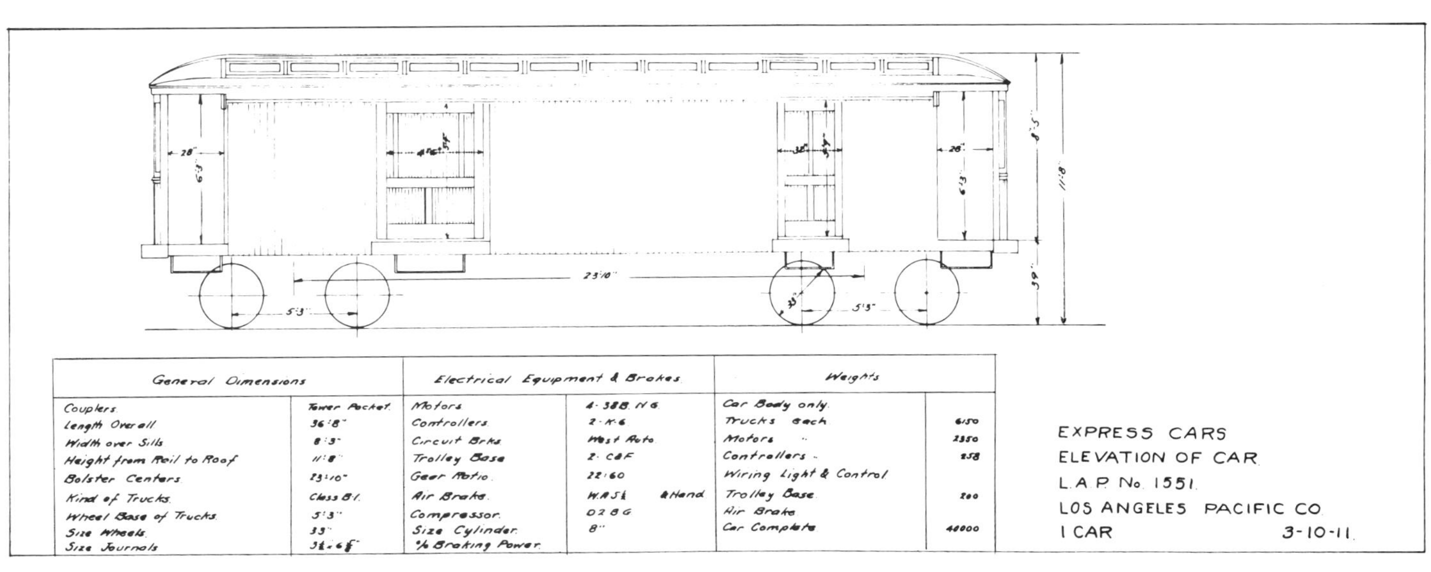

General Dimensions		Electrical Equipment & Brakes		Weights	
Couplers.	Tower Pocket.	Motors	4-38B. N.G.	Car Body only.	
Length Overall	36'-8"	Controllers.	2-K-6	Trucks each	6150
Width over Sills	8'-3"	Circuit Brks.	West Auto	Motors "	2350
Height from Rail to Roof	11'-8"	Trolley Base	2-C&F	Controllers -	258
Bolster Centers	23'-10"	Gear Ratio.	22-60	Wiring Light & Control	
Kind of Trucks.	Class B-1.	Air Brake.	W.A.5½ & Hand	Trolley Base.	200
Wheel Base of Trucks.	5'-3"	Compressor.	D2BG	Air Brake	
Size Wheels.	33"	Size Cylinder.	8"	Car Complete	40000
Size Journals	3¼-6⅞"	% Braking Power.			

EXPRESS CARS
ELEVATION OF CAR
L.A.P. No. 1551.
LOS ANGELES PACIFIC CO.
1 CAR   3-10-11.

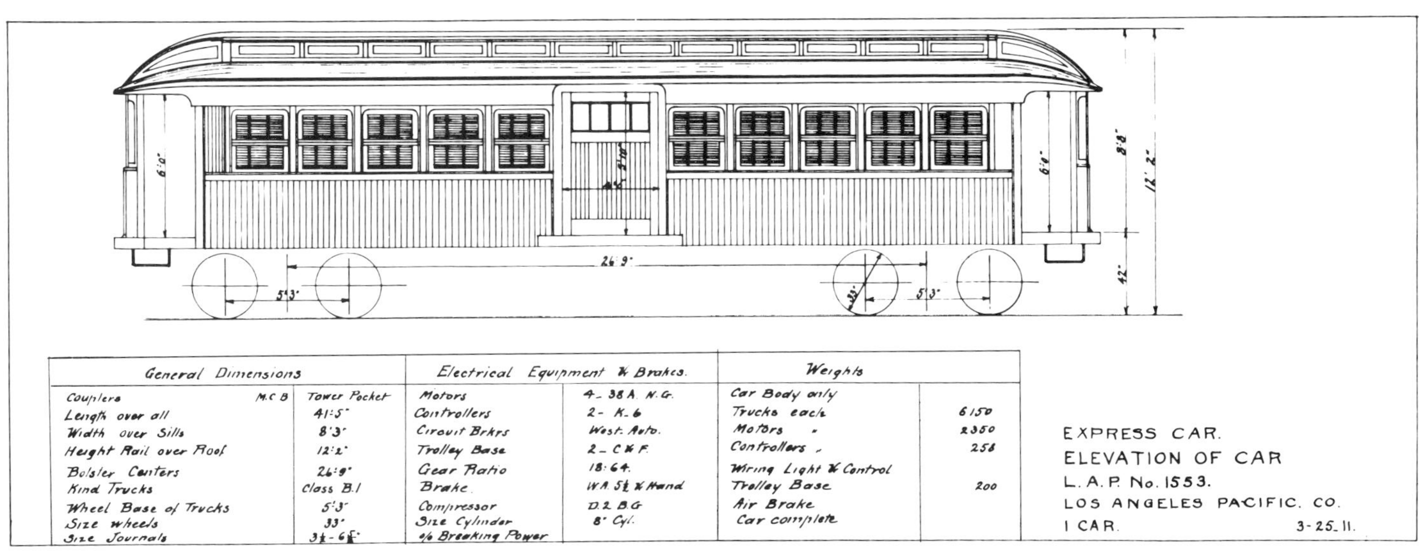

General Dimensions		Electrical Equipment & Brakes		Weights	
Couplers M.C.B	Tower Pocket	Motors	4-38A. N.G.	Car Body only	
Length over all	41'-5"	Controllers	2-K-6	Trucks each	6150
Width over Sills	8'-3"	Circuit Brkrs	West. Auto.	Motors "	2350
Height Rail over Roof	12'-2"	Trolley Base	2-C&F.	Controllers "	258
Bolster Centers	26'-9"	Gear Ratio	18-64.	Wiring Light & Control	
Kind Trucks	Class B.1	Brake.	W.A.5½ & Hand	Trolley Base	200
Wheel Base of Trucks	5'-3"	Compressor	D.2 B.G	Air Brake	
Size wheels	33"	Size Cylinder	8" Cyl.	Car complete	
Size Journals	3¼-6⅞"	% Breaking Power			

EXPRESS CAR.
ELEVATION OF CAR
L.A.P. No. 1553.
LOS ANGELES PACIFIC. CO.
1 CAR.   3-25-11.

A LINEUP OF LAP narrow-gauge freight equipment in Santa Monica. Boxcar 401 and express trailers 1505 and 1506 all were later rebuilt to standard gauge.

(Interurbans)

1509-1511

These three express trailers appear to have been rebuilt from 90-class passenger cars in 1905. Their appearance after this rebuilding cannot be confirmed although undated photos of 1510 at Sherman show a car with a deck roof, no platforms, a center doorway and a body half closed with windows and half slatted like a stock car. By the time LAP's folio drawings were made the cars had evolved into railroad roof closed cars with windowed bodies and center doors, still with exposed steel underframes and no platforms. After the Great Merger these cars were renumbered as follows:

LAP 1509 became PE 1853
LAP 1510 became PE 1950
LAP 1511 became PE 1902

The 1509 was scrapped in 1928; dispositions and dates of scrapping of the other two cars are unknown.

1550

Rebuilt about 1900 from an old steam combine acquired from a predecessor company, the 1550 hauled express trailers and was originally narrow gauge. It became PE 1403 in 1911, a box motor. In 1912 it was rebuilt into tower car 1724 and was dismantled in 1923.

1551

This car was originally a steam baggage car from a predecessor company and was motorized about 1900. It became PE 1404 in 1911. Changed into a bunk car for track gangs in 1913, it was scrapped in 1926.

1553

Steam passenger coach 1553 was motorized about 1900 and had a baggage door cut midway in its side. In 1911 it was renumbered PE 1405 and in 1913 was rebuilt into a dining car for track gangs and renumbered 1863. It was scrapped in 1930.

1554, 1556, 1559

These three ex-passenger motors were rebuilt into box motors in 1905. For their origin, see the 90 class.

Specifications:

Couplers:	Drawbar
Length:	39'0"
Height:	12'0"
Bolsters:	22'0"
Width:	8'2"
Trucks:	1554, 1556: Rigid Bolster
	1559: Peckham
Wheelbase:	5'3" (both types trucks)
Motors:	Four West. 38B (50hp)
Wheels:	33"
Controllers:	K-6
Ratio:	22:60 and 26:60
Brakes:	Westinghouse Automatic
Weight:	42,500 and 42,000

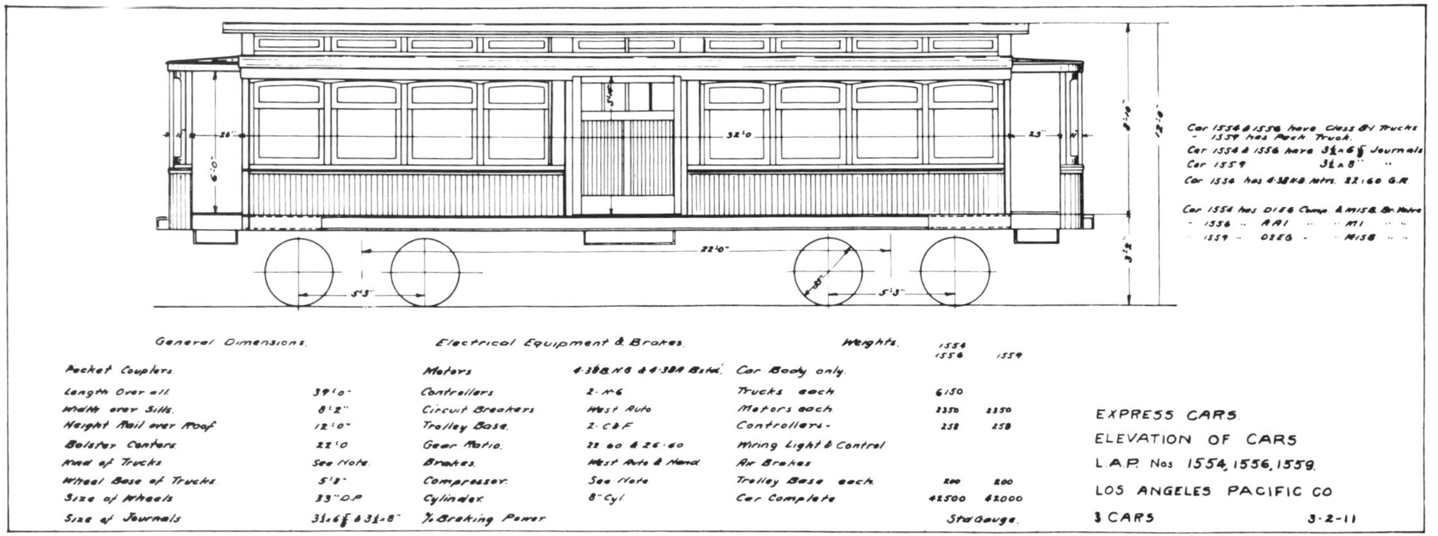

General Dimensions.
Pocket Couplers.
Length Over all.   39'0"
Width over Sills.   8'2"
Height Rail over Roof   12'0"
Bolster Centers.   22'0
Kind of Trucks.   See Note.
Wheel Base of Trucks.   5'3"
Size of Wheels   33" D.P
Size of Journals   3¼×6⅝ & 3¼×8"

Electrical Equipment & Brakes.
Motors   4-38GKG & 4-38A Both.
Controllers.   2-K6
Circuit Breakers West Auto
Trolley Base.   2-C&F
Gear Ratio.   22:60 & 26:60
Brakes.   West Auto & Hand
Compressor.   See Note
Cylinder.   8" Cyl.
% Braking Power.

Weights.   1556   1559
Car Body only.
Trucks each.   6150
Motors each.   2350   2350
Controllers-   258   258
Wiring Light & Control
Air Brakes
Trolley Base each.   200   200
Car Complete   42500 42000
                           Std Gauge.

Car 1554 & 1556 have Class 81 Trucks
" 1559 has Peck Truck.
Car 1554 & 1556 have 3¼×6⅝ Journals
Car 1559   3¼×8"   "
Car 1554 has 4-38KB Mtrs. 22:60 G.R.

Car 1554 has D16G Comp. & M15B Br Valve
" 1556 "   AA1   "   " M1   "   "
" 1559 "   O2EG -   " M15B "   "

EXPRESS CARS.
ELEVATION OF CARS
L.A.P. Nos 1554, 1556, 1559.
LOS ANGELES PACIFIC CO
3 CARS   3-2-11

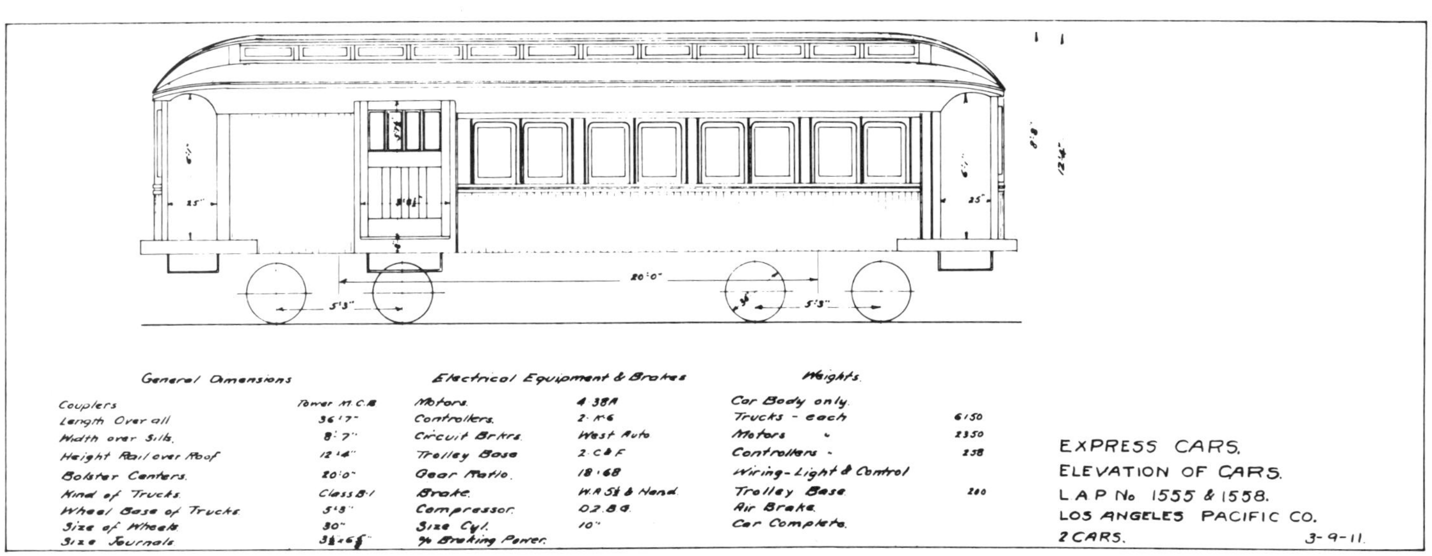

General Dimensions
Couplers   Tower M.C.B.
Length Over all   36'7"
Width over Sills.   8'7"
Height Rail over Roof 12'4"
Bolster Centers.   20'0"
Kind of Trucks.   Class 81
Wheel Base of Trucks.   5'3"
Size of Wheels   30"
Size Journals   3¼×6⅝"

Electrical Equipment & Brakes
Motors.   4-38A
Controllers.   2-K6
Circuit Brkrs.   West Auto
Trolley Base   2-C&F
Gear Ratio.   18:68
Brake.   W.A.S½ & Hand.
Compressor.   O2.8G.
Size Cyl.   10"
% Braking Power.

Weights.
Car Body only.
Trucks - each   6150
Motors "   2350
Controllers -   258
Wiring - Light & Control
Trolley Base   200
Air Brake.
Car Complete.

EXPRESS CARS.
ELEVATION OF CARS.
L.A.P No 1555 & 1558.
LOS ANGELES PACIFIC CO.
2 CARS   3-9-11.

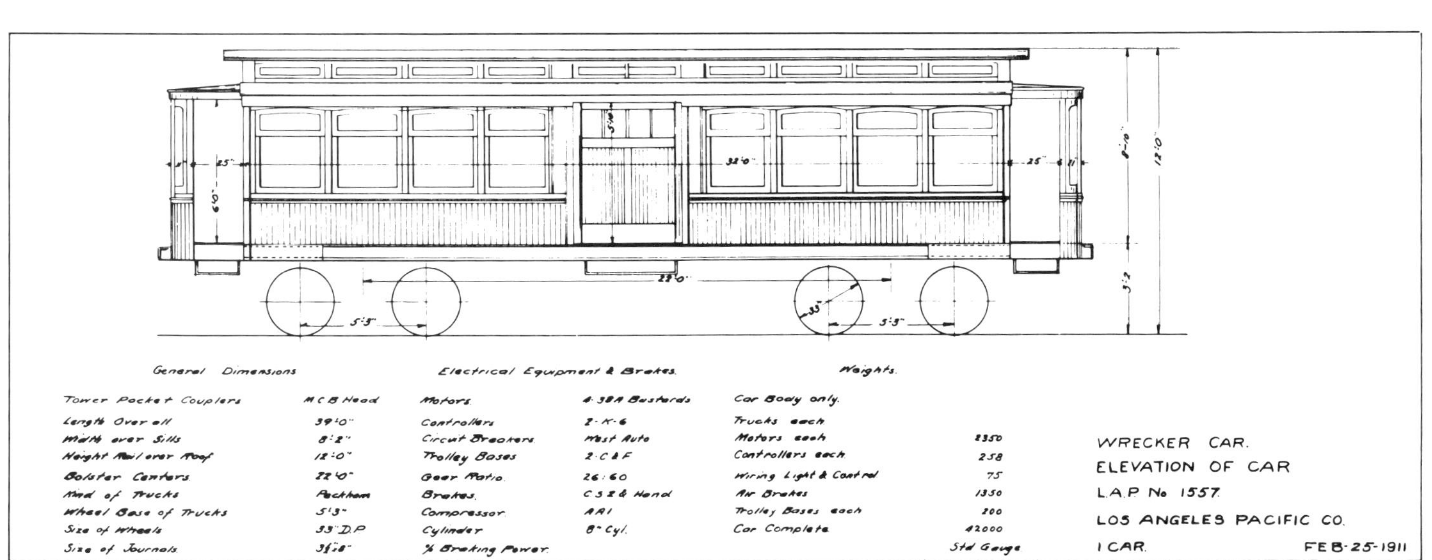

General Dimensions.
Tower Pocket Couplers   M.C.B Head
Length Over all   39'0"
Width over Sills   8'2"
Height Rail over Roof   12'0"
Bolster Centers.   22'0"
Kind of Trucks   Peckham
Wheel Base of Trucks   5'3"
Size of Wheels   33" D.P
Size of Journals   3⅛×8"

Electrical Equipment & Brakes.
Motors.   4-38A Bastards
Controllers   2-K-6
Circuit Breakers West Auto
Trolley Bases   2-C&F
Gear Ratio.   26:60
Brakes.   C S 2 & Hand
Compressor.   AA1
Cylinder   8" Cyl.
% Braking Power.

Weights.
Car Body only.
Trucks each.
Motors each.   2350
Controllers each.   258
Wiring Light & Control   75
Air Brakes   1350
Trolley Bases each   200
Car Complete   42000
                         Std Gauge

WRECKER CAR.
ELEVATION OF CAR
L.A.P No 1557
LOS ANGELES PACIFIC CO.
1 CAR   FEB-25-1911

After the Merger these cars were renumbered PE 1407, 1408 and 1409 respectively. All became tower cars as follows: 1407 became 1731 in 1923; 1408 became 1725 in 1922; 1409 became 1733 in 1924. The 1731 was renumbered 00158 in 1931 and scrapped in 1939; 1725 became 00155 in 1931 and was scrapped in 1948; 1733 was renumbered 00160 in 1931 and retired in 1949.

1555, 1558

These two cars were steam combines acquired by LAP from predecessor companies and rebuilt into electric box motors by Sherman Shops about 1900. PE renumbered them 1406 and 1402 respectively in 1911 and kept them as box motors for but two years for in 1913 both became dining and bunk cars for track gangs with the numbers 1864 and 1861 respectively. The 1864 was scrapped in 1924 and 1861 went in 1926. The 1558 was noted as "stripped of all equipment" in April, 1911.

1557

LAP's wrecker car was this rebuilt passenger motor. It was of the 90-99 class. Other cars in this grouping included 98 and 99, the mail and express combos, and box motors 1554, 1556 and 1558, and express trailers 1509, 1510 and 1511. The 1557 was an express motor in 1905 but was converted to the system wrecker in 1907. Conversion consisted of installing bins for carrying rerailing equipment and the like.

After the merger, 1557 became PE 001 and continued at Sherman at the Western Division wrecker. It was dismantled and burned in 1926 and was succeeded as the West's wrecker by express car 1413 which was then renumbered 005.

WORK MOTORS

1575-1578

LAP owned and operated eight work motor cars: 1575, 1577-1579 and 1581-1584. All were built at Sherman Shops. In addition, two line cars (3 and 5) were sufficiently similar to warrant the supposition that they were either built as work motors or on only slightly modified plans.

1575, 1577-1578 (line car 3 probably was 1576) were all-wood cars. They were built for narrow-gauge operation and had comparatively light weight and light duty motors. Their chief function was to haul work crews and construction trains in the early days; in addition, they performed light switching.

Specifications, Work Motors 1757-1578:

Builder:	LAP Sherman Shops, 1901
Type:	Wood flatbed construction cars
Weight:	39,900 lbs.
Length:	34'0" over buffers
Width:	8'9" over sills
Height:	12'2" rail over roof
Trucks:	Rigid bolster 5'3" LAP type
Motors:	2 38B, 4 69, 4 38B respectively
Controllers:	One K-6
Gear Ratio:	22:60, 14:68, 14:68
Brakes:	West. 5½, D2EG compressor

PE renumbered these cars thusly: 1575 became PE 1522 in 1911 and 1714 (line car) in 1915 (scrapped 1931); 1577 became PE 1523 and remained a work motor until scrapped in

1926; 1578 became 1524 in 1911 and 1716 in 1915; scrapped 1924.

1579

LAP's work motor 1579 was a near-twin of tower car 5. It was built in 1901 at Sherman Shops and was the last of four work motors built that year.

1579 was also the last of LAP's "long" work motors. Freight haulers built after it were about 30 feet long.

Specifications:

Length:	36'0"
Width:	8'3"
Height:	12'2"
Bolsters:	25'2"
Trucks:	B-1 rigid bolster
Truck Wheelbase:	5'3"
Wheels:	30"
Motors:	4 38B (50 hp)
Controller:	One K6
Gear Ratio:	14:68
Brakes:	West. Auto.
Compressor:	D2EG
Cylinder:	8"
Weights:	
Body:	16,575 lbs.
Trucks:	12,300
Motors:	9,400
Control:	250
Wiring:	75
T. Base:	200
Brake:	2,400
Total:	41,200 lbs.

As a PE car, 1579 was in a mixup with the work motor of the San Bernardino Valley Traction Company, SBVT 18. 1579 and 18 switched trucks but the new PE numbers followed the trucks. Hence 1579's body became PE 1543 and was scrapped with that number in 1920. 1579's trucks became PE 1525 in 1911, 1717 in 1915, and scrapped in 1927.

1581-1584

These four work cars were built at Sherman in late 1905 and early 1906. A fifth, 1580, was built on the same work order but was given a more elaborate cab and sloping ends—causing it to be classified on LAP records as a locomotive instead of a work motor, although it was no more powerful than these.

At the time these motors were built, LAP had taken passenger business to the western beaches away from the Southern Pacific and the Santa Fe. Although local travel on steam trains was dead, LAP did not realize it; hence the first two of these motors, 1580 and 1581, were announced as being intended to haul steam trains from Sunset on the SP and from Inglewood on the Santa Fe to Venice and Santa Monica. Needless to say, they rarely, if ever, hauled a passenger train. They were chiefly used to haul rock and gravel trains and after 1908 saw some service in Long Wharf and Air Line trains.

They became PE 1526-1529 respectively; 1526 and 1528 were scrapped in 1933; 1527 became 009 in 1934 and was scrapped in 1941; 1529 became 0010 in 1934 and was scrapped 1940.

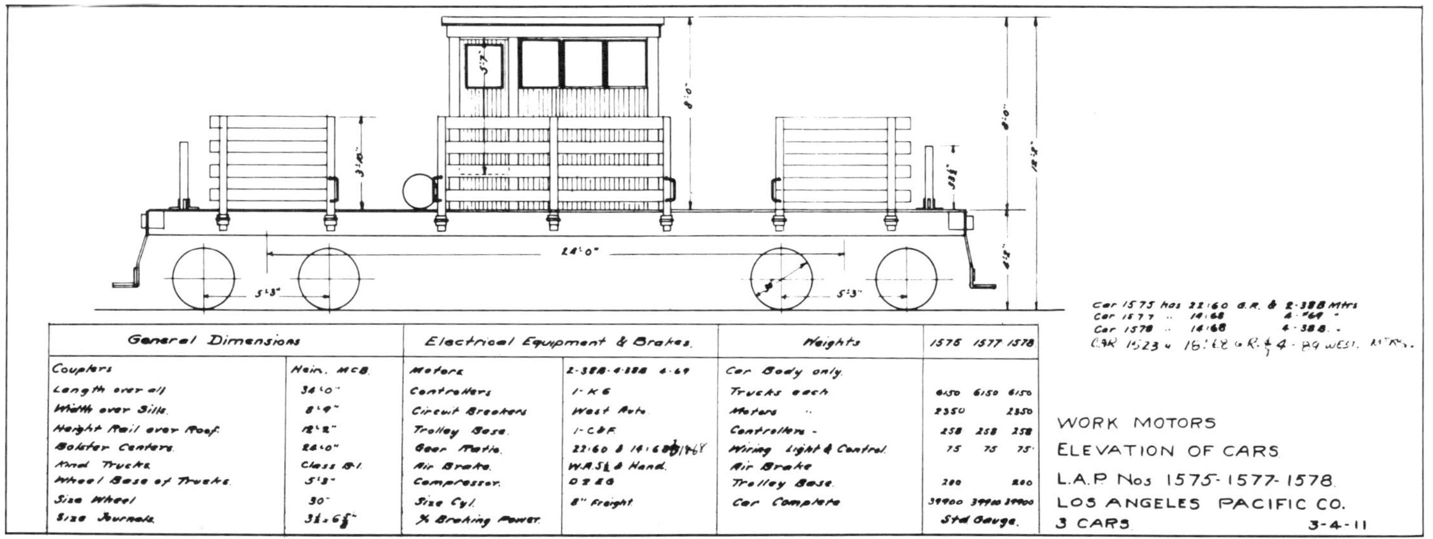

General Dimensions		Electrical Equipment & Brakes		Weights	1575	1577	1578
Couplers	Hein. MCB.	Motors	2-38B-4-38B 4-69	Car Body only.			
Length over all	34'0"	Controllers	1-K6	Trucks each.	6150	6150	6150
Width over Sills.	8'9"	Circuit Breakers	West Auto	Motors ..	2350		2350
Height Rail over Roof.	12'2"	Trolley Base.	1-C&F	Controllers -	258	258	258
Bolster Centers.	24'0"	Gear Ratio.	22:60 & 14:68	Wiring Light & Control.	75	75	75
Kind Trucks.	Class B-1	Air Brake.	W.A.S½ & Hand.	Air Brake			
Wheel Base of Trucks.	5'3"	Compressor.	D2EG	Trolley Base.	200		200
Size Wheel	30"	Size Cyl.	8" Freight	Car Complete	39900	39900	39900
Size Journals.	3½x6⅝"	% Braking Power.		Std Gauge.			

COMPARATIVE SPECIFICATIONS, L.A.P. ELECTRIC LOCOMOTIVES;

No.	Control	Motors	Ratio	Trucks	Brakes	H.P.	Length	Weight	P.E. No.
1580	K6	38-B	14:68	5'3"	W. 7½	172	30'0"	52,000	1552
1585	K34B	GE 73	17:73	6'5"	W. 7½	300	30'0"	84,800	1553
1586	"	"	"	"	"	"	"	74,000	1554
1587	K34D	"	"	"	"	"	"	83,350	1555

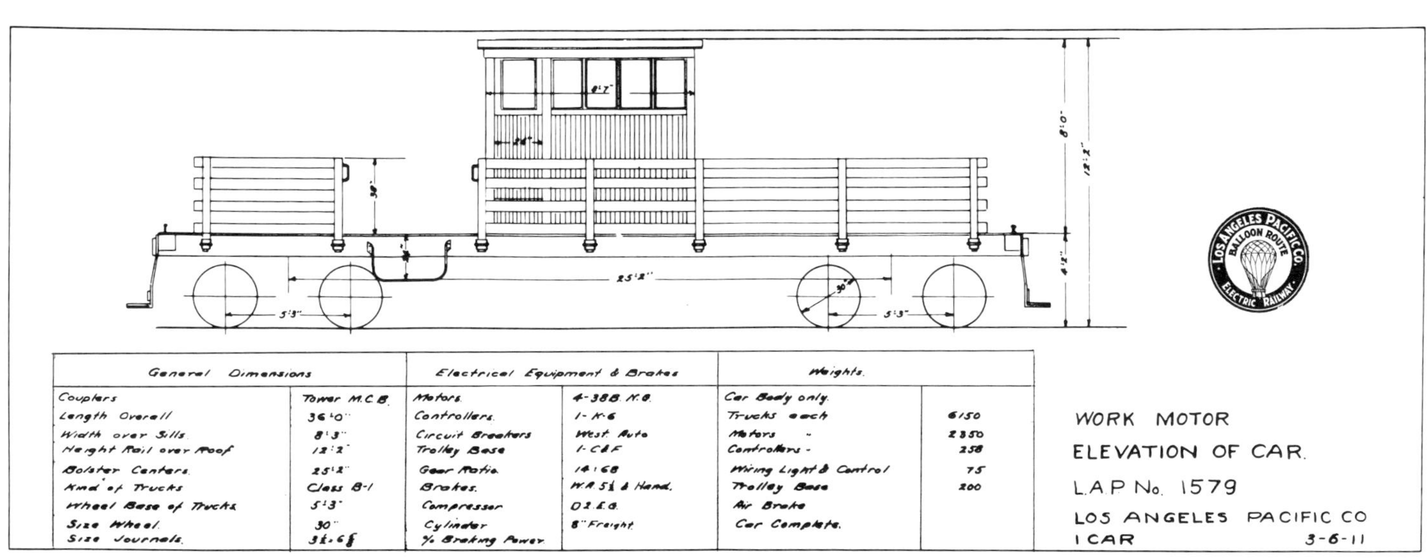

General Dimensions		Electrical Equipment & Brakes		Weights	1579
Couplers	Tower M.C.B.	Motors.	4-38B. N.G.	Car Body only.	
Length Overall	36'0"	Controllers.	1-K6	Trucks each	6150
Width over Sills.	8'3"	Circuit Breakers	West Auto	Motors ..	2350
Height Rail over Roof	12'2"	Trolley Base	1-C&F	Controllers -	258
Bolster Centers.	25'2"	Gear Ratio.	14:68	Wiring Light & Control	75
Kind of Trucks	Class B-1	Brakes.	W.A.S½ & Hand.	Trolley Base	200
Wheel Base of Trucks	5'3"	Compressor	D2EG.	Air Brake	
Size Wheel.	30"	Cylinder	8" Freight	Car Complete.	
Size Journals.	3½x6⅝"	% Braking Power.			

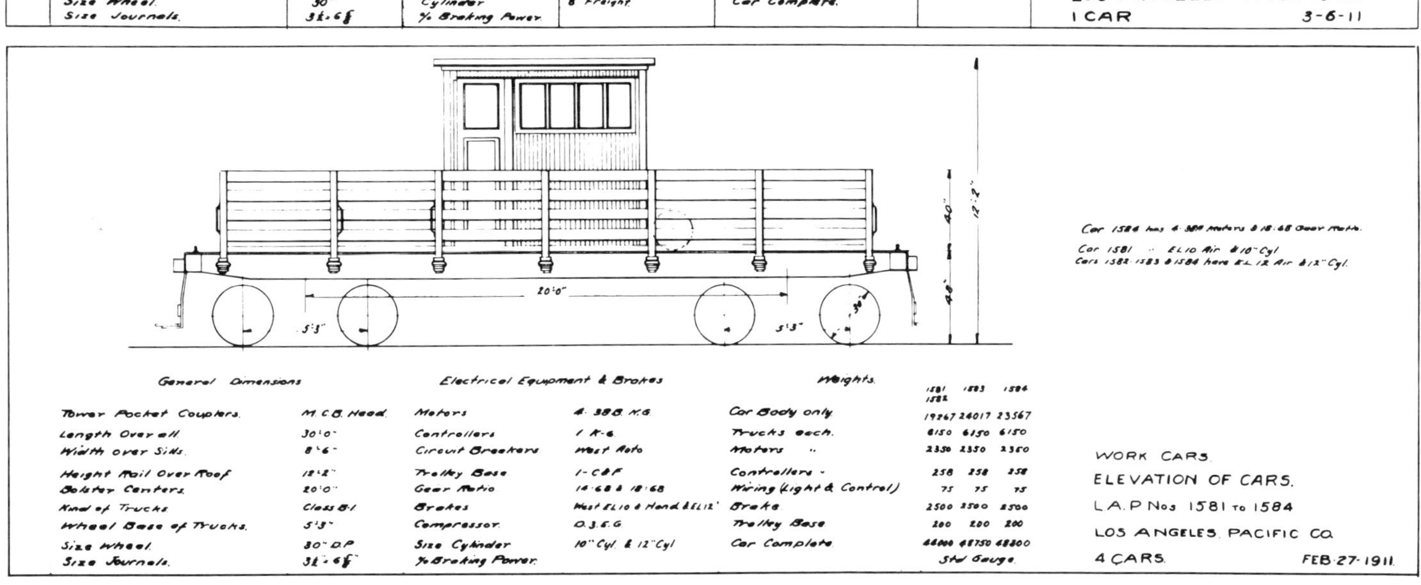

General Dimensions		Electrical Equipment & Brakes		Weights	1581 1582	1583	1584
Tower Pocket Couplers.	M.C.B. Head	Motors	4-38B. N.G.	Car Body only.	19267	24017	23567
Length Over all	30'0"	Controllers	1-K6	Trucks each.	6150	6150	6150
Width over Sills.	8'6"	Circuit Breakers	West Auto	Motors ..	2350	2350	2350
Height Rail Over Roof	12'2"	Trolley Base.	1-C&F	Controllers -	258	258	258
Bolster Centers.	20'0"	Gear Ratio	14:68 & 18:68	Wiring (Light & Control)	75	75	75
Kind of Trucks	Class B-1	Brakes	West EL10 & Hand & EL12'	Brake	2500	2500	2500
Wheel Base of Trucks.	5'3"	Compressor.	O.3.E.G.	Trolley Base	200	200	200
Size Wheel.	30" D.P.	Size Cylinder	10" Cyl. & 12"Cyl	Car Complete.	46000	48750	48800
Size Journals.	3½x6⅝"	% Braking Power.		Std Gauge.			

"OLD MOGUL" freight motor 1582 (above) was one of four similar cars classed as work motors but assigned to general hauling duties. *"Big Mogul"* 1585 (below) was one of two units with bigger dimensions and more pulling power.

(Both: Interurbans)

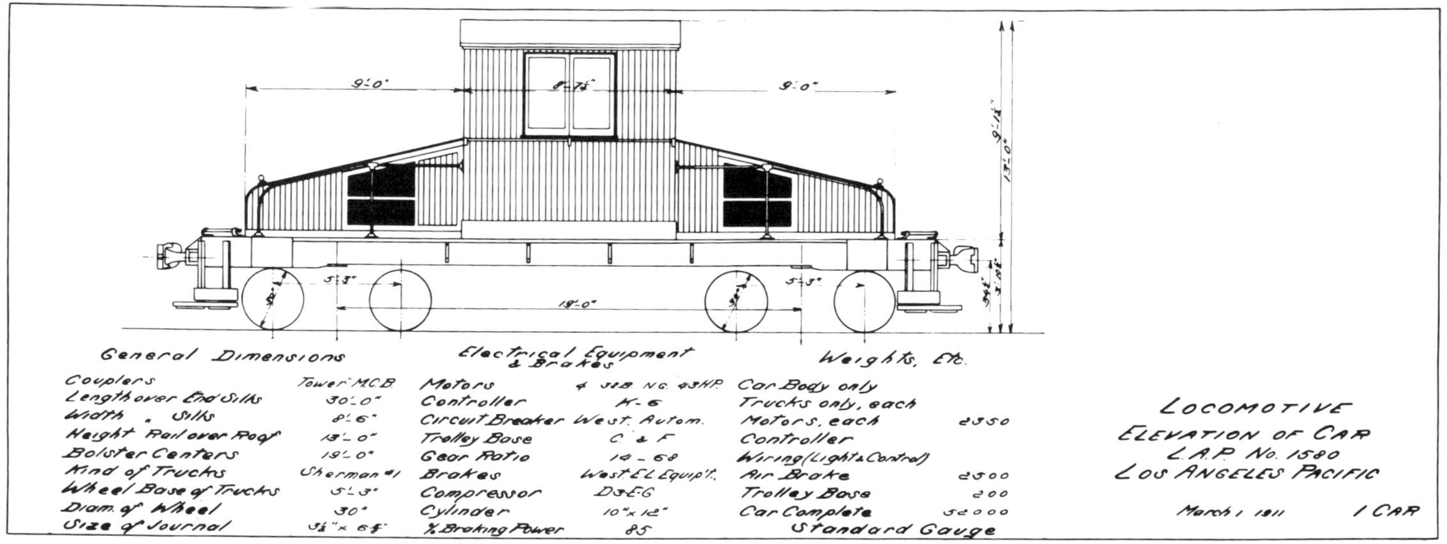

General Dimensions		Electrical Equipment & Brakes		Weights, Etc.	
Couplers	Tower M.C.B.	Motors	4 St8 N.G. 43 H.P.	Car Body only	
Length over End Sills	30'-0"	Controller	K-6	Trucks only, each	
Width " Sills	8'-6"	Circuit Breaker	West. Autom.	Motors, each	2350
Height Rail over Roof	13'-0"	Trolley Base	C & F	Controller	
Bolster Centers	19'-0"	Gear Ratio	14 – 68	Wiring (Light & Control)	
Kind of Trucks	Sherman #1	Brakes	West. E.L. Equip't.	Air Brake	2500
Wheel Base of Trucks	5'-3"	Compressor	D3-E-G	Trolley Base	200
Diam. of Wheel	30"	Cylinder	10" x 12"	Car Complete	52000
Size of Journal	3½" x 6½"	% Braking Power	85	Standard Gauge	

LOCOMOTIVE
ELEVATION OF CAR
L.A.P. No. 1580
LOS ANGELES PACIFIC

March 1, 1911   1 CAR

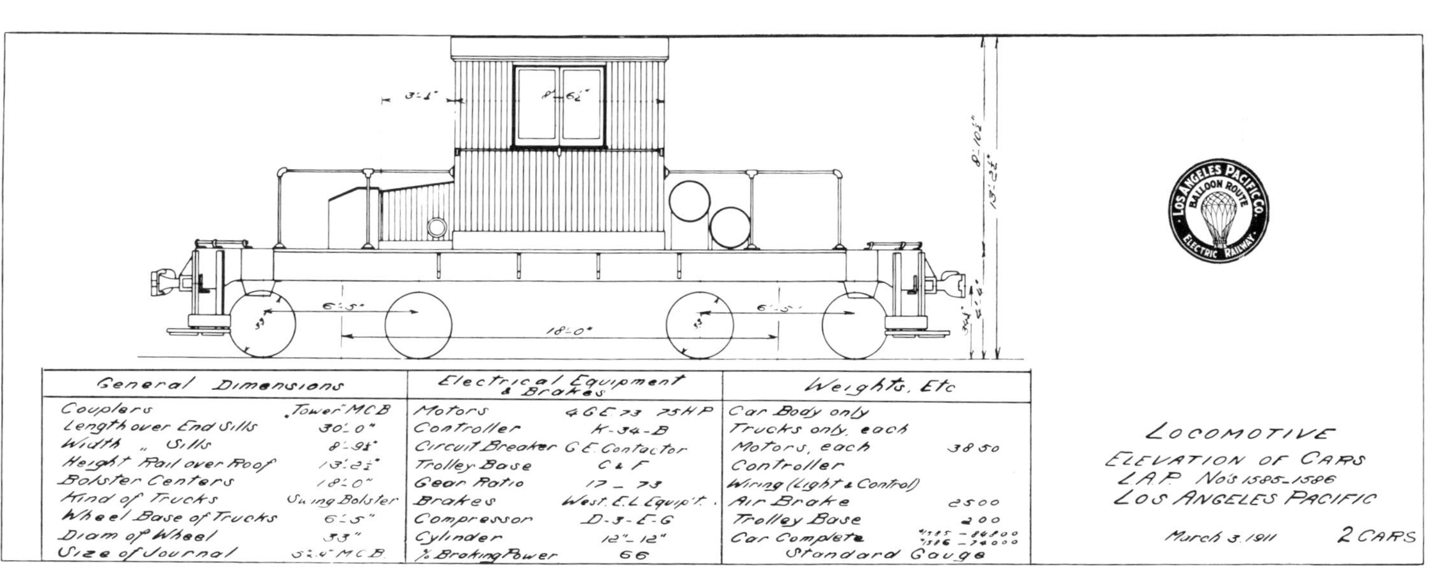

General Dimensions		Electrical Equipment & Brakes		Weights, Etc.	
Couplers	Tower M.C.B.	Motors	4 GE 73 75 H.P.	Car Body only	
Length over End Sills	30'-0"	Controller	K-34-B	Trucks only, each	
Width " Sills	8'-9½"	Circuit Breaker	G.E. Contactor	Motors, each	3850
Height Rail over Roof	13'-2½"	Trolley Base	C & F	Controller	
Bolster Centers	18'-0"	Gear Ratio	17 – 73	Wiring (Light & Control)	
Kind of Trucks	Swing Bolster	Brakes	West. E.L. Equip't.	Air Brake	2500
Wheel Base of Trucks	6'-5"	Compressor	D-3-E-G	Trolley Base	200
Diam of Wheel	33"	Cylinder	12"-12"	Car Complete	1585 – 84800 1586 – 74000
Size of Journal	5¼" M.C.B.	% Braking Power	66	Standard Gauge	

LOCOMOTIVE
ELEVATION OF CARS
L.A.P. No's 1585–1586
LOS ANGELES PACIFIC

March 3, 1911   2 CARS

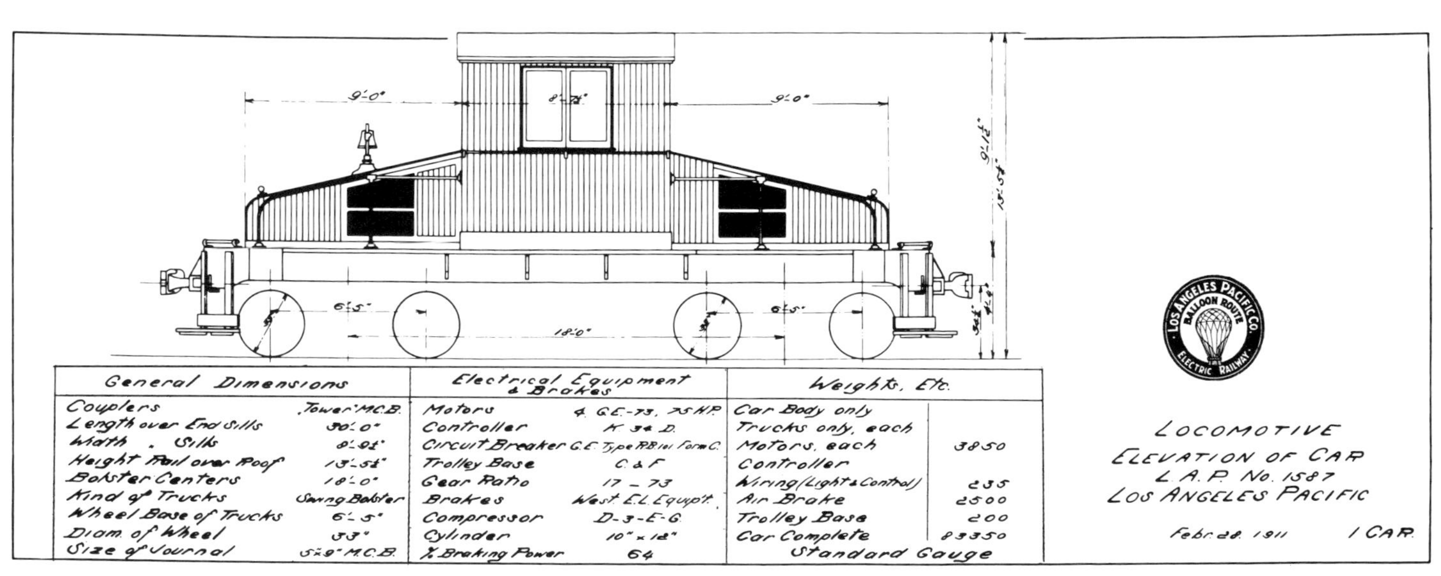

General Dimensions		Electrical Equipment & Brakes		Weights, Etc.	
Couplers	Tower M.C.B.	Motors	4 G.E.-73, 75 H.P.	Car Body only	
Length over End Sills	30'-0"	Controller	K 34 D.	Trucks only, each	
Width " Sills	8'-9½"	Circuit Breaker	G.E. Type R.B. 101 Form C.	Motors, each	3850
Height Rail over Roof	13'-5½"	Trolley Base	C & F	Controller	
Bolster Centers	18'-0"	Gear Ratio	17 – 73	Wiring (Light & Control)	235
Kind of Trucks	Swing Bolster	Brakes	West. E.L. Equip't.	Air Brake	2500
Wheel Base of Trucks	6'-5"	Compressor	D-3-E-G	Trolley Base	200
Diam. of Wheel	33"	Cylinder	10" x 12"	Car Complete	83350
Size of Journal	5¼" M.C.B.	% Braking Power	64	Standard Gauge	

LOCOMOTIVE
ELEVATION OF CAR
L.A.P. No. 1587
LOS ANGELES PACIFIC

Feb 28, 1911   1 CAR

1580

LAP owned and operated four electric locomotives, all of which were built at Sherman Shops. All were of composite construction: steel underframes, wood bodies. All were of the steeple-cab design; 1580 and 1587 had sloping ends but 1585 and 1586 were flatbeds.

Locomotive 1580 was similar mechanically to Work Motors 1581-1584. These five were constructed in 1906 on the same work order. The only difference was the ornate body with which 1580 was adorned.

Specifications, Locomotive 1580

Builder:	LAP Sherman Shops, 1906
Type:	Composite steeple cab
Weight:	52,000 lbs.
Length:	30'0" over buffers
Width:	8'6" over sills
Height:	13'0" rail over roof
Trucks:	Rigid bolster 5'3" LAP type
Motors:	Four West. 38B (43 hp each)
Controller:	K-6
Gear Ratio:	14:68
Brakes:	Westinghouse EL, D3EG comp.
PE Number:	1552 (scrapped 1948)

1585 and 1586 were built at the Sherman Shops in 1908. In design they were an improved 1581; body dimensions were more generous, the horsepower was considerably stepped up, but the offset steeple cab was retained, permitting these motors to carry long objects such as poles.

The influence of the LAP 700 Class passenger cars is obvious in trucks and motors; the trucks were Sherman Shops products, duplicates of the 700s—while motors were obtained by robbing two 700s which thereafter ran as control trailers.

Specifications, Locos 1585 & 1586

Builder:	LAP Sherman Shops, 1908
Type:	Composite steeple cab
Weight:	84,800 and 74,000 lbs.*
Length:	30'0" over buffers
Width:	8'9½" over sills
Height:	13'2½" rail over roof
Trucks:	Swing bolster 6'5"
Motors:	Four GE 73 (75 hp each)
Controller:	K-34-B
Gear Ratio:	17:73
Brakes:	West. EL, D3EG comp.
PE Numbers:	1553 and 1554
Scrapped:	1948 and 1949 respectively

*1585 carried five tons ballast

1587

Here we have LAP's newest and best electric locomotive. Mechanically the 1587 was a duplicate of 1585 and 1586, but its body was given the full treatment, resulting in a locomotive which appeared much more similar to 1580. Indeed, 1587 and 1580 were exactly the same in bodily dimensions insofar as length and height were concerned; the 1587 was wider over sills and cab and twin hoods were likewise wider.

Like the 1585 and 1586, 1587's motors were obtained by robbing a 700; trucks were built at Sherman Shops and were similar to those under the 700s. 1587 had one distinguishing feature: a bell mounted on one of the hoods.

Specifications, Locomotive 1587

Builder:	LAP Sherman Shops, 1910
Type:	Composite steeple cab
Weight:	83,350 lbs.
Length:	30'0" over buffers
Width:	8'9½" over sills
Height:	13'5½" rail over roof
Trucks.	Swing bolster 6'5"
Motors:	Four GE 73 (75 hp each)
Controller:	K-34-D
Gear Ratio:	17:73
Brakes:	West. EL, D3EG compressor
PE Number:	1555
Scrapped:	1935

Freight Cars

LAP's FREIGHT CARS were a utilitarian and homely lot, but they reflected the system's early orientation toward hauling goods as well as people. Photo at left shows boxcar 407 at Buena Vista Freight House being switched by express motor 1553 (out of picture at left) by means of a "reacher" barely visible in the slotted (open) knuckle at left. Car was home-built at Sherman, October 1906.

IN PHOTO ABOVE, a train of standard dump cars is seen at Sherman. Small photo in lower left depicts tank car 1003 at Sherman about 1909. This vehicle was carried in the records as a sprinkling car; a pipe connection is visible in front of the far needle beam and there's a headlight bracket at the near end of the tank.

LAP's ROCK CARS (the Hart Convertible Dump Car) are lined up in photo at right in Brush Canyon.   (All: T.L. Wagenbach)

Of Nuts, Bolts,

Chapter Five

The south portal of the newly completed Hill Street Tunnel, at First St.

and Power Houses

Angel's Flight in LAP Days.

A Railway Like LAP Wasn't Just Tracks and Cars

THE MAJOR rail transit facilities that were to serve the vast part of the Los Angeles basin west of downtown were, with a single major exception, put into operation during the Los Angeles Pacific era. Only the Subway Terminal Building and the mile-long streetcar subway extending therefrom were built later. Thus Sherman and Clark were responsible for some very fundamental and long-lasting transportation landmarks, along with numerous lesser improvements.

The following inventory can be found in the M.H. Sherman file of Miscellanea at the Sherman Foundation Library. The date is definitely no earlier than October, 1905, when the corporate name became Los Angeles Pacific Co., and is probably not before October, 1906, when 13.81 acres were added to the property at Sherman. But the date is almost certainly prior to the spring of 1908, when the Hill Street Station was built in downtown Los Angeles and the Palms Division (Venice Short Line) was standard-gauged.

LOS ANGELES PACIFIC CO.
Property Other Than Rights-of-Way

1. Freight House property at Buena Vista St. & Bellevue Ave., Los Angeles, 165 x 398 feet.

2. Depot grounds, office and freight house at Hollywood.

3. Substation grounds at Sugg St. & Sunset Blvd., about one acre.

4. About 23 acres of land, power houses, shops and car barns, located at Sherman, Cal.

5. Park, depot and grounds, and one acre of sidings (100 ft. x 420 ft.) located at Sawtelle, Cal.

6. Substation and storage battery, two lots on 16th St., Los Angeles, Cal.

7. Substation and grounds at Ivy Park, Ocean Park, Playa del Rey and Hermosa.

8. One lot, freight house, corner Oregon Ave. & Second St., Santa Monica, Cal.

9. About 11½ acres, a strip of land 100 ft. x 5,000 ft. lying between broad gauge and narrow gauge rights of way in Santa Monica and Ocean Park.

10. Old Santa Fe depot grounds, about 200 x 1,600 ft., in Santa Monica.

11. Three acres—car barns and freight yards, Ocean Park, Cal.

12. About 8½ acres at Vineyard; power house, station & grounds.

13. Two and one-half acres—terminal grounds at Venice, Cal.

[Editor's note: Omission of reference to Linda Vista station building and grounds, Santa Monica, built in 1906, may date this list to that year.]

WE NOW DESCRIBE the major properties of Los Angeles Pacific, beginning with the downtown starting point of millions of passenger journeys to Hollywood, the Beaches and points in between.

HILL STREET STATION

THE FIRST MENTION of the Hill St. Station in official LAP records occurs on February 22, 1908, when authority is requested for expenditure of funds for excavating the site, constructing necessary yard tracks, and installing the track connections to the Hill St. line. Work began at once, and was pushed through to completion; the terminal was placed in service on or about June 1, 1908, as LAP's downtown station for standard-gauge trains (those using W. 16th St.). The Fourth St. Station continued in service as the downtown station for narrow-gauge trains (those going out Sunset Blvd.).

In the spring of 1908 LAP (Unit 66) constructed a small lean-to depot structure, which then was intended to be for temporary use pending construction of the subway terminal building, a limit-height building. This temporary station cost $10,000 which was divided as follows: building, $7,000, floors and equipment, $2,000, and superintendence, $1,000. The depot adjoined the old Masonic Temple, built in 1896, which the Los Angeles Pacific Land Company had previously bought, holding it for incorporation into the subway terminal site. The depot was built of wood and stucco and followed LAP's customary Mission style of architecture. LAP also bought the lot adjoining the yard on the north side; on this property was a one-story brick building occupied by the Blue Bell Cafeteria. To the rear of the property on the Olive St. side were several smaller frame structures, one of which was occupied by Wells Fargo & Company; this had one spur track to accommodate box motors.

On November 16, 1908, the Knox Building burned; LAP's losses were considerable, for this building housed not only the Fourth St. Station, but also all of the company's offices. The company at once moved into the Masonic Temple, where it remained until the Great Merger. Thus by the end of 1908, LAP's offices and its principal depot were side by side on Hill Street.

As constructed, Hill St. Yard handled only the W. 16th St. cars. Between February and December, 1909, necessary track

changes and additions were made to handle Hollywood and Colegrove cars. This required installing a new track connecting from south on Hill into the yard. The heaviest expenditures for this work were made in May, June, July and August, 1909. This work cost $9,000, with another $1,000 for trolley overhead construction. Thus on Tunnel Day–September 15, 1909–Hill St. Station was able to replace 4th St. as the Los Angeles terminal of the former narrow-gauge lines.

Almost immediately there began the intolerable congestion which so plagued Hill St. Station throughout its life. All trains left by the southernmost track, loading through four gates cut in the depot walls. Gates 1 and 2 (counting from the main entrance) served all lines except the Venice Short Line; Gate 3 was exclusively for the Venice Short Line; and Gate 4 served the VSL also in rush hours and weekends as well as special movements such as the Balloon Route Excursion. The waiting room was quite small and poorly ventilated. At rush periods it was completely inadequate to handle the crowds and the newspapers and City Hall were bombarded regularly by complaints from irate patrons. The yard, also, was too small for the number of cars using it. Crossovers were poorly located; a three-car train loading for the beach completely paralyzed all incoming train movements from the south. Waiting trains were forced to stand in Hill St.; as a result, cars of the streetcar companies were delayed, thus compounding the injury. Hollywood and Colegrove cars could enter the station, but once inside had to

HILL ST. STATION in downtown Los Angeles, was nerve center of LAP operations.

wait the pleasure of the beach trains before emerging. LAP officials procrastinated expertly and effectively, protesting that Hill St. Station was temporary, that any monies expended on stopgap improvements there would be money thrown away, and that the Fourth St. Subway and its permanent depot building would be built "just as soon as times improve."

Olive St., bounding the rear of the yard, was quite a bit higher than Hill St.; the excavating for the yard brought tracks up against a virtually vertical wall which was not bulwarked. Consequently, vibration of trains loosened great loads of earth which slid down onto cars, at worst breaking vestibules and pilots, at best causing them to pull out for their various destinations with rear ends well dirtied up. Not until 1920 was a bulkhead constructed.

Although LAP's proprietary interest in Hill St. Station ended with the Great Merger, the later interesting developments at this site would be of interest to our readers, so here they are in outline: In 1916, the yard was enlarged and rearranged, giving Hollywood cars their own two tracks for entrance and egress; a small open waiting shelter and ticket booth was built between the two pairs of tracks. In 1925, coincident with the construction of the subway and the Subway Terminal Building, the Masonic Temple and Hill St. Station were razed; a new depot for the W. 16th St. trains was constructed at a cost of $35,000; this, too, was to be temporary until the Vineyard Subway could be constructed. A year later beach patrons were moved into the Subway Terminal as a new concourse, umbrella sheds, and entrance from Olive was thereupon remodeled and leased and became a grocery store. In 1931 came the last big change: a steel and concrete deck 100 ft. x 183 ft. was constructed over the tracks on the Olive St. side, providing a bus deck above, an interurban terminal below. This arrangement continued until the surface terminal was abandoned in 1950. Today both the bus deck and the interurban yard are in use as auto parks.

HILL STREET TUNNELS

THE HILL ST. TUNNELS were built to secure a faster, more direct route into downtown Los Angeles from Hollywood. LAP had trackage rights over the narrow-gauge tracks of the Los Angeles Railway from Sunset & N. Broadway via Sunset, Main, Spring and 4th Sts. to its 4th St. Station. When it was decided to standard-gauge the Hollywood-Colegrove lines, it would have been necessary to: (1) build a combination gauge line over the previous route, gaining nothing in time and freedom from congestion and entailing much costly special track work——, or (2) build two tunnels on the line of Hill St. projected through the two spurs of Bunker Hill which had long barred northward extension of that busy thoroughfare.

LAP wisely cast its vote in favor of the latter project, and preliminary work on the tunnels was started by the Los Angeles Pacific Company (Unit 57) in 1906. Active work on the construction of Tunnel No. 2 began in July 1908 and was completed by December 31, 1908; this was the longer tunnel of the two, being 976 feet in length and extending from Temple St. to Sunset Blvd. Forces were then moved to Tunnel No. 1, 546 feet long, extending from 1st St. to Temple St.; this was virtually completed by August 31, 1909. Operation of Hollywood-Colegrove cars over the standard gauge tracks of the Hill St. tunnel cutoff began on September 15, 1909–a great day for Hollywood as it cut off 10 minutes running time.

Shortly after Tunnel No. 1 was completed, the city of Los Angeles dug a parallel bore for vehicular traffic. The east

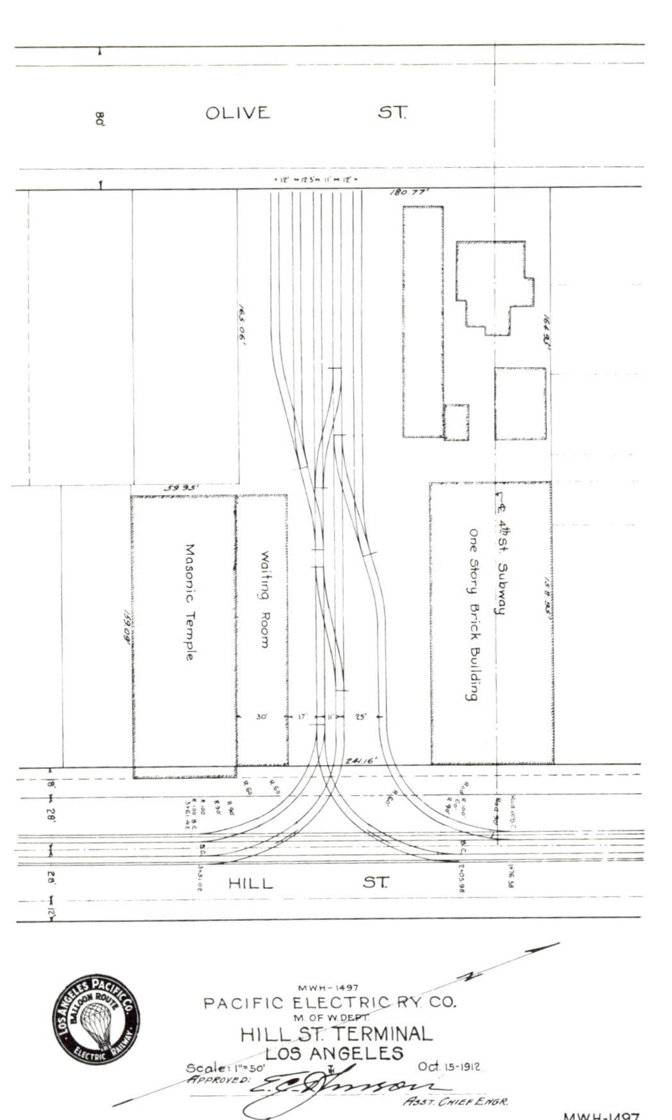

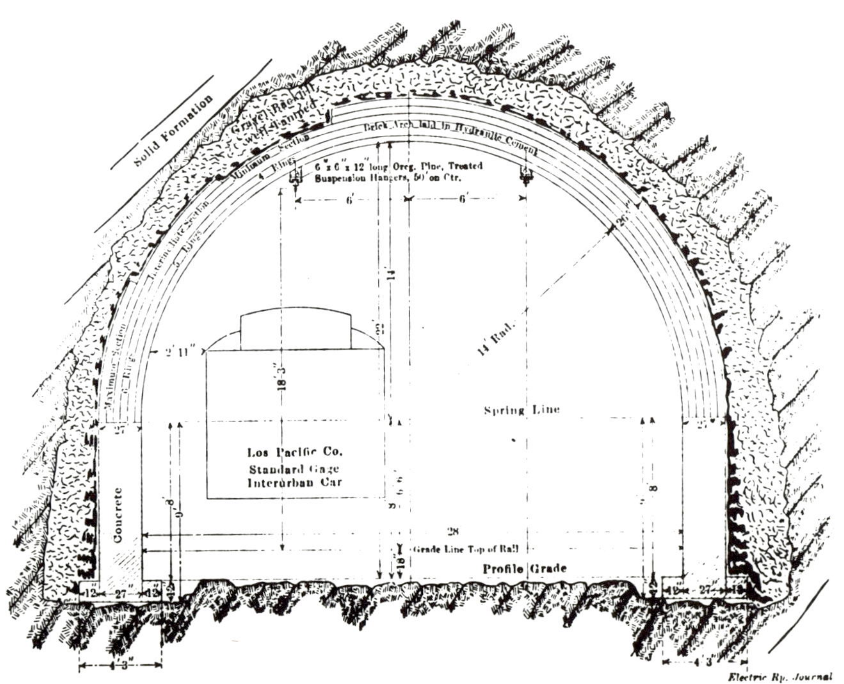

Los Angeles Pacific Company—Cross Section of Hill Street Cut-Off Tunnel

THE NORTH PORTAL of the South Hill Street Tunnel is shown in photo above. Elevation of the tunnel in cross-section shown in diagram at left. (T.L. Wagenbach)

UPPER LEFT DIAGRAM The Hill Street Station Yards in LAP Days.

OCEAN PARK CARHOUSE with the Trolleyway in foreground. A four-car train of 700s is set out on the siding ready to go up to Santa Monica while the 723 and what appears to be a 200 wait in the barn.   *(T.L. Wagenbach)*

bench wall of the LAP tunnel was constructed to the spring line of the city's tunnel so as to be used jointly by the city and the railway company.

Today both tunnels are gone. Tunnel 2 disappeared when the Hollywood Freeway was built in 1951. Tunnel 1 became a vehicular tunnel in 1951 and was removed in 1955 when the hill above it was cut down to grade.

OCEAN PARK

ON FEBRUARY 15, 1901, LAP began work on an extension at Azure & 2nd Sts., Ocean Park, to the Club House via what later was known as the Trolleyway. This appears to be the first use of the Trolleyway by LAP. Midway, land was purchased to serve as the site of a power house, built primarily to serve the projected Palms Division (Venice Short Line). The explosion at Sherman power house the year before had so crippled LAP that this new power house was deemed necessary. The building was erected in the spring of 1901 on Rose Ave. (Sunset Ave.) adjacent to the Santa Fe tracks. A small car house and a wye to turn trailer trains were also built at this location.

A steel strike in the east caused a delay in delivery of machinery so the power house did not go on the line until mid-December, 1901.

Ocean Park power house was rebuilt into a substation in 1904 and was torn down in 1954. The tracks and car barn were removed in 1950 and today a motor coach yard and garage occupy the site.

VINEYARD

IN MAY, 1902, LAP announced it would have a third power house, to be located at the junction of the Palms Division and the old Santa Monica Short Line (W. 16th St. line). This junction point was first called Nadeau but was soon changed to Vineyard, which name it made famous in electric railway circles.

Vineyard power house was built in several units at various times. The original unit was constructed in the last half of 1902 and the first half of 1903. On May 22, 1903, the following article appeared in the Santa Monica *Outlook:*

"The boilers are now being placed at the Vineyard power house. LAP hopes to have the first battery of 1,000 hp in operation in six weeks. Later, batteries of 1,520 hp and 550 hp will be added, giving a total of 2,700 hp more than at present. While it is proposed to increase speed some, the real value will be in the relief it will give when travel is heavy."

On July 25th, same year, the *Outlook:* "LAP expects to have its new power house in operation early in August. The second engine and dynamo have now arrived and are being placed in position. The machinery for the Playa del Rey substation is also being put up."

Outlook, August 18, 1903: "By the end of this month a power plant of three units, two of which are already in place and being adjusted, will be delivering 2,400 volts to the company's substations. The Vineyard power house has sprung up like the proverbial mushroom. Everything in the plant is to be of the very best and the establishment is being erected in accordance with the best and most modern electrical practice of

THE VINEYARD STEAM PLANT. LAP's Vineyard power house was enlarged several times to accommodate a growing need for propulsion power. Interior photo (below) shows, at left, marble switchboards and operators' desk, with the generators in the center. The units are, from front to rear, a 2,750-kw Westinghouse-Parsons steam turbine installed in 1906, a 1,200-kw reciprocating engine, an 800-kw reciprocating engine and a 600-kw reciprocating engine. All units were direct-connected, 2,200-v, 50 cycle AC. The 600 and 800-kw machines dated from 1902-1903 while the 1,200-kw engine and generator was installed in March, 1904. *(Southern California Edison)*

the day. The boiler battery is already installed. Four huge Stirling boilers, rated at 250 hp each, using oil sprayed through Hammel burners and discharging their gases into a big yellow smokestack rising a hundred feet above the grate bars, will furnish the steam. The engines deliver their exhaust into big Wheeler condensers where it is converted back into water and returned to the boilers with comparatively little loss.

In 1906 Vineyard was enlarged; additional boilers, a large transformer room and a high tension switch gallery were added. To old units (a 600-KW, an 800-KW and a 1200-KW direct connected, 2200-volt, 50-cycle AC generators), a 2750-KW Westinghouse-Parsons steam turbine was added. An electric crane for handling machinery and for repairs was also installed.

Vineyard power house was used continuously until 1915 when PE went over to purchased hydroelectric power. In 1924 a drought brought a power shortage and Vineyard generated power again for eight months. In December, 1929, the great smokestack was razed, along with most of the old power house. The stack was of concrete block construction, was 156 feet high, 16'4" wide at bottom and 14'10" wide at top with an inside diameter of 14 feet. A portion of the old power house was in service as a substation until 1950; it was torn down in 1953.

Some of Vineyard's equipment was moved to Torrance Shops in 1919 where it served for many years; included in this category were a steel smokestack seven feet in diameter and a hundred feet high and two 250 hp boilers.

VIEW SHOWING tracks up the coast from Santa Monica to the Long Wharf, seen in distance.   *(T.L. Wagenbach)*

THE LONG WHARF

THE STORY of the great harbor fight is a Los Angeles legend which indirectly affected LAP and therefore merits our attention.

There were three possible locations for the deep-water harbor for Los Angeles: San Pedro (where the government had spent about $900,000 in dredging the Inner Harbor, but which could not accommodate vessels drawing more than 17 feet), Redondo (where a marine canyon ran in close to shore providing deep draft vessels with ample depth), and Santa Monica. All three of the locations had to be provided with large sea walls to insure safety at all times.

In 1892 Congress refused an appropriation for a breakwater at San Pedro; instead, a board of engineers was appointed to review previous recommendations and report on the various merits of Santa Monica, Redondo and San Pedro. The engineers decided in favor of San Pedro.

Previous to this, Senator William B. Frye of Maine, chairman of the Senate Commerce Committee, paid the Los Angeles area a visit. Upon viewing San Pedro, Frye—doubtless a man familiar with the busy harbors of the Atlantic states,

turned to the Chamber of Commerce committee conducting his tour and said: "Why, where are all the ships? I was given to understand there was something of a harbor here! Well, as near as I can make out, you propose to ask the government to create a harbor for you almost out of whole cloth. The Lord has not given you much to start with, that is certain. It will cost four or five millions to build, you say; well, is your whole Southern California worth that much?"

The Southern Pacific, led by Collis P. Huntington, spent a million on behalf of Port Los Angeles, its deep water terminal at the end of the mile-long Long Wharf. Located a mile up the coast from Santa Monica and the competing Santa Fe, Port Los Angeles promised near-monopoly if Washington could be convinced that the future Los Angeles Harbor should be located there. The opposition was equally active, led by the Chamber of Commerce, the *Los Angeles Times*, the Santa Fe and a vast majority of the public. Of these, all were boosting San Pedro except the Santa Fe, which had committed itself to Redondo.

Sen. Frye continued for years to oppose San Pedro. In

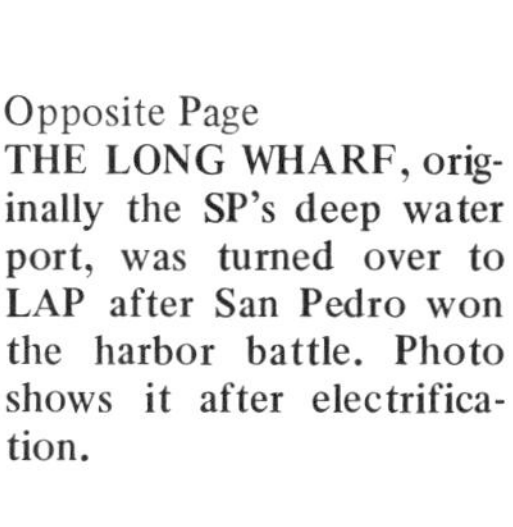

1896, when he introduced a bill appropriating $2,900,000 to build a sea wall at Santa Monica, the memorable struggle reached a climax. So many protests from authoritative sources against the proposed Santa Monica breakwater were sent to Washington, accompanied by demands that it be built instead at San Pedro, that the item was struck out of the House bill and Los Angeles, as in previous years, was left without any appropriation for deep-water work. When the matter came up in the Senate, Sen. Stephen M. White of California, a resident of Los Angeles (and a member of Frye's Commerce Commit-tee), demanded that the money be appropriated for San Pedro; this was refused. He then proposed that a third board of engi-neers be established to go over the whole question of location again. The Commerce Committee refused this compromise and put back in the bill the appropriation for Santa Monica. The fight was then carried to the floor of the Senate, and at the end of a long debate, including White vs. Frye for three hours, White emerged victorious.

Then followed two long years of exasperating delay in the construction of the San Pedro breakwater. Time passed, but the War Department failed to advertise for bids. The people grew impatient. Investigation showed that the Secretary of War, Russel M. Alger, was delaying action apparently with the hope that Congress might again take up the harbor question. Appeals to Alger were met with trivial excuses or indifference. Finally, a Chamber of Commerce committee appealed directly to President McKinley, who then forced Alger to advertise for bids. A Chicago firm, Heldmeier & New, won the contract.

It was only when the contractor dumped the first barge of rock off Point Firmin on April 26, 1899, that the people felt sure their 10-year fight was really won. Then they celebrated for three days—including a giant barbecue at San Pedro.

San Pedro went on to become one of the world's important harbors, while Santa Monica and Redondo, after several years of withering on the vine, gave up the struggle to become com-mercially important; instead, both became outstanding beach resorts and beautiful residential cities. By 1908, when SP leased the Long Wharf and its Air Line railroad to Los Angeles

to LAP, Port Los Angeles had become a ghost of its former self. Thereafter, the Wharf advertised for fishermen, and the big daily event was the arrival of the Balloon Route excursion cars.

Storms and age weakened the Long Wharf; in 1917 the Port Los Angeles outer end was removed, and the remainder went in 1920. Today, only a pile of boulders marks the shore stub of what once was the notable roadbed of "An Ocean Voyage on Wheels."

PORT LOS ANGELES

PORT LOS ANGELES was the business end of the Long Wharf, a 4,720-foot pier jutting out from the coast just north of Santa Monica Canyon. From 1893 until 1903 Port Los An-geles handled the bulk of the coastwise passenger business be-tween the city and points north; this was due to its very favor-able time differential: four hours over Redondo, eight hours over San Pedro.

Port Los Angeles was the dream of old Collis P. Hunting-ton, longtime head of Southern Pacific. "C.P." ordered it built in 1890; on Sunday, May 20, 1890, he and a large group of SP executives descended upon sleepy Santa Monica to make a careful examination of the town and its surroundings. Other SP men followed but the town was kept in a state of uncer-tainty until late 1890 when SP sought a wharf franchise. SP desired such a wharf due to the fact that the Santa Fe would almost certainly build into Santa Monica—also, the new wharf at Redondo, opened in 1888, was seriously cutting into SP's San Pedro wharf and diverting freight to the Santa Fe at Re-dondo.

In August, 1891, a group of SP surveyors arrived and made camp in Santa Monica Canyon and began to make surveys. It was then learned that SP had bought 247 acres on the north side of the canyon with several hundred feet of beach front-age. A right of way had also been secured from SP's reserva-tion at Railroad St. (Colorado Ave.) to the canyon property. On March 6, 1892, the tunnel under Ocean Ave. was put in

LONG WHARF SCENES: Top plate shows yards at outer end; note the extremely long pipe arms used for overhead here. Photo below shows coal bunker including jib crane and scoops for transferring the coal from the collier to the bunker, from which the coal was dumped into hoppers and gondolas for shipment. *(Both: T.L. Wagenbach)*

HOLLYWOOD DEPOT,
at Ivar St.

service. On July 25, the first pile was driven for the Long Wharf. The first steamer landed on May 13, 1893. The last spike was driven on July 14, 1893. In October, the depot at the outer end was completed and the dining room was opened with a banquet. "C.P." was happy.

Port Los Angeles was a miniature town built over the ocean. It had a post office, a custom house, a depot, docks, telegraph, express and freight offices, an elaborate system of waterworks, warehouses, the largest coal bunkers on the Pacific Coast, fully equipped with modern machinery for rapid handling of cargoes. "C.P." dreamed it to be the largest port of entry on the Pacific Coast where might be discharged the rich cargoes of freighters from China and Japan. San Francisco steamers made regular landings Monday, Wednesday, Thursday and Saturday, and huge steam colliers came from British Columbia, lumber vessels from up the coast, and occasionally a full-rigged ship from Europe.

The approach of the wharf proper was 3,120 feet long and the entire wharf was 4,720 feet long. The approach was 26 feet wide which accommodated a double track and an 8-foot walkway on its south side. Material used in the approach were

1,500 selected piles heavily creosoted, 975,000 feet of lumber, 37 tons of bolts and spikes. The main wharf widened out to 130 feet and was over 1,500 feet long. It had seven tracks, plus the bunkers, warehouses, depot, offices, restaurant, etc. The main deck was 20 feet above mean high tide with water depth from 30 to 40 feet.

Los Angeles was made a Port of Entry in 1893, with Port Los Angeles, Redondo and San Pedro as sub-ports. SP's coal was landed at Port Los Angeles; the huge bunkers also served steamships. When conversion to oil of steamers and locomotives took place after 1902, much of the commercial importance of Port Los Angeles waned. "C.P." died in 1900 and his successor, E.H. Harriman, had no particular love for the Long Wharf, which required expensive maintenance. As fewer and fewer ships called, Harriman allowed it to be bruited about (as early as 1902) that SP was considering abandoning the Long Wharf. However, it continued operating, always on a descending scale, until about 1911, when LAP (which had leased it in 1908 and electrified all trackage) abandoned lumber handling. In 1917 the outer end, Port Los Angeles, was removed and the approach continued as a fishing pier. Storms and old age so

SAWTELLE DEPOT. Note
boxcar in side track.
(Both: T.L. Wagenbach)

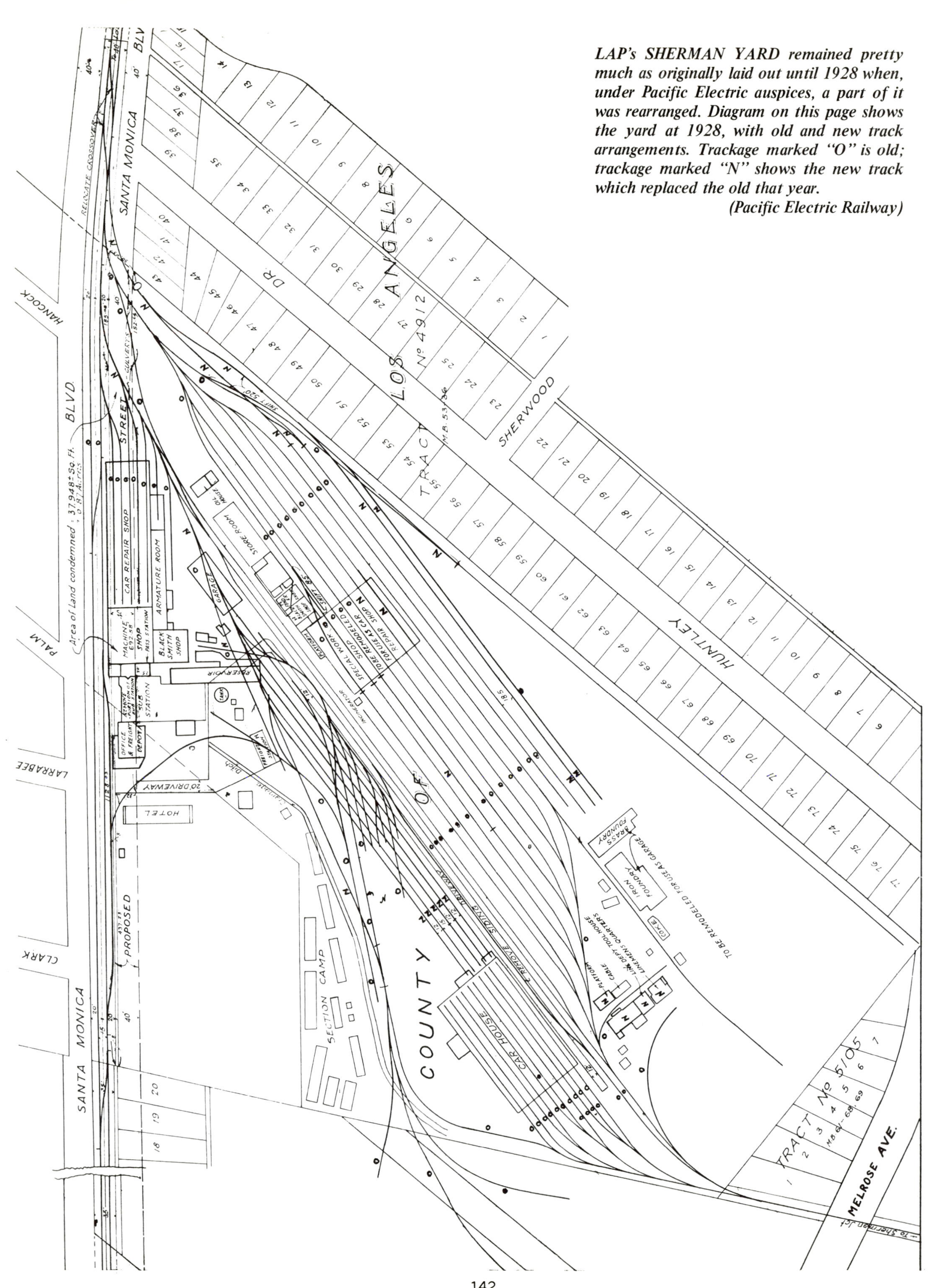

LAP's SHERMAN YARD *remained pretty much as originally laid out until 1928 when, under Pacific Electric auspices, a part of it was rearranged. Diagram on this page shows the yard at 1928, with old and new track arrangements. Trackage marked "O" is old; trackage marked "N" shows the new track which replaced the old that year.*

(Pacific Electric Railway)

THE CARPENTER SHOP at Sherman. Car partially in the picture at the right appears to be express trailer 1510.

(T.L. Wagenbach)

weakened this stub that it, too, was removed in 1920. Today only a pile of granite boulders marks the shore end of the great pier.

Continuing north up the coast from the Long Wharf was the *Hueneme Malibu & Port Los Angeles Ry.,* a private line built by May K. Rindge, widow of Frederick Rindge, to haul produce from the famous Rancho Malibu. From the foot of the Long Wharf, a spur track extended about a mile to the mouth of Temescal Canyon, some 6½ miles short of the Rancho boundary. There was talk in the early days about Sherman, Clark and Rindge collaborating on an electric line up the coast to Ventura; in later years Rindge's widow fought fiercely (and vainly) against a state's highway extension through the Rancho.

FOURTH ST. STATION

THE FIRST downtown L.A. station was located at 222 W. Fourth St., the station of the *Pasadena & Los Angeles Electric Ry.* The two companies continued to share that depot until the sale of the P&LA in early 1898. It is possible that some sort of rental agreement was entered into by Sherman and Clark and the reorganized *Los Angeles & Pasadena Electric Railway,* but facts are vague on this point.

We do know, however, that on November 1, 1899, ground was broken for LAP's own $50,000 station building at 316 W. 4th St. Sherman and Clark were joined by Frederick H. Rindge of Malibu in this venture. The new station building was three stories in height, had a frontage of 78 feet and a depth of 113 feet, and was built of steel and brick with a terra cotta front. LAP's waiting rooms were on the ground floor and its offices were upstairs. This building served as LAP's headquarters until its burning on November 16, 1908. LAP then leased the old Masonic Temple on Hill Street next door to its Hill St. Station and moved its offices there. They remained there until the Great Merger when all offices were consolidated in the P.E. Building.

SHERMAN

SHERMAN SHOPS and Car House were as old as LAP itself. The first mention of this key facility was back in January, 1896. At that time, the *Pasadena & Pacific Railway Co.* (Unit 43) bought 5.56 acres of land adjoining its Santa Monica line about half a mile west of Hacienda Park. It proceeded to lay 2½ miles of yard tracks on the site and built a car barn, a steam power house, and a shop building. This new facility was named "Sherman" after P&P's head man, General M.H. Sherman. It is believed by some that the official name was "Shermanton" but this name never caught on and may safely be disregarded. Sherman was not only the name of LAP's shops and car house—it was used in referring to the entire area now known as West Hollywood.

In the first half of 1897 the W. 16th St. line was built from downtown Los Angeles to Beverly; to effect a connection with this line, the Sherman Cut-off was constructed in June, 1897; this line ran out the back door of Sherman Yards to Sherman Junction, located at what is today La Cienega Blvd. & Third St.

The area in back of Sherman was swampy; dirt trains filled it in in 1905-06 using dirt from the big Sunset Blvd. cuts. The company added 13.81 acres of reclaimed land to Sherman Yard on October 1, 1906, and at once constructed additional shop buildings. These additional buildings were completed in May and June, 1907. When this work was finished, the total mileage of trackage in Sherman Yard and including the Sherman Cut-off had risen to 6.47 in terms of equivalent single track.

Buildings at Sherman included (in LAP's day) two car houses, an iron foundry, a brass foundry, a blacksmith shop, a car repair shop, an oil house, various store houses and the old power house, changed into a substation about 1905. It was LAP's intention to construct a large paint shop and a transfer table to the south of the carpenter shop; neither the paint shop nor the transfer table materialized, but the carpenter shop did and became the general car repair shop in later PE days. The old car house stood in the vacant area just west of the carpenter shop. The old maintenance and repair facilities crowded the main line on Santa Monica Blvd. (Sherman Ave.). When the south roadway was cut through in 1928, these buildings were razed.

Old LAP records give the following data on buildings it erected at Sherman:

Car House: 131'6" x 222'; one story brick; built 1907 at a cost of $30,000. It was torn down in 1955 to make way for a bus parking lot.

Iron Foundry: 54' x 100'; one story, frame building; cost, $2,800.

Brass Foundry: 30' x 90'; one story, frame building; cost, $1,660.

Blacksmith Shop, Office, Fender Shop: 30'6" x 66'3"; one story, brick.

Car Repair Shop: 135' x 135'; one story brick building, built 1907 at a cost of $38,000.

Oil House: 23' x 23'; one story brick, built 1908 at a cost of $5,100.

Store House: 44' x 104'; one story brick, built 1907 at a cost of $15,000.

BUENA VISTA

THERE IS REASON to suspect the existence of some railway activity at Sunset & N. Broadway as far back as the early 1890s. However, among the earliest recorded references to Buena Vista Freight House is dated June 24, 1904: "LAP has received a franchise for three spur tracks off Sunset Blvd. into Buena Vista Freight House." These cost $14,600.

In the summer of 1907 LAP rearranged the tracks, and in 1909 Buena Vista was standard gauged.

A one-story brick and frame building was built in 1905 at a cost of $20,000.

LAP was assessed $7,500 in 1911 for the opening and widening of Sunset Blvd. past the freight route.

When the Air Line was electrified in 1911 and the Merger took place, all LAP freight business was transferred to the PE 8th & Hemlock house.

Gallery Of LAP Substations

(Left) Old Ivy Substation; (Bottom) Ocean Park Substation and onetime steam plant.

RIGHT
New Ivy sub in
Culver City.
BELOW LEFT
16th & Burling-
ton sub in Los
Angeles

ABOVE RIGHT
Hermosa sub
RIGHT
West Olive sub

The Where, Why

Chapter Six

and How of the LAP

Craig Rasmussen

On the

Freight-Conscious LAP,

Lemons Were Almost

As Important As

People

L IKE any railway, the Los Angeles Pacific was in the business of providing transportation—passenger and freight. In this chapter we will touch on how LAP did it in this era when there were few alternative means for getting around— save for the horse, or good old-fashioned footpower.

The basic history of the LAP concentrates on the passenger business, but freight was important too and a general survey of the LAP freight business is presented in this chapter. Reproduction herein of three of LAP's public timetables—for 1902, 1907 and the last one, in 1911—shows the growth of the LAP territory and LAP's means of servicing it.

Finally, a look at the LAP's December 1, 1906, Trainmen's Rulebook covers the line's system of collecting its fares and operating its trains.

Under Sherman and Clark (or in the SP era under Paul Shoup) a trained staff of officers supervised all LAP activities. Heading this staff was the General Manager; such famous LAP men as W.D. Larrabee, T.R. Gabel and D.W. Pontius held this second-in-command job, although it was given different names at different times. The organization of the passenger department was headed by a general agent, then the station agents.

Passenger cars ran under the direct supervision of the dispatcher, whose office was located at Sherman. Telephones at strategic points gave trainmen instant communication with the dispatcher. On double track, no train orders were necessary, cars proceeding under timetable authorization. Employees' timetables were published (unfortunately none seems to have been preserved). On single track, the traffic proceeded under authorization of train orders and/or by timetable rights. Freight trains ran as extras.

FREIGHT

LAP was one of the first electric railways in Southern California to recognize the importance of hauling freight. Perhaps the freight rolling stock it obtained from the *Los Angeles County Railway* and *Cahuenga Valley Railroad* made it think hard about developing a freight business rather than scrapping those cars. At any rate, it motorized certain steam cars and used them as electric locomotives as early as 1898.

One of the most important items shipped in 1898 and 1899 was lemons from the lemon orchards in the Hollywood and Colegrove districts. Lemons bound to Los Angeles were carried in express motors; those destined for eastern cities were loaded onto box cars at Colegrove, taken to Ocean Park and the boxes

BUENA VISTA FREIGHT HOUSE in narrow-gauge days.　　　　　*(Interurbans)*

transshipped into Santa Fe box cars, due to difference in track gauge.

Another important item hauled was decomposed granite; this was loaded into LAP dump cars near Laurel Canyon and hauled to various places along the line, where it was used as ballast. Certain cities, such as Los Angeles and Santa Monica, used this material as street surfacing.

By 1901, LAP's freight service amounted to a very creditable share of its revenue. Eleven freight stations were maintained: Los Angeles, Melrose Jct., Prospect Park (Hollywood Blvd. & Vermont), Colegrove, Hollywood, Laurel Jct., Sherman, Sawtelle, Soldiers' Home, Santa Monica, Ocean Park. Freight was received at and distributed from each of these stations. Wagons were used to provide door-to-door delivery; in Los Angeles, LAP wagons covered the area bounded by Los Angeles St., Hill St., 7th St. and Macy St. and made three trips per day. Wagons called in response to phone calls to Main 923 in L.A. Wagon service in Santa Monica was available; the LAP number there was Main 21. LAP admonished shippers that "Shipments must be received 30 minutes before leaving time."

ANOTHER VIEW OF Buena Vista freight house.   *(T.L. Wagenbach)*

Leaving time was as follows in January, 1901: Lv. Santa Monica & Ocean Park via Colegrove, 6:40 AM; via Hollywood, 3:30 PM; via Colegrove, 3:40 PM. Lv. L.A. via Colegrove, 8:50 AM; via Hollywood, 1:15 PM; via Colegrove, 5:20 PM.

On October 1, 1902, the Santa Monica *Outlook* was quite impressed by an LAP work motor: "The beginning of freight cars by electric motors is now an actual fact. All of the lumber received by the Ocean Park Lumber Company comes that way. The electric motor seems to have no difficulty in doing the work. Yesterday it moved three heavy box cars off the siding at the lumber yard up a grade with little or no trouble and no noise whatsoever. Quite a change from the puffing and blowing of steam and ringing of bells that go with steam cars.

As additional power became available, LAP was able to step up its freight handling. In April, 1903, the company remodeled the old Pavilion in Ocean Park into a freight depot and laid a third rail from Front St. to Hill St. so the standard gauge cars could reach this new depot. 1903 also saw the building of the 26th St. Spur in Santa Monica into a new brickyard; many carloads of freight were obtained from this kiln, as well as affording a new interchange track with the SP's Santa Monica Line. Of course, interchange with the steam lines before LAP was standard gauged (1907-1909) meant transshipping.

On July 1, 1903, LAP announced an improved freight service: A new freight train left L.A. at 5:00 AM, arriving in Santa Monica one hour later; it carried the morning papers, fruit and vegetables. A through freight left L.A. at 7:00 AM and a way freight left at 1:00 PM.

On August 18, 1903, the *Outlook* said: "Within the last few days the Sherman Shops turned out a pair of electric locomotives capable of hauling eight loaded freight cars over any of LAP's grades. More are being pressed into service for the company's freight demands every day, and a surprising quantity of fruit and other goods is being hauled over the north line at present."

The public continued to oppose the standard gauging of street car lines in the Los Angeles area, due to the prevalent fear that a 4'8½" track would bring freight trains down every street. However, LAP went ahead with a modern and convenient freight terminal in Los Angeles. This was the Buena Vista Freight House, located at the corner of N. Broadway and Sunset. This building was one story in height, of the LAP's traditional Mission style of architecture, and covered an area of 400 feet on N. Broadway and 100 feet on Sunset. Ten sets of tracks ran into the grounds which extended another hundred feet up Sunset. Both freight and express were handled at the Buena Vista terminal and a waiting room for passengers was also installed. This new facility was placed in service in April, 1905. A month later, six more express motors were put in service. This increased LAP's express service to four cars daily to and from the beaches.

The shadow of things to come fell across the LAP freight picture in August, 1905, when Sherman Shops turned out two standard gauge electric locomotives. With the advent of standard gauge track LAP would be in a much more favorable position to haul freight. These two locomotives were used on the Inglewood branch and also on combination gauge trackage in Ocean Park and Santa Monica.

In March, 1906, the Southern Pacific, through E.H. Harriman, purchased a controlling interest in LAP. The infusion of new money brought great acceleration to the development of LAP and its freight service was in the vanguard. Broad gauging of the system was pushed forward with vigor, and as this progressed so also did the re-equipping of cars with the necessary 4'8½" trucks.

One of the fixtures of LAP freight service was the newspaper train. This had its beginning in a gasoline speeder on which a young man brought down to Santa Monica the *Morning Herald* from Los Angeles; we discovered this after the young man, evidently looking for a thrill, took a curve too fast one morning and made news as well as distributing same over the adjacent landscape. LAP operated a newspaper car every morning, leaving L.A. at 4:30 AM as of 1907; it operated via Colegrove and Santa Monica to Hermosa and Redondo.

TWO MORE freighthouses: Soldiers' Home (above) and Santa Monica (SP Division).　　　　*(Both: T.L. Wagenbach)*

THE 700s were LAP's only interurbans equipped to operate in trains; here, a four-car train rests at Sherman. (T.L. Wagenbach)

Also in 1907 there was this lineup of express and freight trains leaving L.A.: at 5:00 AM, a freight train for Sentous via Hollywood, Sherman and Vineyard; at 8:20 AM, U.S. Mail to Redondo via Hollywood serving all intermediate post office stations except Palms; at 8:30 AM, express and light freight for Ivy via Hollywood and Venice; 10:45 AM, freight and express for Redondo via Colegrove and Westgate; 2:00 PM, express and light freight for Hollywood; 3:45 PM, express and light freight for Venice via Colegrove; 4:45 PM, U.S. Mail, for Venice via Hollywood; 10:30 PM, freight for Venice via Colegrove; 11:00 PM, freight for Sawtelle via Hollywood.

On July 1, 1908, LAP placed in service the SP Air Line which it had leased from Sentous to the end of the Long Wharf and electrified. This brought considerable freight business to LAP, and also made Sentous its chief interchange point.

By 1909, LAP freight service had matured. Seventeen electric locomotives (the largest of which turned up 300 hp), 221 freight cars (many of which were used in interchange with steam roads), 5 mail and express cars and miscellaneous service cars were in use. At the heart of the LAP freight activity was the Buena Vista Freight House, and in every town of any size on the system there was a freight house adjacent to the passenger depot. Commodities hauled were lumber, oil, crushed rock, citrus products and other items. These moved mostly at night, due to power supply being more adequate then, in trains up to 15 cars in length.

In 1911, LAP operated freight trains as follows: Two trains daily from L.A. to Redondo; four trains from L.A. to Venice via Colegrove; and two daily trains from L.A. to Hollywood (all daily except Sunday). It should be pointed out that no freight trains were routed out W. 16th St. at any time; to serve the Vineyard area, freight trains ran via the Sherman Cutoff or via Palms and Ivy.

This, then, is the story of the development of freight hauling on the LAP system. The business it turned over to PE in 1911 was nowhere near as large as PE's own, but LAP had no harbor to serve and PE did. One of the first acts of the merged company was to connect the LAP with PE via the Air Line; once that was done, Buena Vista Freight House was closed and all LAP freight thereafter went over the PE docks at 8th & Hemlock.

APRIL, 1902

Balloon Route

Los Angeles Pacific
RAILROAD

Santa Monica Scenic Electric Line

TIME TABLE

In Effect December 1st, 1901.   Subject to Change Without Notice

SHORT LINE ROUTE

Leave Los Angeles Fourth Street Station, between Broadway and Hill Streets, via Hill and 16th Streets, **For Santa Monica and Ocean Park.**

*6 35 am	10 35 am	2 35 pm	6 35 pm
7 05 am	11 05 am	3 05 pm	7 05 pm
7 35 am	11 35 am	3 35 pm	7 35 pm
8 05 am	12 05 pm	4 05 pm	8 35 pm
8 35 am	12 35 pm	4 35 pm	9 35 pm
9 05 am	1 05 pm	5 05 pm	10 35 pm
9 35 am	1 35 pm	5 35 pm	11 35 pm
10 05 am	2 05 pm	6 05 pm	

* Daily except Sunday.

All cars stop at the thriving town of SAWTELLE, where one-half mile to the north is the Pacific Branch National Soldiers' Home, an interesting trip. Visitors welcome.

FOOTHILL ROUTES

Leave Los Angeles Via Bellevue Av. **COLEGROVE** and Sherman *For Santa Monica and Ocean Park*

*6 15 am	4 15 pm
7 15 am	*‡4 30 pm
8 15 am	*‡5 00 pm
9 15 am	5 15 pm
10 15 am	6 15 pm
11 15 am	7 15 pm
12 15 pm	8 15 pm
1 15 pm	9 15 pm
2 15 pm	10 15 pm
3 15 pm	11 15 pm
*‡4 00 pm	†12 15 am

* Daily except Sunday
† To Sherman only
‡ To Ida Street only

Leave Los Angeles Via Bellevue Av. **HOLLYWOOD** and Sherman *For Santa Monica and Ocean Park*

*6 45 am	4 45 pm
7 45 am	*‡5 00 pm
8 45 am	*‡5 30 pm
9 45 am	5 45 pm
10 45 am	*†6 00 pm
11 45 am	6 45 pm
12 45 pm	†7 45 pm
1 45 pm	†8 45 pm
2 45 pm	†9 45 pm
3 45 pm	†10 45 pm
*‡4 00 pm	†11 45 pm
*†4 30 pm	

* Daily except Sunday
† To Sherman only
‡ To Ida Street only

Leave Ocean Park and Santa Monica For Los Angeles

(Leave From Ocean Park Casino)

*5 45 am	H 9 55 am	c 2 25 pm	c 6 25 pm
*6 10 am	c 10 25 am	H 2 55 pm	H 6 55 pm
c 6 35 am	H 10 55 am	c 3 25 pm	c 7 25 pm
H 6 55 am	c 11 25 am	H 3 55 pm	X 7 55 pm
c 7 25 am	H 11 55 am	c 4 25 pm	c 8 25 pm
H 7 55 am	c 12 25 pm	H 4 55 pm	c 9 25 pm
c 8 25 am	H 12 55 pm	c 5 25 pm	10 25 pm
H 8 55 am	c 1 25 pm	H 5 55 pm	11 05 pm
c 9 25 am	H 1 55 pm		

Leave Arcadia Hotel 10 minutes later.

*—Daily Except Sunday.

C—Connects at Morroco with cars for Los Angeles via Sherman and COLEGROVE.

H—Connects at Morroco with cars for Los Angeles via Sherman and HOLLYWOOD.

X—Via Sherman and Hollywood and NOT via 16th and Hill Sts.

Local cars via North Loop and South Loop make connections with cars to and from Los Angeles.

TOURISTS

There are no places in all Southern California, where you can more fully enjoy life than at Santa Monica and Ocean Park, during the Autumn and Winter months, the most delightful of all the year. Take a trip there and look over the many cozy furnished cottages for rent at reasonable rates and you will want to arrange for one.

SANTA MONICA...
ALL-THE-YEAR-ROUND RESORT

No other Resort offers so many Attractive Attractions

New Auditorium at North Beach

One of the largest and finest auditoriums for literary, social and general amusement purposes, adds one of the strongest attractions to this popular beach.

North Beach Bath House

With the largest hot water plunge on the Coast. Water changed every day. Surf Bathing, fine safe and clean beach. Fishing and Pleasure wharves, where good sport is always found.

Three Miles

Of wide Plank and Cement Walk along the Beach, connecting Sunset Beach, North Beach, Arcadia, South Beach and Ocean Park.

Hotel Accommodations

Abundant and unsurpassed. Cottages furnished and unfurnished. Golf Links, Tennis Court, Polo Grounds Fine Drives, Camera Obscura, largest in the world. Bowling Alleys, Shooting Galleries, Pool and Billiard Tables.

Balloon Route

LOS ANGELES PACIFIC RAILROAD

Santa Monica SCENIC Electric Line

Balloon Route Train

The Popular Line ✈ To the Popular Beach

EXCURSION RATES EVERY DAY
COMMUTATION TICKETS AS FOLLOWS:

60-Ride Individual, good for current month	$7.50
30-Ride Family, good for sixty days	5.00
10-Ride, good for thirty days, and good for any one and their friends	2.00
Single Round Trip	.50

SPECIAL FOR TROLLEY PARTIES. The "Mermaid" the most elaborate and perfectly equipped. Open to engagements.

BAGGAGE AND EXPRESS SERVICE

Baggage and express called for and delivered. Phone your orders to Main 923, Los Angeles. Main 21, Santa Monica. Main 11, Ocean Park.

General Offices, 316 West Fourth Street

Between Broadway and Hill Street
(Los Angeles-Pacific Railroad Building)
Phone Private Exchange 1

CHAS. C. FIFE,
Gen'l Freight and Pass. Agent

E. P. CLARK,
General Manager

TIME TABLE
No. 3

Effective April 17, 1907

SUBJECT TO CHANGE WITHOUT NOTICE

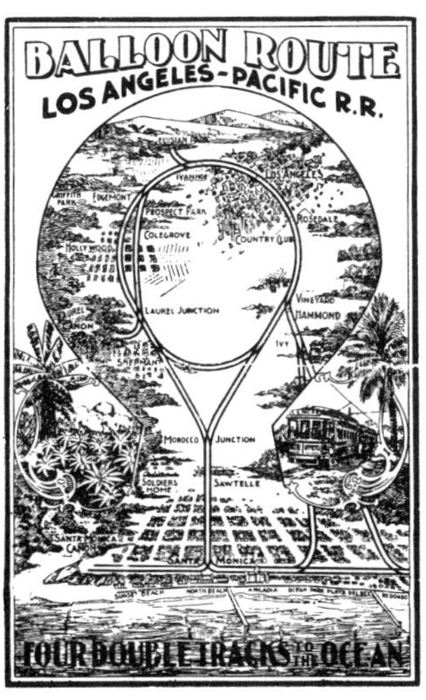

TO

Santa Monica	Ocean Park	Venice
Hollywood	Colegrove	Hermosa Beach
Laurel Canon	Sherman	Redondo
Playa del Rey	Soldier's Home	Manhattan Beach
Santa Monica Canon		Westgate

All Cars Turn at Fourth Street Station

All trains leaving Los Angeles start from Fourth Street Station, Between Broadway and Hill Streets.

Between LOS ANGELES, VENICE, OCEAN PARK and SANTA MONICA Via PALMS

Leave Los Angeles				Leave Ocean Park			
Fourth Street Station				Sunset Ave.			
A. M. 10 20	2 10	*6 10		A. M. 9 39	†1 15	†5 45	
6 20	10 40	2 20	6 20	5 39	† 9 45	1 39	6 09
6 50	10 50	2 40	*6 40	6 09	10 09	†1 45	†6 15
7 20	11 10	2 50	6 50	†*6 15	†10 15	2 09	6 39
7 40	11 20	3 10	7 20	6 39	10 39	†2 15	†6 45
7 50	11 40	3 20	7 50	†*6 45	†10 45	2 39	7 09
8 10	11 50	3 40	8 20	7 09	11 09	†2 45	7 39
8 20	P. M.	3 50	8 50	†*7 15	†11 15	3 09	8 09
8 40	12 10	4 10	9 20	7 39	11 39	†3 15	8 39
8 50	12 20	4 20	9 50	†*7 45	†11 45	3 39	9 09
9 10	12 40	*4 40	10 20	8 09	P. M.	†3 45	9 39
9 20	12 50	4 50	10 50	†*8 15	12 09	4 09	10 09
9 40	1 10	*5 10	11 20	8 39	†12 15	†4 15	10 39
9 50	1 20	5 20	11 50	†*8 45	12 39	4 39	11 09
10 10	1 40	*5 40	12 45	9 09	†12 45	†4 45	11 39
	1 50	5 50		†*9 15	1 09	5 09	12 09
						†5 15	
						5 39	

* Flyer, daily except Sunday.
† Leave North Beach Santa Monica

Between LOS ANGELES AND SUNSET AVE., OCEAN PARK, Via Sawtelle, Westgate and Brentwood Park

Leave Los Angeles				Leave Ocean Park			
Fourth Street Station				Sunset Avenue			
A. M.	A. M.	P. M.	P. M.	A. M.	A. M.	P. M.	P. M.
7 25	11 25	12 25	4 25	5 55	9 55	12 55	4 55
8 25		1 25	5 25	6 55	10 55	1 55	5 55
9 25		2 25	6 25	7 55	11 55	2 55	6 50
10 25		3 25	7 25	8 55		3 55	7 50

Westgate cars will leave Sunset Ave. at 6:50 P.M. and 7:50 P.M. for Sherman making connection at Sawtelle with 7:28 and 8:28 car for Los Angeles. Westgate Division train leaving 4th St., Los Angeles at 7:25 P.M. runs to North Beach only. Leaving North Beach at at 8:50 P.M. and every hour thereafter until 11:50 P.M., connecting at Sawtelle with West Bound car at 9:17 P.M. and every hour thereafter until 12:17 A.M.

LOCAL CARS BETWEEN LOS ANGELES AND VINEYARD Via Sixteenth Street

Leave Fourth St. Station		Leave Vineyard	
A. M.	P. M.	A. M.	A. M.
7 15	4 45	6 45	9 15
7 45	5 15	7 15	
8 15	5 45	7 45	P. M.
8 45	6 15	8 15	5 15
		8 45	5 45

Local cars between Fourth Street and Vineyard daily, except Sunday.

Elysian Park Cars connect with ALL Main Line Cars at Echo Park Hollywood Line.

Additional cars are run Saturdays and ALL Holidays, also other days as the travel requires.

Between LOS ANGELES, VENICE, SANTA MONICA and OCEAN PARK Via HOLLYWOOD

Leave Los Angeles		Leave Venice	
Fourth Street Station			
A. M.	P. M.	A. M.	P. M.
7 15	12 45		15
7 45	1 15		45
8 15	1 45	8 45	3 15
8 45	2 15	9 15	3 45
9 15	2 45	9 45	4 15
9 45	3 15	10 15	4 45
10 15	3 45	10 45	5 15
10 45	4 15	11 15	5 45
11 15	4 45	11 45	6 15
11 45	5 15	P. M.	6 45
P. M.	5 45	12 15	7 15
12 15	6 15	12 45	7 45
		1 15	
		1 45	

Before 8:45 A. M. and after 7:45 P. M. take trains that leave Winward Ave. 5 and 35 minutes after the hour, and transfer at Beverly for Hollywood and Colegrove.

Between LOS ANGELES, MANHATTAN, HERMOSA and REDONDO, Via PLAYA del REY.

Leave Los Angeles			Leave Redondo		
Fourth Street Station					
A. M.	P. M.	P. M.	A. M.	P. M.	P. M.
	12 00	6 00	5 45	12 15	6 45
6 30	12 30	6 30	6 15	12 45	7 15
7 00	1 00	7 00	6 45	1 15	7 45
7 30	1 30	7 30	7 15	1 45	8 15
8 00	2 00	8 30	7 45	2 15	9 15
8 30	2 30	9 30	8 15	2 45	10 15
9 00	3 00	10 30	8 45	3 15	11 15
9 30	3 30	11 30	9 15	3 45	
10 00	4 00		9 45	4 15	
10 30	4 30		10 15	4 45	
11 00	5 00		10 45	5 15	
11 30	5 30		11 15	5 45	
			11 45	6 15	

Connections made at Playa del Rey for Venice, Ocean Park and Santa Monica. Running time between Playa del Rey and Redondo, 25 minutes.

Freight and Express Trains Leaving Los Angeles
Subject to Change Without Notice

4:30 a. m. Paper train, newspapers, perishables and express. REDONDO via Colegrove, return via Hollywood. Intermediate points: Colegrove, Beverly, Sawtelle, Santa Monica, Ocean Park, Venice, Playa del Rey, Manhattan Beach, Hermosa Beach.

5:00 a. m. Freight and express. SENTOUS via Hollywood, Sherman and Vineyard, returning via Sherman and Colegrove. Intermediate points: Hollywood, Sherman, Gaylands, Rosemary, Vineyard, Hauser, Sentous.

8:20 a. m. U. S. Mail. REDONDO via Hollywood, return same route. Intermediate points: all post office stations except Palms.

8:30 a. m. Ex. and light freight. IVY PARK via Hollywood and Venice, return same route. Intermediate points: Hollywood, Sawtelle, Santa Monica, Ocean Park, Venice, Palms.

10:45 a. m. Freight and express. REDONDO via Colegrove and Westgate, return via Santa Monica. Intermediate points: Colegrove, Beverly, Soldiers' Home, Westgate, Brentwood Park, Santa Monica, Ocean Park, Venice, Playa del Rey, Manhattan Beach, Hermosa Beach, Redondo.

2:00 p. m. Ex. and light freight. HOLLYWOOD. Intermediate points: Hollywood and put off points.

3:45 p. m. Express and light freight. VENICE via Colegrove, return via Palms, Vineyard and Colegrove. Intermediate points: Colegrove, Sawtelle, Santa Monica, Ocean Park, Venice, Palms.

4:45 p. m. U. S. mail. VENICE via Hollywood, return same route. Intermediate points: all post office stations except Palms.

10:30 p. m. Freight. VENICE via Colegrove, return same route. Intermediate points: Colegrove, Sawtelle, Santa Monica, Ocean Park, Venice.

11:00 p. m. Freight. SAWTELLE via Hollywood, return via Colegrove. Intermediate points: Hollywood, Sherman, Sawtelle.

Freight and Express Office Tels. Sunset Main 923. Home 8054.

SPECIAL PASSENGER CARS FOR PRIVATE PARTIES
This Company has for charter to special parties luxurious Observation Cars. For rates, apply to General Passenger Department, Room 102, 4th and Hill St. Station, or by phone, Sunset Exch. 1, Home Exch. 355.

TRIP TICKETS
Purchase your tickets from agents established at all principal points. You save money by buying round-trip tickets, limited to ten days.

COMMUTATION AND FAMILY TICKETS
Tickets of 10, 30, 54 and 60 rides, good between Los Angeles and suburban and interurban points and between most all other points, are on sale at all principal points on this Company's lines. These tickets are sold at a reduction, according to the number of rides, limitations, etc.
For further information apply to nearest agent or to General Passenger Department, Room 102, 4th and Hill St. Station.

WHEN THE DOG RIDES
No charge is made if it is a SMALL dog carried in the lap of the owner. For larger dogs the regular ONE-WAY passenger fare will be charged, but not less than 25 cents for any distance, city or interurban. Dogs or other animals will NOT be allowed to occupy car-seat space.

LOST ARTICLES
All articles found by employes on cars of this Company's lines are turned in to the Lost Article Department at Check Room, 4th and Hill St. Station, Los Angeles, where they will be delivered to owner upon identification.

Steam and Electric Launches at Playa del Rey

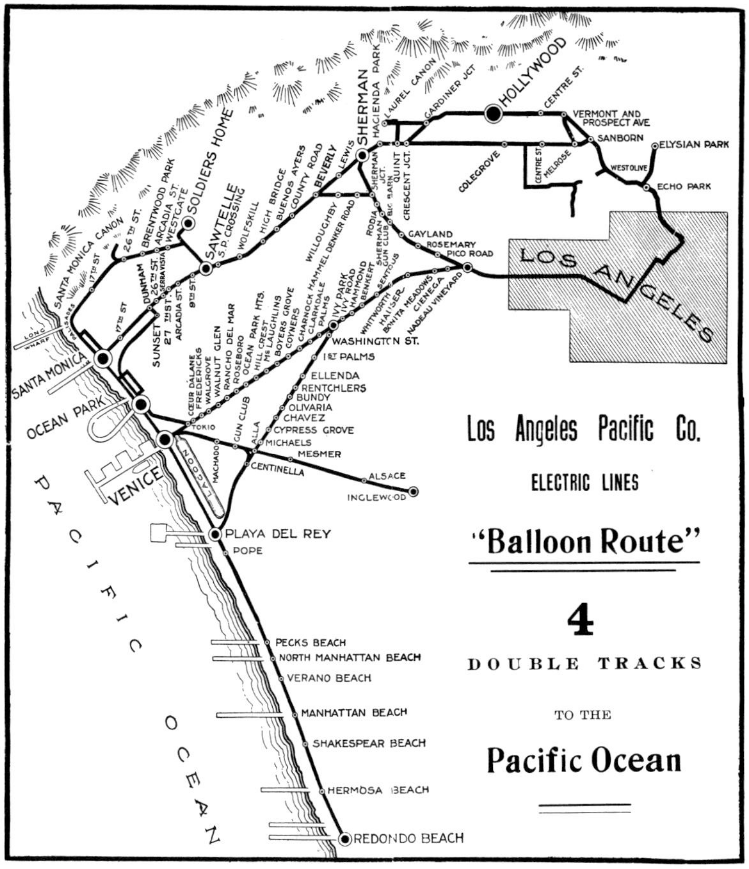

Placid Inland Lake with Still-Water Bathing and Boating at Playa del Rey

Between Los Angeles, Venice, Santa Monica and Ocean Park via Sawtelle (Soldiers' Home Station)

Leave Los Angeles, Fourth Street Station				Leave Ocean Park, Sunset Avenue			
A. M.	A. M.	P. M.	P. M.	A. M.	A. M.	P. M.	P. M.
6 05	11 05	3 35	8 35	5 35	10 35	3 05	8 05
6 35	11 35	4 05	9 05	6 05	11 05	3 35	8 35
7 05	P. M.	4 35	9 35	6 35	11 35	4 05	9 05
7 35	12 05	5 05	10 05	7 05	P. M.	4 35	9 35
8 05	12 35	5 35	10 35	7 45	12 05	5 05	10 05
8 35	1 05	6 05	11 05	8 05	12 35	5 35	10 35
9 05	1 35	6 35	11 35	8 35	1 05	6 05	11 05
9 35	2 05	7 05	A.M.	9 05	1 35	6 35	11 35
10 05	2 35	7 35	12 05	9 35	2 05	7 05	A.M.
10 35	3 05	8 05	1 15	10 05	2 35	7 35	12 05
							12 35
							1 05

Running time between Oregon Avenue, Santa Monica, and Sunset Avenue, Ocean Park, is 9 minutas. Santa Monica local cars make connections with cars to and from Los Angeles.

Santa Monica, Playa del Rey, Ocean Park, Venice and Inglewood via Broad Gauge Line.

Leave Santa Monica, Front Street	Leave Inglewood
A. M.	A. M.
8 00	9 00

Lagoon Line Car from Playa del Rey makes the North Loop, Santa Monica. Connecting at 3rd and Oregon Avenue with cars from Los Angeles via Sawtelle. Leave North Beach Bath House at 6:15 a m., then every thirty minutes until 11:54 p. m. Leave Playa del Rey 6:12 a. m., then every twenty minutes until 11:42 p. m.

Connections made at Playa del Rey with trains from and to Los Angeles and Redondo.

Theatre Trains Leave Los Angeles Every Night For Suburban and Beach Points

Secure one of our Special Stop-over Tickets with Privilege to Stop at all Principal Points on the

BALLOON ROUTE

Going and Returning by DIFFERENT ROUTE

General Offices, 316 West Fourth Street

Between Broadway and Hill Street

T. R. GABEL, General Manager.

F. A. SHORT, G. F. & P. A.

From Los Angeles to Hollywood and Colegrove.

Leave Fourth Street Station

A. M.	A. M.	P. M.	P. M.	P. M.
‡6 05	* 9 15	‖12 40	‡ 4 05	‡ 7 05
§6 15	‖ 9 20	*12 45	‖ 4 10	‖ 7 10
‖6 20	‖ 9 30	‖ 1 00	* 4 15	§ 7 15
‖6 30	‡ 9 35	‡ 1 05	‖ 4 20	‖ 7 20
‡6 35	‖ 9 40	‖ 1 10	† 4 25	‖ 7 30
‖6 40	* 9 45	* 1 15	‖ 4 30	‡ 7 35
§6 45	‖ 9 50	‖ 1 30	‡ 4 35	‖ 7 40
‖6 50	‖10 00	‡ 1 35	‖ 4 40	§ 7 45
†6 55	‡10 05	‖ 1 40	* 4 45	‖ 7 50
‖7 00	‖10 10	* 1 45	‖ 4 50	‖ 8 00
‡7 05	*10 15	‖ 2 00	† 4 55	‡ 8 05
‖7 10	‖10 30	‡ 2 05	‖ 5 00	§ 8 15
*7 15	‡10 35	‖ 2 10	‡ 5 05	‖ 8 30
‖7 20	‖10 40	* 2 15	‖ 5 10	‡ 8 35
†7 25	*10 45	‖ 2 30	* 5 15	§ 8 45
‖7 30	‖11 00	‡ 2 35	‖ 5 20	‖ 9 00
‡7 35	‡11 05	‖ 2 40	† 5 25	‡ 9 05
‖7 40	‖11 10	* 2 45	‖ 5 30	§ 9 15
*7 45	*11 15	‖ 3 00	‡ 5 35	‖ 9 30
‖7 50	‖11 30	‡ 3 05	‖ 5 40	‡ 9 35
†7 55	‡11 35	‖ 3 10	* 5 45	§ 9 45
‖8 00	‖11 40	* 3 15	‖ 5 50	‖ 10 00
‡8 05	*11 45	‖ 3 30	† 5 55	‡ 10 05
‖8 10	P. M.	‡ 3 35	‖ 6 00	§ 10 15
*8 15	‖12 00	‖ 3 40	‡ 6 05	‖ 10 30
‖8 20	‡12 05	* 3 45	‖ 6 10	‡ 10 35
†8 25	‖12 10	‖ 3 50	* 6 15	§ 10 45
‖8 30	*12 15	† 3 55	‖ 6 20	‖ 11 00
‡8 35	‖12 30	‖ 4 00	† 6 25	‡ 11 05
‖8 40	‡12 35		‖ 6 30	§ 11 15
*8 45			‡ 6 35	‖ 11 30
‖8 50			‖ 6 40	‡ 11 35
†8 55			§ 6 45	§ 11 45
‖9 00			‖ 6 50	A. M.
‡9 05			‖ 7 00	‖ 12 00
‖9 10				‡ 12 05
				§ 12 15
				‖ 12 30
				‡ 12 35
				§ 12 45

*To Beach Points via Hollywood.
‖To Laurel Canon via Hollywood.
†To Cresent Junction via Colegrove.
‡To Sherman only via Colegrove.
§To Beverly via Hollywood transfer to Santa Monica.

Connections made at Hollywood with Stage Line for Toluca, 5 miles distant. Fare 25 cents.

Leave Hollywood	Leave Toluca
10 00 A. M.	8 00 A. M.
4 30 P. M.	4 00 P. M.

Corrected to March 1, 1911.

TIME TABLES

LOS ANGELES PACIFIC

Electric Lines to

Santa Monica	Soldiers' Home
Hollywood	Brentwood Park
Laurel Canon	Palms
Playa del Rey	Venice
Santa Mon. Canon	Hermosa Beach
Sawtelle	Redondo Beach
Ocean Park	Manhattan Beach
Colegrove	Westgate
Sherman	Port Los Angeles

Los Angeles Passenger Station
429 South Hill Street

D. W. Pontius, Traffic Manager
Room 217 Pacific Electric Bldg.
Los Angeles   California

Subject to Change Without Notice

EXPLANATION OF CAR SIGNS

Yellow indicates "No Local Stops".
Green and White or Blue and White indicates "Interurban Stops" but "No City Stops".
Blue, Red, Green, Black or White indicates "All Stops".
The colors also represent the lines over which cars travel, which are as follows:
Redondo Line: Blue or Blue and White.
Venice Short Line: Yellow, Green or Green and White.
Sawtelle Line: Red.
Westgate Line: Black.
Hollywood Line-Santa Monica Bay: White.
Hollywood Line-Gardner Junction or Laurel Canyon: Blue.
Hollywood Line via Melrose: Blue.
Colegrove-Hollywood via Western & Franklin Avenues: Red.
Colegrove-Crescent Junction or Sherman: Red.
Los Angeles, Hill & West 16th Streets: White.
Lagoon Line: Blue.

Redondo Beach

Bathing, Hotel Redondo

A beautiful ten-mile ride each way right along the sea—through Manhattan, Hermosa Beach and Moonstone Beach.

FARE LOS ANGELES TO REDONDO BEACH AND RETURN, 50 CENTS

Round trip tickets through Santa Monica, Ocean Park and Venice, permitting stop-over, only 70 cts. You can visit all points in one day.

VENICE SHORT LINE
BETWEEN
Los Angeles—Venice
Ocean Park and Santa Monica

Leave Los Angeles Hill Street Station		Leave Santa Monica North Beach Station	
6 20	3 00	x5 31	2 00
*6 40	*3 20	5 40	*2 20
7 00	*3 40	6 00	*2 40
*7 20	4 00	6 20	3 00
*7 40	*4 20	*6 40	*3 20
8 00	*4 40	7 00	*3 40
*8 20	5 00	*7 20	4 00
*8 40	*5 20	*7 40	*4 20
9 00	*5 40	8 00	*4 40
*9 20	6 00	*8 20	5 00
*9 40	*6 20	*8 40	*5 20
10 00	*6 40	9 00	*5 40
*10 20	7 00	*9 20	6 00
*10 40	7 30	*9 40	6 30
11 00	8 00	10 00	7 00
*11 20	8 30	*10 20	7 30
*11 40	9 00	*10 40	8 00
12 00	9 30	11 00	8 30
*12 20	10 00	*11 20	9 00
*12 40	10 30	*11 40	9 30
1 00	11 00	12 00	10 00
*1 20	11 30	*12 20	10 30
*1 40	12 00	*12 40	11 00
2 00	12 30	1 00	11 30
*2 20	s†1 45	*1 20	12 00
*2 40		*1 40	s1 00

Light Figures A.M. Black Figures P.M.
Extra service on Sundays and holidays according to requirements of travel
*Flyer daily except Sundays and Holidays. Sundays and Holidays regular. Stops at 4th St., Palms, to pick up and discharge passengers.
x Starts from Venice.
S Saturday only.
†To Ocean Park Car Barns only.

Running Time

Los Angeles to		Santa Monica (North Beach) to	
Vineyard	22 min.	Ocean Park (Pier Ave.)	7 min.
Ivy	28 "	Venice	12 "
Palms	31 "	Ocean Park Hts.	16 "
Ocean Park Hts.	33 "	Palms	21 "
Venice	38 "	Ivy	24 "
Ocean Park (Pier Ave.)	44 "	Vineyard	29 "
Santa Monica (North Beach)	50 "	Los Angeles	52 "

All cars on this line stop between Hill Street Station, Los Angeles, and Vineyard to pick up and discharge THROUGH passengers ONLY, and do no local work between Arlington Street and Ivy Park until 7 P.M. After 7 P.M. make all regular stops.

SAWTELLE LINE
BETWEEN
Los Angeles—Venice
Santa Monica and Ocean Park
VIA
Beverly and Sawtelle
(SOLDIERS' HOME STATION)

Leave Los Angeles Hill Street Station		Leave Venice Windward Avenue	
†4 45	3 45	5 32	†3 32
6 15	4 15	†6 02	4 02
†6 45	4 45	6 32	†4 32
7 15	5 15	†7 02	5 02
7 45	†5 45	†7 32	†5 32
8 15	6 15	8 02	†6 02
†8 45	6 45	†8 32	†6 32
9 15	†7 15	9 02	7 02
†9 45	†7 45	†9 32	7 32
10 15	†8 15	†10 02	†8 02
†10 45	†8 45	†10 32	†8 32
11 15	†9 15	†11 02	†9 02
†11 45	†9 45	†11 32	†9 32
12 15	10 15	†12 02	†10 02
†12 45	†10 45	†12 32	10 32
1 15	11 15	†1 02	†11 02
†1 45	†11 45	†1 32	11 32
2 15	*12 15	†2 02	†*12 02
†2 45	*12 45	†2 32	*12 49
3 15	1 00	†3 02	

On this line passengers for Sherman, Hollywood or Colegrove will change cars at Beverly. Last connecting car from Los Angeles for Hollywood and Colegrove, 11:15 p. m. Sherman 12:45 a. m.

On this line passengers for Sherman, Hollywood or Colegrove will change cars at Beverly. Last connecting car from Venice for Hollywood and Colegrove 11:02 p. m. for Sherman 12:49 a. m.

Light Figures A.M. Black Figures P.M.
*To Sherman only
†Connects at 6th Street, Sawtelle, with Westgate line.

Running Time

Los Angeles to		Venice to	
Vineyard	23 min.	Ocean Park (Pier Ave.)	5 min.
Sherman Jct.	28 "	Santa Monica (North Beach)	12 "
Beverly	32 "	Sawtelle	26 "
Sawtelle	38 "	Beverly	33 "
Santa Monica (North Beach)	52 "	Sherman Jct.	36 "
Ocean Park (Pier Ave.)	59 "	Vineyard	41 "
Venice	1 hr. 4 "	Los Angeles	1 hr., 6 "

WESTGATE LINE
BETWEEN
Los Angeles—Santa Monica
North Beach
VIA
Sawtelle, Soldiers' Home
Westgate and Brentwood Park

Leave Los Angeles Hill Street Station		Leave Santa Monica North Beach	
7 25	1 25	6 25	1 25
8 25	2 25	7 25	2 25
9 25	3 25	8 25	3 25
10 25	4 25	9 25	4 25
11 25	5 25	10 25	5 25
12 25	6 25	11 25	*6 25
		12 25	†7 25

Light Figures A.M. Black Figures P.M.
†To Sherman only; transfer at Sawtelle or Sherman for Los Angeles.
*To Sawtelle only; transfer for Los Angeles.

Running Time

Los Angeles to		Santa Monica (North Beach) to	
Vineyard	23 min.	Montana Ave.	03 min.
Sherman Jct.	28 "	26th St.	10 "
Beverly	32 "	Soldiers' Home	14 "
Sawtelle	38 "	Sawtelle	18 "
Soldiers' Home	43 "	Beverly	25 "
26th St.	49 "	Sherman Jct.	28 "
Montana Ave.	54 "	Vineyard	33 "
Santa Monica (North Beach)	56 "	Los Angeles	56 "

BETWEEN
Santa Monica (North Beach) and 6th Street Sawtelle via Westgate Line.

Leave North Beach, Santa Monica 5:55, 6:55, 9:55 a.m.; then every hour until 2:55 p. m.; 3:55 p. m. to Los Angeles via Colegrove; then 7:30 p. m. and every half hour until 11:00 p. m.; last car 12 midnight. Connecting at 6th Street, Sawtelle, with cars to and from Los Angeles.

Leave Sawtelle 5:32, 6:32, 7:32, 9:32 a.m.; then every hour until 3:32 p.m.; then 6:45 p.m.; then 7:56 p.m. and every half hour until 10:26 p.m.; then 11:26 p.m.; last car 12:26 a.m. Connecting at 6th Street, Sawtelle, with cars to and from Los Angeles.

INGLEWOOD LINE
BETWEEN
Santa Monica, Ocean Park, Venice and Inglewood
MIXED PASSENGER AND FREIGHT

Leave Ocean Park 2d and Hill	Leave Inglewood
3 00 PM	4 30 PM

Running time between Ocean Park and Inglewood 1 hour.

SOLDIERS' HOME LINE
BETWEEN
Sawtelle and Soldiers' Home

Leave Sawtelle 6:55 a. m. and every 30 minutes until 6:55 p.m.
Leave Soldiers Home 7 15 a. m. and every 30 minutes until 7 15 p. m.
After 6 55 p. m. westbound and 7 15 p. m. eastbound, Soldiers Home passengers will use the Westgate cars.

Through Beautiful

HOLLYWOOD
...TO...
LAUREL CANON

Then America's only TRACKLESS TROLLEY or a walk over the Mountain Boulevard to
BUNGALOW LAND
BUNGALOW INN
and
PICNIC GROUNDS

30 Minute Trackless Trolley Service 9:45 a. m. to 8:15 p. m. Before and after, hourly service. Fare 10 cents.

Automobile Ride or Trail to
MOUNT LOOKOUT

Automobile trips during the day, round trip fare 50 cents

Affording one of the most picturesque sights in California. A full view of Los Angeles, Hollywood, Colegrove, Sherman, Beverly, Soldiers' Home, Santa Monica, Ocean Park, Playa Del Rey, The Palms and points east of Los Angeles.

A Delightful Outing Any Day in the Year.

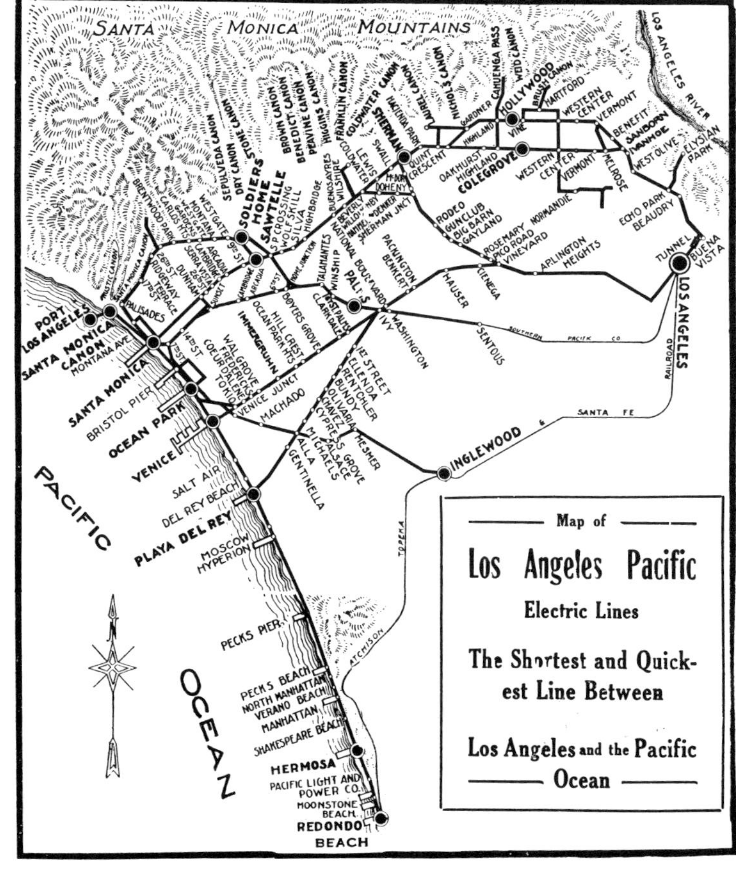

Serves the Most Select Residence Portion of Country Tributary to Los Angeles

Dining Room at Soldiers' Home.
As seen on Balloon Route Excursion.

P.E. TROLLEY TRIP

SUCCESSOR TO TILTON'S TROLLEY TRIP

100 Miles for 100 Cents

The best and cheapest way to see

PASADENA AND THE ORANGE GROVES

SAN PEDRO --- LOS ANGELES HARBOR

Giving FREE ADMISSION to

CAWSTON OSTRICH FARM

FREE ADMISSION to

SAN GABRIEL MISSION
(Founded 1771)

and a stop of 2 hours at

LONG BEACH

Reserved Chairs Free

SECURE THEM IN ADVANCE

COMPETENT GUIDES

Last Car Leaves Pacific Electric Depot, 6th and Main Streets

9:30 A. M. DAILY

REDONDO BEACH LINE
BETWEEN
Los Angeles—Manhattan Hermosa and Redondo Beach
VIA
Playa del Rey

LEAVE LOS ANGELES Hill Street Station		LEAVE REDONDO BEACH	
6 30	2 00	†6 15	1 45
§7 00	†2 30	6 45	†2 15
†7 30	3 00	†7 15	2 45
8 00	†3 30	7 45	†3 15
†8 30	4 00	†8 15	3 45
9 00	†4 30	8 45	†4 15
†9 30	5 00	†9 15	4 45
10 00	†5 30	9 45	†5 15
†10 30	§6 00	†10 15	5 45
11 00	†6 30	10 45	6 15
†11 30	7 30	†11 15	7 15
12 00	8 30	11 45	8 30
†12 30	9 30	†12 15	9 30
1 00	10 30	12 45	10 30
†1 30	11 30	†1 15	11 30

Light Figures A.M. Black Figures P.M. Connections made at Playa del Rey for Venice, Ocean Park and Santa Monica. Running every thirty minutes 6 12 a. m. until 7 12 p. m. From 9 05 p. m. until 12 05 a. m., connections irregular.

§ Connect at Ivy Park for Santa Monica and Port Los Angeles, via Air Line.

†Cars do no local work between Hill St. Sta. and Ivy Park, except Sundays.

Running Time

Los Angeles to		Redondo Beach to	
Vineyard	23 min.	C St. Manhattan	12 min.
Ivy Park	29 "	Playa del Rey	24 "
Playa del Rey	43 "	Ivy Park	37 "
C St. Manhattan	53 "	Vineyard	43 "
Redondo Beach, 1 hr. 3 min.		Los Angeles, 1 hr., 6 min.	

BETWEEN MONTANA AVENUE AND SEVENTH ST., SANTA MONICA AND PLAYA DEL REY

Leave Montana Ave. 6 10 a. m. and every 30 minutes until 9 38 p. m.; then 10 40 and 11 40 p. m.; then 12 40 a. m. to Ocean Park car barn.

Leave Playa del Rey 6 14 a. m. and every 30 minutes until 10 14 p. m.; then 11 14 p. m. and 12 14 a. m. Connections made at Playa del Rey with trains from and to Los Angeles and Redondo, up to 8 14 p. m. From 8 14 p. m. until 12 14 a. m. Connections from Redondo and to Los Angeles irregular.

BETWEEN LOS ANGELES, PALMS & PLAYA DEL REY VIA VENICE

Leave Playa del Rey 6 30 a. m. and every hour there after until 5 30 p. m.; daily except Sunday.

Leave Hill St. Station, Los Angeles, 7 30 a. m. and every hour thereafter until 6 30 p. m.; daily except Sunday.

PICTURESQUE
Santa Monica Canyon

Where the Mountains Join the Sea

Open to Pleasure Seekers, Picnics and Campers

DANCING PAVILION

200--ACRES--200

You can be alone in a Shady Nook, or join the crowd

Playa del Rey

With Its

Auditorium, Placid Inland Lake, Boating, Fishing Wharves, Still Water and Surf Bathing

Here more than half of Los Angeles Sunday schools, public schools and fraternal organizations hold their annual

PICNICS

HOLLYWOOD LINE
FROM
Los Angeles to Hollywood and Laurel Canon

LEAVE LOS ANGELES—HILL STREET STATION

g6 09	c9 21	g12 39	w3 49	v7 14
v6 14	c9 31	v12 44	c3 51	c7 21
c6 21	g9 39	w12 49	c4 01	c7 31
c6 31	v9 44	c12 51	g4 09	g7 39
g6 39	w9 49	c1 01	v4 14	v7 44
v6 44	c9 51	g1 09	w4 19	c7 51
w6 49	c10 01	v1 14	c4 21	c8 01
c6 51	g10 09	w1 19	c4 31	v8 14
c7 01	v10 14	c1 21	g4 39	c8 21
g7 09	w10 19	c1 31	v4 44	c8 31
v7 14	c10 21	g1 39	w4 49	v8 44
w7 19	c10 31	v1 44	c4 51	c9 01
c7 21	g10 39	w1 49	c5 01	v9 14
c7 31	v10 44	c1 51	g5 09	c9 31
g7 39	w10 49	c2 01	v5 14	v9 44
v7 44	c10 51	g2 09	s5 19	c10 01
w7 49	c11 01	v2 14	c5 21	v10 14
c7 51	g11 09	w2 19	c5 31	c10 31
c8 01	v11 14	c2 21	g5 39	v10 44
g8 09	w11 19	c2 31	v5 44	c11 01
v8 14	c11 21	g2 39	s5 49	b11 14
w8 19	c11 31	v2 44	c5 51	c11 31
c8 21	g11 39	w2 49	c6 01	x11 44
c8 51	v11 44	c2 51	g6 09	c12 01
g8 39	w11 49	c3 01	v6 14	x12 14
v8 44	c11 51	g3 09	s6 19	b12 44
w8 49	c12 01	v3 14	c6 21	
c8 51	g12 09	w3 19	c6 31	
c9 01	v12 14	c3 21	g6 39	
g9 09	w12 19	c3 31	v6 44	
v9 14	c12 21	g3 39	c6 51	
w9 19	c12 31	v3 44	c7 01	

Light Figures A. M. Black Figures P.M.

V To Venice via Hollywood and Santa Monica.

G To Gardner Jct. C To Laurel Canon.

W To Vine St. and Hollywood Blvd., Hollywood, via Sanborn, Santa Monica Ave. and Western and Franklin Aves.

S To Sherman via Sanborn, Santa Monica Ave., Western and Franklin Aves. and Vine St. and Hollywood Blvd.

B To Beverly only; transfer for Santa Monica and Venice.

Brush Canon cars connect with cars via Western and Franklin Ave. line.

Extra service morning and evening according to requirements of travel.

xTo Sherman only

Running Time—Los Angeles to

Echo Park Ave.	14 min.	Hollywood [Cahuenga Av.]	31 "
Sanborn	20 "	Gardner Jct.	37 "
Vermont Avenue	23 "	Laurel Canon	40 "

HOLLYWOOD LINE
FROM
Laurel Canon, Gardner Jct. and Vine St. and Hollywood Blvd. Hollywood to Los Angeles

g5 31	v9 35	g1 26	c5 05
g5 49	c9 35	g1 31	c5 15
g6 01	c9 45	v1 35	g5 26
v6 05	g9 56	c1 35	g5 31
c6 05	g10 01	c1 45	v5 35
c6 15	v10 05	g1 56	c5 35
g6 26	c10 05	g2 01	c5 45
g6 31	c10 15	v2 05	g5 56
v6 35	g10 26	c2 05	g6 01
c6 35	g10 31	c2 15	c6 05
c6 45	v10 35	g2 26	c6 15
g6 56	c10 35	g2 31	g6 31
g7 01	c10 45	v2 35	c6 35
v7 05	g10 56	c2 35	c6 45
c7 05	g11 01	c2 45	g6 56
c7 15	v11 05	g2 56	g7 01
g7 26	c11 05	g3 01	c7 05
g7 31	c11 15	v3 05	c7 15
v7 35	g11 26	c3 05	g7 31
c7 35	g11 31	c3 15	c7 35
c7 45	v11 35	g3 26	c7 45
g7 56	c11 35	g3 31	g8 01
g8 01	c11 45	v3 35	c8 15
v8 05	g11 56	c3 35	g8 31
c8 05	g12 01	c3 45	c8 45
c8 15	v12 05	g3 56	g9 01
g8 26	c12 05	g4 01	c9 15
g8 31	c12 15	v4 05	g9 31
v8 35	g12 26	c4 05	c9 45
c8 35	g12 31	c4 15	g10 01
c8 45	v12 35	g4 26	c10 15
g8 56	c12 35	g4 31	g10 31
g9 01	c12 45	v4 35	c10 45
v9 05	g12 56	c4 35	g11 01
c9 05	g1 01	c4 45	c11 15
c9 15	v1 05	g4 56	g11 31
g9 26	c1 05	g5 01	g12 01
g9 31	c1 15	v5 05	

Light figures A. M. Black figures P. M.

G Cars leave Gardner Junction.

C Cars leave Laurel Canon.

V Cars leave Vine St. and Hollywood Blvd., Hollywood.

Extra service morning and evening according to requirements of travel.

Brush Canon cars connect with cars via Western and Franklin Ave. line.

Running Time

Laurel Canon to		Vermont Avenue	17 min
Gardner Jct.	3 min.	Sanborn	20 "
Hollywood [Cahuenga Ave.]	9 "	Echo Park Ave.	26 "
		Hill St. Station	40 "

COLEGROVE-SHERMAN LINE
FROM
Los Angeles to Colegrove Crescent Jct. and Sherman

LEAVE LOS ANGELES, HILL STREET STATION

s5 56	v10 19	c2 06	v5 49
s6 26	s10 26	v2 19	s5 56
v6 49	c10 36	s2 26	c6 06
s6 56	v10 49	c2 36	v6 19
v7 19	s10 56	v2 49	s6 26
s7 26	c11 06	s2 56	c6 36
c7 36	v11 19	c3 06	s7 06
v7 49	s11 26	v3 19	s7 26
s7 56	c11 36	s3 26	s7 36
c8 06	s11 49	c3 36	s8 06
v8 19	s11 56	s3 56	s8 56
s8 26	c12 06	v4 19	s9 26
c8 36	v12 19	c4 36	s9 56
s8 49	s12 26	v4 49	s10 26
s8 56	c12 49	s4 56	s10 56
c9 06	c1 06	c5 06	s11 26
v9 19	v1 19	c5 26	s11 56
s9 26	s1 26	c5 36	s12 40
c9 36	c1 36		
v9 49	v1 49		
s9 56	c1 56		
c10 06	s1 56		

Light figures A. M. Black figures P. M.

S To Sherman via Colegrove.

V To Vine St. and Hollywood Blvd., Hollywood, via Sanborn, Santa Monica Ave. and Western and Franklin Aves.

C To Crescent Junction via Colegrove, daily except Sunday.

Extra service morning and evening according to requirements of travel.

Brush Canon cars connect with cars via Western and Franklin Ave. line.

Running Time—Los Angeles to

Echo Park Ave.	14 min.	Colegrove [Vine St.]	31 min.
Sanborn	20 "	Crescent Jct.	35 "
Western Ave.	25 "	Sherman	39 "

COLEGROVE-SHERMAN LINE

FROM

Sherman, Crescent Jct. and Western Ave.

via

Colegrove to Los Angeles

s5 11	s9 41	w1 35	c5 28
s5 41	c9 58	s1 41	w5 35
w6 05	w10 05	c1 58	s5 41
s6 11	s10 11	w2 05	c5 58
w6 35	c10 28	s2 11	s6 11
s6 41	w10 35	c2 28	c6 28
c6 58	s10 41	w2 35	s6 41
w7 05	c10 58	s2 41	c6 58
s7 11	w11 05	c2 58	s7 11
c7 28	s11 11	w3 05	c7 28
w7 35	c11 28	s3 11	s7 41
s7 41	w11 35	c3 28	s8 11
c7 58	s11 41	w3 35	s8 41
w8 05	c11 58	s3 41	s9 11
s8 11	w12 05	c3 58	s9 41
c8 28	s12 11	w4 05	s10 11
w8 35	c12 28	s4 11	s10 41
s8 41	w12 35	c4 28	s11 11
c8 58	s12 41	w4 35	*s11 57
w9 05	c12 58	s4 41	
s9 11	w1 05	c4 58	
c9 28	s1 11	w5 05	
w9 35	c1 28	s5 11	

Light figures A.M. Black figures P.M.

S Cars leave Sherman.

W Cars leave Vine St. and Hollywood Blvd., Hollywood, via Franklin and Western Aves.

C Cars leave Crescent Junction, daily except Sunday.

*Waits at Sherman until 11:54 p. m., making connection with car from Venice and Santa Monica.

Brush Canon cars connect with cars via Western and Franklin Ave. line.

Extra service morning and evening according to requirements of travel.

Running Time—Sherman to

Crescent Junction	4	Min.
Colegrove, (Vine St....)	8	"
Western Avenue	13	"
Sanborn	19	"
Echo Park Avenue	25	"
Hill St. Station	39	"

Local Cars between Los Angeles and City Limits

Via Sixteenth Street

LEAVE HILL ST. STA.		LV. CITY L'T'S--VINY'D	
4 45	*3 25	†5 43	*2 58
†6 15	§3 30	§5 58	o2 59
§6 30	†3 45	†6 13	†3 13
†6 45	§4 00	§6 28	§3 28
§7 00	†4 15	†6 43	†3 43
†7 15	*4 25	*6 58	*3 58
*7 25	§4 30	o6 59	o3 59
§7 30	†4 45	†7 13	†4 13
†7 45	§5 00	¶7 23	§4 28
¶7 55	¶5 10	¶7 28	†4 43
§8 00	†5 15	¶7 38	*4 58
¶8 05	*5 25	†7 43	o4 59
¶8 10	§5 30	*7 58	†5 13
†8 15	¶5 40	o7 59	§5 28
*8 25	¶5 45	†8 13	†5 43
§8 30	¶5 53	¶8 23	*5 58
†8 45	§6 00	¶8 28	o5 59
§9 00	¶6 10	¶8 38	†6 13
†9 15	†6 15	†8 43	§6 28
*9 25	*6 25	*8 58	†6 43
§9 30	§6 30	o8 59	§6 58
†9 45	†6 45	†9 13	†7 00
§10 00	†7 00	§9 28	†7 13
†10 15	†7 15	†9 43	†7 30
*10 25	§7 30	*9 58	†7 43
§10 30	†7 40	o9 59	§7 58
†10 45	†7 45	†10 13	†8 00
§11 00	†8 00	§10 28	†8 13
†11 15	†8 15	†10 43	†8 30
*11 25	§†8 30	*10 58	†8 43
§11 30	†8 45	o10 59	†9 00
†11 45	†9 00	†11 13	§9 08
§12 00	†9 15	§11 28	†9 13
†12 15	§†9 30	†11 43	†9 30
*12 25	†9 45	*11 58	†9 43
§12 30	†10 00	o11 59	†10 00
†12 45	†10 15	†12 13	§10 08
§1 00	§†10 30	§12 28	†10 13
†1 15	†10 45	†12 43	†10 30
*1 25	†11 00	*12 58	†10 43
§1 30	†11 15	o12 59	†11 00
†1 45	§†11 30	†1 13	§11 08
§2 00	†11 45	§1 28	†11 13
†2 15	†12 00	†1 43	†11 30
*2 25	12 15	*1 58	†11 43
§2 30	†12 30	o1 59	†12 00
†2 45	12 45	†2 13	†12 13
§3 00	†1 00	§2 28	†12 30
†3 15		†2 43	

Light Figures A.M. Black Figures P.M.

§ Through Playa del Rey or Redondo Beach cars.

*Through Santa Monica cars via Westgate.

¶Daily except Sunday.   oVenice-Del Rey

†Through Santa Monica cars via Venice short line.

‡Through Venice cars via Sawtelle.

Franklin Avenue Line—Hollywood.

Western and Franklin Avenue cars leave Santa Monica Ave. at 6:51 p.m. and every half hour until 10:51 p.m. Leave Vine Street and Hollywood Blvd., 7:06 p.m. and every half hour until 11:06 p.m.

Highland Avenue Line—Hollywood.

Highland Avenue cars leave Santa Monica Avenue 6:56 a. m. Leave Highland and Cahuenga Ave. 6:07 a. m. every half hour until 11:07 p. m.

Echo Park Line

Elysian Park cars connect with Hollywood and Colegrove cars at Echo Park Ave. and Sunset Blvd.

WELLS FARGO EXPRESS

Frequent fast express trains between Los Angeles, Hollywood, Colegrove, Sherman, Santa Monica, Port Los Angeles, Venice, Redondo and other points daily except Sundays.

BAGGAGE

Baggage handled by Wells Fargo Express Co. between all points.

PASSENGERS FROM INTERIOR

Do not give your checks to Baggage Transfer representative on train, but deliver to Wells Fargo agent at Southern Pacific, Salt Lake or Santa Fe depots and trunks will be delivered to any point on line, saving 50 cents by arranging in this way.

Los Angeles offices at Los Angeles Pacific Co.'s depots, Hill Street between 4th and 5th and Freight Depot corner North Broadway and Sunset Blvd.

Los Angeles Telephones:

Sunset Main 8034   Home 10143

SPECIAL CARS FOR PRIVATE PARTIES

This Company has for charter parlor cars and coaches at reasonable rates, for picnics, theatre parties and excursions. On trips of this kind, stops may be made along the line at points of interest.

TRIP TICKETS

Purchase your tickets from Agents established at principal points. You save money by securing round trip tickets limited to 10 days.

COMMUTATION TICKETS

Individual tickets of 10 and 54 rides between Los Angeles and any beach point, 30 ride family and 60 ride individual tickets between all points are on sale at all stations at greatly reduced rates.

CASH COUPON BOOKS

Secure one of our $10.00 Cash Coupon Books for $7.50, which are honored on the trains. These books permit stopover at all points on the line and are especially beneficial to traveling men and business houses.

For further information apply to Traffic Department, Room 217, Pacific Building, Los Angeles. Telephones: Home F 1280; Sunset Main 8980, or to regular agents.

LOST ARTICLES

All articles found by employees on trains of the Los Angeles Pacific Company are turned into the Lost Article Department, Hill Street Station between Fourth and Fifth where they may be claimed on identification between 8 a.m. and 11 p.m. Telephones Sunset Broadway 4000, Home 10355.

FREIGHT SERVICE

This Company runs two Freight trains, Los Angeles to Playa del Rey and Redondo and return. Four Freight trains, Los Angeles to Santa Monica, Ocean Park, Venice, Colegrove, Sherman and return. Two Freight trains, Los Angeles to Hollywood and return all daily except Sunday.

QUICK SERVICE AND LOW RATES

Freight Depot corner North Broadway and Sunset Blvd. For particulars see

B. N. PRATT, Agent, Los Angeles Telephones Sunset Main 923, Home A 8054, or apply to

TRAFFIC DEPARTMENT

D. W. PONTIUS, Traffic Manager

F. C. WEEKS, Trav. Frt. Agt., 217 P. E. Building, Los Angeles, Sunset, Main 8980.   Home F 1280

SANTA MONICA
AND
OCEAN PARK

Daily Band Concerts

Dancing :: Bathing

Immense Concrete Sidewalk right along the Ocean for over Two Miles

"The Official Promenade"

BRISTOL PIER CAFE

With a huge Sun Room, giving an unsurpassed view of the RESTLESS SEA.

Balloon Route Excursion

The Greatest Moderate Priced Pleasure and Sight Seeing Trip on the Pacific Coast

One Whole Day for One Dollar

101 Miles for 100 Cents

Showing some of California's finest scenery including 28 miles right along the Ocean, through Hollywood, Soldiers' Home, Santa Monica, Ocean Park, Venice, Redondo Beach. Playa del Rey for dinner.

RESERVED SEATS

An Experienced Guide with Each Car

The Only Electric Line Excursion Out of Los Angeles Going One Way and Returning Another

Free Attractions—At Santa Monica FREE ADMISSION to the CAMERA OBSCURA, an exclusive attraction for Balloon Route Excursionists only. At Venice FREE ADMISSION to the $20,000 Aquarium and a FREE RIDE on the L. A. THOMPSON SCENIC RAILWAY, the longest in the world.

Last Car Leaves Los Angeles

(Hill St. Station Between Fourth and Fifth)

9:40 A. M. DAILY

TRAINMEN'S
RULES. INSTRUCTIONS
AND
PASSENGER TARIFF

EFFECTIVE DEC. 1. 1906

LOS ANGELES PACIFIC CO.

Here are selected pages from the Dec. 1, 1906,
Los Angeles Pacific rulebook and passenger tariff.
Every train crew had to have a copy of this department bible.
(Collection of Craig Rasmussen)

VENICE SHORT LINE DIVISION

0	Vert. & Prosp. Ave.	35
5	Fourth St. Station	35
5	Arlington Ave.	30
10	Nadeau Vineyard	30
10	Cienega	30
10	Bonita Meadows	30
10	Hauser	25
15	Whitworth	25
15	Sentous	25
15	Benkert	25
15	Hammond	20
20	Ivy Road	20
20	Ivy Park	15
20	1st. St. Palms	15
25	Clarkdale	15
25	Charnock	15
25	Coyners	15
25	Boyers Grove	15
25	McLaughlins	15
25	Hill Crest	15
25	Ocean Park Hts.	10
30	Roseboro	10
30	Rancho del Mar	10
30	Walnut Glen	10
30	Walgrove	10
30	Fredericks	5
35	Venice	5
35	Ocean Park	5
35	17th St. S. M.	0

REDONDO DIVISION

0	Vert. & Prosp. Ave.	50
5	Fourth St. Station	50
5	Arlington Ave.	45
10	Nadeau Vineyard	45
10	Cienega	45
10	Bonita Meadows	45
10	Hauser	40
15	Whitworth	40
15	Sentous	40
15	Benkert	40
15	Hammond	35
20	Ivy Road	35
20	Ivy Park	30
20	Washinton St.	30
20	1stSt. Palms	30
25	Ellenda	25
25	Rentchlers	25
25	Bundy	25
30	Olivaria	25
30	Chavez	25
30	Cypress Grove	25
30	Michaels	25
30	Alla	20
35	Centinella	20
35	Playa del Rey	15
40	Pope	15
40	Hyperion	10
45	Pecks Beach	10
45	No. Manhattan	10
45	Verano	10
45	Cent. St. Manhattan	5
50	Shakspear	5
50	Hermosa	5
50	Redondo	0

SAWTELLE DIVISION

0	Vert. & Prosp. Ave.	35
5	Fourth St. Station	35
5	Arlington Ave.	30
10	Nadeau Vineyard	30
10	Pico Road	30
10	Rosemary	25
15	Gayland	25
15	Big Barn	25
15	Sherman Gun Club	25
15	Rodia	25
15	Sherman Jct.	20
20	Hammel Denker Rd.	20
20	Willoughby	20
20	Beverly	20
20	County Road	20
20	Buenos Ayers Bdg'e	15
25	High Bridge	15
25	Wolfskill	15
25	S. P. Crossing	10
25	Sawtelle	10
25	Sawtelle 9th St.	10

VIA WESTGATE

25	Sawtelle	10
25	Soldiers Home	10
25	Westgate	10
25	Arcadia St.	10
30	Brentwood Park	10
30	17th St. S. M.	5

30	Arcadia St.	10
30	27th St. S. M.	10
30	Serra Vista	10
30	Dunham	10
30	17th St. S. M.	5
35	Santa Monica	5
35	Ocean Park	5
35	Venice	5
35	Fredericks	5
35	Salt Air Ave.	0

HOLLYWOOD DIVISION

0	Arlington Ave.	35
5	Fourth St. Station	35
5	Sanborn	35
5	Ver. & Pros. Ave.	30
10	Center St.	25
10	Hollywood	25
10	Gardiner Jct.	25
15	Laurel Canon	25
15	Crescent Jct.	25
15	Quint	25
15	Hacienda Park	25
15	Sherman	20
20	Lewis	20
20	Beverly	20
20	County Road	20
20	Buenos Ayers Bdg'e	15
25	High Bridge	15
25	Wolfskill	15
25	S. P. Crossing	10
25	Sawtelle	10
25	Sawtelle 9th St.	10
30	Arcadia St.	10
30	27th St. S. M.	10
30	Serra Vista	10
30	Dunham	10
30	17th St. S. M.	5
35	Santa Monica	5
35	Ocean Park	5
35	Venice	5
35	Fredericks	5
35	Salt Air Ave.	0

RULES ᴬᴺᴅ REGULATIONS

FOR THE

GOVERNMENT

OF EMPLOYES

OF THE

OPERATING

DEPARTMENT

GENERAL NOTICE

It is of the utmost importance that proper rules for the government of employes of this Company should be literally and absolutely enforced, in order to make such rules efficient. If they cannot or ought not to be enforced, they ought not to exist. Officers or employes whose duty it may be to make or enforce rules, however temporary or unimportant they may seem, should keep this clearly in mind. If in the judgment of any one whose duty it is to enforce a rule, such rule cannot or ought not to be enforced, he should at once bring it to the attention of those in authority.

All persons entering or remaining in the service of this Company are warned that their occupation is hazardous; that they do so with the full knowledge of the dangers incident to the operating of railroads; that in accepting or retaining employment they must assume the ordinary risks attending it; that they are required to exercise great care in the performance of their duties to prevent accidents to themselves or others; and before using tools or apparatus of any kind, they should *know* that they are in a safe condition to perform the service required, and report to the proper officer in writing, defects in tracks, cars, machinery and appliances of any kind liable to cause accidents. The Company does not wish nor expect its employes to incur any risk whatever, from which, by the exercise of their own judgment and by personal care, they can protect themselves, but enjoins upon them to take time in all cases to do their duty in safety, whether they may be, at any time, acting under the orders of superiors or not.

In dealing with the public, especially with the Company's patrons, it is often necessary that employes should observe much patience and self-restraint, always endeavoring to follow the dictates of good sense and prudence, in order to make the most favorable impression, and treating them as any good business man would treat his customers, with a view to making the road popular.

R. P. Sherman,
Superintendent

Approved:
T. R. Gabel,
General Manager.

GENERAL RULES

1. All employes whose duties are prescribed by these rules will be furnished with a copy and will be required to have same in their possession at all times while on duty.

2. Knowledge of Rules: Conductors and motormen are required to be familiar with the rules, and with every special order issued. Employment by the Company binds the employe to comply with the rules and regulations and ignorance thereof will not be accepted as an excuse for negligence or omission of duty. If in doubt as to the exact meaning of any rule or special order, application must be made to the proper authority for explanation and instruction.

In addition to these rules, special orders will be issued from time to time; such orders when issued by proper authority, whether in conflict with these rules or not, must be obeyed while in force.

The Bulletin Board must be examined daily before taking runs, for special bulletins.

3. Enforcement of Obedience: The head of each department must be conversant with the rules, supply copies of them to his subordinates, see that they are understood, enforce obedience to them, and report to the proper officer all violations of same and the action taken thereon.

4. Examination: No employe will be permitted to continue in train service without passing a satisfactory examination of these rules.

5. Violation: The fact that any person enters or remains in the service of the Company will be considered as an assurance of willingness to obey its rules. *No one will be excused for the violation of any of them, even though not included in those applicable to his department.*

6. Promotion: All employes will be regarded as in line for promotion, advancement depending upon the faithful performance of duty and ability for increased responsibility.

7. Gratuity for Lost Time: If an employe should be disabled by sickness, accident or other causes, the right to claim compensation will not be recognized. Any allowance, if made, will be a gratuity justified by the circumstances of the case, and the employe's previous good record

8. Orders: Every employe while on duty connected with the trains on any division of the road, is under the authority, and must conform to the orders of Asst. Supt. pispatchers and inspectors.

9. Uniforms: Employes must wear the prescribed badges and uniforms while on duty and must be clean and neat in appearance.

10. Standard Clocks: The standard time for each division is that of the clock at the general office of the Company at Fourth Street Station.

11. Standard Watches: Each Conductor and motorman must have a reliable watch which has been examined and certified to by a watchmaker prescribed by the Company, and must file his certificate with the Superintendent before he is allowed to take charge of a train. Watches must be examined and certificates renewed when notified.

12. Regulating Watches: Each conductor and motorman must compare his watch each day with the designated standard clock.

13. Comparing Watches: Conductors and motormen whose duties prevent them from having access to the standard clock, must compare daily with, and regulate their watches by, those of conductors and motormen who have standard time.

14. Politeness: Conductors and motormen must treat all passengers with politeness; avoid difficulty, and exercise patience, forbearance and self-control under all conditions. They must not make threatening gestures or use loud, uncivil, indecent or profane language, even under the greatest provocation.

15. Report for Duty: Regular conductors and motormen must report for duty ten minutes before leaving time for their first trip, or if for any good reason unable to so report, must give notice at least ten minutes before such leaving time.

Extra men must report at such time as ordered, or must give notice at least ten minutes before such time. They must not absent themselves after answering roll call without permission.

16. Time Table: A time table is the general law governing the arrival and leaving time of all regular trains at all stations. Time tables will be issued from time to time, as may be necessary. The time given for each train on the time table is the schedule of such train.

(a) Copies of time tables will be furnished to all concerned; conductors and motormen are forbidden to go upon the main track outside of the yards without a copy in their possession, and at the time of change of time tables, train masters must know that they have a copy of the new issue before allowing them to occupy main track.

(b) Each time table from the moment it takes effect supercedes the preceding time table, and all special instructions relating thereto, and trains shall be run as directed therby, subject to the rules.

17. Train Numbers: All West bound trains will be designated by *even numbers;* all East bound trains will be designated by *odd numbers.*

(a) East bound and West bound:—Trains proceeding from Fourth St., Los Angeles, towards Beverly, via Colegrove and Hollywood, towards Ocean Park car barn, via Sawtelle and The Palms, towards Redondo via Playa del Rey, and from Santa Monica to Inglewood, will be called *West-bound;* trains proceeding in the opposite direction will be called *East-bound;* regardless of the points of the compass.

SIGNAL RULES.

18. Signal Appliances: Conductors, motormen, switchmen, switch-tenders, track foremen and bridge watchmen and all other employes whose duties may require them to give signals, must provide themselves with the proper appliances and keep them in good order and always ready for immediate use.

19. Flags and Lamps: Flags of the proper color must be used by day and lamps of the proper color by night.

20. Colors: *Red* signifies *danger,* and is a signal to stop.

(a) *Green* signifies *caution* and is a signal to go slowly.

(b) *White* signifies *safety* and is a signal to go on.

(c) *Blue* is a signal to be used by the car inspectors.

21. Danger Signal: A flag or lamp swung across the track, a hat or any object waved violently by any person on the track, signifies danger and is a signal to STOP.

TRAIN SIGNALS.

22. Head and Tail Lights: Each train running after sunset, or when obscured by fog or other causes, must display the headlight in front, and one or more *red* lights in rear.

23. Blue: A blue flag by day and a blue light by night, placed on the end of a car, denotes that car inspectors are at work under or about the car or train. The car or train thus protected must not be coupled to or moved, until the blue signal is removed by the car inspectors.

When a car or train standing on a siding is protected by a blue signal, other cars must not be placed in front of it so that the blue signal will be obscured, without first notifying the car inspector, that he may protect himself, and not then until the signal is removed.

WHISTLE SIGNALS.

24. Whistle: One long blast is the signal for approaching stations, railroad crossings and junction, (thus ——.)

(a) One short blast is the signal to apply brakes, (thus —.)

(b) Two long blasts is the signal to throw off the brakes, (thus —— ——.)

(c) Two short blasts is an answer to any signal, except 'train parted,' (thus —— .) This signal must be promptly given, unless in city, whenever two taps of the bell are heard, or any signal, and especially flag signals, are seen.

(d) Two short blasts sounded three times (thus —— —— —— ——) is a signal that brakes are sticking.

(e) Three short blasts when the train is standing (to be repeated until answered), is a signal that the train will back (thus — — — .)

(f) Three long blasts is a signal that the train has parted, (thus —— —— —— .)

(g) Four long blasts (thus —— —— —— ——) is the signal to call in the flagman from the west.
Four long followed by one short blast, (thus —— —— —— —— —) is the signal to call the flagman from the east.

(h) Four short blasts is the motorman's call for signals from switch-tenders, watchmen, trainmen and others, (thus — — — —.)

(i) Five short blasts is a signal to the conductor to go back and protect the rear of the train, (thus — — — — —.)

(j) Two long followed by two short blasts is the signal for approaching obscure road crossings and places, (thus —— —— — — .)
Irregular trains and trains behind time, must sound this signal repeatedly in obscure places to warn section and bridge men. The same precaution must be used in fogs.

(k) A succession of short blasts is an alarm for persons or cattle on the track, and calls the attention of train men to danger ahead.

25. Answer all Signals by Sounding Gong or Whistle Twice: A signal from the conductor to start or stop the car, or from some person on the ground, or a signal from a passing train, must be answered by sounding the gong or whistle twice to indicate that signal has been understood.

BELL CORD SIGNALS.

26. Two taps of the signal bell when the train is standing is the signal to start.

27. One tap of the signal bell when the train is running, is the signal to stop at the next regular stopping place.

28. One tap of the signal bell followed at short interval by another, when the train is running, is the signal to stop at once.

29. Three taps of the signal bell, when the train is standing, is the signal to back the train.

30. One tap from motorman to conductor, "Passenger has boarded front end, collect fare."

31. Two taps from motorman to conductor calls conductor ahead.

32. Three taps from motorman to conductor, "Necessary to back train."

LAMP SIGNALS.

33. A lamp swung across the track is the signal to stop.

34. A lamp raised and lowered vertically is the signal to move ahead.

35. A lamp swung vertically in a circle across the track, when the train is *standing,* is the signal to move back.

36. A lamp swung vertically in a circle at arm's length across the track, when the train is running, is the signal that the train has parted.

37. A flag, or the hand, moved in any of the directions given above, will indicate the same signal as given by a lamp.

FIXED SIGNALS.

38. Fixed signals are placed at junctions, railroad crossings and other points that require special protection. Special instructions will be issued indicating their position and use.

39. Imperfect Signals: A signal imperfectly displayed, or the absence of a signal at a place where a signal is usualy shown, must be recorded as a danger signal, and the fact reported to the Assistant Superintendent.

40. Unnecessary Use of Whistle: The unnecessary use of whistle is prohibited.

41. Sounding Whistle: The whistle must not be sounded while passing a train, except in cases of emergency or danger, or when required by the rules.

42. Acknowledge Signal: When a temporary danger signal is displayed to stop a train, it must be acknowledged instantly.

43. Sounding Gong: The gong must be sounded 300 feet before reaching every crossing, and the whistle must be sounded at all *whistling posts.* After whistle is blown, ring gong until over the crossing.

44. White Light in Pushing Trains: When a train is being pushed by another at night (except when shifting and making up trains in the yards) a headlight or lamp must be displayed on the front of the leading car.

45. Look Out for Signals: All signals must be used strictly in accordance with the rules, and trainmen and motormen must keep a constant lookout for signals.

TRAIN RULES

CLASSIFICATION OF TRAINS

46. Designation of Trains: All trains are designated as regular or irregular. Regular trains are those represented on the time table. Irregular trains are those not represented on the time table.

47. Irregular Trains: Irregular trains shall be distinguished as "Work" and "Special" trains.

MOVEMENT OF TRAINS

48. Classification Rights: *Irregular trains must in all cases keep out of the way of regular trains.*

49. Right to Track: *All East bound trains have the absolute right of track over all trains of the same class running in the opposite direction.*

(a) In case of delays, West bound trains may run to siding west of point at which East bound trains are due (flagging obscure places and during heavy fogs), and if trains meet between sidings, they will go to the nearest one to pass. If there is any doubt or dispute as to which is the nearest siding, the West bound train will go back.

(b) Trains arriving at a siding will wait if they see an opposing train coming.

(c) All delayed trains will proceed with caution excepting to meet opposing train at any point.

(d) "Flagging" means that the conductor must walk ahead of the train, so in case he sees the other train coming, he can signal both trains to stop.

50. Distance Apart: *Trains running in the same direction must keep not less than* **1,000** *feet apart, except within the limits of cities and towns, and approaching meeting points where great care must be observed to avoid collisions.*

51. Clear Superior Trains: No train must leave a station expecting to meet or be passed at the next station by a train having the right of track, unless it has ample time to make the meeting of passing point, and clear the track by the time indicated by the time card.

52. Ahead of Time: No train must leave a station in advance of its schedule leaving time, except upon special orders from the Ass't Sup't.

53. Junctions and Railroad Crossings: All trains will come to a *full stop* 30 feet before crossing the tracks of any steam railway and will not proceed until the conductor gives the proper signal from the crossing.

(a) All trains must be under complete control when approaching any electric railway crossing, no matter which train may have the right of way.

No train shall move at a greater speed than four miles per hour while going over Street Crossings within City limits of Los Angeles.

(b) At critical points all trains must be under full control.

(c) If a trolley comes off while on a crossing, do not stop the car to replace trolley until it is clear of the crossing.

54. Leaving Terminals and Junctions: *No train must leave a junction, a terminal, or other starting point, or pass from double to single track until it is ascertained that all trains due which have the right of track against it have arrived.*

55. When a train is stopped by an accident or obstruction, or other causes, at night or during foggy or obscure weather, of where there is not a clear view in both directions, of at least 1,000 feet, red signals must be placed not less than 1,000 feet distant from the location of such train.

56. Irregular Trains: Irregular trains must keep out of the way of all regular trains going in either direction. Freight trains must report to Sherman by telephone when ready to leave any freight stations. All other irregular trains must report to Sherman for orders from all Terminal Points and from all Junctions. Dispatcher must advise irregular trains of all other irregular trains they may meet.

When without definite orders from Dispatcher at Sherman, or when unable to reach Sherman by telephone, irregular trains must protect themselves by flagging obscure points, and during foggy weather against other irregular trains going in either direction, as well as against regular trains.

When possible, irregular trains must have regular trains flag them from point to point.

57. Responsibility for Position of Switches: Conductors will be held responsible for the proper adjustment of the switches used by themselves and their trainmen, except where switch-tenders are stationed.

58. Accidents, Defective Track, and Reporting Same: Accidents, detention of trains, or defects in the track or bridges, must be promptly reported to the train master.

(a) It is the duty of every employe in the service, regardless of departments, to report defects in the tracks or bridges, line or obstructions of any kind wherever met, to the Ass't Sup't, and if possible, to the nearest section or bridge foreman.

(b) All accidents must be reported by telephone from the nearest telephone station to the Ass't Sup't,

and a written report must be forwarded to the Superintendent's office on the proper form, as soon as possible. In making such reports, the facts must be fully, clearly and precisely stated, with all the particulars necessary to a clear understanding of the situation, as known to the person making the report without necessity for inquiries to extract such information. Exaggeration must be avoided. Care must be taken to secure the names and addresses of all witnesses of any accident involving injury to persons or property, or other occurrences where their evidence may be necessary.

(c) In case of accident, conductors may if necessary, demand the services of all employes in the vicinity.

(d) When a conductor discovers anything wrong with the track, bridges or culverts which would be likely to cause an accident to a following train, he must leave a red flag.

59. Accidents---Precautionary Rules: The safety of passengers is the first consideration. All employes are required to exercise constant care to prevent injury to persons or property, and in all cases of doubt, take the safe side.

(a) When a police or fire department vehicle or a runaway or ambulance is observed or heard approaching from any direction, car must be stopped until such vehicle has passed.

(b) Warning to Passengers: Conductors and motormen must (in a polite way) endeavor to keep people from jumping off cars while in motion. If such people attempt to get on or off the car while it is in motion, notify them politely to wait until the car stops. If passengers are leaving car while another car is approaching from the opposite direction, notify them politely to look out for the car on the other track.

(c) Standing on Steps:---Do not permit anyone to stand on the steps or buffers, and never, under any circumstances, permit a woman or child to ride on the steps. They should be fully inside the car before the signal is given to start.

(d) Exercise Care: Motormen are cautioned to exercise great care when a vehicle is passing alongside of track ahead of car. Ring the gong vigorously to attract the attention of the person driving as a warning not to pull in ahead of the car, and run cautiously until the vehicle is passed in safety.

(e) Passing Cars:---When passing standing cars, gong must be rung and car brought to a slow speed.

(f) Render Assistance:---In case of accident, however slight, to person or persons in connection with or near car, the motorman and conductor in charge will render all assistance necessary and practicable. In no case will they leave injured persons without first having seen that they are cared for.

(g) Medical Attendance:---Motormen and conductors are directed not to employ medical attendance to injured persons, except for the first visit, in cases of personal injury; nor will they visit such persons at any time afterward, unless specifically instructed to do so by an officer of the Company.

(h) Give Information to Proper Persons:---No employe shall under any circumstances, give any information concerning any accident, delay, blockade or mishap of any kind to any person except to a properly authorized representative of the Company.

60. Trolley when Backing: When backing on straight line where trolley wheel passes two or more hangers, the trolley must be turned. When on curves or in yards, where there are switches and connections, the trolley must in all cases be turned, if necessary to back. This will also apply to cases where it is necessary to pass any switches or crossings at any point on the road; the only exception being in front of the Fourth Street office, where the motor car is dropping down the grade to couple on to a trailer; but, when taking the cross-over on Fourth Street, the trolly must always be turned, the same as at any other cross-over.

61. Split Switches: Split switches must always be thrown for the locomotives, flat cars and dump cars, as the flanges on the wheels are larger than on regular passenger cars, and they damage the switches when they split them.

62. Stop for all Passengers: Extra or regular cars running into the car barns, must stop for all passengers, taking any the car can carry to their destination, if between that point and destination of car, and explaining to through passengers that the car only goes to the car barn, and advising them when the next car will be along.

63. Starting Signal: No train will start without a signal from its conductor.

64. Conductor and Motorman Equally Responsible: Conductors and motormen will be held equally responsible for the violation of any of the rules governing the safety of their trains, *and they must take every precaution for the protection of their trains, even if not required by the rules.*

65. Trains will be run under the control of the conductor. Although the conductor has charge of the train, the motorman will not be considered blameless if he pro-

ceeds in violation of instructions or orders, even should the conductor, from negligence or misapprehension, direct him to do so.

66. Take Safe Course: *In all cases of doubt or uncertainty, take the safe course and run no risk.*

67. Habits and Personal Conduct: The following are prohibited.

(a) Drinking intoxicating liquors of any kind while on duty.

(b) Entering any place where same is sold as a beverage while in uniform or while on duty, except in case of necessity.

(c) Constant frequenting of drinking places.

(d) Carrying intoxicating drinks on the Company's premises at any time.

(e) Indulging to excess in intoxicating liquors at any time.

(f) Gambling in any form.

(g) Smoking while on duty.

(h) Smoking at any time while in the Company's buildings, (except in the trainmen's room), yards, around oil tanks or reservoirs at Gayland, Beaudry or Temple wells.

68. Absence: No employe whatever may be his rank, will be allowed to absent himself from duty without permission from the head of the department in which he is engaged, nor will employe be permitted to engage in other business without the consent of the Superintendent.

69. Employes leaving the Company's service must return to the Company any property entrusted to their care belonging to the Company.

70. Testimonials: Employes are forbidden to offer testimonials to their superiors either directly or indirectly. Those in authority must not accept such presents or testimonials.

71. Minors: Minors will not be accepted in the train service except as brakemen.

72. Caution in Moving About Cars: Employes are warned not to attempt to get on the end of a car as it approaches them; nor to jump on or off trains in rapid motion or to go between cars in motion to couple them. These and similar acts of imprudence are forbidden.

Every employe is required to exercise great care to avoid injury to himself or to others, especially in the switching or other movement of trains.

73. Avoid Misunderstanding of Signals: It is dangerous to assume that signals given to the motorman have been seen, or if seen that they will be obeyed, when obedience to those signals on the part of the motorman is essential to the safety of an employe in the performance of his duty. He must *know* that the signal has been seen, understood and obeyed before placing himself in a dangerous position. Otherwise, without such knowledge, he assumes all risk of danger arising from any misunderstanding or disregard of signals.

74. Defects in Yard Tracks: Yardmen, trainmen, and other employes are directed to communicate with the train master if they are aware of any defects in the construction of the yard tracks or overhead work whereby an accident might happen while the men are in the discharge of their duties.

75. Care of Passengers: Trainmen must give proper attention to the safety and comfort of their passengers, the heating, lighting and ventilating of cars.

76. Explosive Articles: No gun powder, dynamite, nitro-glycerine, or similar explosive articles, must be transported in any passenger car.

77. Bulletins: Trainmen must consult bulletin board daily before taking trains and must report for duty at least ten minutes before the time of departure.

78. Yard Limits and Stations: *All trains must approach and pass through yard limits under complete control and approach stations carefully.*

79. Flying Switches: Running or flying switches must not be made except where they are necessary or where it would cause great delay to do the work in any other manner.

80. Leaving Cars at Siding: Care must be taken to leave the cross streets and wagon roads unobstructed their entire width.

81. Securing Cars: Trainmen when leaving cars on the main line or side tracks must see that the hand brakes are set. When leaving cars on side tracks, that they are properly secured against running or being blown out on main track by the wind, also that they are far enough from the main track to clear all passing trains safely. If cars are set without a brake, conductors must securely block the wheels.

82. Responsibility for Delays: Conductors and motormen will be held to strict account for delays resulting from bad management, ignorance or carelessness on their part.

83. Killing of Stock: Great care must be taken to prevent the killing of live stock, bringing the train to a full stop if necessary. If stock is killed when it is apparent that it might have been avoided, the value of the stock so killed will be deducted from the motorman's pay.

84. The greatest care must be taken in the handling and delivery of baggage, train mail and Company supplies. Trainmen will be held responsible for any loss or damage resulting from their carelessness.

85. Private Business: Sending personal packages or letters on private business by trains is strictly prohibited. Communications by trains must be exclusively on Company's business.

86. Use of Telephone and Telegraph: The use of the telephone and telegraph lines must be restricted to actual necessity and messages must be short.

87. Medical Fund: All employes are expected to contribute fifty cents to the medical fund each month.

88. Damage: Employes will be held responsible for any damage caused by their neglect or carelessness or by disobedience to rules.

89. Hearing by Superintendent: A hearing will be given by the Superintendent to every employe who desires to complain, and reports or suggestions for the betterment of the service will always receive consideration.

90. Air Hose and Coupling Pins: Air hose and coupling pins must be kept in their places and not allowed to dangle on the ground.

91. Lost Articles: All property found on the cars, on the road or about the Company's premises must be left at the Lost Article Department, Fourth Street office, Ocean Park or Sherman, without delay, and memorandum report made on "Lost Article Tag" which can be procured at the Fourth Street office. After sixty days any article remaining uncalled for will be given to the employe turning in same.

92. Do not allow anyone to put feet on cushions or to spit on floor. However, do not eject any person for not complying with this rule.

RULES FOR CONDUCTORS

100. Be On Rear Platform: Remain on rear platform when not collecting fares, keeping a lookout for persons desiring to board car. Keep careful watch of passengers to observe requests to stop car.

When stops are made at principal places of amusement, churches or any other point where a considerable number of passengers enter or leave the car, conductors must be on rear platform until such point is passed.

(a) Conductors must not ride on front end of car and converse with motorman except when necessary in conforming with their duties.

101. Announcements: Announce distinctly the name of stations, streets, public places and transfer points when approaching the same.

(a) Conductors on Flyers before leaving Fourth Street Station or other terminals, will go through car announcing clearly that car is a "Flyer."

102. Seating Passengers: Passengers should be directed to vacant seats and an effort made to provide them with seats when possible.

(a) Assist elderly and feeble persons, women and children, in getting on and off the car, when possible. Small children, unattended by adults, must not be permitted to ride on the outside seats of any cars.

103. Moving Forward: On cars when passengers are standing, request them to "Please step forward."

104. Collection of Fares: Promptly after leaving terminals or principal stations, conductors will go to the front end of car and announce clearly "Fares please" and collect from the front end.

105. Free Travel: No person will be allowed to ride free. Conductors must collect fare or ticket from all persons travelling, except those authorized by bulletin from time to time, and the register must be rung for every passenger on the car.

106. Ejectments: Ejectments shall be made with the assistance of the motorman or inspector or a policeman after the car has been brought to a stop, using only such force as is sufficient to expel the offending passenger with a reasonable regard for his personal safety. Any person ejected from a car must be put off at a regular stopping place. No passenger will be put off at a point where likely to be exposed to danger. Particular attention must be paid to this rule during bad and inclement weather, late at night or when a passenger is intoxicated.

No passenger will be ejected from a car for mere intoxication, unless said passenger becomes dangerous or offensive; such passenger must then be ejected with great care and must be guided until free from probable injury.

107. Carrying Packages: Passengers must not be allowed to carry bulky or dangerous packages aboard cars.

Do not in any way take possession of, or assume responsibility for, any package which a passenger may bring upon the car.

Do not hang, nor allow articles to be hung, on the brake handles.

108. Care of Car: Advantage must be taken of every opportunity to improve the appearance of cars.

109. Removing Trolley: Do not remove trolley from wire at end of run or elsewhere, at night, until passengers have alighted from the car.

110. Watching the Trolley: Conductors will hold trolley rope at places where trolley is *liable* to leave the wire and when passing switches and crossings in opposite directions to the customary one, and when passing under switches and crossings not often used.

111. Flagging at Buena Vista: Conductors of West bound trains arriving at the switch at Buena Vista Street will go ahead so they can look up Buena Vista St. and see that no cars are coming around the curve before they throw the switch.

112. Resetting Switches: Conductors of all trains will, immediately after taking a siding, spur or cross-over, reset the switch for the main track.

113. Route Signs: See that route signs are properly displayed.

114. Rules for Operating Ohmer Registers.

(a) Before starting from the car barn, see that month and day dials are properly set.

(b) See that the trip dial is set on the number of your trip before taking an impression.

(c) Insert your identification key before attempting to take an impression.

(d) At the beginning of each half trip, insert impression key in register, turn to right one complete revolution and remove key.

(e) Register each fare separately as collected, and ring fare immediately, before the passenger.

(f) See that the pointers on the rod are set to the fare you have collected before pulling the cord.

(g) Always count your change before taking car.

(h) Do not forget your identification key when leaving car. Lost keys will cost you $1.00.

(i) A record will be kept of "overs and shorts" of each conductor and his efficiency will be judged by these results.

RULES FOR MOTORMEN

200. Talking with Passengers and Employees: Motormen while the car is in motion, are strictly forbidden to talk with passengers or employes. Employes must not ride on the front end of cars if there is room for them elsewhere.

201. Speed: Speed must be reduced to six miles an hour in passing all switches and crossings.

202. Bellevue Ave. Hill: All East bound trains must come to a full stop on the west side of Buena Vista St This is a dangerous place, and if a car coming down Bellevue Ave. Hill should get beyond control there might be a serious accident.

(a) Motormen must bring car to full stop at top of hill East bound, and start from the top of the hill with the car under complete control, and keep it so all the way down. Time must not be made up on this hill, or any others east of Beaudry Station.

203. Approaching Cars on Same Track: When approaching any point where a car is standing on the same track, you must slow down so that when near the car you can stop your train by reversing the current, in case brakes do not work, exercising great care when you have trailers. This particularly pertains to terminals and stations.

204. Caution in Coupling: Motormen must exercise great care in handling their cars while yardmen or others are making repairs, and must give close attention to signals. Conductors and yardmen must report to the train master any motorman who fails to obey this order.

(a) Motormen must be at end of car where coupling is to be made. The person making coupling must not go between cars until motorman has stopped his car so that draw-bars will be about one-half a foot apart.

205. Never leave the platform of a car without taking controller handle, throwing off the overhead switch and applying hand brake. Be careful to see that the hands point to the off mark before taking off the controller handle. Always set the hand brake and release the air when car stands over 45 seconds.

206. Trolley Off Wire: When the trolley comes off the wire, you must stop car at once and not start until it is on again, except on railroad crossings.

207. Power Off Line: When from any cause the current is lost, you will immediately throw off the controller and cut in light circuit. When lights show full current, cars with even numbers will start; cars with odd numbers will wait at least sixty seconds. The controller must not be turned beyond the series point until the proper speed for that point is attained. If, on turning on the controller, you find the current weak, turn off controller at once and wait until it is stronger.

208. Blockades: In the event on a blocking of cars from any cause, the cars in such blockade must not all be started at the same time, but singly and at such intervals as will not overtax the power.

209. Water on Track: When there is water on the track, run the car very slowly, drifting without the use of power whenever possible.

210. Spinning of Wheels: Care must be taken to avoid spinning of wheels with no forward or backward movement of the car.

212. Slippery Rails: On a slippery rail do not allow the wheels to slide. As soon as the wheels commence to slip, the brake must be released and reset.

212. Economical Use of Current: In order to effect an economical use of the electric current, it is necessary that the continuous movements of starting and increasing the speed to be made gradually.

(a) In starting a car, let it run until the maximum speed of each point has been obtained before moving the handle to the next point.

(b) Do not apply brakes when the current is on.

(c) Do not apply current when brakes are applied.

(d) Do not allow the current to remain on when car is going down grade, or when passing section breakers'. Endeavor to run car with the least amount of current, allowing the car to drift without the use of the current when it can be done without falling behind time.

(e) A great amount of power can be saved by using judgment and discretion in approaching stopping places and switches by shutting off the power so as to allow the car to drift to the stopping place or switch without a too vigorous use of the brake.

213. All cars must approach crossings under full control and prepared to stop any time to avoid an accident, should a car take a right of way out of order. The car having the first right of way will cross first, the next car to cross it the alternate car. A car must not be considered an alternate car until it has come to a full stop and allowed another car to cross ahead of it.

SUMMARY OF OPERATIVE BULLETINS

1. All trains will reduce speed and be under complete control when approaching Gayland, as oil trains may be switching.

2. Motormen will approach Magnolia Ave. and Hoover St. on the Sixteenth Street line with car under complete control and gong ringing continuously.

3. Conductors must keep themselves supplied with package of slips Form E-11, to be used for names of witnesses in case of accident. Have witnesses write their own names and addresses.

4. Employes riding on badges will be required to show them.

5. All trip sheets must be made ready to turn in before reaching Fourth St. each trip, and cash must be turned in every night and not wait until the next morning.

5. Conductors must not borrow tickets and transfers from other conductors, but must keep a careful check on their stock and see that they do not run short.

7. Trainmen who lay off or absent themselves or leave the employ of the Company from causes other than inability on account of sickness, will lose their rank after thirty days. Should they absent themselves under same conditions and return for re-employment after ninety days, they will lose both their rank and their rate of pay.

8. All trainmen breaking in students will stay with them at all times and not sit down inside the car, allowing the student to "break in" by himself.

9. When any damage is done to a car, such as breaking of windows, etc., by a passenger, collect, if possible, amount sufficient to cover damage. If you cannot collect, get the person's name and address together with names and addresses of witnesses.

10. On all tracks where we operate cars jointly with other companies, in the event of any of the cars of either company being disabled, promptly render any assistance in your power to prevent delay. When necessary, push or pull cars of other companies. Be careful in making connections that no damage occurs.

11. Flyers will make all regular stops between Center Street, Venice, and Montana Ave., Santa Monica.

12. All regular trains will stop without signal in both directions at Temple and Spring, First and Spring, Second and Spring, Third and Spring and Fourth and Spring Sts.

Trainmen will stop cars at any place where there is a standard blue and white stopping sign, "Cars stop Here," to allow passengers to get off and on.

13. Until further notice, only newsboys in Ocean Park and Venice wearing badges of Carter News Co. will be allowed to sell papers on cars.

14. On turning cars into the barn, conductors will take dash signs to the racks. Conductors will be held responsible for the signs.

15. Every conductor when turning his car into a barn or shop must see that heaters are turned off.

17. A green flag along side of track means to run slow. This is a warning that the track is bad, and should never be over looked.

R. P. Sherman,
Superintendent

Approved:
T. R. Gabel,
General Manager

The Balloon

Chapter Seven

The Observation Car "Hermosa," C.M. Pierce at right.   *(Interurbans)*

Route Excursion

C. M. Pierce

How the Crowds Loved

To See the Sea

— By C. M. Pierce's

Excursion Trolley

THE BALLOON Route Trolley Trip was the most famous trolley trip in the west. In its day, few tourists to Los Angeles missed riding the Balloon Route cars, chiefly because of the strenuous efforts of the man who, more than any other, was responsible for the remarkable run of public favor this trolley trip enjoyed. That man was C.M. Pierce. In 1955 the editor had the privilege of interviewing Pierce at his home in the San Fernando Valley where the 90-year-old Pierce owned and operated his own business, the constructing and distributing of health incline boards to large department stores of the nation.

Much of the color of the Balloon Route Trolley Trip is to be found in the various advertising circulars reproduced on the following pages, but Mr. Pierce himself is the best authority for the history of this Southern California institution. Suppose we let him tell this fascinating story in his own words:

"I first came to Hollywood in October, 1900, and opened the Glen-Holly Hotel at the corner of Yucca and Ivar. It was Hollywood's first hotel. We operated a tallyho which met tourists at the car line and took them on a guided tour of the area, then to the hotel for lunch, and back to the car. I noted that many tourists were desirous of keeping in touch with their downtown hotels so I installed a telephone; it was the first telephone in Hollywood and it was a job bringing the pole line over from downtown Los Angeles. In a year or two I grew restive to return to Oregon and did so; it was my privilege to promote the town of Weston, Oregon, doubling its population.

"Hollywood called me back, and when I returned I went into the sightseeing business. The LAP was then operating the Balloon Route excursions but because of lethargic promotion only a very small business was enjoyed. I was offered the position of manager of the Balloon Route and accepted. I took charge of the Balloon Route Trip on the day before Thanksgiving, 1904.

"LAP had turned over the parlor car 400 to this trip; the car was somewhat ornate on the outside with electric lights around the roof as was customary with excursion cars in those days. But the inside had no fixed seats, just folding camp chairs. We went to work assembling a staff of guides and advertising men. For guides I hired big men of commanding presence. When they said anything, the people listened. The advertising men drummed up business for us. We printed thousands of circulars describing the attractions of our trip and these advertising men distributed. One man made the rounds of the large downtown hotels, another rode the Catalina steamer

A TROLLEY PARTY at the DeLongpre Art Gallery, Hollywood, 1905. (Interurbans)

daily, and another rode other excursions, such as the Santa Fe's Kite Trip.

"I remember the trouble the largest of the hotels tried to give us. The Angelus Hotel objected to our advertisements being distributed in its very ornate lobby. My man was escorted out every time he entered but I decided to see what I could do. Sure enough, they kicked me out several times, but I went right back in. The manager got tired of this after a while and we worked out a plan whereby my circulars got through to every Angelus guest.

"These advertising bombardments brought results. Our Balloon Route Trip caught the public fancy as it should, because we gave them the best trip for their money. The old 400 wasn't nearly big enough and we hired more cars and crews; we used to pay LAP $15 a day per car at first, then this went up to $20 and finally to $22.50. We had an arrangement whereby we reported to the dispatcher by 5:00 PM the number of cars we thought we'd need the next day. He then arranged with Sherman car house to have that number of cars at the station in the morning. If we found ourselves short of cars, I had authority to take over any car at the station and add it. Dispatcher Rodenhouse was very cooperative with me and we generally had enough seats.

"At first we operated cars singly, but we did use trailers. We had big banners made and every car we used carried a sign letting everybody know what it was. When the big 700s came, we could operate trains and we did when necessary. In fact, the first four-car train ever to operate out of Hill Street Station was one of our Balloon Route specials. It carried the last of 18 carloads sent out that day, which as I recall was our record day.

"We always went to Hollywood first and there our principal stop was at the studio of Paul De Longpre, the world-famous flower painter. We backed our cars into the spur at our freight station across the street from his home, which stood on Hollywood Blvd. where the Warner Brothers Theater is today. There the cars waited while our excursionists visited De Longpre.

"Then on we went to the Soldiers' Home which was another prime attraction. There we lined our passengers up on the steps of the dining hall for their picture. Our photographer left us then and rode downtown on a regular car, developed

Balloon Route Barkers
Extolled the Wonders
Of Pierce's 101-Mile Trip

and printed his photos, boarded a regular car for Vineyard, met us later there, boarded our cars and sold his photos.

"We took them out on the Long Wharf and they got a big kick out of that. We said it was the only ocean voyage in the world on wheels—and never any seasickness.

"The Camera Obscura at Santa Monica was our next stop and this always impressed. In fact, I understand the city of Santa Monica is constructing a new building to house this unique attraction so it will no doubt be with us for many years to come.

"Then on down the coast to Playa del Rey Pavilion for a fish dinner. I leased this pavilion from LAP and paid the company 10% of what I took in. I put in a good cook and fixed up the dining room and did a good business. We also gave them boat rides in the lagoon and made our large skating rink available at a small fee.

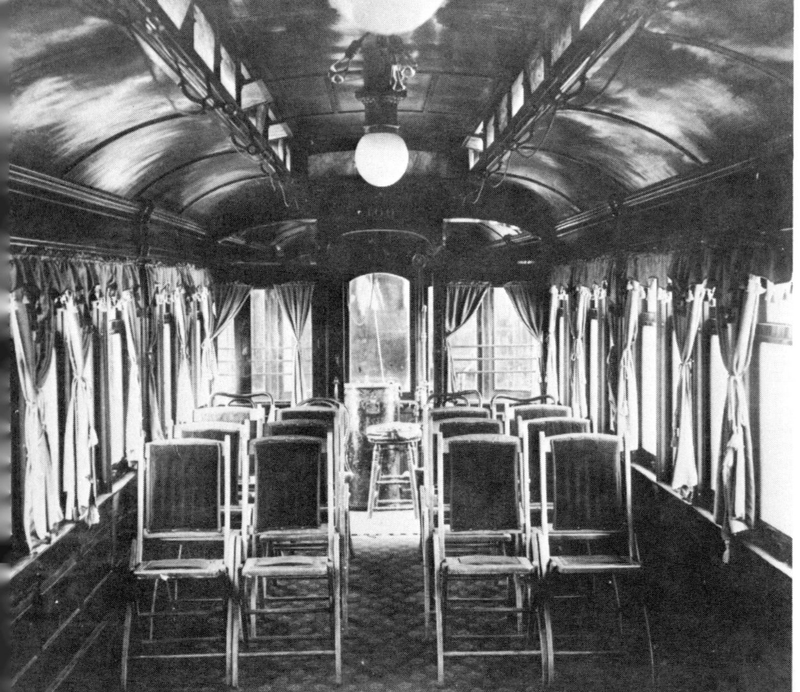

"We then left for the pleasant ride down to Redondo and famous Moonstone Beach. In those days moonstones were sought after and many of our guests turned up excellent specimens after only a short search. These they could later sell, for stores bought them by size, or they could have them polished for a half dollar and have something very nice.

"From Redondo we rode back up the coast to Venice where we stopped for an hour or so to let our people look over the canals, the pier, the Ship Cafe and the numerous other attractions of that most impressive beach undertaking. Then back to our cars for a fast run home via Palms.

"I liked the sightseeing business and knew how it should be run, so I branched out. At the peak I operated 26 different excursions from San Francisco to San Diego. We called them all Balloon Route Excursion Trips; in San Francisco alone I managed eight Balloon Route trips, including the Mt. Tamalpais Trip, the Big Tree Trip, the Mare Island and Bay Trip, an auto trip to Golden Gate Park, a 'Balloon Shaped Trip' which visited the Mint, Golden Gate Park, Lands End, all for 75 cents—the 'Dollar Diamond Trip' which took in Berkeley and Oakland—and others. All these left from our San Francisco office at 789 Market St.

"Other trips I operated in Los Angeles were the 'Seeing Los Angeles' observation car on L.A. Railway, the 'Inside Track' to Riverside and Redlands on SP, and the 'Chinatown Trip'. We operated a steamer trip to San Diego, charging five dollars the round trip including berth and meals.

"In San Diego I operated seven Balloon Route Excursions, including Old Mexico, Coronado, Point Loma, La Jolla, San Diego Mission and others. These were handled from our San Diego office at 1340 'D' St.

"Of course I hired trusted managers to take immediate charge of the San Diego and San Francisco trips, but I made the rounds often enough to be sure they were giving the folks our usual high standard trips.

"We emphasized five reasons why people should go on our trips: (1) You see it all. (2) You see it right. (3) Will save you time. (4) Will cost you less. (5) Our guides are sightseeing specialists, making the trip one of education, comfort and pleasure.

"But the LAP trip was our most famous. I can hear those spielers now: 'Balloon Route Excursion—not up in the air but down on the earth. The Scenic trolley trip, goes one way and returns another. A hundred and one miles for a hundred cents. One whole day for a dollar. Thirty-six miles right along the ocean shore. The only way to see it all and see it right.'

"Every one of our men wore white caps with 'Balloon Route Excursions' on them. We were proud of our excursions and made sure the public knew we were proud. We ran a taut ship, as the saying goes.

"After the 1911 Merger, the PE itself took over the management of its various trolley trips. I remained in the sightseeing business for several years, going over to automobiles and finally to airplanes. But across the years my fondest memories are of the old LAP trolley cars running down country, one after another, taking our tourists down to the beaches and

THE BALLOON ROUTE EXCURSION was a magic attraction in simpler times. In photo at top, the staff of the Excursion posed for this nostalgic portrait in 1909; Pierce is at extreme right in back row. Center photo shows the dining room at Playa del Rey Pavilion, the Excursion's luncheon stop. Bottom photo is an interior study of the unique car 400, flagship of the Balloon Route car fleet for many years.

(All: Magna Collection)

FROM THE MARCH 1907 issue of "Pacific Flyer," LAP House Organ.   *(Pat Ellyson)*

back again. A relative of mine once wrote a poem which we
used extensively in our advertising as I think it captures a great
deal of the spirit of the Balloon Route Excursion; I'd like to
conclude by quoting this poem to you:

> *"Away in the merry Southland,*
> *Far down where the oranges grow*
> *In the land of the great busy city,*
> *Where angels were lost long ago—*
> *There's a way to forget your troubles,*
> *For a day to be brimful of fun,*
> *And the jolly Balloon Route Guide*
> *Will show you how it is done.*
>
> *"Not up in the air he takes you,*
> *Though you'd think you'd left the earth*
> *For weariness, trouble, sorrow or care*
> *Have no place in this car-load of mirth;*
> *Then away and away he will speed you,*
> *Through fairy land down to the shore;*
> *Then back to real life he'll leave you at night,*
> *With a feeling, yes a longing, for more."*

CAHUENGA VALLEY—The excursion goes out on one side and returns on the other of this beautiful valley, through orange, lemon, fig, olive and walnut groves.

SHERMAN—Large power plants, car barns and machine shops of the Los Angeles Pacific Co., whose scenic lines are covered by this excursion. LARGEST OIL DISTRICT IN SOUTHERN CALIFORNIA.

BEVERLY HILLS—A pretty spot.

NATIONAL SOLDIERS' HOME, SAWTELLE—The home of 3,000 noble War Veterans. Massive Barracks; numerous Government buildings; a park covering 700 acres—aptly termed the "Old People's Paradise."

BRENTWOOD PARK AND THE PALISADES—Being rapidly covered with attractive homes overlooking the Sea.

SANTA MONICA—One of the most beautiful residential cities on the Pacific Coast.

PORT LOS ANGELES—The largest pleasure and fishing wharf in the world. An ocean voyage on wheels; an ocean ride unaccompanied by seasickness.

PLAYA DEL REY—(King of Beaches)—Luncheon in the large auditorium dining room 50 cents.

REDONDO BEACH—An attractive seaside resort with shipping interests; immense bath house; auditorium and pleasure piers.

MOONSTONE BEACH—Gathering moonstones and seashells along the sea shore.

OCEAN PARK—An ideal beach resort and a real city on the strand with large pleasure piers; magnificent bath house; a two-mile concrete side walk along the ocean shore. "The Official Promenade."

VENICE OF AMERICA—The most completely equipped amusement and pleasure resort on the Pacific Coast. Immense concrete canals with Gondolas and true Venetian arched driveways; Venetian Villa City. Colonades and arcades along Windward avenue. A large auditorium; dancing pavilion; Oriental exhibits and The Great Ship Hotel are located on the Pleasure Pier.

Take a ride on the Miniature Railway. Visit the New Bath House. Free admission to the $20,000 Aquarium to Balloon Route Excursionists.

INTERESTING POINTS

along the Line of

The Balloon Route Excursion

HILL ST. AND HILL ST. TUNNEL—THE LOS ANGELES OIL DISTRICT ECHO AND ELYSIAN PARKS and Gateway to San Fernando Valley.

HOLLYWOOD—The garden spot of Cahuenga Valley and the prettiest suburb near Los Angeles, with its old pepper avenues, beautiful homes and tropical grounds.

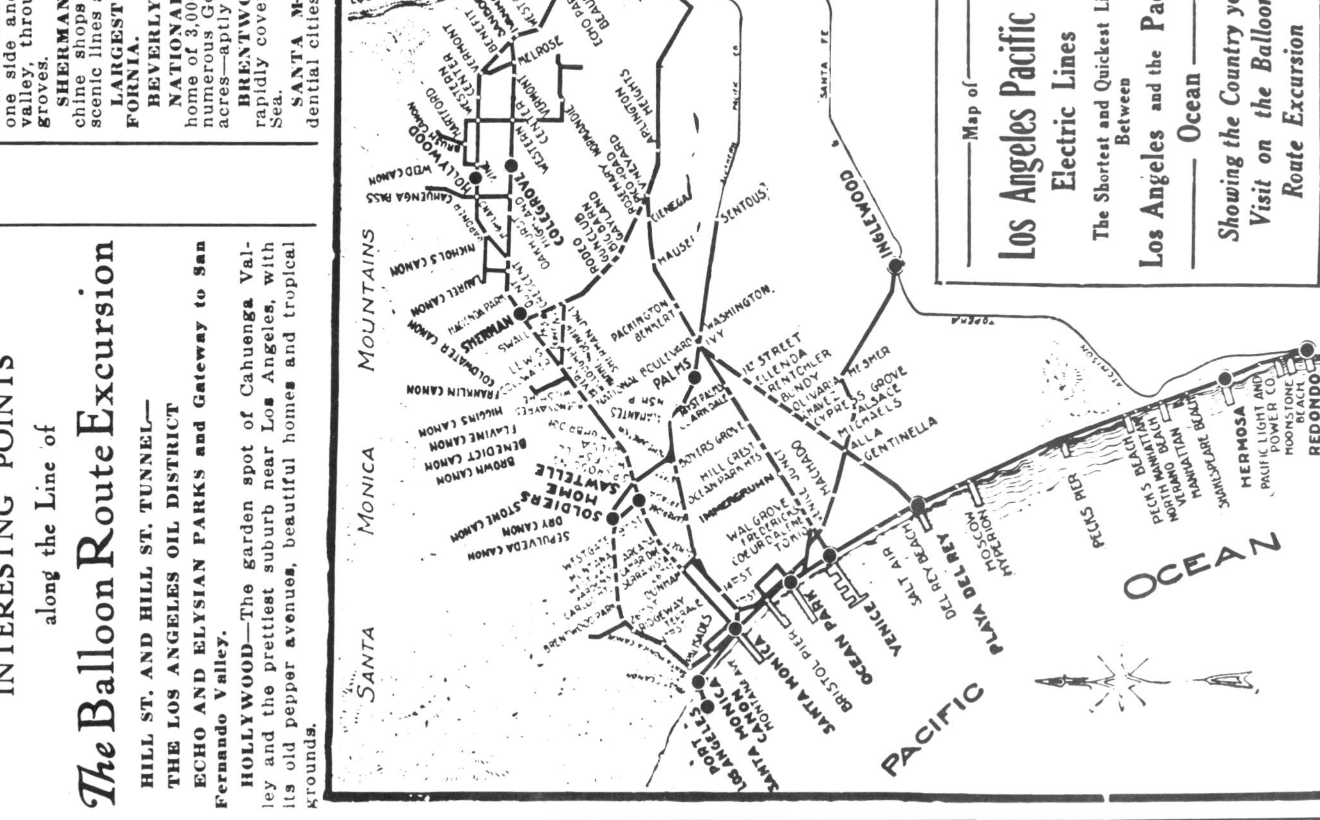

Balloon Route Excursion

The Scenic Trolley Trip

Over the lines of the Los Angeles Pacific Co.

36 Miles Right along the Ocean Shore
:: Visiting 10 Beaches and 8 Cities ::

The Most Enjoyable Day's Outing in all the World in an Observation Car with a Competent Guide

RESERVED SEATS FREE—Get them in advance.

101 Miles of Sightseeing for 100 Cents
ONE WHOLE DAY for ONE DOLLAR

The Only Trolley Trip Going One Way and Returning Another

FREE ATTRACTIONS: An Ocean Voyage on Wheels—The Excursion Cars running a mile into the Ocean on Long Wharf at Port Los Angeles, the longest pleasure and fishing wharf in the world. FREE ADMISSION to the $20,000 Aquarium at Venice and a FREE RIDE ON THE ROLLER COASTER at Ocean Park. Gathering Moonstones and Sea Shells at Moonstone Beach.

LONG STOPS AT

The National Soldiers' Home, Santa Monica, Port Los Angeles, Redondo Beach, Moonstone Beach, Playa Del Rey, Venice and Ocean Park

The Only Way to See it All And See It Right

LEAVES EVERY DAY—9:40 A. M.

429 S. HILL ST.—BALLOON ROUTE STATION

PHONES— Bdwy 4000 Home 10355

Los Angeles

Seeing Los Angeles
BIG RED AUTOS

Balloon Route Excursions
BIG RED PULLMAN AUTOS

Leave 6th and Spring

DAILY—10 A. M., 2 P. M.

A COMFORTABLE, COMPREHENSIVE TRIP, visiting points of interest not covered by electric lines, including the Business Section, Old Mission Church, the Best Residence Sections, Country Club, Westmoreland Place, Westlake Park, Chester Place, Palm Drive, St. James Park, over elegant boulevards and through beautiful parks. A competent guide explains all points of interest. Fare, $1.00 for round trip.

Seeing Pasadena
BALLOON ROUTE EXCURSIONS
Big Red Pullman Autos

Take Pacific Electric Short Line Cars leaving Los Angeles 9:10, 10:30 A. M., 12:14, 1:30 and 2:10 P. M. Get off at Dayton St., near Hotel Green, Pasadena, where Au os meet you.

THE ONLY WAY TO SEE THE BEAUTY OF PASADENA—Visiting Colorado Street and it's many beautiful Churches and Hotels, Busch's Gardens, Merritt's Garden, Orange Grove Avenue—the homes of many millionaires; Marengo Ave., with its huge Peppers; Arroyo Drive, giving a fine view of Mt. Lowe and the Incline Railway.

FREE ADMISSION TO CAWSTON'S OSTRICH FARM

Fare 75c. for the Round Trip

SIX REASONS
'WHY YOU SHOULD TAKE OUR TRIPS

You see it all.

You see it right.

Will save you time.

Will cost you less.

All points are explained.

Our Guides are sightseeing specialists, making the trip one of education, comfort and pleasure.

C. M. PIERCE, Manager of the 26 Balloon Route Trips

"SEEING LOS ANGELES"

Observation Car

It is Cheaper and Better, as all points are explained by a competent guide. Admission to the Ostrich Farm, Pigeon Farm, Refreshments at Bimini, Souvenirs, Attractive Post Cards, are included in this trip.

40 MILES 3 HOURS **All for 50 Cents**

LEAVES FOURTH AND SPRING STREETS

Daily - 10 A. M. and 2 P. M.

POINTS OF INTEREST SEEN AND VISITED

Best Residence Sections

Bimini Hot Springs where

Lemonade is Served

FREE

WESTLAKE
EASTLAKE
ELYSIAN
CENTRAL } PARKS

Largest Pigeon Farm in the World

Los Angeles Ostrich Farm.

This trip is under the management of C. M. PIERCE, Manager of the Famous Balloon Route Excursions. Come and bring your friends. We wil please you.

SIGHTSEEING TRIPS
LOS ANGELES

BALLOON ROUTE EXCURSIONS

NOT UP IN THE AIR - BUT BEST ON EARTH

26 Different Trips
— Seeing —

POINTS of INTEREST

"It is not so much what you see as what you know about what you see."

Reserved Seats Free

GET THEM IN ADVANCE

Main Office *and* Free Information Bureau

429 South Hill Street

Inside the Hill Street Station

C. M. PIERCE, Excursion Manager

Broadway 4000   PHONES   Home 10355

BALLOON ROUTE EXCURSION SOUVENIR
BALLOON ROUTE EXCURSION CAR
OFFICIAL MONTHLY HANDBOOK
WITH COMPLIMENTS OF THE "BALLOON ROUTE EXCURSION CO." LOS ANGELES, CAL.
174

Balloon Route Excursion

(Not up in the Air, but Best on Earth)

Leaves 316 West Fourth Street (near Hill) at 9:40 A. M. Daily...

LOS ANGELES, CAL.

You will find this the most enjoyable day's outing in all the world.

We visit ten of the different beaches and eight cities, along the route of seventy miles, twenty-eight miles of which directly along the grand Pacific Ocean. All points of interest are explained by an experienced and entertaining guide.

Leaving the Fourth Street Station of the Los Angeles Pacific Company, the car travels east on Fourth Street to Spring and north on Spring Street through the main retail section of the city. Spring Street, which was but a few years ago nothing but a trail, is now one of the busiest and most congested commercial streets west of the Mississippi River. You will notice some of the principal hotels and business houses as we pass along. Traveling north, we pass the Los Angeles County Court House and also the new Government building in course of construction, both being on the left of the car. Traveling on north we pass the old Spanish Plaza and the old Plaza

C. M. PIERCE

Mission, built in 1861, with Chinatown, now the largest in the United States, on the right. Here by the old Mission we find one of the bells marking the El Camino Real, the road used by the Catholic missionaries traveling from one mission to the other. These bells are located at intervals along this path throughout Southern California. You will notice one as we go farther on, marking the entrance to Cahuenga Pass. From the Plaza District we turn into old Sonora Town, and pass through the battle grounds of Generals Fremont and Pico, where the contest was made for this territory between the Spaniards and the United States, and pass on out through the oil district, which is interesting to a great many sight seers, and more so from the fact that it is located in the city limits of Los Angeles. Just beyond the oil district we have on the right the Sisters' Hospital. Traveling on out this boulevard along the foot hills through the city limits and into the beautiful

Excursion on Steps of Dining Hall, Soldiers' Home.

suburb of Hollywood, covered with attractive bungalows and homes of Los Angeles business men, whose yards abound in all kinds of tropical plants and flowers, making it in reality a modern Garden of Eden, it is hard to realize that this beautiful suburb was a barley field six years ago, and shows the progressive spirit of the people of Southern California. At Cahuenga Avenue, in Hollywood, to your right is the beautiful home of M. Paul De Longpre, the celebrated French flower artist. You can notice as we pass, his beautiful flower garden to the right of the car. As we go on down through Hollywood we have on the right one of the finest hostelries in Southern California, Hotel Hollywood, and the hostess, Mrs. Anderson,

Ocean Park Bath House

will always be glad to make you welcome, and show you through her beautiful building. She never lacks for patronage, as it is necessary to speak in advance to secure accommodations. Passing a little farther down through the valley, through the vegetable gardens, we go through the little city of Sherman, where the power plant and car barns of this railroad are located, and these little homes you see on the right and left of the car, are the homes of the employees of this company. A little farther on we pass through the largest bean growing district in Southern California. Here, are grown lima beans exclusively, which are a great source of revenue to the ranchers in this section. A little farther on, crossing the Southern Pacific tracks, we arrive at the city of Sawtelle. Turning off to the right here we visit the National Soldiers Home. This is provided by the United States Government for the men who fought the nation's battles and is the most favorably situated of any place of this kind. There are in the neighborhood of three thousand old soldiers located at this home. Our guide will take you you through the principal buildings and fully explain all points of interest. Leaving the

home we pass on by West Gate,
Brentwood Park, where an excellent
view is obtained of the entire valley,
and on past the Santa Monica Canyon we get the first view of the
Pacific Ocean and the longest Pier
in the world, Port Los Angeles,
which is owned by the Southern
Pacific railroad. From this point
we pass down the beach in a
southerly direction to the little city
of Santa Monica, which is situated
on the bluff overlooking the sea.
We depart from the cars nere and go
down to the beach, spending thirty
minutes viewing the panoramic
Camera Obscura, and other points
of interest. Again boarding the
cars we pass on down the beach
through a district covered with very
pretty beach cottages and bungalows to our right and left, to the city
of Ocean Park. This pretty little
beach resort was, five years ago, a
pile of sand, and you can see by the
buildings what a rapid growth it has
made. Besides being the residence
of many Los Angeles business men,
it also contains the summer cottages
of many Eastern people and people

The Colonnade, Windward Avenue, Venice, California

from other parts of the State. Spending a pleasant half hour devouring the beauties of this little city, we pass on through Venice to Playa del Rey, where we have luncheon in the large auditorium, which is, as you will notice, situated directly between the ocean and the large still-water lagoon, and while eating in the dining room you will have a fine view of the ocean and breakers. After we have partaken of our luncheon and enjoyed the scenery at this point, we again board the cars for a ride farther down the beach through to Redondo. We pass through Peck's Beach, North Manhattan, Verano, Manhattan, Shakespeare and Hermosa Beaches, stopping at Moonstone Beach, where many pretty souvenirs in the way of moonstones, agates, etc., may be found. From here we go tothe city of Redondo, and through the Redondo Hotel and gardens, where we get another excellent view of the ocean and harbor. This port handles a great deal of lumber from the North and is quite a shipping point. Leaving Redondo, we retrace our route to Venice, through which we passed before luncheon. We have many things of interest at this point. On the right of the track we have the Miniature Railroad, and Midway, with its animal shows and other varieties of amusement. On the left is Windward Avenue, with its oriental buildings, arcades, colonnades and Venetian architecture. Passing out on the pier we find many curio stores, large auditoriums, the Ship Hotel and other places of amusement. At the end of the pier there is the only private breakwater in the world. This large enterprise was financed by the Abbott Kinney Company, and the entire proposition has been built in about two years. Leaving Venice we travel eastward over the Venetian canals, with Venice Tent City on the left, up through the heart of the Cahuenga Valley over an entirely different route from the one we took in the morning. You will notice the excellent farming land, the many walnut orchards and alfalfa fields on both sides of the car. We pass into the city by what is known as the South Gate, going in on Sixteenth Street, through the Arlington Heights district and by the way of Hill Street; back to our starting point on Fourth Street, arriving about 5 p. m.

We have many times been complimented on this trip and have failed to find a passenger in the many thousands we have carried, that has not been pleased, and we have often been told that it is worth many times the price we charge. We ask you as a favor to us, if you have been pleased with the trip to spread the glad news to your friends, it will be appreciated by us and also by your friends.

In Memory

Chapter Eight

Opening day of Venice line, 1905.   *(Interurbans)*

Lives the LAP

Surely 'Twas Pleasant

To Go a-Trolleying

When All the World

Was Young

Webster defines "memory" as: "That faculty of the mind by which it retains the knowledge of previous occurrences, facts, thoughts, etc., and recalls them."

Few are the men with us today who recall LAP from personal experience. One thing in common they have: an intense desire to convey to us latecomers some of the brilliance, color and dash of "their" railway. We have interviewed as many LAP men as possible and their recollections follow, more or less in their own words.

[Ed.: These interviews, with one exception, were conducted by Ira L. Swett prior to the 1955 publication of Special 18. The interview with Laurence Hiney was conducted by Mac Sebree in February, 1976.]

Recollections

John W. Dodge

BY MID-1908, the lines of the LAP had about reached their final form and beach lines had been changed from narrow (3'6") gauge to standard gauge. The Hollywood and Colegrove lines were still narrow gauge, joining the standard gauge line at Beverly. That junction was not known as Beverly Hills then; it was way out in the country and the station consisted of an open-sided shed. The last of the 700s had entered service and cars 220-249 had been converted to standard gauge. The 700s served the Venice Short Line and Santa Monica via Sawtelle line; other lines were using the older cars.

There were two stations in Los Angeles. The standard gauge station for the beach lines was on Hill near Fifth. The other station was on Fourth between Broadway & Hill for the Hollywood and Colegrove lines which operated over Fourth, Spring and Sunset Blvd. Narrow gauge equipment consisted of 200-219 and similar cars of the 150 and 180 groups which PE made 476-499 without much change. Branch lines such as Echo Park Ave., Cahuenga Pass, etc., used the smaller cars of the 60 series and double ended California type railroad roof short cars of the 30 series. At that time the North Loop local line in Santa Monica and some freight trackage there was still narrow gauge and car 61, isolated, served.

Venice had been established by Abbot Kinney as a very high class beach amusement resort and enjoyed great popularity. The Ship Cafe, Dance Pavilion and other concessions were closely supervised and catered to the best type of patronage. Ocean Park was more the Coney Island type and Santa Monica a very quiet place for families to spend a day on the beach. Playa del Rey had been popular with the better people, but Venice had drawn much of its patronage. Since cars were few and good roads fewer, practically everybody came to the beach on the "Balloon Route," as the LAP was known. The Balloon Route Trolley Trip which was advertised as 101 miles for 100 cents was very popular. It was served by the Hermosa (later PE 020). When traffic required, it was supplemented by regular type cars and later two and finally five of the 700s were modified for this service. The trip took all day and made a stop of a few minutes at the various resorts and other points of interest.

Venice was an unusual spot. East of the tracks, houses fronted on the canals which extended for about half a mile inland. Service roads reached the rear of the houses. Residents could walk beside the canals to the village and trolley station or use the rowboat most of them had, or—better still—ride the Venice Miniature Railroad which ran from the station through and around the canals, about a two-mile loop. There were two Prairie type (2-6-2) locomotives and 10 cars, half red and half blue, forming two trains although I never saw but one in operation at a time.

By 1910, the LAP was entirely standard gauge. The territory served had developed considerably and times were prosperous; the communities had recovered from the 1907 "panic." Multiple unit operation on the Short Line was quite common and Sunday and holiday traffic to the beaches was very heavy. On special occasions, the 700s were supplemented by 200s with trailers (45-57). The 700s were confined to the Short Line and Sawtelle line. 200s served Redondo, Brentwood, Santa Monica via Hollywood and also the Santa Monica-Del Rey local line which had been extended to 7th & Montana in Santa Monica. 200s and older cars ran on the Hollywood and Colegrove lines and branches.

A few of the older cars had been disposed of by 1910. Three cars, evidently of the 150 series went to Phoenix as 30-32 and ran on the Orangewood-Glendale suburban line. One of the trailers was motorized and ran for years on the Brill line in Phoenix as #33. A few of the 30 series went to San Jose and ran for years until the Birneys arrived on the Peninsular's

Bascomb Ave. and Willows lines. At least one LAP car, together with a number of San Diego cars can still be seen at the Pullman Auto Court on East Washington & 20th St. in Phoenix.

The Balloon Route trip had grown greatly in popularity by 1910 and often needed four or five cars. These were not run MU but as sections a few minutes apart.

Venice Had Everything — Even a Miniature Steam Railroad

The original LAP color was light green, about the same as LA & Redondo and LA Interurban, but by 1910 cars were being painted very dark green, about the color of Pullman cars. A little later they began painting them red, no doubt in anticipation of the Great Merger.

By 1910 the Hill Street Tunnels were in use and the Hollywood Station established adjacent to the original "Balloon Route" station. The latter included a building in which waiting room and ticket office were located with gates through which the passengers were admitted to trains. The Hollywood station was merely a shed with a few benches.

At Venice, cars arriving via Santa Monica turned into the tracks which paralleled Grand Canal where they made their layover. The Short Line cars ran to Santa Monica except beach extras, some of which went to Pier Ave., others to Windward Ave. only, then to Ocean Park car house which was then just about the same as it was to the end. The trailer trains, when used, were wyed there.

LAP dash signs always intrigued me—some of them seemed to have a rhythm such as:

Westgate	Beverly	Del Rey
Brentwood	Sawtelle	Manhattan
Palisades	Ocean Park	Hermosa
Venice	Venice	Redondo

The Venice Short Line used green signs; via Sawtelle, red; Redondo, blue; Brentwood, white. The old cars had wooden signs above the front, later replaced by roller signs on the 200s. The 700s had only dash signs.

OFF-TRACK cast welding outfit at Sherman. This one needed a horse for motive power. (Southern California Edison)

Old Fourth St. Station

H. O. Marler

MY EARLIEST recollections of LAP center around the company's original station in Los Angeles, located at 316 W. Fourth St., where stood the Broadway Department Store for many years.

Mr. F.A. Short broke me in. He came to Los Angeles in 1900 and went to work for the Santa Fe. A year later he went to the LAP as its General Passenger Agent and brought me over a little later as office boy. Until 1907, when I became an LAP agent, I held a number of jobs at Fourth Street, and they recall rich memories:

Memories of how we wyed trailers: Fourth Street slopes slightly between Hill and Broadway; the motor car would cut off near Hill Street; run down to Broadway; trailer brakes would then be released, allowing the car to coast down through the crossover to the other track, and the motor would then pull up, back through the crossover, couple on to the trailer for the return trip. One day a certain doctor, a man with a temper and who had long opposed our using a street for a switching yard, parked his buggy on the track and refused to move. We finally got him clear with the aid of the police.

I remember bearded old Abbot Kinney beside the ticket window for hours at a time; for a time the company had an agreement with him whereby he collected a share of every ticket sold to Venice. Woe betide a ticket clerk who dissuaded a prospective Venice passenger to take the other route.

Then on fine summer days we instituted a 25¢ fare to the beach after one o'clock. I well remember a line of people extending out the door of the waiting room, down the street to Broadway, and down Broadway almost to Fifth Street.

Personalities at Fourth Street: T.R. Gabel, General Manager and young Robert Sherman, son of the General, who succeeded Gabel ... M.E. Hammond, LAP's auditor, who gave

A Certain Doctor Objected To Our Using Fourth Street As a Switching Yard

way to G.L. Bugbee, the first SP man in the company (put there, we thought, to keep Harriman informed); later Angus D. MacDonald became our auditor; he later went on to the presidency of the Southern Pacific. ... And, of course, Sherman and Clark themselves; in my time, Sherman was more or less the silent partner, but Clark was very much in the center of things.

Adjacent to the Station was the Sherman Hotel, owned and operated by LAP men, which was operated on a high-class level. Years later the other half of the Sherman-Clark duo was given similar recognition when the great Hotel Clark was built on Hill Street opposite our second station.

TOWER WAGON likewise needed Dobbin for propulsion.
(T.L. Wagenbach)

Those Wonderful Cars!

Russell Westcott

MY UNCLE, Noah B. Sweet, worked at the Sherman Shops as a cabinetmaker; I recall he used some window frames from LAP cars in his house. As a boy I used to visit Sherman Shops frequently and remember well the fascination of watching the men work on the cars. I was especially fascinated by the air brake repair section and spent hours on end watching them test brakes. I rode around the yards in cars and once in a while they would let me work the controller.

At that time the 700s were being built in the east and rumors were that they'd have an elevated cab for the motorman, insulating him completely from passengers. When those cars arrived, I was disappointed in their speed. I have never liked GE motors; years later when I became a motorman on PE I formed this opinion: that for the same rated horsepower, Westinghouse cars seemed to have more zip and pep than GEs. However, everyone in the shops exclaimed over the fine interior woodwork and finish of the 700s. I well remember my uncle's highly favorable comments when he worked over the inside paneling of the 900, 901 and 903 when they were rebuilt. The 700s, and all other LAP cars except the 70s, had large mirrors in the closed section; this added greatly to the feeling of spaciousness. The 700s and all other LAP cars except the 70s had plush seats; the 70s had cane. I always considered the 70s to be somewhat inferior, both in fittings and performance, to other LAP cars.

LAP's 180 class cars performed light city and suburban duties.

(T.L. Wagenbach)

Each class of car had its own separate and distinct characteristics; the little 30s were buzzy at speed; the 60s were smooth, quiet and singing; the 70s were solid and heavy; the 156s were the quietest of all, smooth and comfortable; the 180s were fairly quiet and comfortable; the 190s were my favorite—their four motors made them noisy, fast and "busy"; the 200s gave off considerable noise and were not especially fast; and of course the 700s were solid, heavy and quite comfortable.

About 1910 LAP started repainting its cars in a very dark shade of green. One afternoon I witnessed a funeral procession of perhaps 15 of the dark green cars, each draped in black. The occasion was the funeral for the victims of the dynamiting of the *Los Angeles Times.* The procession started downtown, then out Sunset and Santa Monica Boulevards to the Hollywood Cemetery; there the mournfully draped dark green cars went into the siding and their passengers filed into the cemetery for the service.

Another memory is watching the large electric shovel at work on the Sunset Cut, near Silver Lake Blvd., Benton Way and Occidental. The big shovel worked with mules and scrapers, hand laborers, wagons and dirt trains. The latter ran only at night and were often hauled by 1578. The trains dumped their dirt at spurs across Occidental Blvd. from Olive Substation or took it all the way out to Sherman Shops, where a swamp was filled in to allow more space for tracks. The cut between Coronado and Mohawk amounted to a widening of the old steam railroad cut; this work was done about 1905 and before. Speaking of the Sunset Cut, I remember they put two flagmen up on the top of the hills so the cars could be flagged through safely on the single track kept open. Several times the

flagmen grew careless, and head-on meets were averted only by the alertness of motormen.

I remember the interiors of the cars. The 156s had wonderful Spanish mahogany; the 180s and 190s also had mahogany; the 70s were finished in light oak and the 200s also were lighter; the 60s had the rich dark Spanish mahogany.

That typically LAP railfans' seat on the front platform was always my favorite place to ride. The sign said we couldn't talk to the motorman, but I did, and so did wonderful "Ma" Larrabee, wife of the LAP's superintendent, W.D. Larrabee. She

The Sign Said: 'Do Not Talk to the Motorman.' The Sign Was Ignored.

looked upon the trainmen as her boys, and she did much to make them feel that the company had a personal interest in their welfare.

When air brakes came in, many people were skeptical. They always jumped when the old noisy air pump cut in, but the schedules were improved, due to cars' being able to come up to stops much faster. Straight air was used, and when a trailer was hauled it took a long time to get the air back to the sled. Fortunately, there were not too many stops or LAP would have been out of luck.

LOOKING EAST along Santa Monica Blvd. at Sherman, 1909, we find the LAP office and freight depot, next the substation and in distance the car shops. (T.L. Wagenbach)

The Man Who Made the Cars Run

Jesse B. Green

[Ed.: Green knew the LAP as did few other early-day employes. He went to work for the company on February 23, 1900; he rose to the position of car house and repair shop foreman at Sherman and after the 1911 Merger served as general foreman of PE's 7th & Central Shops, general foreman of the Macy St. Shops, general foreman at West Hollywood until 1941, back to Macy St. in charge of all PE buses and retired in August, 1946.]

I RETURNED from the Spanish-American War (Philippines) in 1900 and found my father working for LAP at Sherman. He died shortly thereafter and I was offered his job. I accepted and was first put to work bonding the rails. After three months I was sent down to Ocean Park to clean and oil cars at the little repair pit located on the northeast corner of Hill & Main Sts. I remained at Ocean Park through the building of the car barn and power house adjacent to the Trolleyway and remember well maintaining the two standard gauge passenger motors and the one standard gauge work motor assigned to the Inglewood line. There was a block of sand between the car barn and the Inglewood line and it was hard work for two of us to get a 350-pound armature from the barn to an ailing Inglewood car. When the Trolleyway was extended to Windward Ave. we put one car on the line to accommodate the rather sketchy traffic; in charge of this car was the son of an LAP official who didn't care if the car ran or not. Usually a telephone call from an irate would-be patron was our first inkling that Junior was not on the job. We would assure the caller that there was a little trouble with the car, that it would soon be fixed and please be patient; then we would find Junior sound asleep on the plush. I remained at Ocean Park until November, 1904, when I quit to enter the real estate business.

LAP called me again in 1906 and on August 1st of that year I again went to work for the Sherman and Clark system. I started at Sherman as a car repairman. My first big job was motorizing and testing the 700 Class cars; they arrived without motors or gears but with all electrical equipment. They told me to rush the work as they were wanted for the crowds who would flock to the beach for the visit of Admiral Evans and the White Fleet in 1908. So I got some men and started to work. We turned out one car a day at Sherman, took them out to Beverly and tested them out there on the Rodeo line.

My next big job was to standard gauge the older cars. No one at Sherman knew a thing about rebuilding narrow gauge trucks to standard gauge, so when I was ordered to take entire responsibility for the work it came as a surprise. I took a narrow gauge truck, studied it, read up on brake linkage and leverages, then experimentally set to work. First the frames had to be widened, then standard gauge axles put in, finally new brakes. Then I got our master car builder—a man named Graham—to inspect the job. He approved it and ordered me to put the cars through just as fast as possible. This we did, turning out a car per day. We would take a car in the morning, jack it up, roll out its trucks, widen them and reinstall them; the electrical men had to connect the control cables and if they were ready when we finished, fine; if they weren't we shoved the car out into the field and let them worry about finding it.

Well do I remember our building trucks at Sherman. We built new A-2 swing bolster trucks for 10 of the 190 Class, making them four-motor cars. We also built the trucks for our electric locomotives and for the "Hermosa." The day the Hermosa was finished Mr. Pontius, then our Passenger Traffic Manager, came out and rode on it. This car was rebuilt from an older car—one of the 70 Class as I recall.

When our system was being standard gauged, a third rail was laid alongside. Our trainmen had to be very careful and more than once I remember trouble occurring because someone forgot. One instance of this occurred on Santa Monica Blvd. near Plummer Park; a new motorman took out a standard gauge car one afternoon, was bowling along at a good rate of speed, and suddenly ran out of standard gauge track, although the old narrow gauge track continued on into the distance. The car shot over into the fields and it took one of my longest cables to reach the runaway and drag it back onto the rails.

Another mishap that I remember occurred one dark night at Rosedale Cemetery on the W. 16th St. line back in 1903. Our car 63, outbound to Santa Monica, was halted by a pile of ties placed across the tracks. As soon as the car stopped, three holdup men boarded, their faces hid by handkerchiefs and guns in their hands. A passenger riding the front section had a gun and opened fire; the holdup men returned his fire and one passenger was instantly killed and three others were seriously wounded. The bandits fled into the darkness and were never apprehended, although LAP offered a sizable reward. Car 63, its woodwork badly ripped by bullets and blood everywhere, was run into Sherman and eventually returned to service.

When we made the big cut on Sunset Blvd. in 1905 we hauled the dirt away in trains of little three-cubic-yard steel dump cars. Some of these trains dumped their dirt at Sherman Yard where we were filling in the back swamp, while others deposited their loads at Olive Substation at Sunset & Occidental, where some stub tracks were located across from the substation. One day some of the little cars were pushed too far and went over the end of the track and down the soft fill. They sent for me and the wrecker and we had a bad time getting them back up onto the rails; there was nothing solid to tie into—just soft dirt everywhere. Finally we got them all back up the slope, but it was a rough experience.

By far the worst wreck we ever had on LAP took place one foggy morning near Sherman and involved a Cholo car carrying track laborers and our lemon train, consisting of an express motor hauling a trailer. The fog on that morning—October 11, 1901—was so bad that neither motoneer could see the oncoming car until five seconds before they hit. The cars were on full

ADVERTISING SECTION

Los Angeles Pacific Company

Electric Lines

The Shortest and Quickest Line between
Los Angeles and the Ocean

See Venice, Santa Monica, Ocean Park, National Soldiers' Home, Playa Del Rey and Redondo.

——— FISH AT ———
Long Warf, Port Los Angeles or Playa del Rey

Take the BALLOON ROUTE EXCURSION   The Greatest Moderate Priced Pleasure and Sight-Seeing Trip in California. One Whole Day for, ... $1.00
Cars leave Hill Street Station 9:40 a. m. Daily.

Los Angeles Passenger Station

HILL STREET, betw. 4th and 5th St.

You Didn't Get Paid Until the Clerk Sold Enough Tickets to Cover Your Wages

speed and there wasn't a chance of stopping them in time. When they hit, the big express motor rode over the floor of the little single truck Cholo car, completely telescoping it. The men, sitting on the floor since there were no seats in the Cholo car, were crushed. Both motoneers were killed. In all, four were killed outright and five badly injured, some dying later. The Cholo car, one of the old 40 Class, was rebuilt into our shop switcher, number 11.

One interesting job we did at Sherman was to rebuild four of our little trailers into motor cars. First we standard gauged their trucks, then applied motors, controls and air brakes (none of our trailers then had air brakes). The little cars were then shipped to the Phoenix Street Railway Company, which was owned by Sherman and Clark and managed by Bob Sher-

man, the General's son. They ran in Phoenix for many years. Both Sherman and Clark were originally from Phoenix; I understand Clark was a school teacher there and Sherman was a member of the school board. Sherman started in Los Angeles about 1890 with the first electric line using overhead trolley, that to Westlake Park via W. First St. Then he and Clark built up the L.A. Consolidated Electric Railway Company, then the Pasadena & Los Angeles interurban, and finally our Pasadena & Pacific which eventually became the LAP.

In the early days, LAP didn't have much ready cash. I recall our carpenter, unable to find the correct piece of wood to repair a car, jumping on a passing car, riding to Los Angeles, buying a single piece of wood, then riding back to Sherman to finish his job. The LAP always paid as it went, which may have been the best policy. However, at one time our men were given a hard time in collecting their pay; things finally got so bad that a man was given an order to pick up five dollars or so at our downtown station; after arriving there he had to stand around until the ticket clerk got five dollars in the till, whereupon he was paid. Just about the only way an LAP man could collect all the wages due him was to quit; one clever young fel-

ANOTHER PORTRAIT of the Parlor Car Hermosa at Playa del Rey, with excursion crowd.   **(Interurbans)**

low at once started quitting every Saturday night, collecting all his wages, and then hiring out again with us on Monday morning. This worked fine until one Monday morning the superintendent recognized him as one he'd personally paid off the previous Saturday; after that he stayed fired.

Our power house at Sherman was notorious for its explosions. One time a boiler came down over on Clark St. Another time it went straight up through the roof. None of us was sorry to see Vineyard replace it.

After the Southern Pacific bought control in 1907 our **LAP** grew into a big system. We never had to worry about running short of money again, but at the same time there was lost the fascination of independence. But even after the 1911 Merger the old **LAP** men continued to regard their Western District of PE as just about the finest electric railway system anywhere. Sometimes I feel like attempting to capture these thoughts in poetry; perhaps it may interest you to read one of these efforts of mine:

When Beverly was a bean field
Some fifty years ago,
We were young and handsome—
Our eyes were all aglow.

But now it is a city,
Old Morocco that we knew;
We gathered at the station
Old friendships to renew.

Their faces all were wrinkled,
Their hair had turned to gray;
Some footsteps rather feeble,
Who once were young and gay.

Old faces passed before us,
Those who had gone to rest—
Men who were the finest,
They who had passed the test.

But we built the railroad
That was called the L.A.P.—
Now retired and resting,
But gathered there were we.

The hours were long and trying,
And we got but little pay;
Still we did our duty,
And worked both night and day.

The cars were painted green then,
They were our joy and pride—

187

HERE IS ANOTHER view of El Viento–"The Wind."

(T.L. Wagenbach)

They ran from Los Angeles
Down to the ocean's side.

The motors they were small, too–
And a trailer on behind,
Loaded to the guard rails;
A handbrake they would wind.

But then they sold the railroad,
The cars were painted red–
From black to red the ink, too;
Lost money then, they said.

But we oldtimers gathered
To bid the cars goodbye;
The buses now take over–

And a tear comes to our eye.

But for fifty years and over
We watched the cars go by;
Their passing makes the heart ache,
'Tis sad to say goodbye.

We clasp the hand of friendship;
Those boys were tried and true;
They were true to the company,
And to their country, too.

Only a few still living
Of those boys of the L.A.P.;
To them a Merry Christmas–
And may they happy be!

Manhattan Memories

George L. Alton, Sr.

AS A BOY I remember spending vacations at the beach. First my parents took me to Santa Monica; when that beach became too crowded we began going to Ocean Park. The crowds found that place and then Manhattan Beach became our summer watering place. We first went to Manhattan Beach in 1906, and liked it so well that we have been living here ever since.

In those early years, LAP's green cars were our only practicable connection with the outer world. Passenger carrying was their main function, but express cars came regularly with life's necessities; one of my uncles was an executive of a brewery in San Francisco and well do I recall meeting an LAP express car at intervals, receiving a barrel containing bottles of beer, and rolling the barrel up the hill from the tracks on the beach to our home—telling inquisitive old ladies that it contained soda pop!

The line down the coast to Redondo was originally narrow gauge. About 1907 LAP decided to standard gauge it. They did the work by laying a third rail along the entire line. About every third or fourth tie was replaced with a standard gauge tie and the new rail was spiked to this tie, and also to the extreme outer ends of the narrow gauge ties. I remember riding down on a Saturday on a narrow gauge car; the next Monday morning everybody was riding the standard gauge cars. As I recall, the 180s and 190s were our regular narrow gauge cars, and when we were changed to standard gauge, the 200s took over. As the narrow gauge ties came due for replacement, standard gauge ties were put in until eventually there was nothing else. Our line never got the big 700s except on Saturdays, Sundays or holidays—and then the press was so terrific that three-car trains were run on frequent schedules—and standing loads were commonplace! Today we have infrequent bus service and there are always seats.

We kids used to go to Redondo regularly and we early learned how to ride LAP free. The cars were so crowded leaving Redondo that the conductor would necessarily have to work his way through slowly. He always started at the front end, so we rode the back platform. By the time we got close to home we would pretty well know if he would get to us or not; if it appeared he would be upon us momentarily, we would drop off at 8th St. or 5th St., but sometimes we'd ride all the way through to 1st St.

QUARRY OPERATIONS in Brush Canyon at their peak, about 1909. Work motors 1582 and 1580 are waiting for their trains of dump cars to load, thence to depart for various parts of the LAP system. (Huntington Library)

When Venice opened, it proved to be the number one attraction, outdrawing all the other beaches. A bunch of us used ؍ go to the Ship Cafe on the Venice Pier. We knew the LAP schedules, and so would stay until the last possible minute; then came a wild dash off the pier, down Windward Ave. and to the Trolleyway where we would usually be just in time to swing aboard the little car that went down to Playa del Rey; there we'd connect with the last Redondo car for the final lap of our journey. Occasionally we cut it too fine and then came a long, cold walk home. Those were the days!

A Tale of Two Conductors

LAURENCE HINEY

BACK ABOUT 1897 I paid just about the highest fare for a single ride the Los Angeles Pacific ever got. I was only 15 at the time, had moved to Los Angeles from my home in Pennsylvania and was already working full time at the Llewelyn Iron Works downtown. My weekly wage was paid in one $5 gold piece, plus $1 in silver, total $6. Not bad for the turn of the century, but one ride on the LAP nearly cost me five-sixths of my entire weekly earnings.

I boarded a Colegrove car and handed the conductor what I thought was a nickel. When I got home I realized it was my $5 gold piece; a gold piece of that denomination was just about the size and weight of a nickel. I was pretty down in the dumps until I boarded an inbound LAP car the next morning and found I was riding with the same conductor! I asked him if he wasn't $4.95 heavy on his receipts for the previous day,

and he admitted he was. I got my gold piece back minus a nickel—and it made my day. LAP conductors were nice men!

The big green cars figured in another minor embarrassment when Los Angeles and I were young. I lived on Hyperion just off Sunset and took my girlfriend to a show downtown on the trolley. Everybody did in those days before automobiles. On the way home, about midnight, the car lurched to a stop near West Olive. No power. We sat. And sat. And sat. I was getting worried, because I had promised the girl's mother I would get her home by midnight. Finally we got off the car and started walking up the hill. Seemed like forever, and just as we were at the top of the hill here came the car—the power had been turned on again. The car stopped for us, but I suddenly realized I had spent my last dime for the fare home and the conductor wouldn't let us on again to complete our ride. So . . . we just had to keep on walking. That was one LAP conductor who wasn't quite so nice.

The LAP had some fine cars. And some not so fine. Some of the old cars that I rode on the Colegrove line were so damn old there were holes in the floor—you could see the street racing backward underneath. Hollywood Blvd. (called Prospect Ave. then) was just a gravel road—a quagmire when it rained. The LAP cars used to carry a pole, so they could push stalled teamster wagons off the tracks. Those were the traffic jams of those days.

The rock crusher up in Brush Canyon always interested me. I used to walk the spur line that ran up there from Franklin Ave. so that LAP could get ballast for its lines. The line didn't run on any street, just followed the wash up to the quarry. The steam engine up at the crusher was especially fascinating; I later built an exact model of it. They told me that there was supposed to be a gold mine up in Brush Canyon, but I never found it.

Appendix

Official Corporate Histories

The following corporate histories are taken more or less verbatim from the official history of the Pacific Electric Railway Company, written in 1914. The history was compiled by the PE Engineering Department and has served as the "bible" whenever the company has been called upon by courts or regulatory bodies to establish historical points of fact.

This version is 95% verbatim. The editor has altered it only in eliminating repetitious passages or in omitting certain financial transactions which would be of questionable value to the average reader.

Each predecessor company was assigned arbitrarily a Unit Number to avoid confusing that company with another when, as often happened, two or more companies chose identical corporate names. A Unit Number was also assigned to a line or lines leased or purchased from outside sources, also to promote clarity.

To make the corporate history more readily understandable, we have worked out the corporate chart which appears on the opposite page, showing constituent and predecessor companies. Dates shown are those when corporate papers were filed with the California Secretary of State or the Secretary of Arizona Territory—and when the subsequent consolidations became effective.

LOS ANGELES OSTRICH FARM RAILWAY COMPANY (Unit 36)

The original line of LAP, on Sunset Blvd., came into being way back in 1886 when the 3-foot gauge Los Angeles Ostrich railroad from a point in Elysian Park Ave. (Sunset Blvd.) opposite the Sisters' Hospital (now St. Vincent's, then at Beaudry & Sunset) in a general northwesterly and westerly direction along present Sunset Blvd. to Childs Ave. (near Sanborn Jct.) and thence northerly, crossing Effie St. and the northern boundary of the city, then up the west side of the Los Angeles River to Kenilworth Station on the Los Feliz Rancho (now Griffith Park), where the ostrich farm then was.

The Ostrich Farm Ry. was incorporated in California on August 5, 1886; among its incorporators was Mr. I.W. Hellman (later to be affiliated with Henry E. Huntington in the famous Huntington-Hellman Syndicate which established the Pacific Electric in 1901). The company's announced purposes were: "To acquire by purchase or otherwise rights of way and lands —and to construct, operate and maintain a narrow gauge steam motor railroad." The proposed road would transport passengers and freight, the cars of which were to be drawn by locomotives or dummies, from some point in L.A. City to the Ostrich Farm, about eight miles. The total capitalization was $60,000, of which $8,000 was paid to Mr. G.J. Griffith, the treasurer.

During the latter part of 1886, Mr. M.L. Wicks of L.A. constructed for this company a line of railroad 6.387 miles in length which followed the route set forth in the first paragraph. Wicks performed the work under a contract with the company by the terms of which he was to receive a subsidy from various landowners along the line and also all of the capital stock of the company. After the construction work had commenced (1886), all of the stock was issued to Wicks except a few shares which were issued to the directors. On July 9, 1887, an agreement was entered into by Mr. Wicks and the *Los Angeles County Railroad Company* whereby the latter company agreed to purchase the Ostrich Farm Ry. Co. for the sum of $50,000, payable to Wicks in bonds of the L.A. County RR Co. During August, 1887, this deal was carried out.

Operation of this line commenced during the latter part of 1886 and was continued until on or about August 15, 1887, at which time the line was turned over to the L.A. County RR Co. under the agreement dated July 9, 1887.

On September 6, 1888, the L.A. Ostrich Farm Ry. Co., together with the L.A. County RR Co. and the L.A. & Pacific Ry. Co., entered into an agreement to consolidate, and to form a new railroad corporation to be known as the *Los Angeles & Pacific Railway Company*. This consolidation was effective on September 11, 1888, on which date the LA&P became the owner of all property formerly owned by this corporation.

THE LOS ANGELES COUNTY RAILROAD COMPANY (Unit 37)

Incorporated in California June 23, 1887. Among the incorporators was M.L. Wicks. This company was capitalized at $300,000. Its proposed road would be from a point in L.A. City to the shore of the ocean on the Bay of Santa Monica, estimated to be 28 miles.

On July 9, 1887, this corporation purchased from Wicks all capital stock of the L.A. Ostrich Farm Ry. Co. and so became the owner of a line of steam motor railroad of 3-foot gauge extending from the Sisters' Hospital to the Ostrich Farm, all single track.

During September and October, 1887, this company changed the gauge of the Ostrich Farm line to 3'6" by setting over one of the rails. During the same period, preliminary work was begun on the construction of a line from the Ostrich Farm line at Childs Ave. (near Sanborn Jct.) to Santa Monica, as well as extending the Ostrich Farm line to Burbank. These lines, as subsequently constructed, were single track, 3'6" gauge lines of steam railroad.

The Santa Monica line extended from the junction with the Ostrich Farm line through the town of Colegrove and the townsites of Cahuenga (Hollywood), Morocco (Beverly Hills), Sunset (Sawtelle)—passing the National Military Home—to the northern boundary of Santa Monica; thence in a generally southwesterly direction along Railroad Ave. (now Colorado Ave.) to a point near Ocean Ave. This line was practically completed and placed in operation during the latter part of 1888.

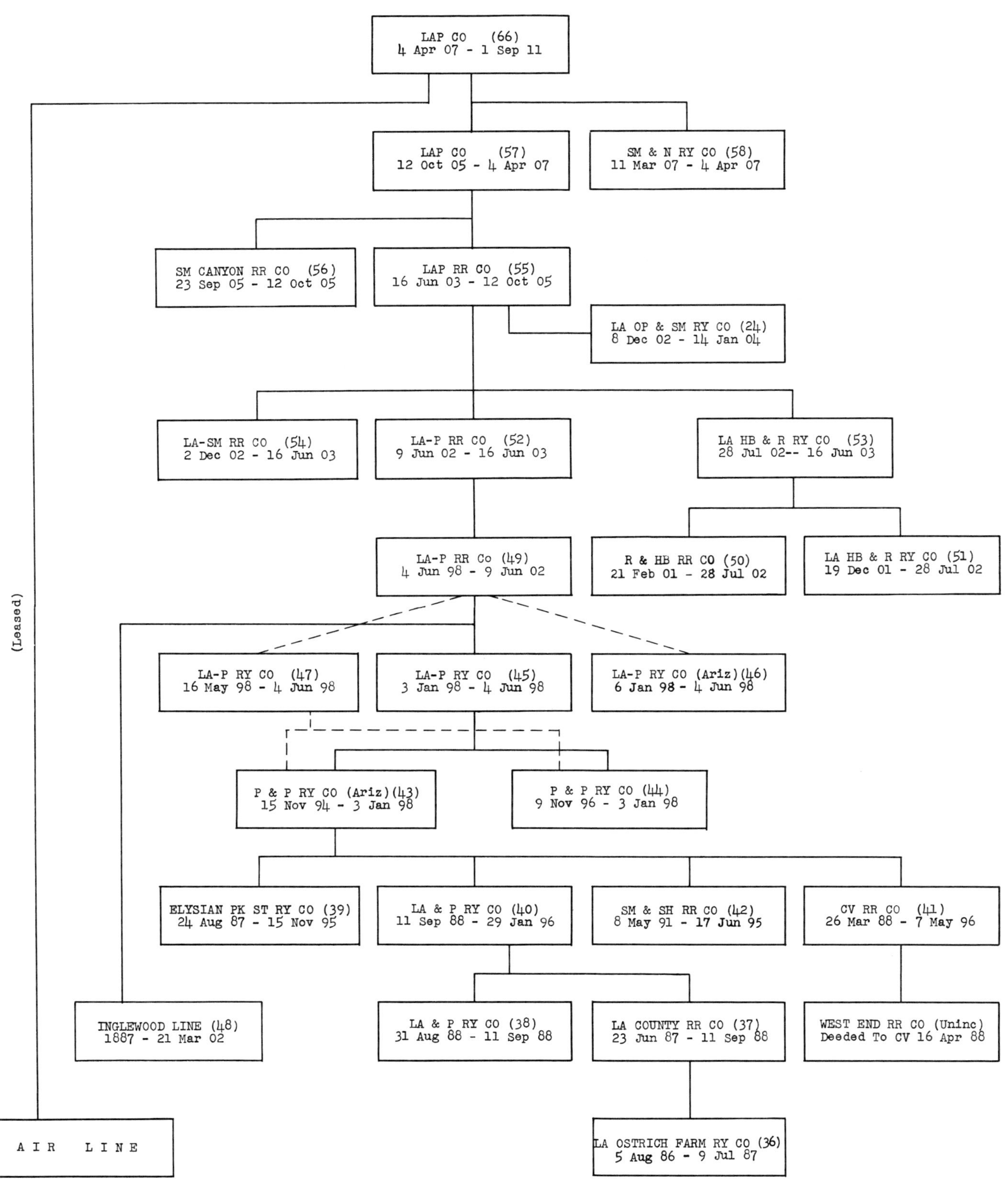

Predecessor Companies

On the extension to Burbank, a bridge was constructed across the L.A. River near the Ostrich Farm and the road constructed in a general northerly and northwesterly direction to Burbank. It was completed early in 1888 and placed in operation.

The mileage of road owned by this company was:

Main Line (L.A. to Santa Monica):	18.599
Burbank Branch:	7.788
Spurs & sidings (no record):	---
Total (single track):	26.387

On September 6, 1888, this corporation and the Los Angeles Ostrich Farm Railway Company (Unit 36) and the Los Angeles & Pacific Railway Company (Unit 38) agreed to consolidate and to form a new railroad corporation under California laws to be known as the *Los Angeles & Pacific Railway Company*. This consolidation was effective September 11, 1888, on which date all property owned by this company at that time passed to and became the property of the Los Angeles & Pacific Ry. Co. (Unit 40), and that corporation took immediate possession.

THE LOS ANGELES & PACIFIC RAILWAY COMPANY (Unit 38)

Incorporated in California on August 31, 1888, with main office located in Los Angeles. It was capitalized at $1,800,000 and the purposes were to construct, maintain and operate a standard gauge steam railroad; also to erect, maintain and operate a telegraph line in connection with said railroad of the estimated length of 75 miles.

The proposed road was as follows:

(1) From a point on the line of the L.A. County RR in the City of L.A. by the most practicable and desirable route to the City of Pasadena, about 9 miles.

(2) From a point on said L.A. County RR within L.A. City in a southeasterly and easterly direction to a point near the southeastern corner of the city; about 6 miles.

(3) From a point within L.A. City by the most practicable and desirable route to the Pacific Ocean at or near Hueneme, in Ventura County; about 60 miles.

This company was thus incorporated for the purpose of building extensions to the lines of the L.A. County RR Co. and eventually to convert all of said lines into standard gauge steam railroads. The preliminary work of obtaining rights of way was performed, but no actual construction work was done by the company and it owned no lines of railroad.

On September 6, 1888, this company agreed to consolidate with the Los Angeles Ostrich Farm Ry. Co. (Unit 36) and the Los Angeles County RR Co. (Unit 37) and to form a new railroad corporation under the laws of California to be known as *The Los Angeles & Pacific Railway Company*. This consolidation was effective on September 11, 1888, on which date the said Los Angeles & Pacific Ry. Co. (Unit 40) became the owner of all property which this corporation owned at that time.

THE ELYSIAN PARK STREET RAILWAY COMPANY (Unit 39)

Incorporated in California on August 24, 1887, with a capitalization of $50,000. The promoters of this line had extensive land holdings in the northwestern part of L.A. City and various subdivisions had been platted and lots in same sold to prospective home builders with the promise of ample streetcar service. Notwithstanding the fact that a great financial depression had settled over Southern California following the real estate boom of 1887-1888, the promoters were obligated to build a street railway to their new additions.

Two ordinances empowered the subdividers to act; the first granted the right to build, operate and maintain a single or double track line from Temple and Echo Park Ave. in a northerly direction on Echo Park Ave. to about 150 feet north of Montana Ave. This was passed on April 14, 1887. On June 24, 1889, another ordinance granted the right to build, operate and maintain a single or double track line from Echo Park Ave. and Sunset Blvd. in a general southeast direction along Sunset to New High St., then south on New High to Sonora St. and east to Main St.

During the latter part of 1889, construction work was commenced on the line on Echo Park Ave. from Temple St. to about 600 feet north of Sunset Blvd.

Early in 1890 the steam railroad (L.A. & Pacific) on Reservoir St. and Elysian Park Ave. (now Sunset Blvd.) which had ceased operation on December 1, 1889, was taken up and that portion of the line abandoned by its owners. During the spring of 1890 this company constructed a one-track line of 3'6" gauge of lightweight rails from Echo Park Ave. and Sunset Blvd. to Main Street, via Sunset, New High, and Sonora St. From Echo Park Ave. and Sunset Blvd. to the Sisters' Hospital it followed the route and used the grade of the steam railroad. That portion of the line on Echo Park Ave. from Temple to Sunset was abandoned during the fall of 1890 and track removed. An extension was then built on Echo Park Ave. to what is now Cerro Gordo St., about one mile. The total length of the road owned by this company (from Main St. to Cerro Gordo St.) was 3.149 miles, single track, all in L.A. City.

The company owned one car and two mules at the start of operation, but the car was subsequently drawn by only one mule; as a result, only two round trips daily were made—one in the forenoon, the other in the afternoon. From the beginning it was never expected that this line would pay more than its operating expenses, and in this the owners were not disappointed.

On November 16, 1891, this company agreed with the Los Angeles Consolidated Electric Railway Company (later LARY) that LACE was to take over the line and electrify that part from Main St. to Echo Park Ave. and operate same as an electric railway; the balance of the line to Cerro Gordo St. would continue as a mule car line. That company failed to electrify the line and on February 27, 1895, it reconveyed the property to this corporation.

By deed dated November 15, 1895, this company conveyed all its property to the *Pasadena & Pacific Railway Co.*, pursuant to a resolution passed by its directors on that date. The consideration named was one dollar and "also that the said grantee and assigns and successors in interest shall cause electric cars to be operated continuously every day giving at least 30-minute service each way for a period of 25 years, such trips to be made during the ordinary hours for running streetcars in the city of L.A."

That part of the line from N. Broadway to Echo Park Ave. on Sunset was abandoned and an electric line was built by P&P during the spring of 1896 and afterwards became a part of the L.A.-Santa Monica line. The balance was operated by horse car for several years. On August 28, 1901, the L.A.- Pacific Co. leased the horsecar line to C.C. Champion on a year-to-year basis. The lessee furnished one car and two horses or mules and received a stipulated amount each month in addition to the total cash fares collected. This lease was in effect until the latter part of August 1902. The line was electrified up to Cerro Gordo St. during the next 90 days and placed in operation on November 20, 1902.

THE LOS ANGELES & PACIFIC RAILWAY COMPANY (Unit 40)

Incorporated in California on September 11, 1888. The lines to be built or acquired were single track or double track, standard gauge steam railroads extending from L.A. City to

Santa Monica Bay; also from a junction with the line of the L.A. County RR Co. easterly to Pasadena; also from a point on same company's line to the easterly corner of L.A. City; also from L.A. City to Hueneme; together with about 75 miles of telegraph lines. All lines of railroad included in this consolidation were to be changed to standard gauge. $2,160,000 was the amount of capitalization.

On September 11, 1888, the constituent companies (L.A. Ostrich Farm Ry., L.A. County RR, L.A. & Pacific Ry.) turned over all lines owned by them of a total length of 26.38 single track miles. This company immediately began standard gauging the Burbank line; new ties were put in, and the gauge changed to 4'8½". This line was opened for regular operation to the Ostrich Farm on September 25, 1888, and to Burbank on May 31, 1889. Narrow gauge steam motors were operated on the Santa Monica line until the rebuilding of the Burbank line was completed. The work of standard gauging the Santa Monica line began in the summer of 1889 and was practically completed by September 1, 1889. Standard gauge trains ran from L.A. to Santa Monica commencing on or about that day.

During September, 1888, this company purchased from the Baldwin Locomotive Works two steam locomotives which were named "Wynetka" and "Cahuenga No. 3" on the installment plan. Two steam motors, ten passenger cars and two flat cars were leased from the firm of Carter Brothers of San Francisco. Owing to financial difficulties, the monthly payments were not made when due, and on November 18, 1889, the two locomotives were turned back to Baldwin in full satisfaction of the purchase price and use of same by this corporation. On December 2, 1889, Carter Brothers took charge of the rolling stock owned by them. By this time the financial depression which followed the "boom" of 1887-1888 had set in, and this company did not run its railroad after December 1, 1889. During the following spring, its tracks were removed from Elysian Park Ave. and Reservoir St. to a point west of Echo Park Ave.

The final sad ending came about in this manner: Two grading contracts totaling about $23,000 became due and the company was unable to pay them. On September 10, 1889, the company was put into the hands of a receiver, and the final result was that the company was thrown into foreclosure on April 2, 1895. On May 4, 1895, the receiver reported to the Court that the Burbank line was very much dilapidated and had been partially destroyed by storms and depredations "committed by divers and sundry persons"—that considerable quantities of ties and rails had been removed without permission. He asked for authority to remove all remaining material in that line to a safe storage place. The Court on the same date ordered him to remove all rails, ties, fastenings and other materials and take them to the junction with the Santa Monica line. This was done, except that material in the line from the river to Burbank was stored at Burbank, due to the company's bridge across the river having washed out.

On April 29, 1895, all property of this company was sold at auction to Mr. A.I. Smith for $190,000. By deed dated January 29, 1896, Smith sold to the *Pasadena & Pacific Railway Company* (for $185,000) the railway and property of this corporation. This transfer covered a constructed railroad from Lake Shore Ave. (Glendale Blvd. today) and Sunset Blvd. at the beginning of a private right of way owned by the company to Santa Monica, 17.245 miles in length, together with all ties, rails and other construction material.

Mr. Smith, in an interview at the time, said: "The road was sold under judgment some time ago and I became the purchaser. I and the bondholders have entered into a contract with the Pasadena & Pacific Ry. Co. by which all of our interests will be vested in that company upon their reconstructing the road and putting it in operation. Under our contract, the Pasadena & Pacific agrees to construct the road, to connect it with the settled part of the county and to operate it with electricity. The company has already purchased a large part of its rolling stock and electric plant and is to commence work within three months and to complete it within twelve months from date."

CAHUENGA VALLEY RAILROAD COMPANY (Unit 41)

Incorporated in California on March 26, 1888 with a capitalization of $100,000. Its proposed road would run from the terminus of the Second Street Cable Railroad to or near Santa Monica, about 18 miles.

On January 11, 1887, James McLoughlin of L.A. acquired a franchise covering the construction, operation and maintenance of a dummy steam railroad from Diamond St. (now Beverly Blvd.) via Texas St. (now Belmont Ave.), Temple and other streets and highways to the southwest corner of the Baptist College, known as the Los Angeles University and located on the high ground near Beverly and Virgil.

On March 9, 1887, McLoughlin agreed with property owners along the line to extend the line from Temple and Hoover in a westerly and northerly direction to the northeast corner of Section 14 (approximately Western and Melrose).

During February and March 1887 McLoughlin constructed a narrow gauge line of single track steam dummy railroad over the route described and placed it in operation as "The Temple and Diamond Sts. Steam Dummy Railroad."

Under the March 9, 1887, agreement, bonus lands to the extent of 22 acres and bonus money amounting to $16,000 in promissory notes executed by property owners along the route were delivered to McLoughlin. During the summer of 1887 he extended the line to what is now the intersection of Western Ave. and Santa Monica Blvd. This extension was known as "The West End Steam Dummy Railroad."

By deed dated April 16, 1888, McLoughlin sold this steam dummy railroad from Diamond and Belmont to Western and Santa Monica to *The Cahuenga Valley Railroad Company* for a consideration of $51,300. Included were franchises, rights of way, and rolling stock (one locomotive and one car).

During the latter part of 1888 McLoughlin secured the necessary rights of way and extended the line northerly along the County Road (Western Ave.) to Prospect Ave. (now Hollywood Blvd.) and thence west on Prospect Ave. to what is now Wilcox Ave.

By deed dated February 1, 1889, McLoughlin sold this last described extension to the Cahuenga Valley company for $10,000. It consisted of a single track line of 3'6" gauge, built of 22-lb. iron rails, running about ¾ mile north on Western Ave., then about 1¼ miles west on Prospect to Wilcox.

In March, 1889, the Second Street Cable RR Co. made an agreement with the Cahuenga Valley RR whereby transfers were exchanged at Beverly and Belmont, where both lines then terminated. This privilege extended only to the L.A. city limits, then at Temple and Hoover Streets.

The steam dummy line was built on Temple St. along the south side from Belmont Ave. to Park View St. When the Temple Street Cable Railway extended its line from Temple and Belmont out to Temple and Hoover (opened April 30, 1889), it was put in the center of the street, which created an impossible situation. The steam line was ordered off the street by the city council, but the Cahuenga Valley RR contended it was a steam railroad line and could not be expelled from the street. However, by deed dated September 16, 1889, this company surrendered its franchise inside the city limits and abandoned its line from Beverly and Belmont to Temple and Hoover. Thereafter the bulk of the company's business was received from the Temple St. Cable line and Temple and Hoover became a rather busy transfer point.

In 1891 or 1892 control of this company passed to Mr. E.C. Hurd and Mr. S.A. Mattison through ownership of a majority of outstanding stock. During the latter part of 1894 the new owners secured the necessary materials for an extension to Laurel Canyon, and placed the track materials along the proposed route. However, property owners were antagonistic toward a steam railroad and made threats to take concerted action to delay or prevent the passage of a franchise by the County Supervisors. The owners, Hurd and Mattison, decided to build the extension first and take up the matter of a franchise afterward. Construction work was commenced after the adjournment of the Courts on a Saturday afternoon and the extension was ready for operation the following morning. This portion of the road extended westerly along Prospect Ave. from Wilcox Ave. to the present Highland Ave., south on Highland to Sunset, and west to Laurel Canyon, where a waiting station and pavilion were subsequently constructed.

After the completion of the extension to Laurel Canyon the company owned a narrow gauge single track steam dummy railroad extending from the western city limits of L.A. to Laurel Canyon, 6.982 miles.

Early in 1895 Sherman and Clark obtained control of the company through majority stock ownership. By deed dated May 7, 1896, the Cahuenga Valley RR Co. sold all its property to *The Pasadena & Pacific Ry. Co.* (Unit 43) for $10.00. P&P and its successors operated the road as a steam line for several years and eventually converted the greater portion into an electric line.

SANTA MONICA & SOLDIERS' HOME RAILROAD COMPANY (Unit 42)

Incorporated on May 8, 1891, with a capitalization of $100,000. Shortly after its incorporation, this company began building a single track narrow gauge horse car line of 20-lb. iron rails over the following route:

From a point near Hill and Main Sts., Santa Monica, in close proximity to the depot of the Southern California (Santa Fe) Railway Company's Inglewood Division, in a northerly direction on Main St. to Fremont Ave.; west on Fremont to Ocean Ave.; north on Ocean to Utah Ave.; east on Utah to Third St.; north on Third to Nevada Ave. (now fabulous Wilshire Blvd.); east on Nevada approximately three miles to the grounds of the Soldiers' Home; thence in said grounds in a northerly and easterly direction to a point near the dining room, where a station was built; together with a branch from a connection with this line on Nevada Ave. in an easterly direction along Seventh St. to the car barn and stables, near Seventh and Arizona Ave.

On June 17, 1895, this company was sold to Sherman and Clark—the property involved consisting of about six miles of track, two bridges, the depot at the Soldiers' Home, four cars, sixteen horses, harness, sheds, and building; also all franchises for electric and steam car lines and all other lines granted to the company. Payment was made in bonds of the Pasadena & Pacific Ry. Co. The parties also agreed that "If by the first day of July 1896 the P&P shall construct and have in operation an electric railway line from Oregon and Ocean Aves. to Front St. (Fremont); thence east on Front St. to Fourth St.; thence south on Fourth to Hill St.; thence west on Hill to Second St.; thence north on Second to Front St. . . . then, and in that case, the (sellers) agree to return to the purchasers five of said (P&P) bonds." This line was constructed, and five bonds were returned to Sherman and Clark.

During the summer of 1896, that portion of the horse car line from Oregon and Ocean Aves. to Hill St. was abandoned and the rails taken up. The balance of the line was operated as a horse car line by the P&P and its successors until the latter part of 1899, when it was abandoned. The rails were taken up and used in temporary tracks by the LA-P RR Co. (Unit 49), successor to P&P.

[Editor's Note: Other sources, including contemporary newspaper accounts, say the line was not abandoned in late 1899, except possibly for that portion incorporated in the North Loop, opened on December 28 of that year. Operations on the Nevada Ave.-Soldiers' Home horsecar line were suspended Friday afternoon, November 25, 1904, when the inbound horsecar discovered that the large wooden bridge had burned. The bridge spanned the first ravine beyond the Half Way House, and was variously described as being 100 or 225 feet long. The county replaced the bridge with a fill, described as near completion in the Feb. 23, 1906, *Outlook*. Horsecar service was never resumed and the tracks were taken up later

HILL STREET looking north from Ninth, circa 1909. Dual-gauge tracks are now a feature of this busy downtown artery.
(Southern California Edison)

in the year. The *Outlook,* October 2, 1906, said: "Quite soon the old horse car line . . . will be only a memory. The double streak of rust . . . are to be removed. The Los Angeles-Pacific is abandoning its franchise. . . . Already the rails and ties at the east end of the line have been removed as far west as the city limits. The work will be followed to the junction with the North Loop line on Third Street. . . ."]

PASADENA & PACIFIC RAILWAY COMPANY
(Arizona) (Unit 43)

Incorporated in Arizona Territory on November 15, 1894, with a capitalization of $1,000,000. E.P. Clark was one of the incorporators and succeeded L.P. Hansen as president. Principal office was Phoenix, with another office located in Los Angeles.

The new company announced its proposed road as follows: either single or double track electric railways from Phoenix via the Asylum to Tempe, 10 miles; also from downtown L.A. to Santa Monica, along or near the line of railway known as the L.A. & Pacific Ry., about 25 miles.

On November 15, 1895, this company acquired all of the railroad property of the Elysian Park Street Railway Co. (Unit 39) consisting of a horse car line (single track) from Main St. to Cerro Gordo St. via Sunset Blvd. and Echo Park Ave. (current street names).

On January 29, 1896, this company acquired all property owned by the L.A. & Pacific Ry. Co. (Unit 40), consisting of a single track line of standard gauge steam railroad between Los Angeles and Santa Monica via Colegrove, Cahuenga, Morocco, Sunset and the National Military Home.

On May 7, 1896, this company acquired all property of the Cahuenga Valley RR Co. (Unit 41), consisting of a single track

line of narrow gauge steam railroad from Temple and Hoover Sts. via Hollywood to Laurel Canyon.

Through ownership of all of the capital stock of the Santa Monica & Soldiers' Home RR Co. (Unit 42), all the property owned by that company consisting of a narrow gauge single track horse car line in Santa Monica and in South Santa Monica (now Ocean Park) and extending from Santa Monica to the Soldiers' Home, passed to this company under an agreement with Mr. E.P. Clark, dated June 11, 1895.

Mileage of road purchased:

Name of Company	Equiv. Single Track
Elysian Park Street Railway Company	3.149
Los Angeles & Pacific Railway Company	17.245
Cahuenga Valley Railroad Company	6.982
Santa Monica & Soldiers' Home RR Co.	6.000
Total:	33.376

On June 11, 1895, an agreement was entered into with E.P. Clark of L.A. covering the reconstruction and electrification of this company's main line between L.A. and Santa Monica, and the acquisition of other railroad property, from which the following notes were made:

The contractor, E.P. Clark, agreed:

(1) To construct and equip and turn over to this company 27 miles of electric railway to be constructed and operated with what was known as the "Trolley Overhead System" commencing in L.A. and running thence via Bellevue Ave., Elysian Park Ave. (both these now Sunset Blvd.), through the Cahuenga Valley on what was known as the Santa Monica Foothill Road, and on the right of way of the old L.A. & Pacific Ry. Co. to Santa Monica by way of Oregon and Utah Avenues.

(2) That long passing tracks would be constructed wherever necessary, and that the construction work would be first class in every particular.

(3) To construct necessary power houses and to install in them the necessary machinery and other equipment.

(4) To use round poles, which had been properly dressed and painted, and to set same in the ground in asphaltum to a depth of six feet.

(5) Overhead construction to consist of No. 0 bare trolley and bare feeder wire of copper, of first-class material; road bed to be of first-class construction and equally as good as that of the L.A. & Pacific Ry. Co.; sixteen redwood ties, 6x8x8, to be used for every 30-foot rail; track to be heavily bonded with heavy copper bonds, to be increased wherever necessary to provide most efficient service.

(6) Contractor to reconstruct all bridges, and put in new bridges wherever needed.

(7) To furnish 10 large double-truck, combination open and closed passenger cars, with the seats inside facing the direction in which the car was moving and those outside to be built lengthwise of the car; said cars to be equipped with Westinghouse #38 motors (40 hp) and controllers.

(8) To have said line in operation to Santa Monica on or before July 1, 1896.

(9) To turn over proper lease and contract covering the joint use of the tracks and overhead trolley wires owned by the Los Angeles Ry. Co. from Bellevue & Buena Vista (now Sunset & N. Broadway) to the center of the business section, running as far south on Spring St. as Fourth; thence west to Broadway, south to Fifth, east to Spring, and north to Fourth.

(10) To secure and turn over the horse car line in Santa Monica known as the Santa Monica & Soldiers' Home RR Co. with all equipment and rolling stock, real estate and improvements.

(11) To secure and turn over all of the capital stock, equipment and rolling stock, road bed, franchises, and all other property of the Cahuenga Valley RR Co., consisting of eight miles of single track and two locomotives.

For its part, the new corporation agreed:

That it deliver to said contractor its entire authorized capital stock and $400,000 worth of gold bonds. The total was 400 bonds of $1,000 each, divided as follows: 53 in payment for property of the old L.A. & Pacific Ry. Co.; 32 for old Cahuenga Valley RR Co.; 25 for the old Santa Monica & Soldiers' Home RR Co.; 40 for purchase of copper wire; 69 for purchase of equipment; 40 for power houses and their machinery; 141 for rebuilding the line from L.A. to Santa Monica, converting same from a standard gauge steam railroad into a 3'6" gauge electric railway, and placing same in operation.

E.P. Clark commenced the work of rebuilding the steam line during June 1895, very shortly after the execution of the above agreement.

A double track was built between Burbank Jct. (Childs Ave.) and Hoover Street, about a half mile; the balance was single track with several sidings and passing tracks. Over the entire line, however, double track overhead was installed. Rails were 40-lb. steel, and the grade was for a standard gauge railroad, having been used as such by the L.A. & Pacific Ry. Co. Approximately a third of the old ties were replaced by new ones.

In building the electric line, Clark did not follow the old steam railroad all the way from Los Angeles to Santa Monica, but straightened out the line in a number of spots, the principal changes being: (1) From a point west of Burbank Jct. the steam road was built in a southwesterly direction to Hoover St.; north on Vermont to a private right of way about two blocks north of the present Santa Monica Blvd. [Ed.: Fountain Ave. today]; thence in a southwesterly direction over said private way to a point near the town of Sherman (now West Hollywood). The electric line was built from a point west of Childs Ave., now known as Sanborn Jct., along the present Santa Monica Blvd. in a westerly direction through Colegrove to the station known as Hacienda Park; thence southwest to Sherman. (2) From the northeasterly limits of Santa Monica, the line was constructed over private way to Oregon Ave.; thence southwesterly along Oregon Ave. (today Santa Monica Blvd.) to Ocean Ave. instead of following the route of the steam road along Railroad Ave. (today Colorado Ave.) in Santa Monica.

During the early part of 1896, the horse car line along Bellevue Ave. (Sunset Blvd.) in Los Angeles was abandoned and taken up and an electric line was built from Echo Park Ave. to Buena Vista St. (North Broadway) along Bellevue Ave. as part of the Los Angeles-Santa Monica Line.

On December 19, 1895, a contract was entered into with the Pullman Palace Car Company covering the construction and delivery of the following rolling stock:

8 Combination open and closed passenger cars	35' long
8 Semi-open motor cars	32' long
12 Semi-open trail cars	32' long
6 Closed motor cars	25' long

This rolling stock was received at Los Angeles during March, April and May, 1896. Air brakes and electric equipment were installed by this company.

During May and June, 1896, this company abandoned the old horse car line to South Santa Monica (Ocean Park) and built a single track narrow gauge electric line from the junction of Oregon and Ocean Aves. in Santa Monica in a southeasterly direction to Front St. (now Pico); thence east on Front St. to 4th St., south on 4th to Hill St., west on Hill to 2nd, north on 2nd to a junction with Main St. and continuing north on Main St. to Front St. Operation over this line, which subsequently was known as the "South Loop," began on July 1, 1896.

The first units of the site for Sherman Shops and yards, on which was also located the power house and car barns, were purchased by this company during January and February, 1896, and consisted of 5.56 acres of land, in two parcels. About 2.5 miles of yard tracks were built.

From a statement of assets issued by the company on January 1, 1896, a total value of road of $1,003,550 was shown. This was broken down as follows:

(1) 38 miles of equivalent single track electric railway with double overhead trolley construction, built and graded for a standard gauge steam road ($505,000);

(2) 4.5 miles of horse car lines with horses and cars, in operation from Santa Monica to Soldiers' Home ($20,000);

(3) 8 miles of steam railroad with three locomotives and coaches, in operation in the Cahuenga Valley ($63,000);

(4) New bridges built in Santa Monica ($7,500);

(5) Power house site, buildings, machinery ($80,000);

(6) 3 Pullman single truck motor cars ($7,500);
     8 Pullman double truck motor cars ($32,000);
     12 Pullman combination motor cars ($52,000);
     14 Pullman coaches ($28,000);
     22 Dump cars ($3,50);
     12 Flat cars ($4,800);

(7) Franchises, rights of way, terminals ($200,000).

(Note: The above 38 miles appears to be in excess of the equivalent single track mileage of electric lines owned by this company. The electric lines owned by the company were approximately 24.5 miles in length, on most of which a double track overhead system had been installed. This does not include spurs and sidings, of which there is no record.)

On May 3, 1895, the Los Angeles Railway Company entered into an agreement with this corporation covering the joint use and operation of that portion of the narrow gauge tracks owned by LARY as follows: From Bellevue Ave. and Buena Vista St. in a southeasterly direction to Main St., to Spring, to 4th, to Broadway, to 5th, to Spring, to 4th, thence back to Bellevue Ave. and Buena Vista; total length, 1.35 miles.

Construction and reconstruction work was practically completed during the month of March, 1896, and regular operation of electric cars between Los Angeles and Santa Monica was inaugurated on April 1, 1896.

Prior to the construction of the "South Loop" during the summer of 1896, that portion of the horse car line in Santa Monica and South Santa Monica between Utah Ave. (Broadway) and Ocean Ave. on the north and Hill St. on the south was abandoned. The balance of the horse car line between Santa Monica and Soldiers' Home was operated by this company and its successors for about three years, then abandoned.

Operation of the Cahuenga Valley Railroad Company's line as a narrow gauge steam railroad was continued by this company and its successors until 1900, just prior to the construction of the Hollywood Line, when certain portions of same were electrified and the balance abandoned.

On December 30, 1897, this company entered into a written agreement with the Pasadena & Pacific Ry. Co. (California) (Unit 44) to consolidate all of its capital stock, bonds, roads, franchises, rights of way, properties, assets and liabilities of every kind with same owned by that company, and to form a new railroad corporation under California laws to be known as *The Los Angeles-Pacific Railway Company* (Unit 45). This consolidation was effective on January 3, 1898.

THE PASADENA & PACIFIC RAILWAY COMPANY (Unit 44)

Incorporated in California on November 9, 1896, with M.H. Sherman, president; A.I. Smith, secretary and treasurer; E.P. Clark and W.D. Larrabee as prominent movers. Principal office: 222 W. 4th St., Los Angeles. Its proposed road was from Altadena to and through Pasadena and Los Angeles to Santa Monica, thence to South Santa Monica; estimated length, 35 miles. The company was capitalized at $500,000.

During the latter part of 1896 this corporation acquired the franchise for the construction, operation and maintenance for fifty years of a single track or double track line of electric railway as follows: From 8th and Hill Sts., Los Angeles, south on Hill to 16th, west to Figueroa, south to 16th, west on 16th to Georgia Bell St., with rails to be not less than 60 lbs. to the yard.

During January, 1897, the franchise granted to E.P. Clark was acquired covering the construction, operation and maintenance for 50 years (from December 1, 1896) of a single or double track electric railway from a point on the westerly boundary of Los Angeles 1,250 feet from the south line of Pico St. and extending east along private way to Cambridge and Western; then along Cambridge to and across Gertrude Ave.; then east on private way to Berkeley St. and Bartlett Ave.; then east on Berkeley to Winthrop and Berkeley; then over private way in an easterly direction crossing New Hampshire, Vermont, Highland and Millard Aves. to the intersection of Highland and Pacific Aves.; then along Highland to Magnolia Ave., then southeast to 16th and Hoover, then along 16th to Bush St. (Burlington Ave.). Also on 4th St. from Hill to Broadway. [Ed.: Above named route traversed what is today Venice Blvd. from Arlington Ave. to Burlington.]

This corporation immediately commenced the construction of a narrow gauge double track line of electric railway over the route above shown to the western boundary of Los Angeles and thence west and northwest to Sherman Jct., passing Pico Heights, Arlington Heights, Nadeau, Laurel Hill and Sunny Slope Park. From Sherman Jct., the line was extended in a westerly direction to Morocco Jct. (Beverly Hills) where it formed a junction with the Los Angeles-Santa Monica Line owned by the Pasadena & Pacific Railway Company of Arizona.

Steel rails, weighing 56 and 60 lbs. to the yard, and new 6x8x8 redwood ties laid on two-foot centers, were used in this construction. The roadbed was graded out to a double width of 33 feet, and the track was ballasted with decomposed granite. Overhead construction was of the center-pole type except on Los Angeles streets, with iron brackets and pipe arms; the trolley was Figure 8, 000 wire; the feeder consisted of one 300,000 C.M. cable, and one 400,000 C.M. cable and one 600,000 C.M. cable.

Construction work was practically completed during the latter part of June, 1897.

During June and July, 1897, a single track line of second-hand 50 and 56 lb. steel rails, with new ties, was built from the present Sherman Jct. to Shermanton, which was subsequently known as the "Sherman Cut-Off."

The double track line formed a part of what was known as the "Santa Monica Short Line." It later became the "West 16th St. Line."

Mileage of road constructed by this company:

Santa Monica Short Line: From 4th & Broadway, L.A. to Morocco Jct. (via Hill, 16th, Vineyard, Sherman Jct., excepting Hill between 4th & 8th Sts. and 16th from Georgia to Bush (Burlington) which trackage was owned by the L.A. Traction Co. but over which P&P of Cal. obtained trackage rights): (Equiv. S.T.) 18.370

Sherman Cut-Off: Single track, from Sherman Jct. to Sherman Car House 1.087

Total mileage owned   19.457

Early in 1897 this corporation entered into an agreement with the Los Angeles Traction Company in which it granted to said LAT the joint right to use and operate over its tracks in Los Angeles as follows:

On 4th St. between Broadway and Hill;

On Hill St. between 8th and 16th Sts.;

On 16th St. between Hill and Georgia Bell Sts.

and in turn was granted the right to use and operate jointly with LAT the tracks of that corporation in Los Angeles as follows:

On Hill St. between 4th and 8th Sts.;

On 16th St. between Georgia Bell and Bush St.

Regular operation of electric cars on the Santa Monica

Short Line over the railway owned by this company to Morocco Jct. and thence over the railway of the P&P of Arizona was inaugurated on July 1, 1897.

Sherman Cut-Off was placed in operation late in July, 1897, and cars of this company were run into the car barns at Sherman over this Cut-Off.

On December 30, 1897, this company agreed to consolidate with the Pasadena & Pacific (Unit 43) and to form a new railroad corporation under California laws to be known as *The Los Angeles-Pacific Railway Company* (Unit 45). This consolidation was effective on January 3, 1898.

THE LOS ANGELES-PACIFIC RAILWAY COMPANY (Unit 45)

Incorporated in California on January 3, 1898, with Clark, Sherman, Larrabee, Smith and others as incorporators. Clark was elected president, Smith became secretary, and M.E. Hammond the treasurer. Its principal office was in Los Angeles and it was capitalized at $1,000,000. It proposed to build single or double track electric railway lines from Los Angeles to Santa Monica, with branch lines to Hollywood, Laurel Canyon, Soldiers' Home and South Santa Monica. Its estimated length: 100 miles. The total capitalization of this consolidated corporation was divided equally between the two constituent companies (P&P of Arizona, P&P of California).

The mileage of road acquired by this corporation on January 3, 1898, was as follows:

From P&P of Arizona:
Horse Car Lines . . . . 5.755 miles
Steam Railroad Lines . . . . 6.982 miles
Electric Railway Lines . . . . .24.661 miles

      37.398

From P&P of California:
Electric Railway Lines 19.457

      19.457
      56.855

On June 2, 1898, this corporation entered into an agreement with the P&P (Arizona), the P&P (California), the Los Angeles-Pacific Ry. Co. (Arizona, Unit 46), and the Los Angeles-Pacific Ry. Co. (California, Unit 47) to consolidate all property of every kind with the same of others, and to form a new railroad corporation under the laws of California to be known as *Los Angeles-Pacific Railroad Company* (Unit 49).

This consolidation was effective on June 4, 1898, on which date the said *Los Angeles-Pacific Railroad Company* became the owner of all property of every kind owned by this corporation at that time.

On June 6, 1902, this company joined in an agreement of consolidation and amalgamation with other companies, for the purpose of correcting possible errors or omissions in former consolidation agreements, and was used as one of the constituent companies of *The Los Angeles-Pacific RR Company* (Unit 52), incorporated June 9, 1902.

This company was not reincorporated during the period June 4, 1898-June 9, 1902, and its corporate existence doubtless ended on June 4, 1898, the date on which the first consolidation was effective.

[Ed.: 1898 was a confused year for Sherman and Clark; on July 7, 1897, their original interurban company, The Pasadena & Los Angeles Electric Railway Co. (Unit 10), which was the stem from which P&P and LA-P sprang, defaulted in the payment of interest due that date upon its bonds; after six months had elapsed, during which time the company failed to pay said interest, the Trustee took charge of P&LA's property which was sold at the County Court House on April 27, 1898. Eventually this property was purchased by Henry E. Huntington, who used it as the foundation of his great Pacific Electric Ry. This cutting out of the P&LA from Sherman and Clark's properties evidently cast doubt on the status of their remaining properties—hence history records the numerous consolidations and incorporations by them in 1898 in an effort to achieve legal stability again. One of said incorporations had the remarkable legal life of 19 days as a going concern!]

LOS ANGELES-PACIFIC RAILWAY COMPANY (Arizona, Unit 46)

Incorporated in Arizona Territory on January 6, 1898. A duplicate copy of the Articles of Incorporation of the Los Angeles-Pacific Railway Company (California) was used as the Articles of Incorporation of this company, and the incorporators, purposes, constituent companies, proposed road, capitalization and bonded indebtedness were the same as those of the California company.

If the consolidation of January 3, 1898, under which the Los Angeles-Pacific Railway Company of California took over the properties of the P&P of Arizona and the P&P of California, was legal—as it appears to be—this company acquired no property.

No road was constructed, and no property was owned by this company, other than that acquired by the consolidation of its two constituent companies, effective on January 6, 1898, if any was so acquired.

On June 2, 1898, this company entered into an agreement with the P&P (Unit 43) the P&P (California, Unit 44), the LA-P (Unit 45) and the LA-P (Unit 47) to consolidate and to form a new railroad corporation under California laws to be known as *Los Angeles-Pacific Railroad Company*. This consolidation was effective on June 4, 1898, on which date the said LA-P RR Co. (Unit 49) became the owner of any and all property of every kind and description owned by this company at that time.

LOS ANGELES-PACIFIC RAILWAY COMPANY (Unit 47)

Incorporated in California on May 16, 1898. The Articles of Incorporation of this corporation were the amended ones of the Los Angeles-Pacific Railway Company (January 3, 1898) with the Board of Directors reduced from 13 to 11 members.

The purposes for which this company was incorporated were listed thusly:

(1) To consolidate properties, assets and liabilities of the Pasadena & Pacific Railway Company (Arizona) and the Pasadena & Pacific Railway Company (California);

(2) To acquire, construct, own, operate and maintain single or double track electric railways in L.A. County.

Setting forth more specifically the reasons for consolidating the above two companies: P&P (Cal.) was organized by stockholders of P&P (Ariz.) for the following reasons:

(1) That it was necessary to have an additional entrance into the city of Los Angeles.

(2) That it was necessary, in order to accommodate travel between L.A. and Santa Monica to build a double-track line.

(3) That it was impracticable for P&P of Arizona to dispose of a second issue of bonds which would constitute only a second lien upon its property.

That, whereas, the second entrance into Los Angeles had been constructed with a double track line which had been placed in operation from L.A. to a point almost midway between L.A. and Santa Monica and grading had been done for an additional track between Morocco Jct. and Santa Monica;

That it was deemed best to consolidate the properties, franchises and business of the two companies.

This company was incorporated at $1,000,000, all subscribed by the same subscribers who had backed the LA-P of January 3, 1898.

AT OCEAN PARK, LAP passengers enjoyed the facilities of this major depot, facing the Trolleyway between Marine and Pier streets. Wells, Fargo & Co. Express was handled, and a few of the local merchants made their business homes here also. *(Both: T.L. Wagenbach)*

CLOSEUP OF THE ex-Santa Fe freight depot at Hill St., Ocean Park, now serving the LAP cars.

The work of grading for the second track between Morocco Jct. and Santa Monica was continued by this company during the period of its corporate existence, but no road was actually constructed.

On May 24, 1898, only eight days after its incorporation, this company entered into an agreement with the P&P (43), the P&P (44), the LA-P (45) and the LA-P (46) to form a new railroad corporation under California laws to be known as *Los Angeles-Pacific Railroad Company* (Unit 49). This consolidation was effective on June 4, 1898.

INGLEWOOD LINE (Unit 48)

The Inglewood Line is a standard gauge, single track line which was constructed during the spring of 1887 by the Los Angeles & Santa Monica Railroad Company, one of the predecessor companies of the AT&SF. It extends from a connection with the Santa Fe's Redondo-San Pedro Line in Inglewood in a west and northwest direction to the southwest line of S. 5th St. in Santa Monica, approximately 9 miles. The line was placed in operation during May, 1887, by said LA&SM RR Co. as a steam railroad, but regular operation of same was inaugurated during June, 1887, by the California Central Railway Company, the successor by consolidation to the original owner. On November 22, 1889, ownership of the line passed to the Southern California Railway Company, the successor (by consolidation) to the California Central.

By order of the Railroad Commission of California, dated April 10, 1901, the Southern California Railway Company was authorized to abandon operation of this Inglewood branch, from Inglewood to Santa Monica. At a special meeting of stockholders of the SCRC, held March 21, 1902, the proper officials were authorized to sell said line to the Los Angeles-Pacific Railroad Company.

By deed dated March 21, 1902, the Southern California Railway Company sold to the Los Angeles-Pacific Railroad Company the Inglewood Line, including all right of way, tracks and other fixtures; also the franchise to maintain and operate said road; also a depot and pavilion grounds owned by said SCRC.

This line was converted into an electric railway during 1902 by the LA-P RR Co. (Unit 52), the successor to LA-P (Unit 49), and became the first standard-gauge electric line to bear the LA-P name.

LOS ANGELES-PACIFIC RAILROAD COMPANY (Unit 49)

Incorporated in California on June 4, 1898, by Sherman, Clark and associates. Principal office: Los Angeles. The company was originally capitalized at $1,000,000, but on March 15, 1901, this was increased to $1,500,000 with General Sherman subscribing for all the increase, payment being made by him by transferring to this corporation additional franchises, rights of way, extensions to existing lines and additional equipment.

The road acquired by this corporation from its constituent companies consisted of a narrow gauge steam railroad from the west city limits of Los Angeles City via Hollywood to Laurel Canyon; a narrow gauge electric line from Buena Vista and Bellevue via Colegrove, Sherman, Morocco and Barrett (Sawtelle) to Santa Monica, mostly all single track; a narrow gauge electric line from 4th & Broadway via S. Hill and W. 16th Sts.; Vineyard and Sherman Jct. to Morocco, all double track; a narrow gauge single track line from Sherman Jct. to Sherman; and various yard tracks and sidings at the Sherman Car House; also these horse car lines: (1) From Echo Park Ave. and Sunset to Echo Park Ave. and Cerro Gordo St.; (2) From Santa Monica to Soldiers' Home.

During the latter part of 1899, the Soldiers' Home horse car line and a portion of the steam railroad formerly owned by the Cahuenga Valley Railroad Company running through Hollywood to Laurel Canyon were abandoned and the tracks taken up. Immediately following said abandonment, electric lines were built, as follows:

At the time this company was formed, grading was in progress between Ocean Ave., Santa Monica, and Morocco for the second track. This work was rushed to completion and an additional track of 60-lb. rails laid between these points, except that a second track was not laid over the crossing with the Southern Pacific at Soldiers' Home at this time. This work was completed during the latter part of 1898, after which the double track line between Santa Monica and Morocco became a part of what was known as the Main Line, extending from Los Angeles to Santa Monica via Hill and W. 16th Sts.

At different times during this company's corporate existence, short stretches of the second track on the line via Colegrove and Sherman were built, and during 1900 this second track was completed between Morocco Jct. and Sherman, and also between Sherman and Los Angeles about four miles of second track were built.

During the latter part of 1899 the "North Loop" in Santa Monica was constructed, opening Dec. 28. This was a single track narrow gauge line beginning at Ocean and Utah (Broadway), thence east on Utah to 3rd, north to Montana Ave., west to Ocean Ave., and south over private way along Ocean Ave. to Utah Ave. This loop covered a portion of the route followed by the horse car line to Soldiers' Home.

Work was commenced on the construction of the Hollywood Line on December 15, 1899, and the line was completed and placed in operation during April, 1900. This line extended from Melrose on the Colegrove Line in a northwesterly direction to Prospect Ave. (now Hollywood Blvd.) over what was known as the Melrose Cut-Off; then west along Prospect from Vermont Ave. to La Brea (then Sutherland St.), then on private way southwest, crossing Sunset Blvd., to a junction with the Santa Monica Line at Crescent Jct. (Fairfax Ave.). As originally built, this line was double track for about a quarter of its length; a second track was laid during the latter part of 1900 and early part of 1901 with the exception of the Melrose Cut-Off which remained single track.

During the latter part of 1900 a narrow gauge single track spur, known as the "Oil Spur," was built from the old Ca-

LAP's STANDARD passenger shelter: a touch of the ornate.

(T.L. Wagenbach)

huenga Valley Line at a point in Temple St. (extended) west of Virgil Ave. in a southerly direction to 4th St. Also, the Quint Cut-Off to Laurel Canyon from Santa Monica Blvd. along Crescent Heights Ave. was built. Both these short lines were operated in connection with the remainder of the Cahuenga Valley Line as steam roads.

This company also built part of the single track line extending from Fremont Ave. (Pico) in Santa Monica in a southerly direction through Ocean Park and Venice to the Short Line Beach Tract; this line later became the Lagoon Line.

In January, 1902, grading began on the Venice Short Line, and a double track was laid between Tokio (near Venice) and Fredericks by February 26, 1902. With the exception of the ballasting, this line was practically completed by June 1, 1902. As originally built, this line was single track from Tokio to a connection with the Inglewood Line, which it used to reach Ocean Park.

On March 21, 1902, this company purchased from the Southern California Railway Company (Santa Fe) the single track standard gauge steam railroad line extending from the Redondo Line in Inglewood to S. 5th St. in Santa Monica, about 9 miles. This was known as the Inglewood Line.

Here is a summary of equivalent single track mileage of the railroad owned by this corporation, exclusive of spurs and sidings, of which there is no record:

Road acquired by consolidation:		56.855
Less lines abandoned:		
Santa Monica-Soldiers' Home horse car line		
Steam road, Western Ave. from Santa Monica		
Blvd. north and west to Hollywood Line	7.628	
		49.227
Road constructed:		
Second track on original line	12.234	
North Loop, Santa Monica	2.128	
Hollywood Line, Melrose-Crescent	9.398	
Oil Spur	0.544	
Quint Cut-Off	0.553	
Lagoon Line	1.940	
Venice Short Line	17.611	
		44.408
Total		93.635

On June 6, 1902, this company, together with the P&P (Arizona), P&P (California), LA-P (Arizona), and the LA-P (California) and the LA-P (Unit 47), entered into an agreement to consolidate all their properties of every kind and description, and to form a new railroad corporation under California laws to be known as *The Los Angeles-Pacific Railroad Company* (Unit 52). This consolidation became effective on June 9, 1902.

REDONDO & HERMOSA BEACH RAILROAD COMPANY (Unit 50)

Incorporated in Arizona Territory on February 21, 1901, with principal office located at Phoenix, but another office was maintained in Los Angeles. E.P. Clark was elected president and A.I. Smith, secretary. Capitalization was $400,000 and the proposed road was a single or double track railroad from Redondo to Port Ballona (near Venice) of an estimated length of 10 miles.

On December 2, 1901, a contract was entered into by and between this company and the Redondo Improvement Company and Newark, Venable & Cleghorn, contractors, covering the grading of an extension to Hermosa Avenue from the south line of the Hermosa Beach Company's property near Redondo in a southerly direction to the intersection of Diamond & La Alameda Streets in Redondo, being 70 feet and 100 feet wide. This work was completed during February,

1902, and was paid for by this corporation and the Redondo Improvement Company in equal part.

In this manner, right of way for a double track electric line was obtained between Hermosa and Redondo. Prior to the completion of the work, this company acquired the necessary franchise for its line from Diamond & La Alameda Sts. south along La Alameda to Opal St., southeasterly to Camino Real, thence continuing southeasterly to the city limits in Redondo; it also purchased construction material for about three miles of single track railway, which material was distributed along the line from Redondo to a point north of Hermosa.

However, before any track was laid this company sold its rights of way, franchises and track materials and therefore owned no constructed road.

By deed dated March 12, 1902, this company sold to the *Los Angeles, Hermosa Beach & Redondo Railway Company* all of its railroad property of every kind.

LOS ANGELES, HERMOSA BEACH & REDONDO RAILWAY COMPANY (Unit 51)

Incorporated in California on December 19, 1901, by Clark, Sherman, Smith and others. Sherman was elected president, and Smith became secretary. Its principal office was in Los Angeles. This company had a capitalization of $1,000,000, and it proposed to build a railroad from Los Angeles to Redondo via Hermosa, with a branch line to Santa Monica, connecting there with the LA-P; also to connect with LA-P at "some convenient point between Los Angeles and Santa Monica, all in Los Angeles County, of an estimated length of fifty miles."

On March 12, 1902, this corporation purchased from the Redondo & Hermosa Beach Railroad Company all of the railroad property owned by that company, consisting of franchises, rights of way and construction materials for a proposed line between Redondo and Playa del Rey, over a portion of which grading had been done but no tracks built.

With the exception of some grading on the Redondo end of the line, no construction work was done by this company.

During the latter part of July, 1902, a consolidation agreement was entered into with the Redondo & Hermosa Beach Railroad Company, according to the terms of which the two companies consolidated all their properties of every kind and formed a new railroad corporation under California laws known as *The Los Angeles, Hermosa Beach & Redondo Railway Company* (Unit 53).

This consolidation was effective on July 28, 1902.

LOS ANGELES-PACIFIC RAILROAD COMPANY (Unit 52)

Incorporated in California on June 9, 1902. Incorporators were Clark, Sherman, Pope, Larrabee, Hammond and Smith. Clark was elected president, with Smith secretary and Hammond treasurer. The purpose of this company was to consolidate the stocks, bonds, assets, liabilities, and all other property of every kind and description of these companies:

Pasadena & Pacific Railway Co. of Arizona . . . (Unit 43)
Pasadena & Pacific Railway Co. of California . (Unit 44)
Los Angeles-Pacific Ry. Co. (California) . . . . . (Unit 45)
Los Angeles-Pacific Ry. Co. (Arizona) . . . . . . (Unit 46)
Los Angeles-Pacific Railway Company . . . . . . (Unit 47)
Los Angeles-Pacific Railroad Company . . . . . . (Unit 49)

Also to construct, own, operate and maintain railway lines within Los Angeles County; to carry passengers, express, mail and freight on and over said lines, for hire.

The new company was capitalized at $2,500,000. It

acquired the lines of its constituent companies, of which the following is the approximate mileage:

Horse car line (Elysian Park line) 1.255
Electric railways 87.429
Steam railroads (Cahuenga Valley RR, Inglewood) 13.951
                                          102.635

Very shortly after its incorporation, this company began the work of converting the Inglewood Line into an electric railway. Certain changes were made in the line in Venice, and a complete overhead system was installed along this single track standard gauge line. Electric cars began operating over same during the latter part of 1902 between Inglewood and Santa Monica. [Ed. This appears to be the first electric operation on standard gauge trackage by LA-P.]

During September, October and November, 1902, the horse car line on Echo Park Ave. was electrified. It was placed in operation as a single track narrow gauge electric line on November 20, 1902.

The Venice Short Line was ballasted during the latter part of 1902, and considerable work was done in improving the other lines owned by this company.

With the exception of a portion of the Cahuenga Valley Line, over which narrow gauge steam locomotives were operated, the road owned by this corporation on June 10, 1903, consisted of single and double track, narrow and standard gauge electric lines of which the following is the approximate mileage, equivalent single track, exclusive of spurs, sidings and yards of which there is no record:

Electric Lines: (Colegrove Line, W. 16th St. Line,
    Hollywood Line, Elysian Park Line, Sherman Cut-
    Off, Sherman Yards, North and South Loops, La-
    goon Line, Venice Short Line, Inglewood Line)   97.684
Steam Lines: (Cahuenga Valley RR from Temple St.
    to Colegrove Line, Oil Spur, Quint Cut-Off; all nar-
    row gauge)   4.951
                                                   102.635

On June 10, 1903, this corporation entered into an agreement with the Los Angeles, Hermosa Beach & Redondo Railway Company (Unit 53) and the Los Angeles-Santa Monica Railroad Company (Unit 54) to consolidate all their properties and to form a new railroad corporation under California laws to be known as *Los Angeles Pacific Railroad Company of California* (Unit 55).

This consolidation was effected on June 16, 1903.

LOS ANGELES, HERMOSA BEACH & REDONDO RAILWAY COMPANY (Unit 53)

Incorporated in California on July 28, 1902. Sherman, Clark, Pope, Hammond and Smith were the incorporators, and the principal office was in Los Angeles. Sherman became the president, Smith secretary, and Hammond treasurer.

This corporation was formed by the amalgamation and consolidation of the properties of the Redondo & Hermosa Beach Railroad Company of Arizona (Unit 50), and the Los Angeles, Hermosa Beach & Redondo Railway Company (Unit 51).

Its announced proposed road was a single or double track steam or electric railway line commencing at 4th & Broadway in Los Angeles, thence in a westerly and southwesterly direction to Ballona Harbor (Playa del Rey); then southwesterly along the coast to Redondo. Also, a branch to Santa Monica to connect with LA-P; also, to connect with LA-P at some convenient point between Los Angeles and Santa Monica. The estimated length of said proposed road: fifty miles.

This company was capitalized at $1,000,000 (10,000 shares at $100 each). Sherman took 4,999 shares; Clark subscribed for 4,998 shares, and Pope, Hammond and Smith bought one share each.

The constituent companies owned various franchises, construction materials and rights of way, but no constructed road at the time their properties were taken over by this corporation.

During September, 1902, work was commenced on a narrow gauge, double track electric line from a junction with the Venice Short Line at Ivy Park (now Culver City) and running thence southwesterly to Port Ballona and thence southeasterly along the coast to Redondo. This line was constructed of 50 and 56 lb. relaying rails with new ties, and was completed with the exception of ballasting and placed in operation to Port Ballona during December, 1902.

The line in Redondo, and from Redondo as far north as North Manhattan was built during November and December of 1902 and January, February and March, 1903.

During the period December 1, 1902-May 31, 1903, the double track line was constructed between Playa del Rey and North Manhattan, with the exception of ballasting.

Regular operation of through trains over this and other lines between Los Angeles and Redondo was inaugurated late in the summer of 1903 by the Los Angeles Pacific Railroad Company, the successor to this company.

Total length of the narrow gauge, double track line constructed by this company from Ivy Park to Redondo, exclusive of spurs and sidings, was as follows:

Ivy Park-Redondo (double track 14.394) 28.788
In Redondo (single track line on Pacific Ave.) 0.383
                                                      29.171

On June 10, 1903, this company agreed with the Los Angeles-Pacific Railroad Company (Unit 52) and the Los Angeles-Santa Monica Railroad Company (Unit 54) to consolidate all properties, and a new railroad corporation known as the *Los Angeles Pacific Railroad Company of California* was formed.

This consolidation was effective on June 16, 1903, on which date the consolidated corporation, LAP RR of California (Unit 55) became the owner of all property of every description owned by this company at that time.

LOS ANGELES-SANTA MONICA RAILROAD COMPANY (Unit 54)

Incorporated in California on December 2, 1902, with unknowns as incorporators. Subsequently, Sherman was elected president and A.I. Smith, secretary.

This company's proposed road was from some suitable place in Los Angeles to Santa Monica; also, from the Soldiers' Home in Sawtelle by the most practicable route northwest on the coast some 40 miles.

This company was capitalized at $2,000,000 but built and owned no road.

On June 10, 1903, this company agreed to consolidate with the Los Angeles-Pacific Railroad Company (Unit 52) and the Los Angeles, Hermosa Beach & Redondo Railway Company (Unit 53) to form a new California corporation: *The Los Angeles Pacific Railroad Company of California* (Unit 55).

On June 16, 1903, this consolidation became effective.

LOS ANGELES PACIFIC RAILROAD COMPANY, OF CALIFORNIA (Unit 55)

Incorporated in California on June 16, 1903, with Sherman, Clark, J. Ross Clark, Pope, Larrabee, Hammond and A.I. Smith as incorporators. Clark was elected president, Sherman was vice-president, also treasurer—and Smith became secretary. The principal office was located in Los Angeles.

This corporation was capitalized at $5,000,000.

This corporation acquired through the consolidation of

GRACEFUL, though weatherstained, is this LAP bridge over the Grand Canal, Venice.   *(Southern California Edison)*

June 16, 1903, all lines of railway owned by its constituent companies: Los Angeles-Pacific Railroad Company (Unit 52), Los Angeles, Hermosa Beach & Redondo Railway Company (Unit 53), and the Los Angeles-Santa Monica Railroad Company (Unit 54); the total length was about 131.806 miles.

During the summer of 1905, those portions of the old Cahuenga Valley steam road lying between the Hollywood Line and Laurel Canyon and from the Colegrove Line at Western Ave. south and east over private way to Alexandria Ave. were converted into electric lines. The balance of this line east of Mariposa Ave., including the Oil Spur, was subsequently standard-gauged by the Los Angeles Pacific Company (Unit 66) but was never operated as an electric railway.

On January 14, 1904, this company agreed to buy all the outstanding stock of the Los Angeles, Ocean Park & Santa Monica Railway Company (Unit 24), together with a contract between the said company and the Los Angeles Traction Company covering the use of certain tracks owned by LAT in Los Angeles. [Ed.: W. Jefferson St. to city limits). Payment for this property was made in bonds of this corporation. In September, 1905, this company sold all of the above described property acquired through ownership of capital stock of the LA,OP&SM Ry. Co. to Sherman and Clark.

[Ed.: To fill in the picture: In April, 1903, Southern Pacific entered the Los Angeles electric railway scene by purchasing the Los Angeles Traction Company for $1,715,000. The following month, SP (E.H. Harriman, president) secured Hellman's half of Pacific Electric Railway. In March, 1906, SP purchased a majority of shares of LA-P.]

During July and August, 1903, this company completed the Redondo Line by ballasting, surfacing and lining the track, after which the line was placed in regular operation.

During the spring of 1904, after the property of the Los Angeles, Ocean Park & Santa Monica Railway Company had been acquired, it reconstructed its overhead system on the lines between Santa Monica and Venice, and put in long pipe-arms extending from center poles to the track of its Lagoon Line on one side and to the line of the LA,OP&SM on the other side, after which the line of the LA,OP&SM Ry. was placed in operation as an electric line.

Effective August 26, 1904, it extended the Lagoon Line as a double track line from the Short Line Beach Tract, just south of Venice, to Playa del Rey where a connection was made with the Redondo Line.

In the spring of 1905, the Hollywood Cut-Off, which extended along Sunset and Hollywood Blvds. between Sanborn Jct. and Vermont Ave. was constructed, forming a part of the new Hollywood Line and connecting the Colegrove and Hollywood Lines.

During the summer of 1905, the balance of the double tracking between Sherman and Los Angeles on the Colegrove Line was completed.

This company also built the Vineyard Power Plant and the new freight house at Buena Vista and Sunset in Los Angeles.

Prior to October 12, 1905, all of the lines owned by this corporation which were not built as such had been converted into electric lines. The total length of lines owned in equivalent single track on the same date was 145.456 miles.

On October 2, 1905, this company and the Santa Monica Canyon Railroad Company (Unit 56) consolidated, forming a new corporation named *Los Angeles Pacific Company* under California laws. This consolidation was effective on October 12, 1905.

SANTA MONICA CANYON RAILROAD COMPANY (Unit 56)

Incorporated in California on September 23, 1905. Subsequent to its incorporation, Sherman was elected president, Smith secretary. Principal office: Los Angeles. Capitalized at $5,000,000.

The proposed road of this corporation was to be from a suitable point in Los Angeles to Santa Monica, with branch lines to Hollywood and Colegrove; also from Sawtelle and Soldiers' Home to Santa Monica, thence by most practicable route northwest along the coast. Estimated length: 100 miles.

Notwithstanding the fact that this company's entire capitalization was issued and outstanding, presumably in the acquisition of franchises, rights of way or other railroad property, there is no record of its having acquired any road, either by purchase, construction or otherwise, during the short period of its corporate existence.

On October 2, 1905, this corporation agreed to consolidate with the Los Angeles Pacific Railroad Company of California (Unit 55) and a new corporation known as *Los Angeles Pacific Company* (Unit 57) was formed under California laws. This consolidation was effective on October 12, 1905.

LOS ANGELES PACIFIC COMPANY (Unit 57)

Incorporated in California on October 12, 1905, with Sherman, Clark, Pope, Larrabee, Hammond, Smith and others as incorporators. Principal office, Los Angeles. Clark became president; Sherman, vice-president and treasurer; Smith was secretary. The new corporation was capitalized at 15 million dollars.

The proposed road was to be 18 main and branch lines of single track or double track steam or electric railway in the vicinity of Los Angeles; estimated length: 500 miles.

The constituent companies turned over various single and double track electric railway lines, all of which (with the exception of the Inglewood Line) were narrow gauge. The approximate mileage of road thus acquired in equivalent single track miles was 145.456.

During the latter part of 1905, this company built the Short Line Cut-Off from Tokio Station on the Venice Short Line to a connection with the Lagoon Line at Center Street in Venice. This was a double track construction.

During October, November and December, 1905, the narrow gauge double track Westgate Line was constructed and was ready for operation February 14, 1906.

The work of standard-gauging its road and equipment was begun by this company prior to the consolidation of April 4, 1907, and about $12,000 was spent on same.

Sherman Yards were enlarged by the acquisition on October 1, 1906, of 13.81 acres of land, and additional shop buildings were constructed.

The preliminary work on Tunnel No. One on Hill Street in Los Angeles was done by this company.

All this company's lines of railroad were operated by electricity. The aggregate length, equivalent single track, was about 157.482 miles, exclusive of spurs and sidings of which there is no record.

On March 30, 1907, this company voted to consolidate with the Santa Monica & Northern Railway Company (Unit 58) and to create a new railroad corporation under California laws to be known as *Los Angeles Pacific Company* (Unit 66). This consolidation was effective on April 4, 1907.

SANTA MONICA & NORTHERN RAILWAY COMPANY (Unit 58)

Incorporated in California on March 11, 1907. Subsequent to incorporation, Sherman and Smith were elected president and secretary respectively. Principal office: Los Angeles; capitalization, $1,000,000.

This corporation's proposed road was to be from some suitable point in Los Angeles in a westerly direction to the Pacific Ocean at Santa Monica; thence in a northerly direction to the northern line of Los Angeles County where same joined the ocean. Also, from some suitable point on the main line, in a northwesterly direction to and through Hollywood and the Cahuenga Pass or some other pass to the San Fernando Valley; thence in a northwesterly direction to the northern boundary of Los Angeles County, where the same joined the ocean. The length of the proposed road was estimated to be 100 miles.

Prior to the incorporation of this company, the LAP Company (Unit 57) spent considerable money in running a preliminary survey from the Long Wharf at Port Los Angeles along the coast to a point approximately 15 miles northwesterly from said Port Los Angeles, as a part of a proposed line to the northern boundary of Los Angeles County.

Subsequent to its incorporation, said work was turned over to this corporation by LAP Company. Practically all of the preliminary engineering work was done on this proposed line, including the making of line maps, topographical maps, estimates covering the cost of tunnels, pile and frame trestles, and other structures. No actual work of construction was done by this company, and the project was subsequently abandoned.

During March, 1907, an agreement was entered into with the LA, OP&SM Ry. Co. (Unit 24) under which this corporation was to purchase certain franchises and various parcels of right of way owned by that company along the line of its constructed and proposed road between Santa Monica and Los Angeles. Before the final consummation of this deal, this company was merged into the LAP Company (Unit 66). The LA,

OP&SM Ry. Co. executed a corporation grant deed, dated December 30, 1910, to said LAP Company, covering 49 parcels of right of way between Santa Monica and a point east of Ellenda Station on the Redondo via del Rey Line, connected in places, but for the most part forming a disconnected right of way.

This corporation owned no constructed road, and no lines were operated by it under lease or otherwise.

On March 30, 1907, this corporation and the Los Angeles Pacific Company (Unit 57) agreed to consolidate and a new railroad corporation was created under California laws which was subsequently known as *Los Angeles Pacific Company* (Unit 66).

This consolidation became effective on April 4, 1907.

LOS ANGELES PACIFIC COMPANY (Unit 66)

Incorporated in California on April 4, 1907; its two constituent companies were Los Angeles Pacific Company (Unit 57) and Santa Monica & Northern Railway Company (Unit 58). The following Directors were elected: Epes Randolph of Tucson, and E.P. Clark, M.H. Sherman, R.C. Gillis, John D. Pope, T.R. Cabel, R.P. Sherman, M.E. Hammond, W.H. Logan, M.F. Finkenstein and A.I. Smith, all of Los Angeles. At the first meeting of this Board of Directors, held on May 4, 1907, the following officials were elected: E.P. Clark, president; M.H. Sherman, vice-president and treasurer; A.I. Smith, secretary; R.P. Sherman (Sherman's stepson), general superintendent.

The company was incorporated for a term of 50 years. Its principal office was maintained in Los Angeles until February 3, 1908, when it was changed to Sherman, California.

[Ed.: The Southern Pacific's majority stock ownership was reflected in the membership of the Board of Directors; of the Directors listed above, Colonel Epes Randolph was a Southern Pacific representative.]

The following lines were already built, or proposed to be built by this company; their total length was estimated to be about 750 miles:

1. Colegrove-Santa Monica
2. Hollywood
3. Laurel Canyon
4. An extension of Laurel Canyon Line (west)
5. W. 16th St.
6. Venice Short Line
7. Redondo via Playa del Rey Line
8. North & South Loops, Santa Monica
9. Santa Monica to Soldiers' Home via Nevada Ave.
10. Inglewood
11. Cahuenga Valley
12. Elysian Park
13. Lagoon Line
14. Westgate Line
15. Line in Santa Monica Canyon
16. Subway from Los Angeles to Vineyard
17. Hill St. Station north thru tunnels to Sunset Blvd.
18. From W. 5th St. & Vermont Ave. over private way in a westerly direction 5.09 miles to Sherman Jct.
19. From Highland and Hollywood Blvd. south on Highland on private way 2.41 miles to 5th St.
20. From 5th and Western north on Western 2.41 miles to Prospect Ave. (now Hollywood Blvd.)
21. From Sunset and Occidental Blvds. southwesterly 1.77 miles to the intersection of the 4th St. Subway near 5th and Vermont
22. From western terminus of Laurel Canyon Line, southwesterly along Sunset Blvd. and private way 6.95 miles to Montana Ave. and San Vicente Blvd.
23. From intersection of SP's Long Wharf Line and Santa Monica Canyon easterly up said canyon 3 miles, connecting with the Gravel Pit Spur of Westgate Line

24. From same point of intersection in a northerly direction paralleling the ocean shore about 20 feet above high-water line 25.8 miles to the intersection of the L.A. County Line and the ocean

25. From same point of intersection at Santa Monica Canyon northeasterly up Rustic Canyon about two miles; then west four miles to Santa Ynez Canyon

26. From Sunset and Occidental in L.A. northerly and westerly 36.8 miles to Russell Canyon.

This company was capitalized at $21,000,000 (210,000 shares at $100 each). All was subscribed, as follows: Epes Randolph, 107,100 shares; W.M. Buffum, 102,889; the 11 Directors, one each.

The road acquired by this corporation on April 4, 1907, consisted of single and double track, narrow gauge and standard gauge electric lines of the approximate length of 157.482 miles (equivalent single track) with their appurtenances, exclusive of spurs and sidings of which there is no record.

The work of standard-gauging the LAP system was begun by one of the constituent companies and was completed by this corporation. The heaviest expenditures were made on all lines except Colegrove and Hollywood between April 4, 1907 and August 31, 1908.

On May 20, 1907, this company purchased from SP second-hand steel rails weighing 61 lbs. per yard, together with the necessary fastenings, to the value of approximately $30,000, and during the periods shown, third rails were laid over the following lines, making of them combination standard-narrow gauge lines:

Main Line	From Sawtelle to 26th St., S.M.,	June, 1907
Hollywood	From Sanborn Jct. to Crescent Jct.,	June, 1909
Colegrove	From Colegrove to N. Broadway, L.A.,	May, 1908

On S. Hill St. and W. 16th St. in L.A., this company reconstructed the narrow gauge double track line, a portion of which was owned by the L.A. Interurban Railway as successor to the L.A. Traction Company and subsequently by the L.A. Railway—and converted same into a combination narrow-4'8½" gauge double track line as follows:

W. 16th St. from Hill to Burlington: July-Oct. 1907; Jan.-April, 1908;

S. Hill St. from 4th to 16th: July, 1907; Feb.-May, 1908.

During April and August, 1909, third rails were installed in the double track line on S. Hill St. between 1st and 4th by this corporation.

The standard-gauging of the LAP system was completed between March 1 and December 31, 1910, and all third rails were released with the exception of the combination narrow-standard gauge tracks on S. Hill St. from 1st to 16th and on W. 16th from Hill to Burlington.

Preliminary work on the Western Ave.-Franklin Ave.-Brush Canyon Line, which was known at that time as the Brush Canyon Line, was completed between June 1 and December 31, 1907, by the L.A. Stone Company for and on behalf of this corporation. Actual construction work, which consisted of the building of a narrow gauge single track line from a junction with the Colegrove Line at Western Ave. north along Western to Franklin, a narrow gauge double track line west on Franklin to Argyle and thence via Argyle, Yucca St. and Vine St. to Hollywood Blvd.; a narrow gauge single track line from a point on Franklin Ave. between Bronson and Tamarind Aves. to the rock crusher plant of the L.A. Stone Company in Brush Canyon—was performed during January, February, March and April of 1908. An extension in Brush Canyon was completed in April, 1909. The second track (standard gauge) on Western Ave. from Santa Monica Blvd. to Franklin Ave. was built during the period January 1-August 31, 1910, with most of the work being done in April and May.

The Highland Ave. Line was constructed as a standard gauge line from Santa Monica Blvd. to the northern city limits of Hollywood and was laid shortly thereafter.

A single track narrow gauge line extending from Beverly to Coldwater Canyon, known as the Rodeo Line, was constructed during the period April 1-July 31, 1907. It was standard-

THE OLD CAR HOUSE, Sherman, which burned in 1913.
(T.L. Wagenbach)

gauged during the latter part of the following year.

The Hollywood-Van Nuys Extension was a double track and single track standard gauge line extending from the northern limits of Hollywood to Hanna. Preliminary engineering work was begun on same during October, 1909, but was not completed until December, 1910. Grading was commenced during December, 1910. Work on bridges and tracklaying began in January, 1911. The first overhead construction work was done during May, 1911. This line was about 50% completed at the time it was turned over to the Pacific Electric Railway Company (Unit 73) by this corporation on September 1, 1911.

In Santa Monica, the preliminary work on the single track standard gauge line known as the 8th St. Line was done by this company, but it performed no actual construction work on same with the exception of installing the turnout at Oregon Ave. (Santa Monica Blvd.) and 8th St. This line was completed by PE during January, 1912. The extension on Montana Ave. from 3rd St. in an easterly direction to 7th St. was built during 1910 after the North Loop was abandoned, as follows: During the latter part of 1910, that portion of the North Loop on Montana Ave. between Ocean Ave. and 3rd St., together with all of the South Loop, were abandoned and the tracks taken up.

In Los Angeles, the Hill St. Tunnels were a big job. The preliminary work on Tunnel No. 1 (between 1st St. and Temple) was done by one of the constituent companies (LAP Company, Unit 57). Actual construction work on same was practically completed by this company between January 1 and August 31, 1909, although the expenditures on account of this tunnel extended over the whole period of its corporate existence. Sidewalks, stairs and curbs were built during June and July of 1910. Construction of Tunnel No. 2 was commenced in August, 1907, and extended to June, 1910. The principal part of this work was done between July 1 and December 31, 1908. A double track standard gauge line was constructed on N. Hill St. from 1st St. through Tunnels 1 and 2 to a connection with the tracks of this company on Sunset Blvd. during August, September and October of 1909, and operation of LAP cars through the Hill St. Tunnels was commenced on September 15, 1909. Very shortly after this date, it took up the tracks on 4th St. between Hill St. and Broadway.

Other construction included new shop buildings at Sherman during May and June, 1907; new yard and storage tracks at the Buena Vista Freight House during the summer of 1907; the Hill St. Station was built between February 1 and May 31 of 1908.

The following is a statement of the mileage of lines owned on September 1, 1911, the date on which same were turned over to the Pacific Electric Railway Company, including the Hollywood-Lankershim-Van Nuys Line which was not completed but which was essentially an LAP line. The termini of the lines do not in all cases agree with the limits of said lines at the time same were constructed, and in some instances the names of the lines were changed subsequent to their construction.

Name of Line	Double	Single	Spurs	E.S.T.
W. 16th & Sawtelle:				
(4th & Hill-Ocean & Oregon)	17.00	--	2.38	36.38
Hollywood (4th & Hill-Beverly)	12.23	--	0.68	25.14
Colegrove	4.71	--	0.50	9.92
Melrose Cut-Off	--	0.84	0.05	0.89
Cahuenga Valley Line	--	1.55	0.10	1.65
Franklin Ave. Line	2.18	0.07	0.02	4.45
Brush Canyon Line	--	1.56	0.95	2.51
Hollywood-Van Nuys Line:				
(S.M. Blvd.-Hanna Station)	7.34	5.86	0.62	21.16
Buena Vista Freight Yard	0.19	--	0.48	0.86
Elysian Park Line	--	1.26	--	1.26
Laurel Canyon Line	--	0.96	0.08	1.04
Venice Short Line:				
(Vineyard-Center St., Venice)	9.03	--	0.29	18.35
Del Rey-Redondo Line:				
(Ivy. Jct.-Diamond Ave.)	14.40	0.11	2.99	31.90
Lagoon Line:				
(Ocean & Oregon-Del Rey)	4.67	0.03	1.39	10.76
Westgate Line:				
(Oregon Ave., Sawtelle-Ocean & Oregon, Santa Monica)	5.81	0.07	0.66	12.35
Sherman Cut-Off & Yards	--	1.21	5.26	6.47
Venice Freight Branch	0.41	0.46	0.87	2.15
Montana Ave., Santa Monica	--	1.34	0.02	1.36
Rodeo Line	--	1.38	0.10	1.48
Inglewood Line	--	8.93	3.44	12.37
Unused Tracks, Various Lines	--	--	2.22	2.22
Total, All Track Owned	77.97	25.63	23.10	204.67

The Santa Monica Air Line, with the Long Wharf and appurtenances, passed by consolidation to the Southern Pacific Railroad Company of April 12, 1898, and later to the S.P. Railroad Company of March 10, 1902. At all times hereinafter mentioned, the last named was the owner of said line, which was operated by the Southern Pacific Company as lessee until 1908.

An agreement, dated April 4, 1908, effective July 1, 1908, was entered into by and between the S.P. RR Co. (owner), the S.P. Company (lessee) and the Los Angeles Pacific Company for a period of 50 years, covering the rental of the main line, spurs and sidings between Sentous (near Culver Jct.) and Port Los Angeles, together with the Soldiers' Home Branch. The S.P. Company reserved the right to operate trains over leased portion of the line. LAP agreed to electrify same and to operate the line in conformity with charter obligations; it also agreed to pay all taxes and assessments and to make all necessary expenditures for maintenance; also to pay a stipulated sum annually as rental for said line.

LAP installed a complete overhead system on the leased part of the line, including the Soldiers' Home Branch, bonded the rails and placed same in operation as an electric line during the summer of 1908.

LAP electrified the balance of the line, extending from Sentous to Clement Jct. (Alameda St.) during the period December 1, 1910-July 31, 1911, including spurs and sidings, but never operated same. At about the time this portion of the Air Line was ready for operation, all property of every kind owned by LAP was acquired by consolidation by PE (Unit 73).

An agreement dated January 27, 1912, effective the next day, was entered into by and between the S.P. RR Co., the SP Company and PE covering rental of the tracks between Sentous and Clement Jct.

Mileage of Air Line	Main Line	Sidings	Equiv. S.T.
Sentous to Long Wharf	10.880	11.580	22.460
Soldiers' Home Branch	2.610	1.130	3.740
Sentous-Clement Jct.	7.866	4.606	12.472
Total	21.356	17.316	38.672

This company owned 172 passenger (and combination passenger mail and express) cars, 194 freight cars, and 25 service cars at the time of consolidation hereinafter mentioned.

On May 28, 1910, the Board of Directors was reduced from 11 to 7 members and the following Directors were elected: R.C. Gillis, M.H. Sherman, A.D. McDonald, Paul Shoup, Epes Randolph, William F. Herrin, and E.E. Calvin. R.C. Gillis was elected president; Shoup and Sherman, vice presidents; George L. Bugbee, secretary; and the Farmers & Merchants National Bank of Los Angeles acted as treasurer. [Ed.: This signalized the total assumption of control by SP; of the above-named Directors, all were SP retainers or friends. It is of interest to note further that in the Great Merger of September 1, 1911, the new Pacific Electric's five Directors were Herrin, Gillis, Randolph, Shoup, and W.C. Martin.]

On February 15, 1911, resolutions were adopted by this company setting forth its intention to consolidate with the

PRE-OPENING SHOT of the south portal of Hill Street Tunnel No. 2, September, 1909. Feeder cable wasn't yet attached to insulators and tracks were still being ballasted. View taken from Temple Street. *(T.L. Wagenbach)*

companies hereinafter named and to create and incorporate a new railroad corporation under the laws of the State of California to be known as *Pacific Electric Railway Company.*

The companies with which this corporation agreed to consolidate were:

Pacific Electric Railway Company (old company)
Los Angeles Interurban Railway Company
Los Angeles & Redondo Railway Company
Riverside & Arlington Railway Company
San Bernardino Valley Traction Company
Redlands Central Railway Company
San Bernardino Interurban Railway Company
This consolidation became effective on September 1, 1911.

[Ed.: So ends the history of the Los Angeles Pacific as an independent company. However, due to geographical considerations, the LAP portion of PE was operated to the end as a semi-separate entity, being known as the PE Western District. As a matter of fact, any old LAP man would have felt right at home on the Western District up until the Subway Terminal was opened (December 1, 1925) and the Glendale-Burbank Line added. However, LAP did experience one major invasion of its territory when the Los Angeles Traction Company joined with Abbot Kinney to build a competing electric railway line from Los Angeles to Santa Monica via Venice. Although not part of the LAP official history, this colorful chapter in the history of Southern California's interurbans is too important to be omitted and follows.]

LOS ANGELES, OCEAN PARK & SANTA MONICA RAILWAY CO. (Unit 24)

Incorporated in California on December 8, 1902. William S. Hook, Abbot Kinney and others were the incorporators. Kinney was elected president, Hook vice-president. The company's proposed road was to have been steam or electric, double or single track railroad from Los Angeles to and through Ocean Park to Santa Monica, an estimated length of 15 miles. The company was capitalized at $1,000,000.

On December 18, 1902, this company accepted a proposition made by Kinney and Hook to transfer to this corporation those certain franchises granted by the City of Los Angeles covering the construction, operation and maintenance of a double track line of street railway on West Jefferson St. from Wesley (University) Ave. to the west city limits (400 feet west

of Arlington Ave.); and also certain franchises granted by the city of Santa Monica to Hook authorizing the construction, operation and maintenance of a line of railroad over and along certain streets and private rights of way; also all of the title held by Kinney and Hook in and to private way; and also that certain private right of way about 25 feet wide lying immediately west of the right of way of the LA-P Co. and extending from Hollister Ave. to Front St. in Santa Monica. For the above, this company paid Kinney and Hook in equal portions: $80,000 in paid-up capital stock and $80,000 in bonds of this company.

Owing to the fact that the bonded indebtedness was not created by this company, the above agreement could not be carried out. On July 16, 1903, the above agreement was abandoned and annulled. Investigation has developed the fact, however, that Hook and Kinney expended considerable money in the construction of the lines owned by this company—notwithstanding the fact that the above agreement was not carried out. Due to transfers which were made subsequent to the date first mentioned, it is considered that Hook and Kinney were acting for, and on behalf of this corporation in the joint construction of the railroad lines subsequently owned, namely:

(In any reference to construction work performed by this company, it is understood that Hook and Kinney, either jointly or individually, acted for and on behalf of this company.)

West Jefferson St.: Construction materials were purchased during the summer of 1902 for this line by the Los Angeles Traction Company (Unit 27), which was owned or controlled by Hook, his wife, and his brother. Construction work was begun during August or September of 1902 and carried on to completion by LAT forces during the latter part of November, 1902. This was a narrow gauge, double track electric railway line extending from Jefferson and Wesley Ave. in a westerly direction along Jefferson to the west city limits. It consisted of two miles of double track. Steel rails weighing 70 pounds to the yard and a good grade of 6x8x6 ties were used. The LAT placed the line in operation on December 1, 1902, and continued the operation of same until November 13, 1903, under an agreement (either verbal or written) according to the terms of which this corporation was charged with the total operating expenses and credited with the total operating revenues. Included in the operating expenses were charges covering the rental from LAT of two cars at $2 per day each, and power for the two cars at $4 per day each. Conductors and motormen were paid 22 cents and 22½ cents per hour. Operating revenues were from $11 to $16 daily, while operating expenses were from $28 to $35 daily.

L.A.-Santa Monica: On January 5, 1903, this corporation and the LAT entered into a trackage and traffic agreement which provided for the operation of this company's cars over the tracks of the LAT from Vermont and Jefferson to the business section of Los Angeles. At a meeting of the Directors held at the office of the manager of the LAT near the corner of Georgia and Girard Sts. in Los Angeles on March 14, 1903, this company passed a resolution adopting definite location for its line between Santa Monica and Los Angeles:

"Extending from a point in the intersection of Jefferson St. with the westerly boundary line of the City of Los Angeles thence in a general westerly direction across the Santa Monica branch of the SP's railroad and across the line of the Los Angeles, Hermosa Beach & Redondo Ry. Co. (Unit 53), and across the right of way and railroad of the Inglewood Branch of LAP and also across the right of way and railroad track of LAP extending south from Santa Monica to the Short Line Beach Tract; thence northerly along the westerly side of the last mentioned line of railway to Santa Monica."

Kinney and Hook (jointly or individually) secured the necessary franchises covering the construction, operation and the maintenance of an electric railway in Santa Monica and purchased private rights of way from the intersection of Fremont (Pico) and Ocean Aves. in a southerly direction through Ocean Park and Venice and thence parallel to what is now Washington Blvd. to a point at or near Ellenda on the Redondo Line of the LA,HB&R Ry. Co. (Unit 53) with several disconnected parcels of land closer to Los Angeles.

During March, April, May and June of 1903 grading was done for a single track line from Fremont Ave. in Santa Monica to Windward Ave. in Venice, and for a double track line from Windward Ave. to a point at or near Ellenda on the Del Rey Redondo Line, and tracks were laid as follows: A narrow gauge single track line from Bicknell Ave. (two blocks south of Fremont) in Santa Monica to Windward Ave. in Venice, and from Windward Ave. to a connection with the Inglewood Line

near Washington Blvd. in Venice—this latter being later known as a portion of the "Venice Freight House Branch."

The rails, ties and fastenings were placed along the graded portion of the right of. way, and a single track line was constructed over approximately half the distance between the Inglewood Line in Venice and a point at or near Ellendale Station on the Del Rey-Redondo Line of LAP. The track was laid from the Del Rey-Redondo Line in the direction of Venice for some distance, over which a construction train was operated to haul in the necessary materials, but a connection was not made with the track which was built from the Inglewood Line in Venice towards Los Angeles. Work on the line came to a standstill during July, 1903, after Hook sold his half of the company, along with all his LAT holdings, to SP interests.

The foregoing constitutes the sum total of construction work done by the company on this line. In the following summary of mileage, it is estimated that 50% of the track between Windward Ave., Venice, and Ellenda Station had been laid, although the actual percentage cannot be given:

Bicknell Ave.-Windward Ave. 1.584
Windward Ave.-Ellenda Station 2.287

               Total mileage   3.871

On April 14, 1903, Hook, his wife and his brother entered into a written agreement with W.A. Clark of Butte to sell and convey to Clark all stock of this corporation owned by them, amounting to 75 shares, and also all of the issued and outstanding capital stocks owned by them in the following corporations: L.A.-Pasadena Traction Company (Unit 26), L.A. Traction Company (Unit 27), and California Pacific Ry. Co. (Unit 28).

On June 9, 1903, W.A. Clark transferred all right, title and interest in and to said contract and agreement and to all of said stock to the Union Trust Company of San Francisco, which company subsequently assigned all of its right, title and interest in same and in and to all of said stocks of the other companies named to the Los Angeles Interurban Railway Company (Unit 62). In this manner, the LAIU became the owner of 75 shares, same being one half of all of the issued and outstanding capital stock of LA,OP&SM Ry. Co.

[Ed.: Clark acted for and on behalf of President Harriman of SP in the above purchase. Harriman's goal was to force President Huntington of Pacific Electric to come to terms. With the control of the Hook properties and with his victory in the $110,000 W. 6th St. franchise battle with Huntington on May 4, 1903, Harriman forced Huntington to compromise. The LAIU was set up as a joint Harriman-Huntington company, and a by-product of this clash of the titans was the leaving of Kinney high and dry—PE continued to respect its gentlemen's agreement with LAP not to invade the other's territory and Kinney had no entry into Los Angeles.]

On March 9, 1904, LAP (Unit 55) became the owner of all of the issued and outstanding stock of this corporation, amounting to 150 shares. On April 21, 1904, Kinney resigned as president and was succeeded by M.H. Sherman of LAP. By deed dated June 7, 1904, the W. Jefferson St. line was sold to the Los Angeles & Glendale Electric Railway Company (Unit 25) and subsequently was taken over and operated by LAIU until the Great Merger (1910) when it was turned over to L.A. Railway.

[Ed.: So ends the abortive attempt of Kinney and Hook to compete with LAP for the lucrative Venice-Ocean Park traffic. From April 14, 1903, to March 9, 1904, Kinney held on to his half of the company; when he did sell, LAP ripped up his single track on the Trolleyway, spread its tracks to the extreme width of that thoroughfare and laid a 10-foot walk down the center. The LA,OP&SM's tracks from Windward Ave. to the Inglewood Line were retained and were used for years as layover and freight tracks. The partially completed tracks between the Inglewood Line and Ellenda Station were removed.]